The Civil Rights Act and the Battle to End Workplace Discrimination

The Civil Rights Act and the Battle to End Workplace Discrimination

A 50 Year History

Raymond F. Gregory

ROWMAN & LITTLEFIELD
Lanham • Boulder • New York • London

Published by Rowman & Littlefield
A wholly owned subsidiary of The Rowman & Littlefield Publishing Group, Inc.
4501 Forbes Boulevard, Suite 200, Lanham, Maryland 20706
www.rowman.com

16 Carlisle Street, London W1D 3BT, United Kingdom

British Library Cataloguing in Publication Information Available

Library of Congress Cataloging-in-Publication Data

Gregory, Raymond F., 1927- author.
The Civil Rights Act and the battle to end workplace discrimination : a 50 year history / Raymond F. Gregory.
pages cm
Includes bibliographical references and index.
ISBN 978-1-4422-3722-3 (cloth : alk. paper) -- ISBN 978-1-4422-3723-0 (electronic)
1. Discrimination in employment--Law and legislation--United States. 2. Discrimination in employment--Law and legislation--United States--History--20th century. 3. United States. Civil Rights Act of 1964. I. Title.
KF3464.G743 2014
344.7301'133--dc23
2014010593

∞™ The paper used in this publication meets the minimum requirements of American National Standard for Information Sciences Permanence of Paper for Printed Library Materials, ANSI/NISO Z39.48-1992.

Printed in the United States of America

For Mary

Contents

Introduction

On the evening of June 11, 1963, President John F. Kennedy addressed the nation by television and radio, informing Americans that he was about to propose to Congress legislation providing African Americans and other minority groups with rights that should have been granted them years before. His proposals, if enacted, would bar limitations on voting rights, initiate nondiscriminatory measures in public education, guarantee the right of free access to public accommodations, and prohibit discrimination in the workplace. Kennedy centered his speech on the nation's longstanding commitment to attain equal rights for all its citizens:

> This Nation was founded by men of many nations and backgrounds [and] on the principle that all men are created equal, and that the rights of every man are diminished when the rights of one man are threatened. . . . Today we are committed to a worldwide struggle to promote and protect the rights of all who wish to be free. . . . It ought to be possible, in short, for every American to enjoy the privileges of being American without regard to his race or his color. . . . But this is not the case. . . . We are confronted primarily with a moral issue. It is as old as the scriptures and is as clear as the American Constitution. [1]

Kennedy enlarged on this theme in his message accompanying the proposed civil rights bill he later forwarded to Congress:

> The legal remedies I have proposed are the embodiment of this nation's basic posture of common sense and common justice. They involve every American's right to vote, to go to school, to get a job and to be served in public without arbitrary discrimination—rights most Americans take for granted. In short, enactment of [a civil rights act] at this session of Congress is imperative.

The civil rights legislation that President Kennedy proposed in 1963 contained a provision that later would come to be known as Title VII. As enacted by Congress, Title VII of the Civil Rights Act of 1964 would play an indispensable role in the implementation and enforcement of the right guaranteed to all Americans to labor in a workplace free of discrimination by reason of race, color, religion, sex, or national origin.

Three years after enacting the Civil Rights Act of 1964, Congress passed the Age Discrimination in Employment Act of 1967 (ADEA), extending the bar against discrimination in the workplace to discriminatory conduct directed at older Americans.

The fiftieth anniversary of the 1964 Civil Rights Act appears to be a particularly appropriate time to examine how the courts have applied the provisions of the act while resolving workplace discrimination claims and also to assess the progress that has been attained in eradicating employment discrimination based on race, color, sex, national origin, and religion.

For the past fifty years, a relatively small contingent of America's lawyers have battled in the nation's courts to provide all Americans the rights secured to them through Title VII and—for nearly as long—through ADEA. This book records the details of that battle.

Four of my previous books have traced the details of specific aspects of that battle:

1. *Age Discrimination in the American Workplace: Old at a Young Age* (2001)
2. *Women and Workplace Discrimination: Overcoming Barriers to Gender Equality* (2003)
3. *Unwelcome and Unlawful: Sexual Harassment in the American Workplace* (2004)
4. *Encountering Religion in the Workplace: The Legal Rights and Responsibilities of Workers and Employers* (2011)

Sections of those books have been reported or summarized in this book.

Students studying for admission to the bar acquire knowledge of the law through the *casebook method*. They learn the law by reading groups of court cases assembled in book form. In this work, as in my previous books, I employ a modified form of that method. I have selected court cases that illustrate various aspects of employment disputes and have summarized them for the reader. The modified form of the casebook method is not without its limitations. While law students read actual court cases, readers of this book will read case summaries. Nearly every judicial decision examines more than a few relevant issues, but we will generally focus on the single issue in the case that is central to the point of law under consideration. Quoting the exact language of the court is the best approach to gaining a correct understanding of its ruling, but quoting the court is generally not feasible when we are examining only one of the many issues it considered. In most instances, these circumstances require the relevant aspects of the opinion to be summarized rather than cited word for word. In the interest of accuracy, when summarizing a ruling, I have closely tracked the court's language whenever possible.

The second limitation of the modified form of the casebook method, in some instances, may lead to a bit of frustration for the readers, for while they may learn the law relevant to the court's determination, they may not always learn the ultimate outcome of the case under discussion. Actual trials of employment discrimination cases occur less frequently than the public supposes. More frequently, legal claims alleging discrimination are settled by the parties at some point in the litigation process, most often before the case reaches the trial stage. Because jury trials present substantial risks for employers, they generally attempt to avoid the courtroom and a sitting jury whenever possible. The motion for summary judgment affords the employer the opportunity to procure an early dismissal of a worker's case, thus avoiding a trial before a jury. A motion for summary judgment requires the court to assess the evidence that the employer and the worker intend to offer during the course of the trial so as to determine whether a genuine need for a trial actually exists. If the court finds that the evidence to be offered is insufficient to allow a jury to reach a verdict for the worker, the court will grant the employer's motion for summary judgment. At that point, the court dismisses the worker's complaint. Unless the worker appeals, the case is over. But on the other hand, if the court finds the worker's evidence to be sufficient, it will deny the employer's motion for summary judgment and direct the parties to proceed to trial. In those circumstances, more often than not, an employer will opt to settle the dispute rather than face a jury.

The reader must be cautioned about one other matter. In cases decided at the summary judgment stage, all evidence is interpreted by the judge in the light most favorable to the party opposing the motion—in nearly all cases, the plaintiff. Thus the reader should be aware that the facts summarized in summary judgment opinions *assume* that the facts alleged by the plaintiff are true. If the court denies the motion and the case proceeds to trial, it is possible that a jury may conclude that the plaintiff's version of the facts is not accurate and in those circumstances the jury's verdict will likely be in favor of the defendant.

Employers nearly always require that secrecy be maintained in the settlement process, and they generally demand, as a term of the settlement, that its provisions not be published. Some of the cases discussed in this book end in that posture, and thus the reader does not learn the details of the settlement. This can be frustrating, but readers may be assured that in nearly all instances of this nature, the terms of settlement are favorable to the worker. To avoid a jury trial, an employer will often make a far more generous settlement proposal at this point in the litigation than it would have made earlier in the proceedings.

This book has been written for laypersons and those lawyers who do not specialize in employment law. Every attempt has been made to eliminate technical language and legal jargon and to preclude immersion in legal intricacies and technical data having less than general application. In the discussion of areas where some technical knowledge of the law is required, emphasis has been placed on the law's general applicability without regard to its exceptions. The broad picture takes precedence over special circumstances that may be relevant only in a limited number of instances.

In 1966, the Equal Employment Opportunity Commission reported that workplace discrimination was widespread and that its impact could be found throughout the American workplace in nearly every occupational group and industry. "[I]t is a profound condition, national in scope, and it constitutes a continuing violation of the American ideal of fair play in the private enterprise system."[2] Since that time, the United States has been engaged in a national effort to eliminate discrimination from the workplace. This is the story of that effort.

I

Employment Discrimination Prior to 1964

Chapter One

Employment Discrimination Prior to 1964

The Thirteenth Amendment to the Constitution abolished slavery in 1865, but for decades afterward African Americans found themselves relegated to an economic underclass that limited them to employment in agricultural or domestic service jobs. In 1896, the Supreme Court, in effect, sanctioned the existence of this underclass when it ruled that the "equal protection of the laws" clause of the Fourteenth Amendment allowed a state to provide "separate but equal" facilities for the emancipated slaves.[1]

At the outset of the twentieth century, nearly 90 percent of working African Americans were employed in low-income jobs, and even those conditions deteriorated during the depression years of the 1930s. For years, monthly employment statistics showed significantly higher unemployment among African Americans than whites, manifesting widespread discrimination in hiring and firing.[2] Generally, employers excluded African Americans from traditionally "white" positions, hiring them only for less desirable, lower-paying jobs. In 1962, nonwhite male workers earned a salary less than 60 percent of that of white males. Nonwhite females fared even worse, earning a salary less than 25 percent of that of white male workers.[3] Racial discrimination in employment—dominant, commonplace, and all-inclusive—marked those times.

Before and after the Civil War, women had limited access to the workforce. The exclusion of women dated back to the beginning of the industrialization era in the early nineteenth century. For the following 150 years, employers openly discriminated against women by either refusing to hire them under any circumstances or by rejecting them if they were married or had children. Exclusion from the labor market was often reinforced by state statutes. Illinois barred women and felons from becoming lawyers. In 1872, the Supreme Court affirmed Illinois's rejection of a woman's application to practice law and purported to fix women's proper place in American society: "The natural and proper timidity and delicacy which belongs to the female sex evidently unfits [women] for many of the occupations of civil life. . . . [T]he family institution is repugnant to the idea of a woman adopting a distinct and independent career from that of her husband." To make certain that all citizens understood clearly women's proper place in society, the court added: "The paramount destiny and mission of woman are to fulfill the noble and benign offices of wife and mother. This is the law of the Creator."[4]

The Supreme Court's attitude toward women persisted well beyond the nineteenth century. As late as 1948, the court upheld a Michigan statute barring a woman from employment as a bartender, unless the male owner of the bar in which the woman intended to work was either her father or her husband.[5]

New Deal programs advanced by President Roosevelt brought significant numbers of women into the workplace, but women continued to confront oppressive employer discriminatory conduct. But reluctance to hire women completely eroded during World War II when millions of men departed the workplace for the military, allowing manufacturing firms no option other than to rely upon women to fill positions vacated by departing males. The number of working females doubled between 1941 and 1944, but they remained subjected to discriminatory policies as employers paid women, on average, only 60 percent of the salary paid their male coworkers.[6]

Widespread employment discrimination against African Americans, women, immigrants, and the aged prevailed as Americans prepared for and then proceeded to war. Defense manufacturers and government agencies were then engaged in hiring hundreds of thousands of workers to run the developing war machinery, but prevailing racial attitudes excluded many workers, primarily African Americans, from this expanding workforce. African American leaders—among them, A. Philip Randolph—tried to force President Roosevelt to eliminate these racist attitudes. They planned a demonstration march on Washington, a march that would likely have attracted more than 100,000 African Americans to the capital to protest their exclusion from employment in government and defense industries. Administration officials urged the leaders of the march to cancel the event, but they refused to comply unless Roosevelt first agreed to employ his presidential powers to eliminate racist hiring policies.

Faced with a determined African American force of thousands of workers, the president capitulated and promulgated Executive Order 8802, prohibiting discrimination in government and defense industry hiring practices.[7] Roosevelt was clear and direct:

I do hereby reaffirm the policy of the United States that there shall be no discrimination in the employment of workers in defense industries or government because of race, creed, color, or national origin, and I do hereby declare that it is the duty of employers and of labor organizations in furtherance of such policy and of this order, to provide for the full and equitable participation of all workers in defense industries without discrimination because of race, creed, color, or national origin. [8]

Leaders of the planned march cancelled the event, but perhaps they should have first considered how the administration planned to implement the order, as its terms failed to provide for legal sanctions for violations of its provisions. The Committee on Fair Employment Practices, charged with implementation of the order, utilized settlement negotiation, conciliation, and persuasion to advance the employment of African Americans during the course of the war; but, once the war ended, Congress refused to continue the funding of the activities of the committee, and it ceased to exist in 1946.

Barriers to female employment went up again after the war. Law firm interviewers were typical of employers and did not hesitate to tell female applicants that their firms did not hire women or that "they already had one." Some firms simply posted "No Women" notices in their entrances and in their help wanted ads. [9] When future Supreme Court Justice Sandra O'Connor graduated Stanford Law School, the only offers of employment she received when she applied for a position as an attorney were for the position of legal secretary. Nanette Dembitz—who later served as a New York judge—was unable to obtain a position with a Wall Street law firm, even though she had been an editor of the *Columbia Law Review* and, as the niece of Supreme Court Justice Louis Brandeis, had excellent family connections. [10]

Employers experienced greater success in integrating persons of different national origins than in integrating persons of race or color. Nonetheless, early in the nineteenth century, job posting often boldly stated "NINA"—"No Irish Need Apply"—and Irish workers could rarely obtain employment in any job above that of a common laborer. Latino workers also typically earned far less than white workers, suffered higher unemployment rates, and labored under discriminatory workplace rules and regulations.

Age bias was generally not addressed in the American workplace prior to 1967, as the population at large failed to recognize that ageism was outdated and irreconcilable with civilized society and American cultural values. Consequently, discrimination against older workers was unaddressed and remained rampant.

President Truman also employed executive orders to advance equal employment opportunities for African Americans. After ordering the desegregation of the armed forces, he issued executive orders (1) prohibiting discrimination in federal employment [11] and (2) creating a Committee on Government

Contracts, which was charged with initiating efforts to prevent discrimination in government contracting.[12] President Eisenhower followed suit, also issuing executive orders prohibiting discrimination in federal employment and government contracting.[13]

All presidents from Roosevelt to Johnson supported the view that the US government should refuse to conduct business with commercial concerns that discriminated on the basis of race. However, outside of the government sector, little changed. Congress failed to act to eliminate discrimination from the private sector workplace, but state legislatures were more active. In 1945, New York enacted the first fair employment law covering private employment and created a state agency to eliminate and prevent further discrimination in employment "because of race, creed, color, or national origin."[14] Noticeably absent from the statute was any reference to discrimination by reason of sex.

The New York law became the prototype for statutes enacted in twenty-four other states.[15] These statutes, however, generally lacked adequate enforcement procedures and thus were of limited effectiveness.

These were the conditions that prevailed at the beginning of 1964. For African Americans, women, the foreign-born, and older workers, the American workplace was not a very nice place.

Chapter Two

Enactment of the Civil Rights Act of 1964 and the Age Discrimination in Employment Act of 1967

President Kennedy's purpose in addressing the nation in June 1963 was to explain the legislation he was about to propose to Congress. It would bar any limitation on African Americans' voting rights, initiate nondiscriminatory measures in public education, guarantee the right of African Americans to free access to public accommodations, and prohibit discriminatory conduct in the workplace. Kennedy centered his speech on the nation's longstanding commitment to attain equal rights for all its citizens.

> This Nation was founded by men of many nations and backgrounds [and] on the principle that all men are created equal, and that the rights of every man are diminished when the rights of one man are threatened. . . .
>
> Today we are committed to a worldwide struggle to promote and protect the rights of all who wish to be free. And when Americans are sent to Vietnam or West Berlin, we do not ask for whites only. It ought to be possible, therefore, for American students of any color to attend any public institution they select without having to be backed up by troops. . . . It ought to be possible for American consumers of any color to receive equal service in places of public accommodation, such as hotels and restaurants and theaters and retail stores, without being forced to resort to demonstrations in the street, and it ought to be possible for an American citizen of any color to register and to vote in a free election without interference or fear of reprisal. . . . It ought to be possible, in short, for every American to enjoy the privileges of being American without regard to his race or his color. . . . But this is not the case. . . . The Negro baby born in America today, regardless of the section of the Nation in which he is born, has about one-half as much chance of completing high school as a white baby born in the same place on the same day, one-third as much chance of

completing college, one-third as much chance of becoming a professional man, twice as much chance of becoming unemployed, about one-seventh as much chance of earning $10,000 a year, a life expectancy which is seven years shorter, and the prospects of earning only half as much.

We are confronted primarily with a moral issue. It is as old as the scriptures and is as clear as the American Constitution. . . . One hundred years of delay have passed since President Lincoln freed the slaves, yet their heirs, their grandsons, are not fully free. They are not yet freed from the bonds of injustice. They are not yet freed from social and economic oppression. And this Nation, for all its hopes and all its boasts, will not be fully free until all its citizens are free. . . . We preach freedom around the world, and we mean it, and we cherish our freedom here at home, but are we to say to the world, and much more importantly, to each other that this is a land of the free except for the Negroes?

Next week I shall ask the Congress of the United States to act, to make a commitment it has not fully made in this century to the proposition that race has no place in American life or law. . . . The old code of equity law under which we live commands for every wrong a remedy, but in too many communities, in too many parts of the country, wrongs are inflicted on Negro citizens and there are no remedies at law. Unless the Congress acts, their only remedy is in the street. [1]

In Kennedy's message accompanying the civil rights bill he forwarded to Congress, he stated:

The legal remedies I have proposed are the embodiment of this nation's basic posture of common sense and common justice. They involve every American's right to vote, to go to school, to get a job and to be served in public without arbitrary discrimination—rights most Americans take for granted. In short, enactment of [a civil rights act] at this session of Congress is imperative.

Prior to 1963, twenty-five states had adopted employment practice laws that barred some element of workplace discrimination.[2] None of these states, however, was included in the Old Confederacy. Congress, then dominated by southern senators and representatives, had steadfastly resisted all efforts to enact federal legislation barring employer discriminatory conduct. But changes in attitude of people across the country began to appear.

Americans had been sickened by Nazi claims of racial superiority. The revelation of what bias could produce when carried to an extreme contained a sobering reminder that the United States had its own sad record of bias and that reform was long overdue.[3] Black and white Americans had fought side by side against the Nazis, and some had died together in battle. These occurrences caused the growth of a more sympathetic forum for those who were then engaged in challenging racial discrimination and also gave rise to a new generation of African Americans who were determined to end that discrimination.

The Supreme Court, in its 1954 decision in *Brown v. Board of Education*, ruled that state laws that mandated racially segregated schools violated the Fourteenth Amendment.[4] Thus the court gave support to those in the civil rights movement challenging racial discrimination in other areas such as in the workplace. One year later, Rosa Parks, an African American living in Montgomery, Alabama, refused to move to the back of the bus to make way for a white man. The police were summoned and Parks in short order was arrested, convicted of violating local law, and jailed. She quickly became a symbol of social impulse toward African American equality, and the Montgomery bus boycott that followed catapulted Martin Luther King Jr. into a leadership role in opposing segregation and discrimination in the southern states and throughout the country.

Early in his administration, President Kennedy had opposed any broad-based civil rights legislation as he was convinced that such a proposal was doomed to failure because of southern resistance. But the social impulse toward political, economic, and dignitary equality for African Americans[5] that had steadily gained strength after the war now appeared to present a new opportunity to pursue federal legislation banning racial discrimination in education, public accommodations, voting, and employment.

Two and a half months after Kennedy's television and radio address, 250,000 African Americans and their supporters marched on Washington, DC, where they assembled at the Lincoln Memorial. Their aim was to draw attention to the nation's longstanding problem with racial bias and to forcefully express their demands that the legislation proposed by Kennedy be greatly strengthened. Folk singer Joan Baez led the crowd in singing "We Shall Overcome," and moving speeches by some of the nation's most vocal racial equality advocates reached a climax when Martin Luther King Jr. gave his "I Have a Dream" speech.

Leaders of the march later met with President Kennedy at the White House, but Kennedy was reluctant to accede to their demands that the proposed bill be strengthened, as he felt such a move would only induce greater opposition. But two weeks later, another event changed the course of the bill.

Early on a Sunday morning a bomb exploded in an African American Baptist church in Birmingham, Alabama, killing four girls and injuring many others. Birmingham, one of the most segregated cities in the South, was a prime target of the civil rights movement, and the church that was bombed that day was well known as a meeting place for civil rights leaders, including Martin Luther King Jr. The bombing represented one of the most horrific acts of extremists opposed to advancement of the civil rights movement.

Then, not long after, President Kennedy was assassinated. The assassination of the president on November 22, 1963, added to the growing public support for the proposed civil rights legislation. Five days after the assassination, President Johnson addressed a joint session of the Congress:

The greatest leader of our time has been struck down by the foulest deed of our time. . . . No words are strong enough to express our determination to continue the forward thrust of the America that he begun. . . . On the 20th day of January in 19 and 61, John F. Kennedy told his countrymen that our national work would not be finished "in the first 1,000 days, not in the life of this Administration, nor even perhaps in our lifetime on this planet." "But," he said," let us begin."

Today in this moment of new resolve, I would say to all my fellow Americans, let us continue. . . . This is our challenge: Not to hesitate, not to pause, not to turn about and linger over this evil moment, but to continue on our course so that we may fulfill the destiny that history has set for us.

Our most immediate tasks are here on this Hill:

First, no memorial oration or eulogy could more eloquently honor President Kennedy's memory than the earliest possible passage of the civil rights bill for which he fought so long. We have talked long enough in this country about equal rights. We have talked for a hundred years or more. It is time now to write the next chapter, and to write it in the books of law.[6]

It was up to President Johnson to carry the fight forward, and he did not fail those who supported the pending bill. Johnson directed his formidable skills, attained through many years' experience in the Congress, in guiding the legislation through the Congress.

Title VII of the proposed bill dealt with discrimination in employment. Two themes emerge from the legislative history of Title VII. It was adopted because it was consistent with the nation's ideals and principles and also because it would eliminate workplace discrimination, the basic cause of the disparities that had developed between African American and white workers.

Opponents of the bill committed two fundamental errors, each of which resulted in a greatly expanded and an enormously strengthened bill. First, they proposed that discrimination by reason of sex be added to the prohibitions of Title VII. One of the bill's outspoken opponents was Representative Howard Smith of Virginia. Smith epitomized all that was obsolete in the Congress of the day. A thirty-three-year veteran of the House, he had repeatedly imposed his own will by delaying or weakening progressive legislature, and Kennedy had been well aware that, as the filibuster would be the major problem to passage of the bill in the Senate, Smith would be the major problem in the House.[7]

It was Smith who proposed amending the proposed bill by adding sex to the prohibitions against employment discrimination. His intent was not to advance the interests of women but to defeat the entire bill by complicating the debate and confusing some Representatives who, although fully supportive of the provisions ensuring equality for African Americans, were less certain of the need to expand the legislation to include protections for women.

Showing contempt for his own amendment, Smith related having received a letter from one of his female constituents complaining of the "grave injustice" of there being more females than males in the country, which resulted in some women not having a husband. This story was greeted with laughter on the floor of the House but also with anger from the few women serving in the Congress at the time. But Smith's ploy backfired. Once the question of discrimination against women was placed on the House floor it was difficult for many representatives to ignore it, and ultimately Smith's amendment was adopted by the House. Thus, what began as a joke ended in legislation providing one of the broadest set of legal protections ever granted American women.

The second fundamental error committed by opponents of the bill was their opposition to any provision that would provide the Equal Employment Opportunity Commission with any effective powers of enforcement. The EEOC was created by the legislation to administer the provisions of Title VII. As originally conceived, the EEOC would be empowered to enforce its rulings through its authority to issue cease-and-desist orders. In order to gain support for the bill, supporters of the proposed legislation concluded they had to accede to opposition demands that the EEOC be stripped of cease-and-desist authority. Ultimately, opponents of the bill also were able to deny the EEOC the authority to initiate its own lawsuits. At the time, this was considered a great victory, as the final bill failed to provide the EEOC with any effective enforcement tools.

But their victory was short-lived. Overlooked in their rush to strip the EEOC of enforcement powers was a provision in Title VII authorizing individual claimants to initiate legal actions through their own attorneys. Workers did not require the participation of the EEOC to obtain relief from employers who would discriminate against them. The efforts of private attorneys later became the enforcement power that was to make Title VII the force that ultimately would make great strides in eradicating discrimination from the American workplace.

The Civil Rights Act of 1964 was signed into law by President Johnson on July 2, 1964. In general terms, Title VII of the act prohibited discrimination in employment on the basis of race, color, religion, sex, or national origin. When Title VII was first proposed, Congress had also included age in the bill's protections, but it was later excluded. The final version of the legislation, however, directed the secretary of labor to "make a full and complete study" of the factors underlying age discrimination in employment and its consequences to older workers and to the economy.

One year later, Secretary of Labor W. Willard Wirtz submitted his report to Congress setting forth five basic conclusions:[8]

1. Many employers impose specific age limits upon those they will employ.
2. These age limitations markedly affect the rights and opportunities of older workers.
3. Although age discrimination rarely is based on the sort of animus that motivates racial, national origin, or religious discrimination, it is based upon stereotypical assumptions of the abilities of the aged, unsupported by objective facts.
4. The evidence available at the time showed that the arbitrary removal of older workers from the workplace was generally unfounded and that, overall, the performance of the older worker was at least as good as that of the younger worker.
5. Age discrimination is profoundly harmful in that it deprives the national economy of the productive labor of millions of workers and substantially increases the costs of both unemployment insurance and Social Security benefits; and it inflicts economic and psychological injury upon workers deprived of the opportunity to engage in productive and satisfying occupations.

A congressional committee studying the problem of age bias in the workplace later concurred with Wirtz's findings. Congress then drafted and adopted the Age Discrimination in Employment Act (ADEA), and President Johnson signed that law on December 16, 1967. The newly adopted ADEA joined Title VII of the Civil Rights Act of 1964 in Congress's continuing effort to eradicate discrimination from the workplace. Both laws reflect, as the Supreme Court later noted, "societal condemnation of invidious bias in employment decisions."[9]

The Civil Rights Act of 1964 has been described as "one of the most monumental achievements in the history of the United States."[10] I prefer a more realistic assessment: "The Civil Rights Act of 1964 . . . became the cornerstone of modern civil rights law, including equal employment opportunity law."[11]

The operative language of Title VII provides that it shall be an unlawful employment practice for an employer:

> (1) To fail or refuse to hire or to discharge any individual, or otherwise to discriminate against any individual with respect to his compensation, terms, conditions, or privileges of employment, because of such individual's race, color, religion, sex or national origin; or
>
> (2) To limit, segregate, or classify his employees or applicants for employment in any way which would derive or tend to deprive any individual of employment opportunities or otherwise adversely affect his status as an employee, because of such individual's race, color, religion, sex, or national origin.[12]

The ADEA has similar broad operative language.[13]

Title VII and ADEA are broad in scope, covering every aspect of employment—hiring, discharge, promotion, demotion, transfer, compensation, benefits, working conditions, harassment, retaliation, and nearly everything else connected with the employment relationship. Crucial to the successful implementation of these legislative acts was the decision to enlarge the role of the right of the individual worker to sue his or her employer for violations of these laws. The decision to empower the individual worker rather than an administrative agency to enforce the terms of these statutes made a great deal of sense in light of previous failures of state agencies to enforce state antidiscrimination laws.[14] The individual right to sue in federal court has proved by far to be the most effective tool for implementing the broad precepts of both Title VII and ADEA and in reducing employment discrimination throughout the country.

Whether Americans can completely eliminate racial, color, gender, national origin, religious, and age discrimination from its workplace is an issue that will be resolved only in the future.[15] The remaining chapters of this book will examine how far we have proceeded in achieving that goal.

II

Early Employment Discrimination Cases

Chapter Three

Proving Employment Discrimination

Congress created the Equal Employment Opportunity Commission to administer Title VII and, more particularly, to process race, color, national origin, religious, and sex claims filed pursuant to the statute. Franklin D. Roosevelt Jr., the first chairperson of the agency, recognized the difficulties the EEOC would confront in carrying out its functions, primarily because of its limited enforcement powers. Those difficulties loomed even larger on the day that Title VII became effective, as at that time the agency had neither staff nor offices. [1]

EEOC officials anticipated 2,000 discrimination claims would be filed during the agency's first year, but over 14,000 complaints were filed within the first six months. Most of those complaints alleged race discrimination. In 1964, the unemployment rate of nonwhite workers was twice that of white workers. Earlier Bureau of Census statistics disclosed that only 12 percent of nonwhite workers held professional, managerial, and other white-collar jobs, whereas 42 percent of white workers were employed in those positions. Almost one-half of all nonwhites were employed as unskilled workers. Because African Americans had for years experienced continuous workplace discrimination, they were among the first to take advantage of the new anti-discrimination law. The EEOC had no alternative but to focus its initial efforts on the resolution of race complaints. Moreover, at first, the EEOC did not consider seriously the proposition that sex discrimination constituted a substantial issue for women in the workplace. Reflecting upon the manner in which sex discrimination had been added to the Civil Rights Act through the antics of Virginia congressman Howard Smith (see chapter 2), an EEOC director characterized the prohibition against sex discrimination as a statutory "fluke . . . conceived out of wedlock."[2] As a consequence, in the early days of its existence, the EEOC devoted far less effort to eliminating sex discrimination than to eliminating race discrimination from the workplace.

Because Congress had deprived the EEOC of any significant enforcement authority, agency personnel were limited to investigating claimants' charges and, when appropriate, entering into conciliation or settlement discussions with employers. The EEOC had been given the power to conciliate but not the power to compel. It had been given no teeth.[3] The EEOC was a "poor, enfeebled thing."[4]

Claimants quickly learned that the EEOC did not possess the authority or power to litigate their claims. Realizing that the burden of bringing suit was in their hands, many claimants opted to abandon EEOC jurisdiction and turn directly to the courts. Although a claimant first had to file a discrimination claim with the EEOC, at several points in the administrative process that followed a claimant could elect to quit the process and proceed to the federal court. And therein lay the genius of Title VII and the Civil Rights Act of 1964.

The most significant difference between the state fair employment laws and Title VII lay in the procedures designed to adjudicate employment discrimination claims. Rather than relying upon the assignment of enforcement procedures to an administrative agency, Congress gave a much larger role to the claimant worker. It gave the worker the right to sue in the federal courts. The preference for litigation over the administrative process arose out the failures of the state agencies, extending over a period of a quarter century, to attain effective relief for victims of employment discrimination. The legal structures that have developed as a consequence of that decision have empowered individual workers to pursue their own claims in the federal courts, and over the years they and their attorneys have created a workplace environment far more adverse to discriminatory employer conduct than what preceded them.[5]

During the first years of Title VII, thousands of discrimination claimants elected to litigate their claims in the federal courts. Within a year of Title VII's effective date, the federal courts located in many of the nation's major cities were inundated with such lawsuits, presenting major problems for these courts. Few lawyers were available to manage this litigation, as the legal profession was unprepared to handle claims asserted under this newly minted law, a law that was complicated and confusing to most onlookers, including lawyers. When a lawyer was unavailable, a claimant would often resort to representing himself. "Pro se" plaintiffs, as they are referred to by the courts, present enormous difficulties for the judge presiding at the litigation of their claims. As these plaintiffs are not versed in the intricacies of the litigation process, the judge to whom a pro se claim has been assigned must guide the pro se plaintiff through that process. This consumes a great deal of time and usually ties up the judge's trial calendar, much to the chagrin of other plaintiffs and defendants litigating other cases.

In 1967, Judge Sidney Sugarman, chief judge of the federal court in New York City (the District Court of the Southern District of New York) confronted those circumstances. He issued a plea to lawyers who tried cases in his court to come to his aid. Pro se Title VII claimants were overwhelming his court, and he asked lawyers to volunteer their services to represent these claimants. This was a lot to ask. It was pro bono work, requiring a volunteer to steep himself in the intricacies of a law that for the most part remained nearly unknown to most lawyers. Yet the New York bar immediately responded to Judge Sugarman's plea, and in short order he had a lengthy list of volunteers to whom court officials thereafter regularly assigned pro se Title VII cases.

After a year or so, Judge Sugarman terminated the program as increasing numbers of lawyers were then undertaking the representation of Title VII claimants and pro bono lawyers were no longer required. When the judge terminated the program, he ordered court officials to turn over to the EEOC the list of pro bono lawyers who had come to his assistance, thus presenting the agency with a ready-made assemblage of attorneys experienced in Title VII law. Many of the lawyers on the list, including myself, continued to represent claimants who, after having filed a discrimination claim with the EEOC, turned to the courts for legal relief. Thus there developed a body of lawyers who specialized in Title VII law, in New York and soon across the nation. It was these lawyers who would later engage in fighting bruising litigation contests with employers. It was these lawyers who would utilize Title VII as a powerful tool in the battle to eliminate discrimination from the American workplace.

The number of claims filed with the EEOC continued to increase—to 12,000 in 1969 and to more than 71,000 by 1975. Thus, from the beginning, the agency was overwhelmed by claims, and in responding to these claims, it began to fall further and further behind. With the vast number of charges filed and the lack of expertise among most of the agency's personnel, its investigations were often inadequate.[6]

Nonetheless, the EEOC continued to play an important role, using its limited authority to good advantage. In processing a discrimination claim, it possessed the authority to issue a "reasonable cause finding," and in that process it often issued written opinions, supported by underlying legal rationale. Consequently, it became involved in developing guidelines that often established the framework for court decisions that followed upon suits filed by individual workers.[7]

The EEOC was also served well by the willingness of its officials to hold public hearings that dramatized discrimination issues. "The bright light of publicity was not a substitute for judicial action—but many business and labor leaders were sensitive about airing their dirty linen before a critical public."[8] The mere prospect of a public hearing oftentimes proved sufficient to move an employer to settle a discrimination claim.

One of the first tasks of the EEOC and the federal courts was to define, with some specificity, the types of employer conduct that were actionable under Title VII and how a worker claiming to have been a subject of such conduct should go about proving it. Proving that an employer *intended* to discriminate against an employee was critical to establishing its liability in cases of this nature—referred to by the courts as "disparate treatment" cases. Except in "disparate impact" cases (discussed later in this chapter), proof of the employer's intent to discriminate is a basic element of a discrimination charge. The worker and his lawyer must produce evidence sufficient to prove that a discriminatory intent was a determining factor in the employer's decision adversely affecting that worker.

In a disparate treatment case, proving that an employer's intent was discriminatory is never an easy task. Employers have learned to mask acts of employment discrimination with the appearance of business propriety. As the Supreme Court observed, they neither admit discriminatory animus nor leave a paper trail disclosing it. Thus, few employment discrimination cases turn on direct or "smoking gun" evidence of racial, color, sex, national origin, or religious bias. Employers simply do not place memoranda in their files, openly admitting to a biased employment decision. Even the least sophisticated of employers are careful not to leave a trail of discriminatory conduct, and it would be rare indeed for a corporate executive to take the witness stand and freely affirm he acted adversely to the interests of a female worker because of her race, color, sex, national origin, or religion.[9]

Employment discrimination litigation involves numerous, complex legal procedures that render it difficult for a claimant to establish a discrimination case and provide employers with opportunities to create barriers blocking plaintiff workers from achieving their litigation goals. In addition, these procedures do not readily lend themselves to the resolution of employment discrimination cases. For example, the complexities of corporate decision making oftentimes cannot be adequately analyzed in the adversarial framework of the courtroom. But the litigation process nevertheless insists on an either/or explanation—a discriminatory motive either was or was not the basis of a particular employment decision. Moreover, in employment discrimination litigation, unambiguous villains and victims are increasingly more difficult to identify.[10] How then does a discrimination complainant—while simultaneously avoiding employer-initiated barriers and contending with unwieldy legal procedures—prove that a discriminatory intent, rather than a legitimate business reason, motivated an employment decision adversely affecting her employment status?

DIRECT EVIDENCE OF DISCRIMINATION

Direct evidence of discrimination is most often unavailable to assist the plaintiff worker in proving discrimination. Due to current legal and social sanctions, people generally repress demonstrations of overt bias. Thus, even if an employer is aware of his own bias, he is unlikely to express it openly. It is highly unlikely that direct evidence of discrimination will ever appear in the form of an employer's direct and unequivocal admission that his employment decisions were based on race, color, sex, national origin, or religion. Even if a fellow worker of the complainant were to observe discriminatory acts committed by their employer, and thus be in the position to offer the court direct evidence of these acts, he may be reluctant to come forward to testify on behalf of the complainant for fear of jeopardizing his own career. As a result, cases that turn on direct evidence of discrimination are the exception rather than the norm.

Debbie Moore's sex discrimination case against Alabama State University was one of those exceptions. After working in the university's admissions office for eight years, Moore was promoted to admissions staff assistant, functioning as "second in command" to the director of the admissions office. When the director's office became vacant, Dr. Roosevelt Steptoe, the university's vice president of academic affairs, asked Moore to assume increased responsibilities, and for a time she shared the duties of the director's position with another employee. Moore had every expectation that she would be awarded with further promotion, and she eagerly awaited advancement to admissions office director. Her application for the director's position, however, was rejected by a committee appointed to screen and interview candidates for the position. Moore alleged that Steptoe's bias against women led him to interfere with the application process to undermine her candidacy.

Steptoe had a major role in the university's hiring process; he appointed the committee that screened and interviewed applicants for the director's position and, after receiving the committee's recommendations, made the final decision. Moore relied upon two incidents she claimed epitomized Steptoe's bias against female workers. On one occasion, while Moore was walking across campus, she met Steptoe who, noticing Moore's pregnant condition, commented, "I was going to put you in charge of that office, but look at you now." Later, Steptoe told Moore he would not consider her for the director's position because she was married with a child, that the director's job entailed far too much traveling for a married mother and, in any event, a woman should stay home with her family.

After her rejection for the director's position, Moore sued the university for sex discrimination. The primary trial issue evolved around Steptoe's comments regarding Moore's pregnancy and her duties as a mother. Did these comments constitute direct evidence of a discriminatory bias against

Moore? In order for statements of this type to be considered as direct evidence of discrimination, the law requires that the plaintiff demonstrate that the comments are capable of only one interpretation—that they reflect a discriminatory attitude correlating to the discrimination complained of—and that they were made by a person involved in the decision affecting the worker. The court ruled that Steptoe's comments did indeed qualify as direct evidence of discrimination. The comments were made by an official with decision-making authority, neither statement was subject to multiple interpretation, and "neither required any leap of logic or inference" to conclude that an act of discrimination had occurred. [11]

INDIRECT EVIDENCE OF DISCRIMINATION

Since direct evidence of sex discrimination is most often not available, a lawyer representing an employment discrimination claimant must search out indirect or circumstantial evidence of the employer's discriminatory conduct. Soon after congressional enactment of Title VII, the Supreme Court established ground rules for evaluating indirect evidence of discrimination.

McDonnell Douglas Corp., an aircraft manufacturer headquartered in St. Louis, Missouri, employed over 30,000 people. Percy Green, an African American, worked for the company as a mechanic and laboratory technician for eight years when he was laid off during the course of a workforce reduction. Green, a long-time activist in the civil rights movement, protested that his discharge was racially motivated. As part of his protest, he deliberately stalled his car on the main road leading to the plant, blocking access to it as the morning shift arrived. The police arrived shortly and requested him to move his car. He refused, the car was towed away, and he was arrested for obstructing traffic.

Some weeks later, McDonnell Douglas advertised for qualified mechanics. Green applied for re-employment, but the company rejected his application, purportedly because of his participation in the protest. Green claimed that the rejection of his application was racially motivated, but the court dismissed his claim. When his case eventually reached the Supreme Court, the critical issue before the court concerned the order and allocation of proof in a disparate treatment employment discrimination case.

Green charged that he was denied employment "because of his involvement in civil rights activities" and "because of his race and color." McDonnell Douglas denied discrimination of any kind, asserting that its failure to re-employ Green was based upon and justified by his participation in an unlawful protest against the company. With these factual assertions before the court, it proceeded to set out a structure for proving an employment discrimination claim supported solely by indirect evidence:

The complainant in a Title VII trial must carry the initial burden under the statute of establishing a prima facie case of racial discrimination. This may be done by showing (i) that he belongs to a racial minority; (ii) that he applied and was qualified for a job for which the employer was seeking applicants; (iii) that, despite his qualifications, he was rejected; and (iv) that, after his rejection, the position remained open and the employer continued to seek applicants from persons of complainant's qualifications.

Clearly, Green established a prima facie case. The burden then shifted to the employer to articulate a legitimate, nondiscriminatory reason for Green's rejection. Here McDonnell Douglas assigned Green's participation in unlawful conduct against it as the reason for his rejection. The Court ruled that this sufficed to discharge the company's burden to meet Green's prima facie case of discrimination, but the inquiry did not end there. While Title VII did not compel the rehiring of Green, neither did it permit McDonnell Douglas to use Green's conduct as a pretext for discriminatory conduct prohibited by the statue. Green should be afforded the opportunity to show that McDonnell Douglas's stated reason for his rejection was in fact pretextual. Especially relevant to such a showing would be evidence that white employees involved in acts against McDonnell Douglas of comparable seriousness were nevertheless retained or rehired. An employer may justifiably refuse to rehire one who has engaged in unlawful, disruptive acts against it, but only if this criterion is applied alike to members of all races. Green had to be given the opportunity to demonstrate by competent evidence that the presumptively valid reasons for his rejection were in fact a cover-up for a racially discriminatory decision.

The Court ruled that Green's claim should not have been dismissed and that he should have been allowed to pursue his claim under Title VII. The Court remanded the case to the trial court for a retrial. On the retrial, Green had to be afforded the opportunity to demonstrate that McDonnell Douglas's assigned reason for refusing to re-employ him was a pretext to cover up its discriminatory conduct. If the trial judge so ruled, he should then order a prompt and appropriate remedy. In the absence of such a finding, McDonnell Douglas's refusal to rehire should stand.[12]

The procedure established in this case was based upon the court's observation that an employer invariably responds to a charge of discriminatory behavior with the argument that the employment decision adversely affecting the worker was based upon a legitimate, nondiscriminatory reason. If the worker establishes that the purported nondiscriminatory reason was not the actual reason motivating the employer, or that the employer's reason simply is not credible, the court may assume that the employer proffered such a reason only to cover up an unlawful motive. In a subsequent case, the Supreme Court explained why it was justified in making such an assumption:

We are willing to presume this largely because we know from our experience
that more often than not people do not act in a totally arbitrary manner, without
any underlying reasons, especially in a business setting. Thus when all legitimate reasons for an [employer's decision] have been eliminated as possible
reasons for [its] actions, it is more likely than not the employer, who we
generally assume acts only with *some* reason, based [its] decision on an impermissible consideration such as race [or sex, color, national origin, or relig-
ion]. [13]

Thus, the task of the worker's attorney is to prove that the employer's stated
reasons for its actions adversely affecting his client were not its true reasons.
He must show that the employer, rather than disclose its real reasons, has
concealed them. The attorney must prove that the employer's expressed reasons are "pretextual," offered by the employer only to cover up its discriminatory intent.

As thus sanctioned by the Supreme Court, one method of proving intentional discrimination is through the disclosure, by indirect evidence, that an
employer offered a false explanation for its decision adversely affecting the
worker. A court or jury may infer from the falsity of the explanation that the
employer has disassembled or misrepresented the facts in order to cover up a
discriminatory purpose.

Once the employer's explanation, because of its falsity, is eliminated
from consideration, discriminatory conduct may well be the most likely alternative explanation for the employer's decision, especially since the employer
is in the best position to assert the actual reason for its decision and it failed
to do so. Thus, as the Supreme Court later ruled, in some if not most circumstances a court or jury may infer the ultimate fact of discrimination from the
falsity of the employer's explanation. [14] A federal appellate court has succinctly explained this rationale: "Resort to a pretextual explanation is like
flight from the scene of a crime, evidence indicating consciousness of guilt,
which is, of course, evidence of illegal conduct." [15]

Nearly all disparate treatment cases involve indirect evidence. These
cases focus upon the employer's motivation underlying an employment decision. Are the reasons expressed by the employer for an employment decision
its actual reasons, or was the decision motivated by an impermissible factor,
such as the worker's race, color, sex, national origin, or religion? Or, on the
other hand, are the reasons advanced by the employer credible? Even if an
employer's asserted reasons did, in fact, serve as one of the bases for its
decision adversely affecting the worker, was the employer also motivated to
make that decision because of the worker's race, color, sex, national origin,
or religion? Are the reasons asserted by the employer merely pretexts, proffered by the employer for the purpose of covering up the true nature of its
decision, namely, that it was discriminatory? These are the issues that typically confront juries hearing employment discrimination cases.

When unsupported by direct evidence, pretext cases are likely to fail unless the evidence of pretext is clear and persuasive. Pretext in a myriad of forms is often detected only through the vigilance of the affected worker. Because the worker is better informed than anyone else regarding the particulars of her own job, she generally is in the best position to evaluate the accuracy and truthfulness of the reasons advanced by her employer, purportedly justifying its adverse employment decision. Her ability to root out the facts underlying the employer's decision often determines whether a pretext case will succeed or fail.

PROVING AGE DISCRIMINATION CLAIMS

The general principles of proof applied to Title VII cases are also applicable to age discrimination cases alleged under the Age Discrimination in Employment Act of 1967 (ADEA). Almost all age discrimination suits focus on the issue of pretext. Are the reasons expressed by the employer for its decision its actual reasons, or was the employer's decision motivated by an impermissible factor, such as the employee's age? Are the reasons advanced by the employer credible? Even if an employer's reasons did, in fact, serve as a basis for its decision that adversely affected the worker, was the employer also motivated to make that decision because of the worker's age?

Pretext may be established in an age discrimination case in a number of ways, including the following:

1. By showing that the employer's reasons for its decision adversely affecting the worker had no basis in fact. For instance, if an employer advances "poor job performance" as the basis for its decision to fire a worker, the worker may be able to show that her performance was wholly acceptable during the entire period of her employment, and it was not until *after* the decision to fire her was made that her job performance was placed in issue. In one case, an older worker was not notified of any performance problem, and her supervisors had commented favorably upon her performance until just prior to her termination; but the employer nevertheless tried to justify the worker's termination on account of "poor job performance." There was no basis in fact for its position, and the employer lost the case.
2. By showing that the employer's reasons for its decision were not the actual reasons that motivated it to act.
3. By showing that the reasons given by the employer are insufficient to have motivated it to act in the manner that it did. An older worker may establish this by offering evidence that younger workers exhibited the same shortcomings but were not terminated. The treatment of older

workers less favorably than younger employees—a clear case of disparate treatment—is one of the most common forms of age discrimination.

4. By showing that the employer altered or manipulated its own rules and procedures so as to create the circumstances that purportedly justified the adverse action taken against the older worker.
5. By showing that hostility toward or mistreatment or harassment of the older worker underlay the employment decision affecting that worker.
6. By showing a reduction in the responsibilities of the older worker or a transfer of responsibilities to younger workers just prior to the older worker's termination. Evidence that the employer has been grooming a younger employee to assume the duties of an older worker also strongly points in the direction of pretext.

During the seven-year period following the effective date of Title VII, the courts constructed general guidelines for establishing both disparate treatment and disparate impact employment discrimination claims. In the years following, the courts continued to examine and, on occasion, refine those principles, but the basic work had been completed. The role of the EEOC was yet to be fully defined, but the work and office of the lawyers representing individual workers had been clearly established. We now proceed to examine in some detail the claims that first appeared in the courts and follow the course of development of Title VII and ADEA in the early days of those antidiscrimination laws.

Chapter Four

Early Race Discrimination Cases

The manpower shortages that occurred during World War II allowed African Americans to gain employment positions previously denied them. Early in the war, at a time when nonwhites comprised about 10 percent of the population, less than 3 percent of war industry workers were nonwhite. By the end of the war, over 8 percent of these workers were nonwhite—an enormous increase, attained over a relatively short period of time. But these gains were short-lived. By mid-1946, one year after the war, the employment gains of African Americans had mostly dissipated as a result of an unchecked revival of discriminatory practices.[1]

In the course of the following ten years, matters failed to improve. In 1955, while 31 percent of white workers held professional, managerial, and other white-collar positions, only 12 percent of nonwhite workers found themselves in those positions. Only 14 percent of white workers were employed in service and other nonskilled positions, but 47 percent of nonwhites worked in those positions. Many nonwhites worked part time, largely because they were unable to find full-time jobs as unemployment among African Americans was prevalent. They comprised 10 percent of the workforce, but 20 percent of the unemployed.[2]

In 1964 employment in federal government agencies remained segregated. Despite the adoption of fair employment laws by twenty-five states, discriminatory practices remained widespread in state and local government offices and work units. Employment in the private sector was much the same as in prior years. The unemployment rate of nonwhites was twice that of whites, as jobs available to African Americans were sharply limited. Of those African Americans who were employed, few held white-collar positions, most others worked in semiskilled blue-collar jobs, and few held foreman

27

positions, These were the circumstances African Americans confronted when the 1964 Civil Rights Act became the law of the land.

African Americans had grown increasingly impatient with the slow progress—indeed, in most instances, the total lack of progress—of governmental endeavors aimed at eradicating discriminatory employer conduct from the workplace. Title VII provided them with the means to undertake that task themselves. As shown in chapter 3, soon after enactment of Title VII, African American complaints of workplace discrimination inundated the courts.

Many of the cases reviewed in this book fall into the category of discrimination cases referred to as disparate treatment. *Disparate treatment* refers to an employer policy or practice that treats some workers less favorably than others, and it is the most common form of employment discrimination.

One of the most persistent issues raised in the earliest Title VII cases was whether the statute prohibited only intentional discriminatory conduct, such as conduct that is the subject of disparate treatment cases, or in addition policies and practices that appeared to be neutral but still had a discriminatory impact. Disparate impact, as distinguished from disparate treatment, comes into play in a discrimination case when an employment policy or practice, appearing on its face to be nondiscriminatory, falls more harshly upon some workers than upon others.

In a case involving a group of African Americans employed by Duke Power Company in North Carolina, the Supreme Court ruled in 1971 that disparate impact discrimination was barred by Title VII. At the time, Duke Power had ninety-five employees at its Dan River Station, fourteen of whom were African Americans. They had sued the company, alleging that they had been subjected to racially discriminatory employment practices. The case was tried before a federal district court that ruled that, prior to July 2, 1965, the effective date of the Civil Rights Act of 1964, the company openly discriminated on the basis of race in the hiring and assigning of employees at its Dan River plant.

The plant was organized into five operating departments: (1) Labor, (2) Coal Handling, (3) Operations, (4) Maintenance, and (5) Laboratory and Test. African Americans were employed only in the Labor Department where the highest-paying jobs paid less than the lowest-paying jobs in the other four departments in which only whites were employed. Promotions were normally made within each department on the basis of job seniority.

In 1955 Duke Power instituted a policy of requiring a high school education for initial assignment to any department except Labor. Ten years later, the company introduced another policy that made the completion of high school a prerequisite for transfer from Labor to any other department. White employees lacking a high school education who were hired before the introduction of the high school education requirement continued to perform their jobs satisfactorily.

On the date Title VII became effective in 1965, the company added a further requirement for new employees. To qualify for hire to any department except the Labor Department, a job applicant, in addition to having a high school education, had to register satisfactory scores on two professionally prepared aptitude tests. Completion of high school alone continued to render employees eligible for transfer to any of the four desirable departments from which African Americans had been excluded provided the incumbent employee had been on the job prior to the time of the new requirement. In September 1965 the company began to permit incumbent employees lacking a high school education to qualify for transfer from Labor or Coal Handling by passing the two aptitude tests—the Wonderlic Personnel Test, which purports to measure general intelligence, and the Bennett Mechanical Comprehension Test. Neither was directed or intended to measure the ability to learn to perform any particular job.

The district court had found that while Duke Power, prior to the Civil Rights Act, had followed a policy of overt racial discrimination, such conduct had ceased. On appeal, the court of appeals noted that the district court was correct in its conclusion that there was no showing of a racial purpose or invidious intent in the adoption of the high school diploma requirement or general intelligence test and that these standards had been applied fairly to whites and African Americans alike. It held that, in the absence of a discriminatory purpose, use of such requirements was permitted by Title VII. Thus the court of appeals rejected claims asserted by the African American workers that because these two requirements operated to render ineligible a markedly disproportionate number of them, these requirements were unlawful under Title VII.

The Supreme Court began its review of the case by rejecting Duke Power's contention that it ceased acting in a discriminatory fashion once the Civil Rights Act was enacted in 1964. The Court then adopted the view that an employer who perpetuates an act of discrimination committed prior to the enactment of Title VII again commits a discriminatory act. Chief Justice Burger, speaking for the court, noted that one of the objectives of Title VII was to achieve equality of employment opportunities by removing barriers that had operated in the past to favor white over African American employees. Under Title VII, practices and procedures, neutral on their face, and even neutral in terms of intent, cannot be maintained if they operate to "freeze" the status quo of prior discriminatory employment practices.

The court ruled that Title VII proscribes not only overt discriminatory conduct but also practices that are fair in form but discriminatory in operation. The touchstone is business necessity. If an employment practice operates to exclude African Americans and it cannot be shown to be related to job performance, the practice is prohibited.

> On the record before us, neither the high school completion requirement nor the general intelligence test is shown to bear a demonstrable relationship to successful performance of the jobs for which it was used. Both were adopted, as the court of appeals noted, without meaningful study of their relationship to job-performance ability. Rather, a vice president of the Company testified, the requirements were instituted on the Company's judgment that they generally would improve the overall quality of the work force.
>
> The evidence, however, shows that employees who have not completed high school or taken the tests have continued to perform satisfactorily and make progress in departments for which the high school and test criteria are now used. The promotion record of present employees who would not be able to meet the new criteria thus suggests the possibility that the requirements may not be needed even for the limited purpose of preserving the avowed policy of advancement within the Company. . . . [G]ood intent or absence of discriminatory intent does not redeem employment procedures or testing mechanisms that operate as "built-in headwinds" for minority groups and are unrelated to measuring job capability.[3]

Thus, disparate impact gained the approval of the Supreme Court. Workers could now rely on the disparate impact approach to eliminate employment policies or practices that deprived them of job opportunities and advancement or in some other fashion seriously disadvantaged them. In these cases, an employment policy or practice may have been adopted without a deliberate, discriminatory motive, but it may nevertheless constitute the functional equivalent of an act of intentional discrimination. As one court explained it, "In essence, disparate impact theory is a doctrinal surrogate for eliminating unproven acts of intentional discrimination hidden innocuously behind facially neutral policies or practices."[4]

Workers using the disparate impact approach are not required to prove that the employer was motivated by a discriminatory purpose in implementing the targeted policies or practices. The motivation of the employer is irrelevant to the outcome of this type of case. If the workers establish that an employment policy disproportionately affects them because of their race, the employer must show, if it is to prevail, that the policy is essential to its business needs. But even if it is essential, the workers may nonetheless prevail if they are able to show that the employer has available to it other policies that it could implement, if it wished, that would impact the workers less disadvantageously.

An African American alleging disparate impact in connection with an employer's hiring practices must establish three elements: (1) a significant disparity exists between the proportion of African Americans available for a particular position and the number of African Americans hired for that position; (2) the employer's specific, facially neutral employment practice that allegedly causes that disparity; and (3) a causal nexus exists between the employment practice and the disparity.

Once the plaintiff worker has established these three elements, the employer may attempt to justify the challenged practice by showing that it serves a legitimate, nondiscriminatory business objective. But as noted, even if the employer succeeds in establishing a business necessity, the worker may still prevail by showing that another practice, impacting African Americans less harshly, is available to the employer to satisfy its business objectives.

The Supreme Court, in effect, approved a new approach to litigating employment discrimination claims. It shifted the focus from an individual worker's claim of discriminatory conduct to the claims of a group of worker claimants. Suppose the lead plaintiff in this case—Griggs—had acted alone as the thirteen other African American workers did not join in the litigation against Duke Power. If Griggs had sued the company on the grounds that it intentionally discriminated against him by applying the high school education requirement, his case would have been rather weak and he probably would not have prevailed. However, when all fourteen African American employees claimed that the high school education requirement disproportionately rejected them for transfer or promotion to the company's better-paid positions—that the application of the high school education rule disparately impacted them as a group—their claims were materially strengthened.[5]

The lower courts had little time to digest these rulings before the Supreme Court again considered a race discrimination in employment case. The plaintiffs in this case, again African Americans, were a certified class of present and former employees of a North Carolina paper mill owned by defendant Albemarle Paper Co.[6] In August 1966, after filing a complaint with the Equal Employment Opportunity Commission and receiving notice of their right to sue, the plaintiffs brought a class action in the United States District Court for the Eastern District of North Carolina, asking the court to grant permanent injunctive relief against "any policy, practice, custom or usage" at the plant that violated Title VII.

At the trial, the court found that the company had "strictly segregated" the plant's departments, reserving the higher-paying and more skilled jobs for its white workers and relegating its African American workers to lower-paying job classifications. Accordingly the court ordered the company to implement a system of plantwide seniority. The court refused, however, to award back pay to the plaintiff class for losses suffered under the segregated seniority program. On appeal of the ruling denying backpay, the Court of Appeals for the Fourth Circuit reversed the district court decision and ruled that back pay should have been awarded.

Because of the compensatory nature of a back pay award and the strong congressional policy embodied in Title VII, a district court must exercise its discretion as to back pay . . . . Thus, a plaintiff or a complaining class who is successful in obtaining an injunction under Title VII of the Act should ordinarily be awarded back pay unless special circumstances would render such an award unjust.

The Supreme Court agreed with the court of appeals. It held that the district court's decision denying back pay must be measured against the purposes that inform Title VII. As the court observed in *Griggs v. Duke Power Co.*, the primary objective was a prophylactic one:

It was to achieve equality of employment opportunities and remove barriers that have operated in the past to favor an identifiable group of white employees over other employees. Backpay has an obvious connection with this purpose. If employers faced only the prospect of an injunctive order, they would have little incentive to shun practices of dubious legality. It is the reasonably certain prospect of a backpay award that "provide[s] the spur or catalyst which causes employers and unions to self-examine and to self-evaluate their employment practices and to endeavor to eliminate, so far as possible, the last vestiges of an unfortunate and ignominious page in this country's history.[7]

The court hammered home its point: It had not merely the power but the duty to render a decree that would, so far as possible, eliminate the discriminatory effects of the past as well as bar like discrimination in the future. And where a legal injury of an economic character has occurred, the law gives a remedy, "the compensation shall be equal to the injury." The injured party is to be placed, as near as may be, in the situation he would have occupied if the wrong had not been committed. The district court's stated grounds for denying back pay in this case must be tested against these standards.

The first ground was that Albemarle's breach of Title VII had not been in "bad faith." This is not a sufficient reason for denying backpay. . . . But, under Title VII, the mere absence of bad faith simply opens the door to equity; it does not depress the scales in the employer's favor. If backpay were awardable only upon a showing of bad faith, the remedy would become a punishment for moral turpitude, rather than a compensation for workers' injuries. This would read the "make whole" purpose right out of Title VII, for a worker's injury is no less real simply because his employer did not inflict it in "bad faith." Title VII is not concerned with the employer's "good intent or absence of discriminatory intent" for "Congress directed the thrust of the Act to the consequences of employment practices, not simply the motivation. . . . To condition the awarding of backpay on a showing of "bad faith" would be to open an enormous chasm between injunctive and backpay relief under Title VII. There is nothing on the face of the statute or in its legislative history that justifies the creation of drastic and categorical distinctions between those two remedies.

In these two decisions, the Supreme Court set a tone that guided the implementation of Title VII in the early days of its existence. It adopted the view that Title VII did not protect discriminatory policies and practices effectuated prior to its enactment. An employer who perpetuates the effects of policies and practices put in place prior to the enactment of Title VII again commits a discriminatory act.

The Supreme Court also clearly stated that Title VII was to be broadly interpreted, that court-ordered relief granted in the wake of discriminatory conduct must be sufficient to deter subsequent illicit conduct. The goal of Title VII is to eliminate discriminatory policies and practices from the American workplace.

In the early days of Title VII, African American women confronted different issues than those faced by African American men. Viewed from one perspective, African American women suffered the same types of workplace discrimination as African American men:

- They were less likely than white workers to be promoted, and when they were promoted, they were more likely to have waited a far longer period of time for their promotions.
- They were more likely to receive lower performance evaluations.
- They were paid less than their white coworkers.
- They were generally excluded from executive and other high-paying positions, and few ever achieve senior management positions.

But viewed from other perspectives, African American women were treated more adversely than African American men. Historically, African American women have been paid less than either white men or white women and they generally have been paid less than African American men.

Early court decisions interpreting Title VII failed to recognize that the employment experiences of African American women often reflect an interaction of sexism and racism. In 1976, five African American women sued their former employer, the St. Louis Assembly Division of the General Motors Corporation, and their former union, the United Automobile Workers, alleging that GM's seniority system and its "last hired–first fired" layoff policy, mandated by GM's collective bargaining agreement with the union, perpetuated the effect of GM's past acts of race and sex discrimination.

Prior to 1970, GM employed only one African American woman at its St. Louis plant. Emma DeGraffenreid, an African American, applied for employment at the Assembly Division in 1968 and again in 1973. She was denied employment in 1968 but was hired in 1973. The following year, however, she lost her job in a companywide layoff. DeGraffenreid alleged that if she had not been discriminated against at the time of her first application for employment in 1968, and instead had been hired, she would not have been laid off in 1974 pursuant to GM's "last hired–first fired" policy. Four other African American women filed similar claims, all claiming that GM's past discriminatory conduct in failing to hire African American women had caused them to lose their positions in the 1974 layoff. The judge hearing the case, however, refused to permit them to continue the litigation in his court. He first noted that the five complainants were suing "on behalf of black women," and thus they were attempting to combine two legal actions—one for sex discrimination and one for race discrimination—into a "new special sub-category, namely, a combination of racial and sex-based discrimination":

> The court notes that plaintiffs have failed to cite any decisions which have stated that black women are a special class to be protected from discrimination. The court's own research has failed to disclose such a decision. The plaintiffs are clearly entitled to a remedy if they have been discriminated against. However, they should not be allowed to combine statutory remedies to create a new 'super-remedy' which would give them relief beyond what the drafters of [Title VII] intended. Thus, this lawsuit must be examined to see if it states a cause of action for race discrimination, sex discrimination, or alternatively either, but not a combination of both.[8]

Once the court limited consideration of the case to one that alleged separate claims of sex and race discrimination, it concluded that the sex claim was deficient, because GM had hired women prior to 1970, albeit all but one were white. It then ruled that the African American women could pursue their race claims against GM, but only in combination with African American men who were then engaged in suing the company for race discrimination.

Thus, the court rejected discrimination claims based on an interaction of race and sex bias. It left the complainants without a remedy for discrimination directed against them simply because they were African American women. Apparently, the court believed that in enacting Title VII, Congress either failed to contemplate that African American women would be subjected to discriminatory conduct as "African American women" or that it failed to offer them any protection if such discrimination did occur. As University of California law professor Kimberle Crenshaw has pointed out,

> The court's refusal in [the DeGraffenreid case] to acknowledge that Black women encounter combined race and sex discrimination implies that the boundaries of sex and race discrimination doctrine are defined respectively by white women's and Black men's experiences. Under this view, Black women are protected only to the extent that their experiences coincide with those of either group.[9]

Just four years after the *DeGraffenreid* case was decided, another court arrived at a radically different conclusion. Dafro Jefferies, an African American, was employed by the Harris County Community Action Association in Texas, first as secretary to the director of programs and later as a personnel interviewer. In the latter position, she applied for promotion to various positions, but on each occasion was unsuccessful. Subsequently, her employer posted a notice announcing vacancies for two field representative positions, and Jefferies immediately filed applications for both. The vacant positions had previously been staffed by a white female and an African American male.

Shortly after Jefferies submitted her applications for the field representative positions, she saw a personnel department form indicating an African American male had already been hired for one of the positions. Believing she was a victim of discrimination, Jefferies filed a discrimination charge with the EEOC and later commenced a legal action against her employer.

Testimony elicited at the trial disclosed that approximately 70 percent of the association's employees were female, that women held sixteen of the thirty-six supervisory positions in the agency, and several women occupied positions on the association's board of directors. Jefferies undisputed testimony established that every position for which she had applied had been filled either by a white woman or by a man, black or white.

Jefferies pursued her case along three avenues, alleging separate acts of race and sex discrimination as well as acts of discrimination based on a combination of race and sex. The court rejected Jefferies's race discrimination claim since the person hired for one of the field representative positions was also African American. Because both the person seeking the position and the person achieving the position were of the same race, the court held that it would be implausible to view the association's decision with regard to filling the position as discriminatory. The court also rejected Jefferies's sex discrimination claim. Evidence showed that (1) several women served on the association's board of directors, (2) of the thirty-six supervisory positions, sixteen were held by women, and (3) one of the field representative positions for which Jefferies had applied had been filled by a woman. The court determined that the association did not discriminate generally on the basis of sex.

With the rejection of the race and sex discrimination claims, the court was left with the decision whether to allow Jefferies to pursue her claim that the discrimination she experienced resulted from a combination of sex and race bias. Should Jefferies be allowed to sue the association for discrimination she experienced by reason of the fact that she was an African American *and* a woman?

Jefferies argued that an employer should not escape liability for acts of discrimination against African American women merely by demonstrating that it neither discriminated against African American men nor white women. The court agreed. Its decision was based in part upon its view of the scope of Title VII. The statute provides a remedy for employment discrimination on the basis of a worker's "race, color, religion, sex, or national origin."[10] Congress's use of the word "or," in the court's view, showed that Congress intended to prohibit employment discrimination based on any or all of the listed characteristics. Moreover, the court noted, that at the time of the enactment of Title VII, the House of Representatives rejected a proposed amendment that would have limited evidence of sex discrimination to that based "solely" upon sex, thus opening the door to claims based on sex as well as on one of the other of the statute's characteristics, such as race. Thus, the court concluded:

> Black females represent a significant percentage of the active or potentially active labor force. In the absence of a clear expression by Congress that it did not intend to provide protection against discrimination directed especially toward black women as a class separate and distinct from the class of women and the class of blacks, we cannot condone a result which leaves black women without a viable Title VII remedy. If both black men and white women are considered to be within the same protected class as black females for purposes [of proving discrimination,] no remedy will exist for discrimination which is directed only toward black females.[11]

The court, recognizing African American women as a distinct subgroup, granted them protection from acts of discrimination barred by Title VII. As an African American woman, Jefferies stood in a class separate and apart from African American men and white women. Under this court ruling, when an African American woman charges her employer with committing acts of discrimination against her *as an African American woman*, the fact that African American males and white females were not also subjected to discrimination is irrelevant to her claim.

The fact that an African American male was granted promotion to the position for which Jefferies had applied is not relevant to her claim, since he was not a member of the class of workers that included Jefferies. Stated in other terms, Jefferies may prove that the association's reasons for not promoting her to the field representative positions were discriminatory by showing that persons outside her class—African American men and white women—were treated more advantageously than she was as an African American woman.

In contrast to the *DeGraffenreid* decision, the *Jefferies* decision clearly holds that discrimination against African American women may exist in the absence of discrimination against African American men or white women. The *Jefferies* decision provides a rational basis affording protection to those workers experiencing discrimination as a combination of factors, such as sex and race.

In the years immediately following the enactment of the 1964 Civil Rights Act, the Supreme Court and the federal courts across the nation found themselves immersed in Title VII legal issues, and chief among those issues was racial discrimination. We now turn to other acts of discrimination that were also demanding the attention of the courts.

Chapter Five

Early Sex Discrimination Cases

Congress enacted the 1964 Civil Rights Act at a time when the status of women in the workplace had rested on the bottom rung of the employment ladder for many decades. Only 10 percent of managerial positions and fewer than 15 percent of professional jobs were filled by women. Although women represented one of three workers in the labor force, nearly 45 percent of low-paying service jobs were held by women.[1] Thousands of women were relegated to dead-end jobs without hope of promotion. Discrimination against women was profound and pervasive.

Initially, the EEOC was hesitant to address these issues. In the deliberations leading to the adoption of the Civil Rights Act, Congress placed great emphasis on race discrimination as the issue requiring immediate attention, while sex discrimination was considered almost as an afterthought. Although Congress did not specifically direct the EEOC to place less emphasis on sex discrimination than on race discrimination, this is precisely what occurred as a consequence of the nature of the deliberations leading to the enactment of Title VII.

Nor at first did the EEOC take seriously female worker claims that sex discrimination constituted a substantial issue for women in the workplace. As earlier noted, this attitude motivated the EEOC staff to devote far less effort to the elimination of sex discrimination than to the elimination of race discrimination from the workplace.

The EEOC's irresolution in addressing issues regarding discrimination against women was reflected in the original EEOC guidelines on sex discrimination. The guidelines did not favor women. The EEOC assumed that when Congress enacted Title VII, it had not intended to disturb existing state protective laws, such as those limiting women's working hours and restricting their places of employment. Employers had responded to these laws by

39

assigning female workers to "women's jobs," and jobs thus classified generally paid less than those designated as "men's jobs." Early on, the EEOC announced it would not consider a state law prohibiting women from working in jobs requiring them to lift more than a specified weight as a violation of Title VII.[2] Thus, in the early stages of the EEOC administration of Title VII, state protective laws remained significant barriers to the equal treatment of women in the workplace.

Eventually, the EEOC corrected its earlier stance and redirected its attention to Title VII's prohibitions against sex discrimination. It remained for the courts, however, to determine whether to interpret the statute broadly or restrictively, whether to limit the application of the statute to the most blatant, and therefore the most obvious, forms of discriminatory conduct or to extend the reach of the statute to employer conduct less obviously discriminatory. In 1971, the Supreme Court was presented with this issue.

After reading a local Florida newspaper help-wanted advertisement placed by the Martin Marietta Corporation, Ida Phillips submitted an employment application for the position of assembly trainee. Shortly thereafter, she was notified that female applicants with preschool-age children were not being considered for the job. When she later learned that men with preschool-age children had been interviewed and hired for employment in that position, Phillips sued the company for sex discrimination.

In response to Phillips's lawsuit, Martin Marietta alluded to its high hiring rate of women for the assembly trainee position, arguing that it had refused to hire Phillips not because she was a woman but solely because she had preschool-age children at home. An employer may not be found guilty of sex discrimination, the company urged, unless it utilized sex, and only sex, as the basis for its action. Martin Marietta concluded that because Phillips's gender had not been the basis for its refusal to hire her, it had not committed an act in violation of the statute.

The Supreme Court rejected Martin Marietta's argument and ruled that an employer that promulgates one hiring policy for women and another for men violates Title VII, even though the difference in the hiring policies relates to a factor other than sex—in this case, the presence of young children in the home.

If the court had acceded to Martin Marietta's argument, the scope of the statute would have been materially limited. As stated by Justice Thurgood Marshall in his concurring opinion:

> By adding the prohibition against job discrimination based on sex to the 1964 Civil Rights Act, Congress intended to prevent employers from refusing "to hire an individual based on stereotyped characterizations of the sexes.". . . Even characterizations of the proper roles of the sexes were not to serve as predicates for restricting employment opportunity. . . . When performance

characteristics of an individual are involved, even when parental roles are concerned, employment opportunity may be limited only by employment criteria that are neutral as to the sex of the applicant.

Thus, the Supreme Court firmly placed its stamp of approval on the side of an expansive, rather than a restrictive, interpretation of the statute, establishing the rule that the differential treatment of women on the basis of her child-caring responsibilities constitutes a violation of Title VII.[3]

Another issue soon surfaced that threatened to undermine the scope of Title VII. Congress had added an exception to the statute's proscriptions of sex discriminatory practices by permitting employers to deny employment to women when the nature of the job required the physical attributes of a man to perform the job's functions: "Notwithstanding any other provision of this [statute], it shall not be an unlawful employment practice for an employer to hire or employ employees on the basis . . . of sex . . . in those certain instances where . . . sex . . . is a bona fide occupational qualification reasonably necessary to the normal operation of that particular business or enterprise."[4] If broadly interpreted, the bona fide occupational qualification exception would justify the exclusion of large numbers of women from some jobs, particularly those requiring the performance of manual tasks.

Dianne Rawlinson, a rather small woman, applied for the position of prison guard in the Alabama prison system. Her application was rejected as she failed to meet the state's minimum 120-pound weight requirement as well as its minimum five-foot, two-inch height requirement. Rawlinson sued, claiming that the weight and height requirements disproportionately excluded women from eligibility for employment as prison guards.

Data submitted to the trial court showed that the five-foot, two-inch minimum height requirement excluded over 33 percent of working women from prison guard positions, while excluding only slightly more than 1 percent of male workers. Similarly, the 120-pound minimum weight requirement eliminated 22.29 percent of female workers but only 2.35 percent of male workers. When the height and weight requirements were combined, over 41 percent of female workers would fail to qualify for the position, while less than 1 percent of working males would be barred.

In defense of the weight and height requirements, the Alabama Board of Corrections argued that these physical requisites were bona fide occupational qualifications directly related to the prison guard position, thus justifying Rawlinson's rejection for the job. However, the board made the mistake of not offering the court any data correlating the height and weight requirements with the requisite amount of strength essential to perform the functions of the prison guard job. When the case reached the Supreme Court, the justices pointed out that if the strength of a prison guard was truly job-related and constituted a bona fide occupational qualification (BFOQ), the board could have adopted specific tests to measure directly each applicant's strength: "Such a test, fairly administered, would fully satisfy the standards of Title VII because it would be one that measures the person for the job, and not the person in the abstract."[5]

The Supreme Court ruled that if the board wished to rely on the BFOQ defense to deny a position to a woman, it would be required to conduct individual evaluations of each female applicant to determine that applicant's qualifications for the position.

This was the first of many court rulings holding that an employer must evaluate a female worker as an individual rather than rely upon stereotypical characterizations of female worker capabilities. An employer may not validly assert the BFOQ defense on the assumption that all women, as a class, possess identical or even similar attributes. As the Supreme Court emphasized, the BFOQ defense is based on an extremely narrow exception to the general prohibition of discrimination on the basis of sex, and for an employer to rely upon that exception, it must prove a female job applicant is specifically unqualified for the position in question. It is impermissible under Title VII to refuse to hire a woman on the basis of a stereotypical characterization of the female sex.

When may the BFOQ exception be validly asserted? Under Alabama law, Dianne Rawlinson had a second hurdle to surpass before she could qualify for the prison guard position. The Supreme Court noted that Alabama's prison system was "a peculiarly inhospitable one for human beings of whatever sex." Because of insufficient staffing and inadequate penal facilities, the Board of Corrections had not undertaken to segregate inmates according to their offenses and, as a result, male prisoners incarcerated as sex offenders, constituting 20 percent of the prison population, were scattered throughout the prison's dormitory facilities. Were these circumstances such as to render the prison guard job too dangerous for women? Ordinarily, as the court observed, whether a particular job is too dangerous for women is a decision that an individual woman should make for herself. But in this case, more was at stake. The court felt that sex offenders who had criminally assaulted women in the past would be moved to do so again if they had access to women within the prison. There also was the risk that other inmates, deprived of a normal heterosexual environment, would assault women guards.

> In a prison system where violence is the order of the day, where inmate access to guards is facilitated by dormitory living conditions, . . . and where a substantial portion of the inmate population is composed of sex offenders mixed at random with other prisoners, there are few visible deterrents to inmate assault on women custodians.

Therefore, the court concluded, Rawlinson's "very womanhood" undermined her capacity to provide the security that is a primary responsibility of a prison guard. Since the use of female guards under the conditions existing in the Alabama prison system would pose a substantial security problem—a problem directly linked to the sex of the prison guards—being male was a bona fide occupational qualification for the prison guard position.[6]

There are not many positions in the business world where "womanhood" constitutes a disqualifying factor. The court's decision in the Rawlinson case, along with other early court decisions emphasizing the narrow application of the BFOQ defense, have opened up many positions for women that formerly were reserved for men. On each occasion that we observe a police woman at her post, a female school bus driver, train engineer, conductor, construction or utility worker, or other female workers performing tasks that prior to the enactment of Title VII had been reserved for men, we have the courts to thank for the limitations that have been placed upon the application of the BFOQ defense.

Beginning with the Rawlinson case, the Supreme Court has repeatedly held that a woman must be evaluated as an individual and not as a member of a class or as a woman in the abstract. Stereotypical characterizations of female attributes may in certain instances be true of some women, but they are not true of all women.

The issue of sex stereotypes next came before the court in connection with a challenge to the pension plan provided the employees of the Los Angeles Department of Water and Power. The department's pension plan was based upon mortality tables and its own experience that women live longer than men. Because the department's female workers lived longer in retirement, the cost of a pension for the average female retiree was greater than that for the average male retiree. To compensate for the difference, the department required its women employees to make larger contributions to the plan. Because greater amounts were withheld from their paychecks to finance their pension benefits, female workers received less take-home pay than their male coworkers. The women objected to this policy and sued the Los Angeles Department of Water and Power.

The Supreme Court struck down the pension plan as an instance of sex stereotyping. The water department's rationale for requiring larger pension contributions from women was based upon the assumption that all women live longer than men. But *all* women do not live longer than *all* men. As a group, women live longer than men as a group, but this may not be true of many members of each group and it is certainly not true of all members of either group. It is simply impossible for an employer to forecast the life span of any particular woman. The Department of Water and Power was not justified, therefore, in using a group's average longevity in the computation of the cost of that woman's pension benefits. To do so was to consider her not as an individual but as a group member. Employment decisions based upon stereotypical assumptions pertaining to a group or class rather than upon an individual's particular circumstances are antithetical to gender equality.[7]

Other courts, following the Supreme Court's lead, rejected employer initiatives based on sex stereotypes. United Air Lines made the mistake of adopting a no-marriage rule for its female flight attendants but declined to make the rule applicable to male flight personnel, including male flight attendants. United justified its no-marriage rule on the ground that it had received complaints from husbands of its flight attendants concerning their wives' working schedules and irregular working hours. The federal court of appeals sitting in Chicago rejected United's position, noting that Title VII required employers to treat their employees as individuals: "United's blanket prophylactic rule prohibiting marriage unjustifiably punishes a large class of prospective, otherwise qualified and competent employees where an individualized response could adequately dispose of any real employment conflicts."[8]

Subsequent to these early cases, most courts have consistently rejected stereotype-based employment rules and regulations based on group rather than individual characteristics. But despite these rulings, stereotypes still frequently underlie current employment decisions adversely affecting women.

Even though an employer may refrain from discriminating against women in general, it may nonetheless be guilty of acts of discrimination committed in violation of a particular woman's rights. Thus, if an employer generally treats its female employees fairly and advantageously, it can never be justified in discriminating against a particular female worker. Each claim of discrimination must be examined in the circumstances confronted by the particular woman involved. It must be emphasized that Title VII and the principles of nondiscrimination require that an employer consider a female worker on the basis of individual capabilities and not on the basis of any characteristics attributable to women in general. Stereotypical assumptions may play no role in this process.

In addition to adjudicating cases involving sex stereotyping, soon after the enactment of Title VII the courts again were required to consider the validity of the state protective laws. These laws originally were intended for the general benefit of women, but restrictions on working conditions of female workers seriously undermined the career prospects of many women. The initial EEOC guidelines were based on the assumption that Congress, in enacting Title VII, had not intended to invalidate these laws. The courts, however, believed otherwise, and most of the state protective laws soon met their demise.

Another issue arose soon after enactment of Title VII. Pregnant workers who were adversely treated once their employers learned of their pregnancies began to file claims for sex discrimination. The statute provided that it was unlawful for an employer to discriminate against a woman *because of sex*, but it was silent with regard to pregnancy.[9] Thus the courts were confronted with the question whether "because of sex" included "because of pregnancy." The early pregnancy cases concluded with victories for the complainants,[10] but the Supreme Court, sometimes reluctant to assume a leading role in matters relating to civil rights in employment, declared in a case involving the General Electric Company that discrimination against pregnant women was not barred by Title VII.

After GE adopted a disability plan that afforded its employees with sickness and injury benefits, but excluded any benefits for disabilities arising from pregnancy, a group of female workers brought a class action against the company, claiming that the exclusion of pregnancy from the terms of the disability plan amounted to an act of sex discrimination in violation of Title VII. The trial court agreed, declaring that discrimination against pregnant women is a form of sex discrimination and thus the disabilities plan's pregnancy exclusion was discriminatory. But the Supreme Court thought otherwise. The court, speaking through Justice Rehnquist, first noted that pregnancy is merely a physical condition, and an employer is free to include or exclude disability coverage for this physical condition just as it may with respect to any other physical condition. In Justice Rehnquist's view, the GE plan did not afford coverage for any disability or illness from which women were excluded. Nor did it include any disability or illness from which men were excluded. "There is no risk from which men are protected and women are not. Likewise, there is no risk from which women are protected and men are not." Since the plan did not exclude anyone from coverage because of gender, it complied with Title VII. For that reason, the Supreme Court rejected the position generally adopted in the lower courts that discrimination based on pregnancy was a form of sex discrimination.[11]

Sexual harassment was another matter that the courts and the EEOC were required to confront. The sexual harassment of a woman by a man located higher up on the corporate ladder conveys to that woman that the message that she is primarily perceived not as a workplace colleague and a valuable asset but rather as a sexual object. The sexual harassment of women expresses the age-old belief that women should be sexually available to men, and it simultaneously reminds them that they are neither respected nor viewed as workplace equals.[12]

Because sexual harassment reflects an unequal status existing between a man and a woman, it generally involves a power relationship affecting the terms and conditions of the woman's employment. Sexual harassment may culminate in a hostile and offensive work environment, an environment the harassed woman must confront each day of her work life. Women, therefore, perceive sexual harassment as a reflection of a status that emphasizes their sex roles over their work roles, thus threatening their economic livelihood. [13]

Catharine A. MacKinnon, who first argued that workplace sexual harassment constitutes a major problem for women, stated in her seminal book *Sexual Harassment of Working Women* that "[s]exual harassment is seen to be one dynamic which reinforces and expresses women's traditional and inferior role in the labor workplace." MacKinnon was the first to contend that sexual harassment in the workplace is a form of sex discrimination. [14]

In 1976, in one of the earliest sexual harassment cases decided after the advent of Title VII, the complainant alleged that her supervisor had retaliated against her when she refused his request for an "after hours affair." The District of Columbia federal court held that the substance of the complainant's allegations centered on her claim that she was discriminated against not because she was a woman but because she had declined to engage in a sexual affair with her supervisor. According to the court, this was not sex discrimination: "This is a controversy underpinned by the subtleties of an inharmonious personal relationship. Regardless of how inexcusable the conduct of plaintiff's supervisor might have been, it does not evidence an arbitrary barrier to continued employment based on plaintiff's sex." [15]

Less than a year later, an Arizona federal court arrived at a similar conclusion. The court ordered the dismissal of the complaints of two women who alleged they had been verbally and physically harassed by their supervisor and that his sexually harassing behavior continued unabated until they were compelled to resign their employment. The court stated that, although Title VII bars discrimination against a woman by an employer, nothing appears in the statute to apply to sexual advances of a supervisor in its employ:

> In the present case, [the supervisor's] conduct appears to be nothing more than a personal proclivity, peculiarity, or mannerism. By his alleged sexual advances, [he] was satisfying a personal urge. Certainly no employer policy is here involved. . . . Nothing in the complaint alleges nor can it be construed that the conduct complained of was company directed policy which deprived women of employment opportunities. [16]

The court also expressed its concern that the outgrowth of a ruling that such activity was actionable under Title VII would be a federal lawsuit "every time a worker made amorous or sexually oriented advances toward another." In such circumstances, the court opined, the only certain way an employer could avoid such charges would to be to hire only employees who were asexual.

One year later, a District of Columbia federal appellate court ruled that women subjected to acts of sexual harassment are discriminated against not because of their refusal to engage in sexual acts demanded by a supervisor as the first court had held but simply because they are women: "But for her womanhood . . . her participation in sexual activity would never have been solicited. To say, then, that she was victimized in her employment simply because she declined the invitation is to ignore the asserted fact that she was invited only because she was a woman."[17]

Soon after, another federal appellate court ruled that if a supervisor, with the knowledge of his employer, makes sexual demands of a subordinate female employee and conditions her employment status on a favorable response to those demands, he and his employer acts in violation of Title VII.[18]

Thus, in the years immediately following the adoption of Title VII, the courts and the EEOC often formulated broad legal principles applicable to issues relating to discrimination against women. But in some areas—pregnancy and sexual harassment—the courts often adopted much more restrictive views of women's workplace rights.

Chapter Six

Early National Origin Discrimination Cases

Shortly after the beginning of World War II, President Roosevelt issued an executive order authorizing certain designated military commanders to exclude persons from prescribed geographical areas as a protection against espionage and sabotage. The military commander of the Western Defense Command designated the entire Pacific coast as an area possibly subject to an invasion by Japan and thus an area that could very well be targeted for espionage and sabotage. All Japanese aliens and persons of Japanese ancestry were then ordered to evacuate the area.

Longstanding racial animosity against the Japanese was a salient feature of prewar attitudes of white Americans living along the West Coast. The evacuation order followed several months of blatant anti-Japanese sentiment expressed by newspaper columnists, radio commentators, and California politicians who agitated for some form of proscriptive action against persons of Japanese ancestry living in the United States.

Over the next eight months, 120,000 men, women, and children of Japanese descent were forced to leave their homes in California, Oregon, Washington, and Arizona and move to internment camps. More than 80,000 of them were American citizens. The government did not charge them with criminal activity, and it conducted no trials or hearings prior to their evacuation. The military authorities did not tell these people why they had to leave their homes or how long they would be barred from returning to them.

Military commanders had no reasonable basis for selecting this group of people for evacuation and internment. Their action was motivated by bias against those of Japanese ancestry. Army officers referred to persons of Japanese ancestry as "subversive," as "potential enemies," as a people belonging to "an enemy race," and whose "racial strains were undiluted." They further claimed, without substantiating evidence, that persons of Japanese lineage were accustomed to practice "emperor worshiping ceremonies."[1] These people were condemned because they constituted a large, unassimilated, tightly knit racial group, allegedly bound to an enemy nation by strong ties of race, culture, custom, and religion. The reasons alleged by the military as justifying these evacuations were based on misinformation, half-truths, insinuation, bias, and the assumption that because a few persons of Japanese ancestry may have tried to aid the Japanese war effort, the entire group could not be trusted to be or remain loyal to the United States.

Americans have a lengthy history of discriminating against peoples of other nations who abide in the United States. Most of these people are eventually assimilated into the national mores, as were the Italians, Poles, and Irish, but prior to their assimilation they were targets of long years of discriminatory animus.

The targeted peoples of 1964, the year Congress moved to enact Title VII, were workers with Spanish surnames, who numbered in excess of 600,000 at the time. These workers were generally barred from white-collar and blue-collar craftsmen positions and were concentrated in unskilled, semiskilled, and service jobs.[2]

The inclusion of national origin as a protected basis in the Civil Rights Act of 1964 caused little debate in Congress, explained by reason of the fact that subsequent to the forced evacuation of people of Japanese ancestry from the Western states during the war, various executive orders expressly prohibited discrimination on the basis of national origin in the hiring of federal government employees.

Once Title VII was adopted, cases challenging employer conduct, allegedly infected with national origin bias, followed the disparate treatment and disparate impact lines of proof used in race and sex cases. One of the first questions to arise with respect to the scope of the national origin prohibition was whether it included discrimination on the basis of citizenship.

Cecilia Espinoza, a lawfully admitted resident alien who was born in Mexico, resided in San Antonio, Texas. She sought employment as a seamstress at the San Antonio division of Farah Manufacturing Co., but her employment application was rejected on the basis of a longstanding company policy against the employment of aliens. Espinoza then sued the company on the ground that it had discriminated against her because of her national origin in violation of Title VII.

The district court granted Espinoza's motion for summary judgment, holding that a refusal to hire because of lack of citizenship constituted discrimination on the basis of national origin. The court of appeals reversed that ruling, concluding that the statutory phrase "national origin" did not embrace citizenship. The issue then passed to the Supreme Court. The court noted that the plain language of the statute supported the company's position that the

Title VII ban of national origin discrimination did not include discrimination by reason of citizenship:

> The term "national origin" on its face refers to the country where a person was born, or, more broadly, the country from which his or her ancestors came. . . . Congress itself has on several occasions since 1964 enacted statutes barring aliens from federal employment. The Treasury, Postal Service, and General Government Appropriation Act, 1973, for example, provides that "no part of any appropriation contained in this or any other Act shall be used to pay the compensation of any officer or employee of the Government of the United States . . . unless such person (1) is a citizen of the United States . . . ." To interpret the term "national origin" to embrace citizenship requirements would require us to conclude that Congress itself has repeatedly flouted its own declaration of policy. This Court cannot lightly find such a breach of faith. So far as federal employment is concerned, we think it plain that Congress has assumed that the ban on national origin discrimination in Title VII did not affect the historical practice of requiring citizenship as a condition of employment. And there is no reason to believe Congress intended the term "national origin" . . . to have any broader scope.

The district court had drawn primary support for its holding that Title VII's ban on national origin discrimination included a ban on citizenship discrimination from an interpretative guideline issued by the Equal Employment Opportunity Commission that provided: "Because discrimination on the basis of citizenship has the effect of discriminating on the basis of national origin, a lawfully immigrated alien who is domiciled or residing in this country may not be discriminated against on the basis of his citizenship."[3] The court recognized that in some instances an employer's use of a citizenship requirement could be a part of a larger scheme to conceal unlawful national origin discrimination, and in those circumstances, Title VII would prohibit discrimination on the basis of citizenship. But those were not the circumstances of this case. Farah Manufacturing accepted applications of persons of Mexican origin, provided the individual concerned had become an American citizen. Indeed, the district court found that persons of Mexican ancestry made up more than 96 percent of the employees at the company's San Antonio division and 97 percent of those doing the work for which Mrs. Espinoza applied. Espinoza was denied employment, not because of the country of her origin, but because she had not yet achieved US citizenship.

The district court agreed with the court of appeals that neither the language of Title VII nor its history nor the specific facts of the case indicated that Farah Manufacturing engaged in unlawful discrimination because of national origin.[4]

While the Supreme Court initially took a somewhat restrictive view of national origin discrimination, the EEOC adopted an extremely broad view. In the EEOC perspective, no one can be denied equal employment opporttunity because of his or her "birthplace, ancestry, culture, linguistic characteristics common to a specific ethnic group, or accent." In addition, equal employment opportunity cannot be denied "because of marriage or association with persons of a national origin group; membership or association with specific ethnic promotion groups; attendance or participation in schools, churches, temples or mosques generally associated with a national origin group; or a surname associated with a national origin group."[5]

The EEOC also acted to severely restrict English-only rules. An employer can require its employees to speak English on the job only if English is necessary to perform job functions effectively. An English-only rule is allowed only if required to ensure the safe or efficient operation of the employer's business and is put in place for nondiscriminatory reasons.[6]

The 1970 census showed that national origin discrimination was still widespread. This was particularly true of Asian workers. The average income of a Japanese worker with four or more years of college was 83 percent of the average income of a comparable white male worker. For a Chinese worker, it was 74 percent; for a Filipino worker, 52 percent. With Asian women, the discrepancy was even greater. Their income on average varied between 44 percent and 54 percent that of white males.[7]

Title VII's prohibition of national origin discrimination is closely allied with its ban of employment discrimination by reason of a worker's color. Race and color also clearly overlap. Thus color discrimination can occur between persons of different races or ethnicities. An employer who adversely treats a brown-complexioned Latino worker may be guilty of national origin, racial, and color discrimination.

Chapter Seven

Early Religious Discrimination Cases

As originally written, Title VII did not define religion. The EEOC filled in the gap, specifying in its guidelines that the term *religion* included "all aspects of religious observance and practice, as well as belief." *Religious practices* included "moral or ethical beliefs as to what is right or wrong which are sincerely held with the strength of traditional religious views." A belief is religious not because it is professed by a religious group but because the individual espousing it sincerely holds that belief with the strength of traditional religious views. [1]

In nearly all instances, the courts have rejected efforts to denominate an individual's personal beliefs as nonreligious. The fact that no religious group accepts such beliefs is not decisive. Rather, the courts have endeavored to determine the issue by asking a single question: Do the person's beliefs occupy the same place in his or her life as an orthodox belief in God holds in the life of a member of one of the traditional religions?

William Frazee refused a temporary retail position because the job would have required him to work on Sundays. He then applied for unemployment benefits, but his application was denied because, as the Illinois authorities announced, a refusal to accept a position on account of religious conviction must be based upon "some tenets or dogma accepted by . . . some church, sect, or denomination," and a refusal based solely on an individual's personal belief is irrelevant. Therefore, the Illinois officials ruled, Frazee's contention that as a Christian he believed it wrong to work on Sunday was not enough. As you might expect, this reasoning did not sit well with the Supreme Court, which dismissed the Illinois ruling with one sentence: "Undoubtedly, membership in an organized religious denomination, especially one with a specific tenet forbidding members to work on Sunday, would simplify the problem of identifying sincerely held religious beliefs, but we reject the notion that to claim the protection of the [law], one must be responding to the commands of a particular religious organization."[2]

Although the courts have steadfastly held to the position that legal protection for personally held nonreligious beliefs must be denied, they rarely enter a situation that requires them to distinguish between a personal or nonreligious belief and a religious belief.

Title VII's prohibition of discriminatory acts based on a person's race, sex, or national origin relates to particular classes of workers, whereas its ban against religious discrimination applies to all workers, regardless of their race, sex, or national origin. It obligates an employer to act in a specified manner in two designated areas. First, an employer must eliminate all religious discriminatory animus from employment decisions involving the hiring, promotion, layoff, transfer, discipline, job assignment, compensation, discharge, and other working conditions of its employees. Second, it must reasonably accommodate workers who notify it of the existence of a conflict between their religious observances and practices and the employer's work rules and directives, unless in doing so it would incur an undue hardship.

The employee is obligated to monitor her religious conduct to determine whether it is appropriate to the workplace. The worker who keeps his religious beliefs to himself will not cause a problem for others or himself, but the worker who believes she has the right to openly express her religious beliefs, or attempt to convince others to join her in her religious beliefs or practices, may offend her fellow workers, thus causing problems for the other workers, her employer, and herself.

As in other forms of discrimination prohibited by Title VII, a worker alleging workplace religious discrimination may establish a claim by submitting direct or indirect evidence of the employer's discriminatory intent in advancing an employment decision adverse to the worker's interests. In the majority of cases, an employer manages to conceal its religious prejudice, and thus it remains wholly or partially hidden from the view of the worker. To successfully establish a legal claim where there is no direct evidence of prejudice, the complaining worker must rely on indirect evidence to establish the employer's discriminatory bias.

After serving for several years as an assistant professor of history at Jackson State University in Mississippi, Leslie Citron complained that his department head and other university officials had made several decisions that proved adverse to his interests and reflected a bias against his Jewish faith. Among other complaints, Citron alleged he had been denied the opportunity to teach in the graduate school while other professors, who were not Jewish and were less qualified, were granted those assignments. The university rebutted his claim with evidence that assignments to the graduate school had been made in favor of professors who possessed a particular form of academic training that Citron lacked.

Citron also claimed he had been discriminated against when he was assigned to teach a disproportionate number of freshman courses, while non-Jewish professors were permitted to limit their assignments to these courses. But again the university easily rebutted his claim by showing that department heads exercised professional judgment in determining the needs of their particular departments and in assessing the capabilities of their faculty. Commenting that no faculty member had a vested right to teach any course he desired, the court ruled that Citron had failed to sustain his burden of proving that discrimination played any role in the university's decisions with regard to work assignments.[3]

Employer decisions involving the exercise of professional judgment are generally immune to attack unless the complaining worker is capable of proffering direct evidence that religious bias infected the decision-making process. Without persuasive evidence of that nature, religious discrimination claims generally end in defeat for the worker. But one Texas worker successfully avoided that outcome.

When Martha Young first began working for the Bellaire, Texas, branch of the Southwestern Savings and Loan Association, she was aware that all Southwestern employees were required to attend monthly staff meetings in the Houston office. She knew that various business matters were considered at these meetings—organizational policies, current economic conditions, and plans for the future—but she did not know that those business discussions were preceded by religious homilies, followed by prayers, both led by a local Baptist minister.

Young was an atheist. At first she attended these meetings without complaining, but later concluded that her forced attendance violated her freedom of conscience. Instead of registering a complaint, she simply stopped going to the meetings, but after a time her absence was noted and reported to the Bellaire branch manager. When confronted, Young admitted she had repeatedly skipped the meetings because of their religious content. Her manager reminded her of her obligation to attend these meetings and that if she objected to the religious content, she should "close her ears" during those portions of the meetings. When Young persisted in not attending the meetings, the manager again reminded her that her attendance was mandatory. Young then notified him that she was leaving Southwestern. When he asked her for a letter of resignation, she refused his request, noting that she was not resigning but was in fact being forced out of the bank.

Several months later Young filed suit against Southwestern, demanding reinstatement, back pay, and reimbursement of her attorney's fees. Young had enjoyed her work and Southwestern valued her services. The only possible reason for her resignation was her resolution not to attend religious services that were repugnant to her conscience, coupled with the knowledge that her attendance at the monthly staff meetings was mandatory and that if she failed to attend, she would be terminated. In these circumstances, Young was forced to resign so as to escape an unlawful, religious employment requirement. The court awarded judgment in her favor.[4]

At the time of the enactment of Title VII, religious discrimination among certain religions was prevalent. Catholics were denied executive positions in several industries, Seventh-Day Adventists were not allowed to attend Saturday Sabbath services, and anti-Semitism remained a significant issue.

Wallace Weiss, who was Jewish, was employed as a research analyst by the US Defense Logistics Agency (Logistics). His supervisor, who was not Jewish, was not aware at the time he hired Weiss that he was Jewish. After his hire, Weiss was the only Jew working in the Logistics office.

Soon after Weiss started working at the agency, his supervisor and a coworker openly used religious slurs in his presence. They referred to him as the "resident Jew," "Jew faggot," and "rich Jew" and daily taunted him, accusing the Jews of having killed Christ. Although continuously subjected to anti-Semitic remarks of that nature, Weiss still achieved high performance evaluations and, as a consequence, salary increases.

Weiss developed stress and anxiety-related disorders. Ultimately, after deciding that enough was enough, he complained to company executives about the anti-Semitic remarks. When his supervisor learned of those complaints, he immediately changed course, ceased making anti-Semitic remarks, and made certain that the coworker did also. His prejudice against Jews, however, resurfaced in another mode. He severely criticized Weiss's job performance, gave him unreasonably difficult assignments, unfairly blamed him for delays in the completion of work projects, and subsequently lowered his job performance evaluation.

Although the agency's executive personnel were aware of these occurrences, they neither ordered disciplinary action taken against Weiss's supervisor nor directed him to cease his harassing conduct; and even though they could have readily arranged Weiss's transfer to another supervisor, they declined to take that step. As Weiss's anxiety-related disorders intensified, his job performance deteriorated, and eventually he was fired. Weiss then sued Logistics for religious discrimination under Title VII.

An occasional offensive religious epithet most often will not rise to the level justifying a Title VII claim. But when a worker is repeatedly subjected to demeaning and offensive religious commentary, the conditions of his employment are necessarily altered, and thus this type of conduct almost always gives rise to a valid discrimination claim against the employer. The Logistics executives took no action to eliminate religious discriminatory animus from Weiss's work environment or from decisions made with respect to his working conditions. They simply ignored his complaints.

After considering this evidence, the court ruled that the supervisor's conduct violated Weiss's right to work in an environment governed by the nondiscriminatory terms and conditions of employment guaranteed by Title VII.[5]

Although anti-Semitic and other forms of religious bias were the subjects of early Title VII cases, the great bulk of those early cases entailed the refusal of an employer to accommodate a worker's religious beliefs or practices, and many of those cases arose out of conflicts relating to the attendance of the worker at Sabbath services.

As enacted in 1964, Title VII failed to specifically provide for accommodation; but in the EEOC's first promulgated guidelines, employers were directed to accommodate the "reasonable religious needs" of their employees "where such accommodation can be made without serious inconvenience to the conduct of [their] business." One year later, the EEOC revised its guidelines to provide that accommodation is required whenever it "can be made without undue hardship on the conduct of the employer's business."[6] Six years later, in 1972, Congress inserted a provision for accommodation to Title VII itself. The newly added language, awkward in construction, reflected the EEOC guidelines: "The term 'religion' includes all aspects of religious observance and practice, as well as belief, unless an employer demonstrates that he is unable to reasonably accommodate to an employee's or prospective employee's religious observance or practice without undue hardship on the conduct of the employer's business."[7]

Unfortunately, in amending the statute, Congress failed to specifically define the terms "reasonable accommodation" and "undue hardship." There the matter stood until 1977, when the Supreme Court agreed to consider the case of *Trans World Airlines, Inc. (TWA) v. Hardison.*[8]

TWA operated a large maintenance base in Kansas City, Missouri. Larry Hardison worked as a clerk on the night shift in the stores department at the base. Because of its essential role in the Kansas City operation, the stores department operated 24 hours a day, 365 days a year, and whenever a position in that department was not filled because of illness or other absence, an employee from another department or a supervisor was assigned to cover that job, even when work in other areas of the base would suffer. Like all employees at the base, Hardison was subject to a seniority system provided by the terms of TWA's collective bargaining agreement with the International Association of Machinists and Aerospace Workers.

Approximately one year after the commencement of his employment with TWA, Hardison became immersed in the study of the teachings of the Worldwide Church of God. One of this religion's tenets required Sabbath observance of its members by abstention from work from sunset on Friday to sunset on Saturday. When Hardison informed the manager of the stores department of his newly acquired religious convictions regarding observance of the Sabbath, the manager authorized a change in shift to allow him to meet his Sabbath requirements. Shortly after, Hardison asked for and was granted a transfer to a day-shift position. After the transfer, he was assigned to work on a Saturday as a substitute for an employee on vacation. Lacking sufficient seniority to avoid the Saturday assignment, he asked the union to waive the seniority provisions set out in the collective bargaining agreement, thus allowing another worker to be assigned to that position, but the union refused on the ground that were it to agree to a waiver, it would in effect be undermining the contractual rights of other employees.

In an attempt to avoid future Saturday assignments, Hardison proposed that his work week be limited to four days. TWA rejected that proposal because Hardison's job was essential, and on weekends he was the only person on his shift to perform it. To leave the position vacant would have impaired supply-shop functions that were critical to airline operations. To fill Hardison's position with a supervisor or an employee from a different area would have left another plant operation understaffed. And to employ someone not regularly assigned to work Saturdays would have required TWA to pay premium wages.

When TWA and Hardison could not agree upon any course of action that would relieve him of working on Saturdays, Hardison simply refused to report for work on Saturdays. TWA discharged him on grounds of insubordination for refusing to work during his designated shift. Hardison then claimed that his discharge constituted religious discrimination in violation of Title VII.

When the case reached the Supreme Court, the court first noted that TWA had made significant efforts to accommodate Hardison's religious needs, conducting several meetings with him in attempts to find a solution to his Sabbath problem. In addition, it had made efforts to find him another job and had authorized a union steward to search for workers to swap shifts with him.

Hardison argued, however, that TWA should have done more. He insisted that Title VII provisions obliging an employer to accommodate the religious observances of its workers took precedence over both the collective bargaining contract and the seniority rights of TWA's other employees. But the court disagreed. The duty to accommodate did not require TWA to take steps inconsistent with the terms of its agreement with the union, and an established seniority system need not give way to the accommodation of a worker's religious observances:

> The foundation of Hardison's claim is that TWA . . . engaged in religious discrimination . . . when [it] failed to arrange for him to have Saturdays off. It would be anomalous to conclude that by "reasonable accommodation" Congress meant that an employer must deny the shift and job preference of some employees, as well as deprive them of their contractual rights, in order to accommodate or prefer the religious needs of others, and we conclude that Title VII does not require an employer to go that far.

The court also rejected Hardison's contentions that TWA should have permitted him to work a four-day week or replace him with supervisory personnel or workers from another department, as both alternatives would involve costs to TWA, in the form of either lost efficiency or higher wages. The court concluded that to require TWA to bear more than a "de minimis cost" in order to give Hardison Saturdays off was an "undue hardship."

Justices Marshall and Brennan dissented from the decision on the ground that from that point onward the courts need not grant even the most minor accommodation to religious observers in order to enable them to follow their religious beliefs and practices. Justice Marshall concluded that despite Congress's enactment of Title VII, one of this country's "pillars of strength—our hospitality to religious diversity—has been seriously eroded."[9]

After the Supreme Court's decision in the Hardison case, the EEOC revised its guidelines in some areas, including the following:

> *Reasonable accommodation.* A refusal to accommodate is justified only when an employer can demonstrate that an undue hardship will result from all available forms of accommodation. The assumption that many employees with the same religious practices as the person being accommodated may also need accommodation is not evidence of undue hardship. Some alternatives for accommodating religious practices may disadvantage the person accommodated with respect to employment opportunities, such as compensation. Therefore, when there is more than one means of accommodation, the employer must offer the alternative with the fewest disadvantages.
> *Undue hardship.* An employer may assert undue hardship to justify a refusal to accommodate only if it can demonstrate that the accommodation would require more than a de minimis cost. The EEOC will determine what constitutes "more than a de minimis cost" by giving due regard to the identifiable costs in relation to the size and operating costs of the employer and the number of individuals who require the accommodation.[10]

The Hardison decision and the EEOC guidelines call for both the employer and the employee to fulfill certain responsibilities when engaged in the process of finding an appropriate accommodation. The employer is solely responsible for initiating a good-faith discussion to determine whether the employee's religious beliefs and practices can be accommodated, while the employee is required to make a good-faith attempt to satisfy her needs through the means offered by her employer. In endeavoring to work out a solution, the employer and the worker have a duty to cooperate with each other.

The number of religious discrimination claims increased in subsequent years. The primary reasons for this continuing growth in religious discrimination claims has been attributed to several factors: (1) the desire of workers to practice and apply their religious beliefs at work, (2) the "spread the faith" rationale of evangelical Christians, (3) the aging of the workforce, (4) the growth of a more diversified workforce, and (5) the expanded public role of religious experience. These factors will be examined in chapters 17 and 19.

Chapter Eight

Early Age Discrimination Cases

Employers commonly make decisions affecting older workers that assume those workers are no longer capable of performing adequately. Older workers are thus subjected to adverse employment decisions, motivated by false and stereotypical notions relating to age, without regard to the actual state of their physical or mental capabilities.

Older workers confront employment problems of two sorts. One older worker may experience difficulties in performing job responsibilities because of actual deterioration in physical or mental ability. Another may work for an employer who assumes the worker, whom it has employed for many years, has suffered physical or mental deterioration even if, in fact, this is not the case. Employers readily assume that physical and mental deterioration occurs concurrently with advancing age, as it is far less expensive to act on that assumption than it is to test the general capability and work proficiency of each of their older workers.

Age closes doors, severely limiting the range of employment options available to the older worker. She may have reached the highest point in her career and feel she has more to offer her employer than at any previous time in her life and yet find that her age presents a formidable barrier to any further advancement. The position to which she may aspire will more likely be awarded to a much younger person, lacking the experience and, probably, the enthusiasm and dedication of the older worker. The younger worker has only her youth to recommend her, but that will prove more than sufficient. The younger worker will be awarded the promotion. A year later the older worker may be downsized or forced into retirement on some pretext. Her chances then of finding another position are nearly zero, and she will remain in retirement, like it or not.

The first legislative action outlawing age discrimination in the workplace was undertaken in Colorado in 1903. Over the next fifty years, a few states followed suit, such as Massachusetts in 1937, but it was not until the 1950s and 1960s that a broad-based movement developed in state legislatures to afford these protections to older workers. In 1958, age was added to the New York statute barring discrimination in employment, and similar statutes were adopted in Connecticut and Wisconsin (1959); California, Ohio, and Washington (1961); New Jersey (1962); and Michigan and Indiana (1965).

Enactment of federal legislation barring age discrimination lagged behind, as initially these protections lacked broad public support. It has been suggested that other programs for the elderly, such as Social Security, Medicare, and Medicaid, offered little controversy and invited little public opposition because these laws also benefited the children of the elderly, who might otherwise be forced to assume the burden of their parents' retirement and medical costs, whereas laws barring age discrimination less directly benefit the young. In fact, younger workers are more likely to be affected adversely, as statutory protections against age discrimination often result in more jobs held by older workers and, in turn, fewer jobs available for their younger colleagues.[1]

When Title VII of the Civil Rights Act of 1964 was first proposed, Congress included age in the bill's protections, but it was later excluded. The final version of the legislation, however, directed the secretary of labor to "make a full and complete study" of the factors underlying age discrimination in employment and its consequences to older workers and to the economy.

One year later, Secretary of Labor W. Willard Wirtz submitted his report to Congress.[2] Wirtz's study focused primarily on the common employer practice of setting age limits in the hiring process. Previous studies had shown that approximately 55 percent of all job openings were closed to applicants over age fifty-five, and even workers as young as forty-five were barred from 25 percent of those positions.[3] Thus, the original impetus for the enactment of a federal statute barring age discrimination in employment emerged from discriminatory hiring practices rather than from discriminatory terminations or retirements of older workers.

A congressional committee studying the problem of age bias in the workplace later concurred with Wirtz's report, affirming his findings that employers generally operated under false assumptions regarding the effects of aging in older workers, that these assumptions led to the common usage of age barriers in the hiring process and that, consequently, a disproportionate number of older workers were among the unemployed. Testimony before the committee described age discrimination as "inhuman," "unjust," and "cruel" and at the root of the high national unemployment rates.[4]

Congress then drafted and adopted the Age Discrimination in Employment Act (ADEA), and President Johnson signed the law on December 16, 1967, to become effective June 12, 1968.[5] The newly adopted ADEA joined Title VII of the Civil Rights Act of 1964 in Congress's continuing effort to eradicate discrimination in the workplace. Both laws reflect, as the Supreme Court later noted, "societal condemnation of invidious bias in employment decisions."[6]

The preamble to the ADEA emphasizes the individual as well as the social costs of age discrimination in employment. It confirmed the secretary of labor's findings that employers had commonly established age limits for the hiring and retention of employees, regardless of their potential for job performance, and that older workers found themselves materially disadvantaged in preserving their employment status and, more particularly, in regaining employment after having been displaced. The ADEA was intended to promote employment opportunities of older workers by requiring employer decisions affecting job status to be based upon the capability of the individual worker rather than upon his or her age.

The ADEA makes it illegal for an employer to fire, refuse to hire, or take any other adverse action against a worker because of his or her age. Thus, the ADEA prohibits age discrimination in nearly the same terms as Title VII's prohibition of race, sex, national origin, color, and religious discrimination. Judicial interpretations of Title VII provisions have been relied upon by the courts in construing the ADEA, and interpretations of provisions of the ADEA have been used in explicating Title VII provisions.

While barring employers from engaging in unlawful acts of age discrimination, Congress also made certain that the ADEA permitted employers to use neutral criteria, not directly dependent on age, in employment decisions affecting older workers. Regardless of age, a worker may always be dismissed for inadequate or poor job performance. Even decisions based on age may be justified where age is a bona fide occupational qualification, such as in positions affecting public safety. Airline pilots, policemen, and firemen fall into that category.

After its enactment in 1967, the ADEA at first remained an obscure, little-used piece of legislation. Beginning in the late 1970s, however, ten years after its enactment, workers began to file age discrimination claims with increasing frequency. By the mid-1980s, workers were filing age claims with the Equal Employment Opportunity Commission at the rate of over 20,000 per year, nearly equaling the number of race and sex discrimination claims filed annually. Thus, the ADEA developed into a significant factor in the American workplace, soon becoming a major source of litigation in the federal courts.

From the inception of the ADEA, most age discrimination claimants have been white males. They are more often between the ages of fifty and fifty-nine, have held professional or managerial positions, and are more likely than any other group of workers to file suits in connection with their terminations of employment. Initially, far fewer blue-collar workers and women appeared as age discrimination claimants.

Once enacted, the ADEA quickly dominated and surpassed reliance upon previously adopted state statutes barring age discrimination. For age complainants, the ADEA became the law of choice. Whether the law has performed as the lawmakers originally intended is a matter that will be examined later (chapter 20).

Employers have learned to mask acts of age discrimination with the appearance of propriety, neither admitting discriminatory animus nor leaving a paper trail disclosing it. Thus, few age cases turn on direct or "smoking-gun" evidence of discrimination. Exceptions have occurred. A fifty-five-year-old licensed engineer applied for a mechanical engineering position with a US Navy shipbuilding facility in Bath, Maine. During his interview, he was advised by the chief engineer that he was looking for a "younger engineer." When pressed as to whether age really made a difference, the interviewer responded, "I think so. We have a couple of older engineers that will be retiring in a couple of years, and we want to hire a younger engineer and train him to take their places."[7]

Most employers are far more discreet and less likely to express their age bias in such explicit terms. Employers simply do not place memoranda in their files openly admitting that an older worker was fired "because she was too old." Even the least sophisticated of employers are careful not to leave a trail of discriminatory conduct, and it is the rare corporate executive who will take the witness stand at trial, freely affirming that he was motivated to fire a worker because of her age.[8]

The burden of proving age bias lies with the older worker. It is the older worker who must prove that discriminatory intent, rather than a legitimate business reason, motivated an employment decision adverse to the worker. Almost all age discrimination suits focus on the issue of pretext. Are the reasons expressed by the employer for its decision its actual reasons, or was the employer's decision motivated by an impermissible factor, such as age? Are the reasons advanced by the employer credible? Even if an employer's reasons did, in fact, serve as a basis for its decision that adversely affected the worker, was the employer also motivated to make that decision because of the worker's age? Are the reasons asserted by the employer merely pretexts, proffered by the employer for the purpose of covering up the nature of its decision, namely, that it was discriminatory? These are the issues that typically confront juries hearing age discrimination cases.

A. N. George worked for Mobil Oil Corporation and its subsidiary, Mobil Europe, Inc. Four years after George was hired, Mobil promoted him to general manager of Mobil Europe's affiliate in Greece. Five years later he was promoted to area executive, the third highest position in Mobil Europe, and charged with supervising seven European affiliated companies. In this position, George reported to John Simpson, vice president of Mobil Europe, who in turn reported to its president, P. W. Wilson.

Each year, Mobil evaluated the performance of its employees, and throughout his tenure as area executive, George was rated "MR+," meaning that he exceeded the requirements of his position, a rating highly regarded by Mobil executive personnel.

When the oil industry began to experience economic problems occasioned by falling oil prices, Mobil Europe undertook a restructuring, ordering large cuts in staff and transferring some of its responsibilities to Mobil headquarters in New York. These changes affected George's area executive position in that he no longer could rely upon staff assistance to the same extent that he had prior to the restructuring.

George continued to receive a MR+ performance evaluation, he was described as a "results-oriented executive," and his superiors recommended that he remain in his position as area executive. At the time of his final appraisal, the affiliates under George's supervision were profitable and were outperforming projections. The appraisal contained neither negative comments nor suggestions that George was experiencing any difficulty adjusting to the restructuring that had been put in place the previous year. Despite the positive tone of the appraisal, Simpson later testified that at the time he conducted the appraisal, he had begun to doubt George's effectiveness in the restructured organization.

Within a few weeks of the appraisal, Wilson recommended that George be replaced as area executive. Wilson's recommendation was accepted at Mobil headquarters, and he was directed to find a replacement. Subsequently, Mobil considered five high-ranking employees for the position, and Simpson was directed to review their employment histories to determine who was best qualified to assume the position. Simpson designed a ranking form, ostensibly free of age bias, that assigned numerical values for various attributes necessary to perform the functions of the area executive position. For some reason, never explained by Mobil, Simpson also included George in this ranking exercise; and although George had satisfactorily performed as the area executive for eight years and had consistently been rated MR+, Simpson gave him the lowest score of the six employees who were ranked, while he awarded a much younger employee, who was then working under George's supervision in a subordinate position, the highest ranking. This younger worker was selected by Mobil to replace George.

Mobil then informed George that his term as the area executive would end and that his employment with Mobil would be terminated at the end of the year. In November of that year, after George had been relieved of his position, Simpson prepared a performance appraisal of George's final year.

This appraisal, totally negative in tone, rated George's performance MR–, sharply attacked George's affiliate strategy and guidance, and noted his failure to adapt to the restructuring. This appraisal was totally inconsistent with Simpson's assessment of George's performance made earlier that year.

After his termination, George sued Mobil for age discrimination. Mobil later asked the court to grant it summary judgment, dismissing George's case. The primary issue before the court was whether the reasons given by Mobil for George's termination were pretextual. The court first expressed doubt as to the validity of Mobil's assertion that George had failed to adjust to the restructuring. If he had failed, why did Simpson not note the failure in George's earlier appraisal, since the restructuring had been fully implemented by the time of the appraisal? The court labeled the appraisal later conducted by Simpson as "suspect," not only because it was performed after George had been relieved of his position but "because it reversed all of George's prior evaluations." The court also questioned the objectivity of Simpson's ranking procedure. "The inclusion of [George] in this exercise after the recommendation to separate him was adopted suggests that his dismal rating may have been a foregone conclusion." How was it possible for George to have received the lowest rating when he was the only one of the six candidates who had any experience serving as the area executive? The apparent lack of objectivity in this procedure supported George's position that the reasons given by Mobil for removing him from his position were pretextual. The court rejected Mobil's bid to dismiss George's case, and his claims against Mobil were resolved soon thereafter.

If George had not received consistently high performance appraisals over a period of several years, the court undoubtedly would have given Mobil's position greater credence. But Mobil's attack on George's performance was wholly inconsistent with his past appraisals. This is the type of evidence that claimants pray for. They also pray that the evidence will uncover employer manipulation of the performance evaluation process. Mobil's wholly negative performance appraisal, conducted after George had been relieved of the area executive position, was certainly ill advised. Since Mobil lacked a good business reason for conducting such an appraisal, it, at the very least, created the appearance of impropriety.

This case illustrates the onerous nature of establishing pretext. Other than the fact that Mobil appeared to have perverted the performance appraisal and the ranking processes, George was unable to offer evidence suggesting that age discrimination was the reason for his termination. Although Mobil replaced George with a younger worker, he was sixty-two at the time, and any replacement selected by Mobil would likely have been younger than George. Thus, George relied solely upon proof of pretext to establish his case. Since the evidence supporting pretext was strong, he achieved a successful outcome.

A pretext case is likely to be decided in favor of the employer unless the indirect evidence relied upon by the claimant worker is clear and persuasive or is buttressed by at least some direct evidence of employer unlawful bias. Jack Spence's age discrimination suit against Maryland Casualty Company illustrates the point. Maryland Casualty was an insurance company head-quartered in Baltimore. Spence began working with the company after graduating from college in 1950 and, except for a short period, continued as one of its employees for more than thirty-five years. In 1977, the company promoted Spence to manager of its office in Buffalo, where he proved to be very successful; he succeeded in increasing the volume of policy premiums received by that office from $5 million in 1977 to $39 million ten years later. But all was not well with the Buffalo office.

Spence, who was then fifty-eight, reported to William Loden, the branch manager supervisor of the company's Mid-Atlantic region, who in turn reported to Thomas Fitzsimmons, vice president for the region. Both Loden and Fitzsimmons grew critical of Spence's management of the Buffalo office. On one occasion, Loden visited the Buffalo office and harangued Spence and his staff. On his next visit, Loden criticized Spence's management style "as unduly soft," and he told Spence he wanted him to "kick people in the ass, as I do it." Spence tried to explain to Loden that his management style differed and that he had been successfully motivating his staff for thirty-five years without resorting to the type of tactics advocated by Loden. Loden responded that if Spence wanted to remain with the company, he would have to change his management style.

Loden and Fitzsimmons continued to pressure Spence to alter his management style to conform with their perception as to what was required to raise the level of proficiency of the Buffalo staff. Throughout all of this, Spence was placed under a great deal of stress, and his doctor later discovered he was suffering from a dangerously high blood pressure condition. As his problems with Loden and Fitzsimmons worsened, Spence elected to take sick leave. Spence's lawyer later wrote to the company stating that Spence could return to work under normal conditions but not so long as he was required to work under Loden's direction. Thereafter, as a result of a complaint from another branch manager, both Loden and Fitzsimmons were demoted, and Spence was advised that he would no longer have to report to either of them. Since Spence was now relieved of the stress of dealing with Loden and Fitzsimmons, the company asked him to return to work. Spence refused, claiming that his doctor had advised against it. Spence, however, never informed his doctor that he would no longer be required to report to Loden and Fitzsimmons. Spence then commenced and age discrimination suit against Maryland Casualty, claiming that the company had abused him because of his age, ultimately forcing him into an early retirement.

Spence's case was dismissed on the company's motion for summary judgment. The court questioned Spence's failure to register complaints against Loden and Fitzsimmons, especially in light of the fact that the company had acted promptly in relieving them of their responsibilities after another branch manager complained about them. The fact that the company asked Spence to return to the Buffalo office militated against the validity of his claim that he was forced into an early retirement because of his age. The facts were not in dispute. Summary judgment was appropriate; case dismissed.[9]

As workers may rely upon both the disparate treatment and disparate impact approaches to establish a Title VII employment discrimination case, both approaches are also available to workers claiming age discrimination. As noted in chapter 3, disparate impact may result from an employment practice or decision that—although it appears to be nondiscriminatory—falls more harshly upon one set of workers than upon another. The circumstances that confronted a Connecticut teacher is a case in point.

Miriam Geller, a fifty-five-year-old teacher, sued the Bugbee School in West Hartford, Connecticut, for age discrimination. Before applying for a position at Bugbee, Geller had gained considerable teaching experience in New Jersey. After moving to Connecticut and filling some substitute teaching positions, she applied for a permanent position at Bugbee. After her interview, she was hired to fill a vacant position and was directed to report for work at the beginning of the school year. The school officials, however, continued to interview other candidates for the position. After ten days in the classroom, Geller was replaced by a twenty-five-year-old who had applied for the position and was interviewed *after* Geller had started teaching. The Bugbee School officials justified the replacement of Geller and her subsequent dismissal on the ground that the local school board had adopted a cost-cutting policy limiting the hiring of new teachers to those having fewer than five years of teaching experience. With her years of teaching in New Jersey and in Connecticut, Geller had far more than five years of experience.

At the trial of her age discrimination claim, Geller's attorneys placed in evidence statistical data showing that nearly 93 percent of Connecticut teachers who were over forty years of age had in excess of five years' teaching experience, while only 62 percent of teachers under forty had taught more than five years. Thus, under the local school board's cost-cutting policy, the likelihood of the selection of a teacher over forty was substantially less than the selection of a teacher under forty. Although the purpose of the school board's policy was to economize by hiring less-experienced teachers, it also opened more teaching opportunities for younger, less experienced applicants and substantially limited the opportunities for older, more experienced teachers.

This is a classic example of an employment policy that, although nondiscriminatory and appearing totally neutral on its face, disproportionately affected, or disparately impacted, older workers. Even if the school board had no intention of discriminating against older teachers, the direct result of its hiring policy was to make it impossible for nearly all older teachers to obtain a teaching position at the Bugbee School.

The school still could have defeated Geller's claim if it were able to establish that its cost-cutting policy was consistent with its business needs and no other selection methods existed that less directly impacted older teachers; but it failed in that regard, and the jury ruled in Geller's favor.[10]

The older worker, who has the disparate impact approach available to her, need not prove that the employer intentionally discriminated against her. The motivations of the employer are simply irrelevant in this type of case. If the worker is able to establish through statistics or other means that an employment policy disproportionately affected her because of her age, the employer will be confronted with proving that the policy was required by its business needs. But even if it succeeds in establishing this, the worker will nonetheless prevail if she can show that the employer also had available to it other policies that affected the older workers less disadvantageously.

The disparate impact approach has proved to be a significant legal tool for older workers because it challenges systemic impediments to the hiring, advancement, and extension of employment of older workers. However, the appropriateness of this approach soon came under attack as several federal appellate courts cast doubt on the viability of disparate impact claims in age discrimination cases. It was argued that the domain of the ADEA is confined to employment policies and practices based upon inaccurate stereotyping of older workers. In a disparate impact case, however, the employer's policy in question is not motivated by unlawful stereotypes or by the ages of the workers. Neither an illicit motivation nor a discriminatory intent plays a role in these cases. Thus, some authorities concluded that the disparate impact approach fell outside the purview of the age statute.

Even those courts that allowed the disparate impact approach in age discrimination cases limited its applicability. The same appellate court that awarded Miriam Geller a victory later denied it to two other teachers in a similar case.

Annmarie Lowe and Marie Delisi were teachers in the Commack Union Free School District in New York. In 1976, the school district, facing a declining student enrollment, decided to abolish some teacher positions, and both Lowe and Delisi were "excessed." Under New York law, they were placed on a preferred eligibility list for vacancies that thereafter occurred. While Lowe and Delisi waited for vacancies to occur, they both accepted teacher assistant positions that paid substantially less than their former positions. No vacancies occurred, and after seven years they were removed from the preferred list, as required by New York law. Two years later, the school district adopted the New York State Retirement Incentive Program providing retirement incentives for teachers fifty-five and older. With the adoption of this plan, and the anticipated voluntary retirements of teachers age fifty-five and older, it was expected that vacancies for teacher positions in the district would soon become available. Lowe and Delisi, both fifty-two years old at the time, immediately submitted their applications for a teacher position.

As anticipated, some of the older teachers elected to accept retirement, and thirteen teaching positions became available the following year. But when neither Lowe nor Delisi was hired for any of those positions, they cried foul and filed age discrimination suits. They claimed that the school district had decided not to replace the retiring fifty-five-year-old and older teachers with newly hired teachers close to the same age. The school district's defense centered around the procedures that were designed for the selection of the thirteen new teachers, and there was no evidence that these procedures were age biased. But Lowe and Delisi pointed out that those procedures disparately impacted applicants who were over the age of fifty. In essence, they claimed that the number of successful candidates ages fifty and over was disproportionately low. The court rejected their position. The ADEA, the court reminded Lowe and Delisi, protects workers ages forty and over, and eight of the thirteen newly hired teachers were over forty. When viewed from that perspective, there was no disproportionate impact.

The court's position, however, failed to recognize the validity of the argument that if the group of successful candidates over age fifty is compared with the group of successful candidates under age fifty, the group of older teachers was disproportionately disadvantaged by not being hired. The court, however, insisted that the only relevant age groups to be considered were those under and over forty, and under these circumstances, the older group was not disadvantaged. [11]

The court's rationale in declining to accept the position espoused by Lowe and Delisi has been soundly criticized by other courts. [12] The disagreement on this issue is joined, as noted, by the failure of the courts to agree upon whether the disparate impact approach is ever applicable to an age discrimination case. These issues were later resolved by the Supreme Court (see chapter 22)

One other issue troubled those courts that considered the early ADEA cases. After establishing the employer's liability for acts of age discrimination, what is the nature of the relief that should be granted the worker as a consequence of the employer's unlawful conduct?

Despite the near universal application of the "make-whole" standard of relief to victims of employment discrimination, the remedies made available to victims of age discrimination are materially deficient in two respects: (1) the worker is denied compensatory damages for pain and suffering, and (2) punitive damages are not available. Both types of damages are available to victims of race, color, sex, national origin, and religious discrimination, but victims of age discrimination are barred from recovering these types of damages.

Pain and suffering correlate with discrimination, regardless of its nature. Anger, guilt, indignation, bitterness, frustration, humiliation, shame, depression, emotional distress, emotional instability, and massive loss of self-esteem are discrimination's natural consequences. A worker cannot be made whole if precluded from recovering damages for this type of injury. But the ADEA neither specifically provides for nor denies this type of recovery, and the courts have proved to be sorely lacking in courage and in plain common sense in failing to extend a worker's monetary recovery to damages for pain and suffering. Although specific authority is lacking, the statute defines the relief obtainable in the broadest of terms: "In any action brought to enforce this Act the court shall have jurisdiction to grant such legal or equitable relief as may be appropriate to effectuate the purposes of this Act."[13]

Early in the life of the ADEA, some courts did, indeed, interpret this broad statutory language to encompass recovery for pain and suffering.[14] But the pendulum swung to the other extreme, and the courts thereafter concluded that pain and suffering damages are excluded from an age discrimination recovery.

Punitive damages stand in the same stead as compensatory damages for pain and suffering. The make-whole standard of relief requires an award of punitive damages when the discriminatory conduct of the employer is shown to have been outrageous. Again, the statute does not specifically authorize the recovery of punitive damages, but the broad authority granted to the courts by the statute allows them to order their recovery, if the courts are so inclined. Since they appear not to be so inclined, an amendment to the statute is required if age claimants are to be afforded all the relief necessary to make them "whole."

Injunctive relief, an appropriate Title VII remedy, is equally available to an age discrimination claimant. As an injunction requires the employer to obey the law, it is an effective enforcement device for preventing future acts of discrimination against older workers.

The First Federal Savings & Loan Association of Broward County, located in Florida, had six offices. At any given time, it normally employed about thirty-five tellers, a position having a high turnover rate. Over a period of fourteen months, First Federal hired thirty-five tellers, all but three of whom were either in their teens or twenties, and none as old as forty. During that fourteen-month period, Betty Hall, age forty-seven, applied for a position with First Federal. Hall did not specify in her application any particular position that she was seeking, and a personnel officer interviewed her with regard to all positions then available, including that of teller. The interviewer noted on Hall's application that she was "too old for teller." Hall was not hired for any position.

At the time, another applicant over the age of forty also was rejected for a teller position because she was "too old." A legal action brought on behalf of Hall against First Federal sought back pay for Hall and injunctive relief barring First Federal from discriminating against future job applicants over the age of forty.

The court had no difficulty in awarding Hall back pay, since the evidence clearly demonstrated the existence of a discriminatory hiring policy. Other evidence also showed that this policy was not limited to the teller positions. Accordingly, the court also granted injunctive relief, enjoining First Federal from continuing to implement illegal employment practices, not only in reference to the teller positions, but to all positions in First Federal's offices. [15]

The ADEA stands alone among the employment discrimination statutes in providing for the recovery of "liquidated damages," damages that are computed by doubling the back pay award. Liquidated damages may be granted if the court determines that the employer was guilty of a "willful" violation of the statute. The courts long struggled with the definition of "willfulness" as well as with the identification of those circumstances that will allow a liquidated damage award.

In a disparate treatment case, an employer may be found liable for age discriminatory conduct if the worker proves that the employer intended to commit a discriminatory act. Proof of intentional conduct is crucial. But if an employer intended to discriminate, would not its conduct be willful? In that case, every proven act of age discrimination would be willful, and every successful worker-litigant would be entitled to liquidated damages. But Congress obviously intended something different. Liquidated damages are not to be awarded in every case but only in those cases that are in some way set apart from the ordinary.

This rationale led some courts to require a worker to show that the employer's conduct had been outrageous before it would declare it to be "willful." The Supreme Court rejected that test and defined an employer's conduct as willful if the employer "knew or showed reckless disregard for the matter of whether its conduct was prohibited by the ADEA." [16] Later, the Court appeared to shift its rationale to favor employers. "If an employer acts reasonably in determining its legal obligation, its action cannot be deemed willful." [17] It is not at all clear that Congress intended to place these limitations on awards of liquidated damages. In fact, it is not at all clear what Congress intended. Thus, the courts continued to struggle with the identification of those circumstances that will permit awards of this nature.

III

Later Trends in the Development of the Employment Discrimination Laws

Chapter Nine

Congressional Amendments of Title VII and the ADEA

Amendments of Title VII and the ADEA generally fall into one of three categories: a clarification of the meaning of a particular provision of one of the statutes, a change in interpretation, or corrective action made in response to an unpopular Supreme Court or lower court decision.

In 1972, Congress amended Title VII to define the meaning of "religion." The statute, as originally drafted, did not define religion. The EEOC, however, drafted its own definition, ascribing to religion "all aspects of religious observance and practice as well as belief."[1] But employers had argued that the statute's prohibition of religious discrimination should be based solely on religious beliefs—not the practices—of a particular religion. The 1972 amendment made it clear that the prohibition covered religious practices as well as religious beliefs.

The 1972 amendments also extended the reach of Title VII prohibitions against employment discrimination to federal, state, and local governmental agencies.[2] Some members of Congress believed that change had occurred too slowly under Title VII, and they proposed speeding up the process by strengthening the EEOC. Once more a movement developed in Congress to grant the EEOC cease-and-desist powers, but again it met with defeat. However, the Congress did empower the EEOC to sue employers in the federal courts, a right Congress had initially denied the agency.

In 1976, the Supreme Court rendered a decision in a sex discrimination case that would raise the ire of female workers and advocates of the antidiscrimination laws and ultimately lead to a major change in the statute. Shortly after the enactment of Title VII, women who were fired after notifying their employers of their pregnancies filed claims for sex discrimination. Thus, the courts were confronted with the question whether discriminatory actions committed "because of sex" also included "because of pregnancy." Initially, these cases concluded with success for the women complainants.[3] However, in the General Electric case (chapter 5), the Supreme Court rejected a lower court's position that discrimination based on pregnancy was a form of sex discrimination.[4]

Congress reacted to the Supreme Court ruling by enacting the Pregnancy Discrimination Act (PDA), which amended Title VII by specifically defining discriminatory acts against pregnant women as sex discrimination: The term "because of sex" includes "because of or on the basis of pregnancy, childbirth, or related medical conditions." Women experiencing "pregnancy, childbirth, or related medical conditions" are to be treated the same for all employment-related purposes as other workers.[5]

Congress designed the PDA specifically to address commonly accepted stereotypical assumptions that women are less desirable employees because they may become or are pregnant. In rejecting these stereotypes, Congress declared that pregnancy must be treated like any other temporary disability. Congress also acted to ensure that the decision to work or not to work during pregnancy would be reserved to each individual woman. But in providing each of these protections, Congress also made it clear that employers are not required to provide pregnant women with any form of special treatment. Employers are merely required to treat pregnant women in the same manner as they treat all other employees.[6]

Subsequently, the EEOC adopted regulations relating to pregnancy:[7]

- An employer may not refuse to hire a woman who is pregnant, so long as she is able to perform the major functions necessary to the job. Any written or unwritten employer policy that excludes from employment female workers because of pregnancy, childbirth, or related medical conditions constitutes a violation of Title VII.
- An employer is required to treat a pregnant employee, temporarily unable to perform the functions of her job due to her pregnancy, in the same manner as it treats other temporarily disabled employees, whether by providing modified job functions, alternative assignments, or disability leaves.
- An employee must be permitted to work at all times during her pregnancy so long as she is capable of performing her job functions.
- Unless a pregnant employee has informed her employer that she does not intend to return to work after giving birth, the employer must hold her job open for her return on the same basis as it holds jobs open for other employees who are on sick or disability leave.
- An employer may not adopt a rule that would prohibit a female employee from returning to work for any predetermined period of time after giving birth to a child.

- Employer policies relating to seniority, vacation benefits, pay increases, and other employee benefits for pregnant workers must be the same as those policies adopted for employees absent for other medical reasons.
- Under the provisions of health, disability insurance, and sick leave plans made available to employees by an employer, all disabilities caused by pregnancy, childbirth, or related medical conditions are to be treated in the same manner as disabilities caused by other medical conditions.

The basic principle underlying the PDA requires an employer to treat pregnant workers in the same manner as it treats other workers who are experiencing a temporary disability. As with other employees, a pregnant woman must be treated on the basis of her ability or inability to perform her job functions. If other employees on disability leave are entitled to return to their jobs when they are again able to work, then women also are entitled to return to their jobs after a maternity leave absence. But it must be emphasized that the PDA does not impose an affirmative obligation on employers to grant preferential treatment to pregnant women.

Congress's explosive reaction to the Supreme Court's decision in the General Electric case and the limitations the court placed on the scope of Title VII's sex discrimination prohibitions was mild in comparison to its reaction and response to a series of negative decisions rendered by the court during its 1988–1989 term.

The decisions rendered by the court at that time reflected "a deeply conservative turn on issues of civil rights, particularly with respect to employment discrimination."[8] Workers did not often prevail in this environment, and even when they did, the court was prone to place material limitations on employment discrimination doctrine.

The decision that provoked the most heated response was *Wards Cove Packing Co. v. Atonio.*[9] In that case, the court, in effect, rewrote its 1971 decision in *Griggs v. Duke Power Co.* (chapter 4). In the *Griggs* case, the court ruled that Title VII proscribes not only overt discriminatory conduct but also employer practices that are fair in form but discriminatory in operation. The touchstone is business necessity. If an employment practice operates to exclude a specified group of workers (African Americans in the *Griggs* case) and it cannot be shown to be related to job performance, the practice is prohibited. Thus, the disparate impact theory was born. Workers could rely on the disparate impact approach to eliminate employment policies or practices that deprived them of job opportunities and advancement or in some other fashion seriously disadvantaged them.

The *Griggs* court also ruled that workers relying on the disparate impact approach were not required to prove that their employer was motivated by a discriminatory purpose in implementing the targeted policies or practices. If the workers could demonstrate that an employment policy disproportionately affected them because of their race, the employer must show, if it is to prevail, that the policy was essential to its business needs.

An African American alleging disparate impact in connection with an employer's hiring practices must establish three elements: (1) a significant disparity existed between the proportion of African Americans available for a particular position and the number of African Americans hired for that position; (2) the employer had in place a specific, facially neutral employment practice that allegedly caused that disparity; and (3) a causal nexus exists between the employment practice and the disparity.

Once the plaintiff workers have established these three elements, the employer may attempt to justify the challenged practice by showing that it served a legitimate, nondiscriminatory business objective. But even if the employer succeeds in establishing a business necessity, the worker may still prevail by showing that another practice, impacting African Americans less harshly, was available to the employer to satisfy its business objectives.

The *Wards Cove* decision undermined this process. It shifted the burden of proving "business necessity" from the defendant employer to the plaintiff workers, thus making it considerably more difficult for the plaintiffs to prevail. Some commentators accused the court of endeavoring to eliminate the disparate impact theory altogether.[10]

Several other of the court's 1988 and 1989 decisions also came under attack, as civil rights and women's groups charged the court with misconceiving the scope of Title VII. A prominent law school professor, William P. Murphy of the University of North Carolina School of Law, observed that not since the New Deal days had the Supreme Court given laws passed by Congress such hostile treatment. Murphy pointed out that of the fourteen employment law cases the court decided at that time, it ruled in favor of the employer in thirteen of those cases. In all fourteen cases, Justices Rehnquist and Kennedy adopted positions advanced by the employer, and they were joined in thirteen of those cases by Justices White, O'Connor, and Scalia. Justices Brennan and Marshall, on the other hand, most frequently supported the worker's positions. Professor Murphy observed, "It seems obvious that the determinant in employment law cases is something other than dispassionate and objective application of neutral principles. The majority and minority were clearly marching to different drummers."[11]

Congress then enacted the Civil Rights Act of 1991, amending Title VII by overturning the court's rulings in many of those cases. Congress, in essence, restored Title VII law to its form that existed prior to 1988.[12] For example, the burden of proof rules in disparate impact cases were restored to those announced in *Griggs v. Duke Power Co.* (chapter 4).

One of the 1991 amendments dealt with an issue we have yet to address. How should a court rule where the defendant employer was motivated by both an illicit and a lawful reason? The "mixed motive" quandary was considered by the Supreme Court in 1989 after Ann Hopkins sued her employer for sex discrimination.

Hopkins was a senior manager at the accounting firm of Price Waterhouse and had worked in the firm's Washington, DC, office for five years when the partners in that office proposed her as a candidate for partnership. They praised her character and her accomplishments, describing her as "an outstanding professional" who had a "deft touch," a "strong character, independence and integrity." Moreover, she had been successful in obtaining new clients. In fact, none of the other candidates for partnership had a record comparable to Hopkins's record of success in securing major contracts for the partnership.

At the time of Hopkins's nomination, only seven of the firm's 662 partners were women. Of the eighty-eight persons proposed for partnership at the time of Hopkins' nomination, Hopkins was the only woman. After the partners voted, forty-seven of the candidates were admitted to partnership, twenty-one were rejected, and twenty—including Hopkins—were held for reconsideration the following year.

The evidence showed that some of the partners had evaluated Hopkins on sex-based terms. Several partners criticized her use of profanity. One partner described her as "macho," another asserted that she "overcompensated for being a woman," and still another suggested that she take "a course at charm school." She was advised that if she wished to improve her chances for partnership she should "walk more femininely, talk more femininely, dress more femininely, wear make-up, have her hair styled, and wear jewelry."

In previous years, other female candidates for partnership had been similarly evaluated on sex-based terms. Female candidates were viewed favorably if they were perceived to have maintained their femininity while becoming effective professional managers. To be viewed as a "women's libber" was regarded negatively.

The following year, all of the male candidates who had been placed on one-year hold were renominated for partnership, but Hopkins was not. When she inquired about her rejection, she was told that difficulties she had experienced in interpersonal skills as well as her aggressive, tough, and macho behavior had contributed to the negative decision. Hopkins then sued Price Waterhouse, alleging that stereotypical views of women and female behavior had played a substantial role in her rejection for partnership.

The lower court that considered the case held that although Price Waterhouse unlawfully discriminated against Hopkins by employing an evaluation process that was corrupted by sexual stereotyping criteria, it also articulated legitimate reasons for rejecting her for partnership. By showing that sex discrimination played a role in the firm's decision, the burden of proof shifted to Price Waterhouse, requiring it to show by "clear and convincing" evidence that Hopkins would have been rejected for partnership even if the firm had not utilized illicit criteria to reject her. The lower court concluded that the firm had failed to meet that burden of proof and awarded judgment in favor of Hopkins.

The Supreme Court agreed with the lower court that in a mixed-motive case, once the plaintiff establishes an illicit motive, the burden of proof shifts to the defendant to demonstrate that it also acted from a lawful motive. But at that point its agreement with the lower court's analysis ceased, as the court ruled that the defendant's burden of proof could be satisfied if a "preponderance of the evidence" rather than "clear and convincing evidence" supported the defendant's contentions. The court, therefore, materially lightened the defendant employer's burden of proof. [13]

The court explained its reasoning. The words of Title VII that forbid an employer to make an adverse decision regarding an employee "because of such individual's . . . sex" requires the court to examine all of the reasons, both legitimate and illegitimate, that contributed to the employer's decision. This means that an employer should not be held liable if it proves that if it had not taken gender into account it would have come to the same decision. The court's prior decisions demonstrate that a plaintiff who shows that an impermissible motive played a motivating part in an adverse employment decision thereby places the burden on the defendant to show that it would have made the same decision in the absence of the unlawful motive. Thus, Price Waterhouse had to show its legitimate reason, standing alone, would have induced it to deny Hopkins partnership status.

The court, while examining the circumstances confronting Hopkins at the moment of the decision rejecting her application for partnership, homed in on the partners' stereotypical comments about her aggressiveness. The sex-based evaluations used by Price Waterhouse reflected negative stereotypes of women and therefore subverted the evaluation process. Thus, Price Waterhouse discriminated against Hopkins when it relied on these negative stereotypes to reject her partnership bid.

To this point, the court had said little that could justly be criticized. But the court then turned away from previous decisions by ruling that both issues—the employer's discriminatory reason and its legitimate reason—must be considered at the violation, rather than at the remedy, stage of the case. Thus, in the court's view, if a defendant employer establishes a mixed-motive defense, the plaintiff employee cannot be declared the prevailing party and thus will be denied all relief, including prospective injunctive relief and attorney fees.

In enacting the Civil Rights Act of 1991, Congress rejected that rationale. It declared that once the plaintiff proves that an illicit reason was a motivating factor in the employer's decision, it has established a Title VII violation and the employer's proof that it would have made the same decision, even in absence of the illicit reason, cannot alter that fact. Congress removed the mixed-motive defense from the violation stage of a Title VII case and assigned it to the remedy stage. Proof of a mixed-motive may affect the remedy available to a prevailing plaintiff, but it cannot render the defendant the prevailing party. Even if the employer would have taken the same action, the worker may still be awarded declaratory and injunctive relief as well as attorneys' fees.[14]

The Supreme Court was not the only court to fall under congressional scrutiny and harsh criticism during the proceedings leading to the enactment of the Civil Rights Act of 1991. Until that time, victims of sexual harassment were often left without a meaningful remedy as, regrettably, Diane Swanson discovered. Although she established a clear and convincing case of sexual harassment against her employer, the court denied her claim for compensatory damages because the harassment had not resulted in the loss of her job, and therefore she was unable to show a loss of income. Because she was not entitled to any relief, the court ruled that she was responsible for her employer's court costs, which were later deducted from her paychecks.[15]

Other courts had ruled in similar fashion. Even though a Florida federal court had ruled after a trial that a victim of sexual harassment had suffered serious emotional problems, it awarded her only nominal damages amounting to one dollar.[16] Cases of this nature brought to light the existence of a gaping hole in the remedies available to women claiming sexual harassment in the workplace. Title VII lacked provision for awards of compensatory and punitive damages. Damage awards in Title VII cases were limited to loss of pay. If a claimant had no claim for back pay, she basically had no claim for monetary damages.

Prior to this time, race and national origin claimants were able to work around this limitation by combining their Title VII claims with claims asserted under a post–Civil War statute that provided that all citizens had the same rights as a white citizen to make and enforce contracts. Section 1981 (the original Civil Rights Act of 1866) was the first major antidiscrimination employment statute, as it was later interpreted to prohibit employment discrimination based on race, color, and national origin. In contrast to Title VII, under this statute, a claimant is entitled to a jury trial and awards of compensatory and punitive damages. By combining their Title VII claims with Section 1981 claims, race, color, and national origin employment discrimination claimants were able to circumvent Title VII's jury and damage limitations. Sex and religious discrimination claimants did not have that option available to them.

In adopting the 1991 amendments to Title VII, Congress admitted its original errors by providing specifically for the recovery of compensatory and punitive damages. Unfortunately, the amendment failed to completely resolve the issue. As a concession to the American business community, Congress included in the amendment an adjustable scale of upper limits on the combined amounts of compensatory and punitive damages recoverable by a successful litigant. The upper limit, or cap, ranges from $50,000 for small employers, having between fifteen and one hundred employees, to $300,000 for employers with more than five hundred employees.[17] Thus, the recovery of compensatory and punitive damages remained limited for employment discrimination litigants.

The amendments also provided Title VII claimants with the option of having their claims tried before a jury. Initially, early advocates of Title VII opposed jury trials as they feared that Southern juries would react adversely to race discrimination claimants. But, as will be examined in chapter 27, some federal court judges have exhibited a severely negative attitude toward employment discrimination claimants, and thus the option to have one's discrimination claims tried before a jury is exercised far more often than not. The determination of whom to trust—judge or jury—has materially changed with the passage of years.

Since enacting the Age Discrimination in Employment Act of 1967, Congress has amended it on several occasions, each amendment expanding the scope of the ADEA while reaffirming the basic goal of retaining older people in the labor force. The original ADEA did not apply to the federal government or to the states or their political subdivisions. In 1973, a Senate committee declared that those gaps in coverage were serious as "there is . . . evidence that, like the corporate world, government managers also create an environment where young is sometimes better than old."[18] Subsequently, Congress recognized another serious gap in ADEA coverage, a failure to bar age discriminatory acts of employers having fewer than twenty-five employees. In 1974, Congress eliminated the first gap by extending coverage of the law to federal, state, and local governments and partly filled the second gap by excluding from the law's coverage only those employers with fewer than twenty workers.

As originally proposed, the ADEA was designed to bar discrimination against workers of the ages forty-five to sixty-five. Before Congress acted, it changed the lower limit to forty, since the evidence it had at hand showed that forty was the age at which discrimination began to be observable. The upper age limit, however, was not changed. Therefore, as enacted, the statute benefitted the middle-aged, but not the aged. Workers over sixty-five were not protected by the ADEA and could still be forced into retirement. Consequently, even after enactment of the legislation, mandatory retirement remained a common occurrence for workers over the age of sixty-five.

Public opinion polls, however, had shown for some time that the mandatory retirement of sixty-five-year-olds was not popular, as most of the populace felt that workers capable of continued performance on the job should not be forced into retirement.[19] Accordingly, in 1978, Congress raised the ADEA's upper age limit to seventy. In 1986, however, Congress decided that forced retirement at age seventy was no more defensible than forced retirement at age sixty-five. It also recognized that mandatory retirement at any age was detrimental to the Social Security system and, moreover, that the retention of experienced and highly skilled workers in the labor force benefited the national economy. At that point, the upper age limit was deleted from the law, and the long history of legally sanctioned mandatory retirement came to an end.

Through these amendments, Congress converted the ADEA from a statute affording age bias protection for the middle-aged to a statute providing protections for older worker as well. A worker ages seventy-five or eighty, or even older, still capable of performing his job functions cannot be fired or forced into retirement merely because of his age. The amendments outlawing mandatory retirement also reflect a shift in national priorities, from emphasizing the hiring of older workers to that of preserving job security for them.

When employment discrimination matters are in issue, the relationship between Congress and the Supreme Court often becomes contentious. As originally enacted, the ADEA provided an exception to its prohibitions for certain employee benefit plans. But contrary to Congress's intention in adopting this exception, the Supreme Court interpreted it to permit various forms of mandatory retirement. Congress objected to the court's interpretation by narrowing its scope. The Supreme Court then expanded it. Not to be outdone, Congress then overruled that interpretation.[20] No end of this battle is in sight.

At times, Congress has amended Title VII but declined to similarly amend ADEA. As an example, it amended Title VII to provide that an employer's mixed-motive decisions may affect the remedy available to a prevailing plaintiff but cannot render the defendant a prevailing party. Congress did not extend that amendment to the ADEA. Congress's unequal treatment of the ADEA has led to serious disputes in the interpretation of the statute (see chapter 20). Such unequal treatment is wholly unjustified. Corrective action is required.

Chapter Ten

Current Trends in the Law Prohibiting Race Discrimination

After the enactment of Title VII in 1964, workplace equality for African Americans increased dramatically. African Americans now work in virtually every area of the US economy. Many hold well-paying jobs, and their opportunities for advancement are steadily increasing. And yet all is not well.

Racial disparities commonly exist in the workplace. In 2010 the median weekly earnings of full-time wage and salary workers were $611 for African Americans, compared with $765 for white workers.[1] The earnings disparity between male African American and white workers is evident in all major occupational groups. For example, in 2010, the median weekly earnings of white men working full time in management, professional, and related occupations (the highest-paying major occupation group) were $1,273, while the earnings of African American men were $957.[2]

The disparity between the number of white men who hold senior positions in the business world and the number of African American men who hold those positions is stark. Data collected by the EEOC show that in 2011, 530,000 white men held executive, senior-level, and manager positions, while only 12,000 African American men had achieved those positions.[3]

Race remains a serious obstacle for African Americans entering the job market, and as a result joblessness among African Americans is far greater than among white workers. Sixteen percent of African American workers were unemployed in 2010, while the unemployment rate among white workers was 8.7 percent.[4] The *New York Times* recently reported the story of a young African American business school graduate who responded by telephone to an advertisement placed by a Dallas money management firm. The firm's hiring manager seemed ecstatic to hear from him as apparently he had experienced much difficulty in persuading young business school graduates to move to the Dallas area. But when the hiring manager met the young man in person for lunch, he appeared stunned, his interest quickly cooled, and a job offer failed to materialize. The *Times* reporter, after interviewing other job-seeking African Americans, noted that "it is difficult to overstate the degree that they say race permeates nearly every aspect of their job searches."[5]

In excess of 33,000 race discrimination charges were filed with the EEOC in 2012 and over 313,000 were filed during the ten-year period ending that year, making race discrimination the basis for more claims than any other form of employment discrimination.

Racism can be explicit and blatant—sometimes referred to as "old-fashioned racism"—or subtle—sometimes referred to as "modern racism."[6] Currently, racial discrimination is less likely to be as blatant as in the past, but it does surface in this form from time to time. The EEOC, in December 2012, reported that a nationwide apparel retailer for young women had illegally discriminated against one of its store managers after one of the company's executives complained about too many African American employees at the manager's store. The EEOC report stated that the corporate managers had openly stated they wanted employees who "were white, had blue eyes, [and were] thin and blond."[7]

While blatant racism is less prevalent and subtle forms of racism appear more pervasive, another form of race bias, falling between the blatant and the subtle forms, may manifest itself in the workplace. Anthony Ash and John Hithon, both African Americans, were superintendents at a poultry plant owned and operated by Tyson Foods. They both sought promotions to open shift manager positions, but two white males were selected instead. Claiming that Tyson had discriminated against them on account of race, they sued Tyson, alleging Title VII violations.

The trial testimony showed that Tyson's plant manager, who made the disputed hiring decisions, had referred to both Ash and Hithon as "boy." Ash and Hithon argued that this constituted evidence of discriminatory animus. The court of appeals that reviewed the case rejected their claims, holding that "[w]hile the use of 'boy' when modified by a racial classification like 'black' or 'white' is evidence of discriminatory intent, the use of 'boy' alone is not evidence of discrimination." The Supreme Court disagreed. "Although it is true the disputed word will not always be evidence of racial animus, it does not follow that the term, standing alone, is always benign. The speaker's meaning may depend on various factors including context, inflection, tone of voice, local custom, and historical usage. Insofar as the Court of Appeals held that modifiers or qualifications are necessary in all instances to render the disputed term probative of bias, the court's decision is erroneous."[8]

In 1993, the Supreme Court moved in the direction of disfavoring African American and other Title VII claimants who have no direct evidence of discrimination to offer the court. The issue before the court was this: In a suit in which an employer has been charged with acts of racial discrimination in violation of Title VII, does the court's rejection of the employer's asserted reasons for its actions mandate a finding for the claimant? In other words, if the claimant shows that the employer's stated reasons for its actions are pretextual, must the court decide the case in favor of the claimant?

Melvin Hicks, an African American, worked as a correctional officer for St. Mary's Honor Center (St. Mary's), a halfway house operated by the Missouri Department of Corrections and Human Resources (MDCHR). In 1978, Hicks was promoted to shift commander, one of six supervisory positions at the facility. Five years later, MDCHR conducted an investigation of the administration of St. Mary's programs, which resulted in extensive supervisory changes. Hicks retained his position, but another shift commander was promoted to chief of custody and became Hicks's immediate supervisor.

Prior to these personnel changes, Hicks had enjoyed a satisfactory employment record, but soon after these changes were implemented, he became the subject of repeated, and increasingly severe, disciplinary actions. He was suspended for five days for violations of institutional rules and received a letter of reprimand for alleged failure to conduct an adequate investigation of a brawl between inmates that occurred during his shift. He was later demoted from shift commander to correctional officer and ultimately was discharged.

Hicks filed suit in the United States District Court for the Eastern District of Missouri, alleging that MDCHR had violated Title VII by demoting and then discharging him because of his race. After a full bench trial, the district court found for Hicks, finding that the reasons given by MDCHR for the disciplinary actions taken against him were not the real reasons for demoting and discharging him. The court noted that Hicks was the only supervisor disciplined for violations committed by his subordinates; that similar and even more serious violations committed by his coworkers were either disregarded or treated more leniently; and that Hicks's supervisor manufactured a verbal confrontation in order to provoke him and thus create the grounds for his discharge. The court nonetheless held that Hicks had failed to carry his ultimate burden of proving that his race was the determining factor in MDCHR's decision first to demote and then to dismiss him. In short, the district court concluded that, "although Hicks has proven the existence of a crusade to terminate him, he has not proven that the crusade was racially, rather than personally, motivated."[9] The court of appeals reversed that decision, and the case moved to the Supreme Court.

We must pause here for a moment and review previous Supreme Court decisions relating to pretext as a basis for proving discrimination (as discussed in chapter 3). In 1973, soon after congressional enactment of Title VII and the ADEA, the Supreme Court devised what it described as a "sensible, orderly way to evaluate the evidence" in disparate treatment cases, striking a balance between workers and employers by giving both fair opportunities to present their positions in a court of law. The court established two procedures a worker may use to prove an employer's conduct was discriminatory: first, by directly persuading the court that the employer more likely than not was motivated by a discriminatory reason; and, second, by showing that the reasons given by the employer for its conduct were false or not believable or, as more commonly expressed, were pretextual. [10]

The first procedure comes into play less frequently, for the reason that direct evidence of discrimination generally is unavailable to a worker and also because workers have achieved greater success by proceeding under the pretext model. Indirect evidence, demonstrating that the employer has lied about its motivation in acting adversely to a worker's interests, stands at the center of a majority of all employment discrimination cases. In these cases, the basic factual issue to be decided is whether the employer's expressed reasons, purportedly justifying its decision, are true or false. According to early Supreme Court rulings, if the worker proved the employer's proffered reasons to be false or pretextual, he was entitled to a verdict in his favor. If the worker failed to sustain the burden of proving falsity or pretext, the employer was entitled to a verdict in its favor.

For twenty years, the Supreme Court repeatedly reaffirmed and refined this framework for proving workplace discrimination. In the *Hicks* case, the Supreme Court abandoned this practical framework, subverting its previous sensible and balanced approach to proving discrimination.

Prior to the *Hicks* decision, the Supreme Court held fast to the rule that the falsity of the employer's explanation was alone sufficient to compel judgment for the worker. If the worker carried the burden of showing the employer lied, the court was required to decide in the worker's favor: "[The worker] must have the opportunity to demonstrate that [the employer's] proffered reason was not the true reason for the employment decision. This burden . . . merges with the ultimate burden of persuading the court that [the worker] has been the victim of intentional discrimination. [11]

Proof of falsity was equated with proof of discrimination. But in the *Hicks* decision, the Supreme Court discarded this sensible rule and stated that "pretext" really means "pretext for discrimination." Merely proving the falsity of the employer's reasons is not sufficient. The worker still must prove that the employer's decision was discriminatory. [12] This turned the concept of pretext on its head. What advantage does the worker gain by proving the employer lied if he still is required to prove that the employer's conduct was discriminatory?

The *Hicks* decision greatly disfavors the worker who has no direct evidence of discrimination to present to the court. In most instances, the worker must rely upon evidence that his employer has fabricated a defense to cover up its illicit motives, and prior to the *Hicks* case, workers were able to rely upon the presumption that the employer who lied about its reasons for acting adversely to a worker was simply trying to cover up the illegality of its conduct as alleged asserted by the worker. The *Hicks* decision rejects this approach and, by placing an additional burden upon the worker, has made it substantially more difficult to prove that an employer's decision was motivated by a discriminatory intent.

The Supreme Court, however, attempted to ameliorate the full consequences of the *Hicks* decision. Although it ruled that proof of the falsity of the employer's position does not *compel* a verdict for the worker, the jury *may* nevertheless infer a discriminatory motive from the fact that the employer resorted to lying. Thus, if the only evidence offered in support of the worker's case is the falsity of the employer's position, a jury may decide that the employer's conduct was discriminatory, but it is no longer compelled to rule in that fashion.

We now turn to another aspect of racial discrimination that persists in the American workplace. Strangely, racial harassment, which generally flows from crude, boorish, and unlawful behavior, continues to plague African American workers, despite widespread public condemnation of conduct of this nature.

Robert Daniels worked for Essex Group, Inc., for over ten years. The only African American in his division, he was occasionally subjected to racial jokes by coworkers but he did not allow those conditions to affect his work performance. In time, however, the "jokers" grew more numerous and his work environment more toxic. Threatening messages appeared on the restroom walls: "all niggers must die," "hi Bob—KKK." A life-size dummy of a blood-covered African American was hung in his work area. One of his coworkers threatened to beat him up and to injure his young son. When Daniels reported these incidents, his supervisor purported to accede to Daniels's plea for help but failed to undertake any action to alter Daniels's work environment. Daniels continued to tolerate such incidents until a rifle shot was fired into his home. At that point he resigned and sued Essex Group for racial harassment.[13]

The Supreme Court has recognized that hostile environment harassment claims are cognizable under Title VII. To establish a racial harassment claim, the plaintiff must show that the harassing conduct was sufficiently severe or pervasive to alter the terms and conditions of his employment, thus creating a hostile or abusive work environment. A racially hostile environment is one that is both objectively and subjectively hostile. It is objectively hostile if a reasonable person would find it hostile or abusive, and it is subjectively hostile if the victim of the harassment also perceives it to be so.[14] Whether a work environment is sufficiently hostile or abusive to support a racial harassment claim is determined by viewing all the circumstances, including

- the frequency of the acts of harassment
- the severity of the offensive conduct
- whether the offensive conduct was physically threatening or verbal
- whether the victim was humiliated by reason of the conduct
- whether the harasser was a coworker or a supervisor
- the number of other workers who joined in the harassment
- whether the harassment was directed at more than one individual
- whether the harassment unreasonably interfered with the victim's work performance, thus altering the terms and conditions of his employment

In the *Daniels* case, the appellate court that reviewed the case held that he had submitted sufficient evidence to show that he had been subjective to acts of racial harassment, that he had been compelled to labor in a hostile work environment, and that he had carried the burden of proving both by a preponderance of the evidence.[15]

Gregory Williams confronted racial harassment of a different variety. Williams, an African American, worked for the New York City Housing Authority. For reasons that never were explained, Williams's supervisor hung a noose on the wall behind his desk. The noose hung there for three days. After Williams filed a complaint objecting to the display of the noose, his supervisors treated him differently than other employees, strictly applying office work rules with regard to his performance but not to the work performance of others. Subsequently, Williams filed Title VII charges against the Housing Authority, alleging that he had been subjected to a racially harassing and hostile work environment.

The question to which the court was required to respond was whether the display of the noose constituted severe racially harassing conduct.

> [T]here can be little doubt that such a symbol is significantly more egregious than the utterance of a racist joke. . . . [T]he noose is among the most repugnant of all racist symbols, because it is itself an instrument of violence. It is impossible to appreciate the impact of the display of a noose without understanding the nation's opprobrious legacy of violence against African Americans. . . . The effect of such violence on the psyche of African Americans cannot be exaggerated. . . . The hangman's noose remains a potent and threatening symbol for African Americans, in part because the grim specter of racially motivated violence continues to manifest itself in present day hate crimes. Moreover, persistent inequality in this country resuscitates for modern African Americans many of the same insecurities felt years ago. It is for this reason that the Civil Rights Act of 1964 was enacted.[16]

The more severe the harassment, the less pervasive it needs to be. A single incident of harassment—the display of a noose, the burning of a cross, even a favorable reference to the Ku Klux Klan, or use of the N-word—may be sufficient to pass the test of pervasiveness.[17]

African American women also have been the targets of racial harassment, though less frequently than African American men. But, as discussed in chapter 4, they have experienced discrimination of a different sort, one that results from the interaction of sexism and racism. As in early race cases, African American women still confront that issue

June Graham claimed that her employer treated her and other African American women differently than other workers. She was continuously singled out for critical performance reviews. These reviews often were scheduled upon her return to work from authorized absences for illness and other matters. On the trial of her Title VII case, Graham's supervisor admitted that he maintained special time records on Graham, although he did not keep such records for any other workers in his department. He frequently filed absence reports criticizing Graham, even on the occasion when she was absent to attend her child's funeral. On the other hand, white male or female workers were not faulted for frequent absences. Indeed, the only two workers criticized for excused as well as unexcused absences were Graham and another African American woman working in the same department. The evidence clearly showed that African American women were treated more severely in the matter of attendance than all other workers.

The court that considered Graham's case ruled that, as an African American woman, she was protected by Title VII against discrimination on the combined grounds of race and sex. An employer who singles out African American females for less favorable treatment cannot defeat a charge of discrimination merely by showing that its white female workers or its African American male workers were not similarly subjected to unfavorable treatment. Thus, the court affirmed the proposition that African American women, who, as a group, experience adverse treatment, separate and apart from those experienced by African American men on the one hand and white women on the other, are protected by the provisions of Title VII.[18]

An economy that employs workers of all races and colors, male and female, requires a body of law capable of acknowledging and responding to workplace experiences that may be unique to a particular group of workers. Fortunately, as the cases just reviewed clearly demonstrate, the employment discrimination laws have been developed to a degree that the courts are now capable of affording protection to specific groups of workers and to remove workplace acts of discriminatory conduct only those groups encounter.

As a consequence of another development in the laws barring employment discrimination, African American and other minority women are now able to aggregate evidence of racial and sexual bias to show that an employer allowed a work environment, hostile and discriminatory to women of race or color, to exist in its workplace. Even though this evidence may be inadequate to establish separate and distinct race and sex discrimination claims, it may nevertheless be sufficient to show that a pervasive discriminatory atmosphere corrupted the workplace for minority women.

Marguerite Hicks confronted such a workplace while employed by Gates Rubber Co. Hicks worked at Gates Rubber as a security guard. In Gates Rubber's security force of thirty workers, Hicks was the sole African American woman and one of only two African American security guards. Hicks charged Gates with both sexual and racial harassment. Gates workers testified at the trial that their work environment was permeated with racial slurs and jokes. At least one supervisor referred to African American workers as "niggers" and "coons," and on one occasion, the same supervisor referred to Hicks as a "lazy nigger." Another supervisor referred to her as "Buffalo Butt." In addition to claiming racial harassment, Hicks also offered the court evidence that she was sexually harassed by at least two of her supervisors.

Despite this evidence, the trial court rejected Hicks's race and sex discrimination claims on the ground that the evidence was insufficient to establish either claim. On appeal, the appellate court ordered the trial court to reconsider the evidence of discrimination from another perspective. It directed the trial court to undertake an analysis of the evidence to determine whether the trial testimony of race bias and sex bias, when aggregated, was sufficient to demonstrate the existence of a discriminatory workplace environment in which both racial and sexual bias existed in combination. The appellate court stated that Hicks, as an African American woman, should be allowed to rely upon the intersectional character of her alleged sex and race bias claims by establishing a pattern of discriminatory harassment.[19] As one law commentator later expressed it, the appellate court, in effect, authorized Hicks to proceed with her discrimination suit on the ground that Gates permitted "racialized sexual hostility" or "sexualized racial hostility" to exist in its workplace.[20] In other words, the appellate court ruled that evidence of racial bias may assist in establishing a sexually hostile work environment and that evidence of sexual bias may assist in establishing a racially hostile work environment.

After the *Hicks v. Gates Rubber* case, some courts expanded the scope of evidence a complainant may rely on in proving the existence of a discriminatory or hostile work environment. Even evidence of racial and sexual conduct directed against workers other than the complainant—racial and sexual conduct she neither witnessed nor knew of—may be offered to prove the hostility of the work environment in which the complainant worked.

This expansive view of the evidence relevant to a claim of a hostile work environment was accepted by the court in Yvette Cruz's racial and sexual harassment case against her employer, Coach Stores. Cruz worked at Coach as a secretary. She was terminated following an altercation with a male worker who had made a crude sexual comment about her appearance. Cruz later charged Coach with maintaining a race- and sex-based hostile work environment, but the trial court rejected her claim on the ground that she could point to only "vague and unspecified" instances of inappropriate sexual behavior and only one instance of racial misconduct. Thus, the court ruled, she had failed to demonstrate the level of pervasive hostility necessary to support a hostile work environment claim. The appellate court reviewing the decision did not agree.

Cruz described Coach's human resources manager as notorious for his discriminatory attitude toward minorities, an attitude expressed in racial and ethnic slurs. He frequently referred to Hispanics as "spics" and African Americans as "niggers" and stated that "they are only capable of sweeping the floor at McDonalds." Other Coach workers testified to similar remarks made by the manager at a time when Cruz was not present and thus was not the target of his racial epithets. Cruz also testified to instances of daily acts of sexual harassment committed by the same manager. He made repeated remarks that women "should be barefoot and pregnant" and repeatedly stood very close to female workers when talking to them, ogling them and causing them to feel very uncomfortable. When Cruz informed the manager that she found his behavior objectionable, he only laughed or ignored her.

Reversing the decision of the lower court, the appellate court held Cruz to the burden of proving that Coach's workplace was "permeated with discriminatory intimidation, ridicule and insult," sufficiently severe or pervasive to alter the conditions of her employment. Whether the workplace harassment was severe or pervasive depended on all of the circumstances, and in examining all of the circumstances, the court must consider incidences of racial and sexual harassment directed against the complaining worker as well as those directed against other workers. The court expanded the scope of admissible evidence when it ruled: "Nor must offensive remarks or behavior be directed at individuals who are members of the plaintiff's own protected class. Remarks targeting members of other minorities, for example, may contribute to the overall hostility of the working environment for a minority employee."

The court observed that Cruz's hostile workplace claim found additional support in the interplay between the racial and sexual harassment she experienced. Because the evidence disclosed both race-based and sex-based workplace hostility, the manager's racial harassment may well have exacerbated the effect of his sexual harassing conduct and his sexual harassment may have exacerbated the effect of his racial harassment.[21]

The appellate court approved the concept that sexual and racial comments and conduct all contribute to the perception that an employer's workplace is hostile and discriminatory. If an employer permits racial epithets to pervade its workplace, it is likely to condone the presence of offensive sexual conduct as well. Thus, in advancing an expansive rather than a restrictive view of the relevancy of the evidence tending to prove a hostile and discriminatory work environment, the court provided minority women with a powerful weapon to root out workplace harassment directed at them.

In light of the progressive views the courts in recent years have advanced in extending the protections of Title VII to working African American and other minority women, these women should be encouraged to charge their employers with race- and sex-based discrimination whenever the circumstances warrant.

Race remains a serious obstacle for African American workers and it appears as if it will remain an impediment to workplace equality, at least for the immediate future. That's the bad news. The good news is found in the progressive attitudes of many of the federal courts in addressing racial discrimination claims. Apparently, African Americans have not lost confidence in the courts as they continue to file record numbers of workplace discrimination claims. Hopefully, their confidence will be found not to have been misplaced.

Chapter Eleven

Current Trends in the Law Prohibiting Sex Discrimination

Many Americans believe that sex discrimination no longer presents a significant problem for working women. Accounts of women having achieved high-level appointments in academia and the other professions, together with reports of women advancing to upper corporate-level positions, have become increasingly more common. The appointment in July 1999 of a woman as president and CEO of Hewlett-Packard, then the world's second largest computer company, was greeted with pronouncements that "the glass ceiling finally had been shattered," that her appointment reflected the absence of any significant employment barriers deterring women from advancing to middle and senior-level management positions. The appointment of a female CEO, however, clearly is not an everyday occurrence. The glass ceiling may have been cracked in that instance, but it was not shattered.

Although the past fifty years have seen much progress in eliminating discrimination against women in the workplace, little support exists for those who argue that sex discrimination no longer presents a significant issue for working women. Discrimination directed against older women, minority women, and pregnant women—discrimination occurring in all phases of the employment relationship—all too frequently bar women from gaining workplace equality.

Disparities between the compensation paid to women and that paid to men tend to substantiate the continued presence of discrimination against women in the workplace. Some legal commentators argue, however, that the personal choices made by women outside the work environment have important implications for earnings and promotions within the work environment, and these personal choices, not workplace discrimination, account for persistent income disparities between women and men. This argument relies primarily upon the contention that opportunities for promotion may not be as great for women choosing to absent themselves from the workplace for extended periods of time while giving birth or caring for their children. These commentators also observe that women who plan to interrupt their careers to bear children may be motivated to select occupations where job flexibility is high but compensation is low. In either event, it is argued, free choice rather than sex discrimination constitutes the basis for most workplace disadvantages suffered by women. [1]

Undoubtedly, young mothers confront a disproportionate share of job disadvantages, whether these disadvantages exist as a consequence of discriminatory intent or not. However, no existing data supports the proposition that longstanding compensation gaps between male and female workers result in major part from career choices freely made by working women with children. To the contrary, as many court cases discussed in later chapters demonstrate clearly, working mothers are too often intentionally made subjects of employer discriminatory conduct.

Of course, all working women are not mothers, and these women confront workplace problems of another sort. Mary Ann Luciano worked for the Olsten Corporation in New York, an employment agency for temporary workers. The company hired Luciano as director of field marketing, and she performed well in that position. Two years after Olsten hired Luciano, another company offered her a good position that included the office of vice president of the firm. As an inducement to Luciano to remain with the company, Olsten's CEO decided to match the offer. However, several of Olsten's male senior executives were not pleased with the prospect of Luciano's promotion to vice president, and they persuaded the CEO to convince Luciano to temporarily agree to a lower position, with the promise of a promotion to vice president in a year's time, provided she continued to perform her job functions satisfactorily.

During the following year, three of Olsten's senior vice presidents met to formulate a new job description for Luciano, incorporating duties in the description upon which she would be evaluated prior to promotion to vice president. They designed a job description that was impossible to perform, one that would ensure an unsatisfactory performance evaluation. Still not satisfied, they later increased Luciano's job responsibilities, while withholding the support staff she required to perform the additional duties. Even then, Olsten's management refused to proceed with Luciano's performance appraisal. Instead, Luciano was terminated on the ground that her position had been eliminated in a corporate reorganization.

Luciano's job responsibilities were then assigned to two male senior vice presidents, one of whom had been recruited from outside the company. Although she was qualified for both positions, Luciano was not given the opportunity to fill either of them, and even though she also was qualified for other positions in the company that were open, she was not considered for any of them either. After experiencing these adverse actions, Luciano sued the company, claiming she had been the victim of sex discrimination.

At the trial, Luciano's lawyers presented the jury with a vast amount of evidence supporting her sex discrimination claim. In addition to the machinations of the three senior vice presidents, the jury learned that Olsten had promoted men with poor performance records to senior management positions and that, in the reorganization in which Luciano lost her job, new positions were created for male employees whose jobs had been eliminated. The jury also considered statistical data that clearly reflected a glass ceiling firmly in place for Olsten's female employees:

- More than 80 percent of Olsten's 200 Office Services Division field offices were headed by women. These women were denominated "junior management." No woman had ever been elevated to vice president or senior vice president positions in the Office Services Division.
- At its corporate headquarters, Olsten had assigned seventeen vice president and senior vice president positions to men, but only one to a woman. In contrast, although most of Olsten's junior and middle-management workforce was female, women were rarely promoted to positions above those levels.
- In some job categories, a $10,000 wage disparity existed between the average salary paid to men and that paid to women.

With this evidence at hand, the jury encountered little difficulty in arriving at a verdict in Luciano's favor, awarding her substantial damages, and punitive damages as well.[2]

This case is typical in that Luciano confronted obstacles barring her advancement to a higher position, obstacles that were designed to disadvantage her as a woman, while protecting the positions of fellow male workers. But the case is atypical in that the measures undertaken to bar Luciano's elevation to a higher position were made overtly, with little regard given to concealing conduct that clearly was discriminatory. More frequently, decisions contrived to impair the advancement of women are much more subtle in character and are secretly formulated and covertly implemented. Because employers generally conceal discriminatory conduct, it often remains hidden from those against whom the discriminatory act is directed and from other workers who may not be directly involved. Many workers, therefore, erroneously assume that such conduct does not occur in their places of work. This assumption in turn leads to the mistaken belief that discrimination against women no longer presents a material bar to their advancement.

Since its initial formulation, the concept of the glass ceiling has grown to include disadvantaged racial minorities, as well as women, and its focus has expanded to include all promotional opportunities, not merely those pertaining to senior management positions. The concept of the glass ceiling caught the attention of congressional leaders at the time it was considering the 1991 Civil Rights Act, and ultimately Congress created a Glass Ceiling Commission to study and recommend measures to eliminate "artificial barriers to the advancement of women and minorities" and to increase and foster the advancement of women and minorities in the workplace. Four years later, the commission issued its fact-finding report that affirmed the continuing presence of barriers to the advancement of women and minorities.[3]

One of the areas upon which the commission directed its focus was typical employer-held perceptions of working women. Convinced that these perceptions tended to perpetuate the existence of the glass ceiling, the commission undertook to determine whether they had any basis in fact. The commission concluded that these perceptions arose out of commonly held false stereotypes, including notions that women

- are less committed to their work careers than men
- are not tough enough to succeed in the business world
- generally are unable or unwilling to work long or unusual hours
- are unable or unwilling to relocate geographically
- are unable or unwilling to make decisions
- are not sufficiently aggressive
- are too aggressive
- are too emotional

The commission also found widespread stereotypical perceptions of other groups of women. African American women were looked upon as incompetent, lazy, and hostile; Latina women as overly passive; Asian women as inflexible and unassertive.

Why do these stereotypes persist? "In the minds of many white male managers," the commission concluded, "business is not where women . . . were meant to be—certainly not functioning as the peers of white men."[4]

Employers' perception that a serious conflict exists between the child-rearing responsibilities of a working mother and her job responsibilities further undermines the work roles of women. Until these stereotypes are eliminated from the workplace, discrimination against women will continue.

Because sex discriminatory acts are often subtly conceived and not readily detectable, women often remain unaware that sex discrimination constitutes a negative force in their work lives and thus are not motivated to seek legal redress. Other women who may recognize the extent to which acts of discrimination affect their careers are often reluctant to become involved in complex legal proceedings. Others may lack the financial resources to proceed with litigation. Still others believe family responsibilities make it impossible to become involved in extended litigation. Some women fear losing their jobs if they make waves, while others believe that all workplaces are infested with sex discrimination and that it is pointless to contest it. As a result, unlawful employer policies may remain unaddressed. Employers are well aware of these circumstances. Since they often have little to fear if unlawful employment policies are allowed to continue, they may remain unmotivated to undertake any action to rid them from their workplaces. Women themselves, therefore, may unwittingly serve to perpetuate discriminatory conduct, policies, and practices.

Sex discrimination may occur at any point in a woman's employment, at any time between her interview as a job applicant and her termination following long-term employment. The next sections consider discrimination at each of these stages of employment.

HIRING

Prior to the enactment of Title VII, newspaper advertisements for job openings were openly gender oriented. It was a common practice to list help-wanted ads in columns headed "Male" or "Female." Other advertisements specified a preference for one sex or the other: "Excellent opportunity for a young and attractive woman." "Male office clerks wanted." This type of advertisement is now rarely seen.

Prior to Title VII, a female applicant for an entry-level position was often asked about her marital status, the number of her children, whether they were legitimate, her child care arrangements, and her future child-bearing plans. No evidence was offered by the employer suggesting that male job applicants were similarly questioned. Under EEOC regulations, questions of this type now violate Title VII.[5] In addition, an employer may not have in place two interview policies for job applicants—one for men and one for women—without violating Title VII.[6] Thus, on two accounts, job interviews of the sort described are unlawful.

In New York, a Madison County official questioned job applicant Maureen Barbano about her plans for raising a family. As he explained it, he did not want the county to hire a woman who would later become pregnant and then give up her job. He also interrogated her about her husband's attitude toward the type of work she would be required to perform if hired. The court labeled these questions discriminatory. Inquiries about pregnancy, family planning, and a spouse's attitudes concerning those attitudes were totally unrelated to any qualifications for the position.[7]

A job interviewer's questions concerning an applicant's family responsibilities may be proper where a real potential exists for conflict between the applicant's family responsibilities and the responsibilities of the position in question. As an example, a female applicant for a paramedic position that entailed twenty-four hour shifts was asked about her arrangements for the care of her children while she was on duty. In these circumstances, this may have been a reasonable and nondiscriminatory question, as long as it is was asked of both male and female applicants.[8]

Discrimination in the hiring process still occurs in other forms. Employers regularly assign women to lower-paying jobs, delineated as "women's work," generally on the basis of the stereotype that these jobs are "proper" for women. Such stereotypes create a segregated workforce, with men holding the better-paying positions and women filling lower-paying jobs such as bookkeepers, payroll clerks, telephone operators, bank tellers, child-care workers, cleaners and servants, nursing aides, and orderlies. Some women, of course, voluntarily select these types of jobs, but discriminatory hiring practices also account for the recruitment and assignment of many women to these lower-paying positions.

COMPENSATION

Pay inequity for women has long been a common practice, and women, under the umbrella of Title VII, have charged their employers with maintaining discriminatory pay practices. For a case to succeed under Title VII, the complainant must first demonstrate that she was paid less than a man performing similar work. The two jobs in question must be sufficiently similar as to permit the court to confirm that the two workers are "similarly situated." The complainant then must prove that her employer's decision to pay her less than her similarly situated male coworker was an act of *intentional* discrimination. This is a burden of proof not readily sustained.

The continuing existence of disparities in compensation between men and women has been a central issue in the battle to attain workplace equality for women. Even before the enactment of Title VII, Congress passed and President John F. Kennedy signed into law the Equal Pay Act of 1963 ("EPA"), legislation designed to assist women in achieving "equal pay for equal work." Congress's purpose in enacting the EPA, the Supreme Court later commented, was to remedy what was perceived to be a serious and continuous problem of discrimination against women—the fact that the wage structure of many segments of American industry was based on "an ancient but outmoded belief that a man, because of his role in society, should be paid more than a woman even though his duties are the same."[9]

An employer violates the EPA if it pays a man more than a woman who performs a job requiring the skill, effort, and responsibility equal to that of the man's job and if the two jobs are performed under similar working conditions. Unlike Title VII, the EPA complainant is not required to prove that her employer intended to discriminate against her by paying her less. The mere fact that a compensation disparity exists is sufficient to establish her case, unless the employer is able to justify a pay differential by reason of the existence of a seniority, merit, or incentive system or as a result of other factors other than one based on sex. It appears, therefore, that a woman complaining of a compensation disparity should be capable of establishing her case with ease. In practice, however, proving an equal pay case has proved far more difficult than Congress originally intended.

A woman seeking recourse under the statute need not prove that she is being paid less for performing a job that is *identical* to that of a more highly paid male worker, but she must establish that the two jobs are equal or, as some courts have described it, are "substantially similar." EPA cases are frequently lost because female complainants are unable to prove that their jobs require the skill, effort, and responsibility equal, or substantially similar, to those of the more highly compensated male. The EPA provides a remedy only when equal or substantially similar work is involved, and thus the court must dismiss a woman's case if it finds an absence of similarity in skill, effort, or responsibility. If the two jobs are unequal in any one of those respects, the case must be dismissed. On account of the difficulties experienced in demonstrating that the positions in question are equal, the EPA has provided little protection for the vast majority of women asserting pay equity claims.

Several cases demonstrate how the courts have applied the EPA to pay discrimination claims. Dr. Marjorie McMillan was director of the radiology department, one of seven veterinary departments, at Angell Memorial Animal Hospital in Massachusetts. When a local newspaper published a letter relating to the hospital's finances, it listed the salaries of various employees, and McMillan discovered a disparity existed between her salary and that of the other department directors. At the time, she was earning $58,000 a year while her male counterparts had annual salaries ranging from $73,000 to $80,000. With this information in hand, McMillan sued the hospital for violations of the EPA.

At the trial of her case, McMillan offered evidence comparing the skills, effort, and responsibilities of her position, as the director of the radiology department, with those of the male department directors who were more highly compensated, and she demonstrated that the job requirements for each of the department heads were basically the same. Her proof satisfied the demands of the EPA, and the jury's award of substantial damages in McMillan's favor was later affirmed on appeal. [10]

Cherry Houck, a professor at Virginia Polytechnic Institute, sued Virginia Tech for violation of the EPA. In contrast to the approach taken by McMillan, Houck failed to specifically identify the male work colleagues she claimed were paid more than she. She merely testified that in her department, men generally received higher pay than she, even though their jobs were basically the same as hers. Because she failed to compare her job with that of any particular male in her department, the court was unable to determine whether she was in fact paid less for substantially similar work. Houck compared herself with male workers in general instead of comparing herself to a specific male in her department. Her case was fatally flawed.[11]

In an EPA case, care must be exercised by the complainant and her attorney in selecting the particular position for comparison with the complainant's. The wrong selection will most likely culminate in defeat. Josephine Cherrey was an inside sales clerk for the Thompson Steel Company in Maryland. She alleged that Thompson violated the EPA when it paid her, on average, $14,000 a year less than two male employees who she claimed performed substantially the same work as she. Before proceeding to analyze the facts in the case, the court first established a framework to determine whether the jobs to be compared actually required the same skill, effort, and responsibility. The court stated that if the jobs had a common "core of tasks," the inquiry would then turn on whether differing or additional tasks required greater skill or effort or entailed greater responsibilities for the workers in the positions being compared. The court used this framework to measure the degree of equality between Cherrey's job and the two other jobs in the inside sales department that she claimed were comparable to hers. One of the positions that Cherrey used was that of her supervisor. But he regularly conferred with upper management and Cherrey did not. Both positions that she selected required functions that Cherrey was not required to perform, such as market research and the development of sales strategies. In the court's view, the differences in the requirements of the three positions outweighed the common core of tasks, thus rendering the positions unequal in terms of skill, effort, and responsibility. This evidence was more than sufficient to defeat Cherrey's claim.[12]

Prior to the passage of Title VII and the EPA, on average women were paid only 60 percent of the wages paid to men. By 1997, they were earning 74 percent of their male colleagues' compensation.[13] By 2010, they were earning 81 percent.[14] The gains in compensation for women appear to have been consistent, but small. But these statistics may conceal more than they reveal. For example, the pay gap between male and female college graduates has actually widened in recent years.[15]

The failure of the EPA and Title VII to more effectively deal with the pay equity problem has fomented interest in amending the statutes, especially the Equal Pay Act, so as to ease the required burden of proof. Critics of the EPA have long recommended a reduction of the statute's burden of proof requirements by changing "equal skill, effort, and responsibility" to "comparable skill, effort, and responsibility." In fact, the first drafts of the EPA submitted to and considered by Congress used the term "comparable" rather than "equal." Undoubtedly, if the draft language had been retained in the statute, the burden of proof would have proved to be a less formidable barrier to female complainants pursuing pay equity cases. Based on the history of case failures, it appears that an amendment of the statute may be in order.

PROMOTION

Historically, courts have been reluctant to enter into employer–employee frays involving promotions. Even where the presence of flawed promotion procedures is apparent, a court may hesitate to overrule management's decision denying a promotion to an employee, as that decision may have been based on bad judgment rather than discrimination, and bad judgment, in and of itself, will never rise to the level of unlawfulness. "The law forbids invidious distinctions, not mistakes."[16] Unless a worker's qualifications for promotion, when compared with those of the worker who was awarded the promotion, are so far superior that the employer's reasons for the promotion must be viewed as a subterfuge or pretext for discrimination, the worker generally will not prevail, excepting in those instances where she is able to submit independent evidence of a discriminatory motive. Nearly all promotion cases, therefore, turn less on a comparison of the workers' qualifications and more on the weight of the evidence demonstrating a discriminatory employer motive.

This approach to promotion cases is well illustrated in Jane Flucker's sex discrimination case against the Fox Chapel Area School District in Pennsylvania. Flucker, an English teacher, complained that she had not been interviewed for promotion to a middle school position. The school district argued that an interview was unnecessary, as the selection committee was aware of her work and had viewed her performance evaluations. The judge that heard Flucker's case stated that if the decision had been left to him, Flucker would have been selected for the promotion: "As a graduate of Smith College, with over three years' experience in the Princeton, New Jersey high school, with a face out of Botticelli and the charm of Southern speech, how could she possibly lose out in competition "with a graduate of West Liberty State College . . . who . . . had taught 'Mass Media, Revolutionary Lit., Myths & Legends. . .?'" But the mere fact that Flucker was better qualified than the successful male candidate did not necessarily prove sex discrimination. Although the failure of the selection committee to select the better-qualified teacher for the promotion may be considered as evidence of sex discrimination, in this case the court felt that this evidence was insufficient in and of itself to establish a discriminatory intent. The court was not prepared to declare that Flucker's qualifications for the position were so far superior to those of the other candidate that the school district's reasons for not promoting her necessarily had to be considered as pretextual. Thus, for Flucker to prevail, she had to offer the court evidence establishing more than just the shortcomings of the school district's promotion procedures. She had to offer convincing proof that the real reason for the selection of the successful candidate was his gender. But Flucker was unable to offer any corroborative evidence that a discriminatory intent motivated the selection committee, and the judge dismissed her case.[17] As Justice Stevens once expressed it, without corroborating evidence of a discriminatory intent, "[W]e must accept the harsh fact that numerous individual mistakes are inevitable in the day-to-day administration of our affairs."[18]

Some employers appear oblivious to the negative appearance they present to anyone reviewing their promotion procedures; their overt behavior supplies the corroborating evidence missing in the Flucker case. In one case, an employer failed to consider a female managerial employee for promotion on twenty-three separate occasions, and in all twenty-three instances promotions were awarded to males, some of whom were totally unqualified for promotion.[19] Courts have little difficulty in awarding substantial damages to claimants who have been subjected to outrageous acts of discrimination such as these.

As in the case of new hires, inappropriate questions asked of a candidate for promotion may reveal an underlying bias. The male members of an employer's promotion committee were shown to be biased in favor of selecting a male for the position when they questioned a female candidate for the position about night work and the reaction of her spouse to her being absent from the home at that time. The selection committee, however, declined to put comparable questions to male candidates. Clearly, the selection committee exhibited an unlawful bias against women.[20]

Even the US government has been guilty of unlawfully denying promotions to women. Angie Gobert was employed by Minerals Management Services (MMS), a division of the US Department of the Interior, as a GS-12 petroleum engineer. She had a great deal of experience in matters relating to oil spill prevention and cleanup, and on occasion she had served as a spokesperson for MMS in its dealings with other governmental agencies and with industry. When MMS issued a vacancy announcement for a GS-13 petroleum engineer position, Gobert applied for the position and, along with seven other applicants, was found qualified. A male candidate was selected, but he declined to accept the position, as he felt he was better qualified for another position about to become vacant. After Gobert complained that she had not been selected, MMS announced it had decided not to fill the GS-13 position.

Shortly after, MMS issued another vacancy announcement, purportedly for a newly created GS-13 position called oil spill program administrator. Although the job carried a different title, the vacancy announcement was nothing more than a re-advertisement for the previous GS-13 position with no significant differences in job responsibilities. Both positions focused on oil spill prevention and cleanup as well as on the responsibility to serve as an agency spokesperson on these matters. Gobert again applied and once again was found qualified. However, the position was awarded to a male who did not hold a college degree and was not a petroleum engineer. Although the responsibilities of the position had remained unchanged, the qualifications for the position had been altered so as to permit the selection of the male who ultimately was chosen. When Gobert sued MMS for sex discrimination, the court agreed that the entire promotion process had been contrived to permit the selection of the less qualified candidate and thus deprive Gobert of the promotion. The court concluded that the evidence submitted to the court supported Gobert's contention that MMS had unlawfully discriminated against her on account of her gender.[21]

Private industry has acted with equal boldness in denying promotion opportunities to female workers. Svenska Handelsbanken, an international banking corporation with headquarters in Stockholm, Sweden, maintained a branch office in New York City (SH-NY). When the bank hired Victoria Greenbaum for a position in its treasury department, it promised her she would be given the title of vice president after her first annual review. Over the next several years, Greenbaum received the highest possible performance evaluations and her supervisor repeatedly recommended her for promotion, but the bank denied her the vice president position. After each promotion denial, bank personnel offered a different explanation to support the decision that Greenbaum's promotion was inappropriate at that particular time.

Ultimately, Greenbaum sued SH-NY for sex discrimination, and on the trial of her case she demonstrated she had been consistently recommended and repeatedly rejected for promotion, while similarly recommended men were routinely promoted. This evidence strongly suggested that when it came to the promotion of a woman, the bank departed from its ordinary promotion practices and procedures. In the absence of some other explanation for this series of events, this kind of departure from internal office procedures is sufficient to support a finding of discrimination. But Greenbaum had additional evidence of discrimination to offer the court.

SH-NY officials testified that the bank relied upon two principal criteria for promotion to vice president: First, the employee must be able to perform appropriately as a role model for the bank, and second, the bank must be "comfortable" with that individual's role as a representative of the bank. In applying these criteria, bank managers tended to use the word "aggressive" to describe a form of excellence when applied to male candidates for promotion, but as a ground for disqualification when applied to female candidates. Other testimony disclosed that a member of senior management had referred to a female worker as a "tough broad" and he openly stated he did not want any "tough broads"working at SH-NY. This evidence strongly suggested that

Greenbaum was denied the title of vice president, at least in part, because SH-NY applied promotion standards that were stereotypical and gender biased. At the conclusion of the trial, the jury awarded Greenbaum $320,000 in compensatory damages and $1,250,000 in punitive damages.[22]

With the exception of the case involving the female candidate with "a face out of Botticelli," the evidence submitted in each of these cases was both persuasive and forceful in disclosing discriminatory conduct. In each instance, this evidence compelled a verdict in favor of the female candidate for promotion. Less compelling evidence undoubtedly would have resulted in less favorable outcomes, thus illustrating a truth that should guide all discrimination claimants and their attorneys: Do not sue unless the evidence is overwhelmingly in your favor.

DEMOTION

Workers demoted by their employers have infrequently sued their employers for acts of sex discrimination, as it is not uncommon for the damages recovery in these cases to be small. In some instances, a worker may be demoted to a lower position but her compensation may remain unchanged, thus severely limiting the damages that she may recover. The damage award in a demotion case often cannot justify the effort expended and the expense incurred in litigating the case.

TRANSFER

Intracompany transfers have been the subject of sex discrimination litigation at two points in the employment relationship. The first occurs when an employer, because of a discriminatory bias, refuses to grant a female employee a desirable transfer. The second occurs when an employer unlawfully imposes upon a female worker an undesirable transfer—a transfer to a distant locality or a transfer involving the loss of opportunities for promotion, salary increases, or other benefits.

On two occasions, a female postal carrier applied for transfer to a clerk's position, and each time the postmaster denied her request and assigned the position to a male postal carrier. A court later determined, based on the postmaster's changing and inconsistent testimony, that he had failed to offer a legitimate reason for denying the transfers to the female applicant and that the inconsistent explanations were merely pretexts to cover up his discriminatory conduct.[23]

In an older case, a court had to determine whether the transfer of a teacher from a middle school to an elementary school was an undesirable transfer. Carmen Rodriguez had earned master's and doctoral degrees at Columbia

University, where she had focused her studies on art programs for the middle school student. Subsequently, she had taught for twenty years in a middle school located in Eastchester, New York. The school district then decided to transfer her to an elementary school, a move she found wholly undesirable.

Due to declining student enrollment, the Eastchester school district decided to terminate the art teacher with the least seniority in the district. The teacher selected had taught in one of the district's elementary schools, and school administrators decided that she should be replaced with one of the art teachers assigned to the middle school. In addition to Rodriguez, the school district employed two other art teachers in the middle school, both of whom were male and neither of whom possessed Rodriguez's teaching credentials. Still, the school district selected Rodriguez for transfer. When she protested that one of the male art teachers would be better suited for the assignment, her principal responded, "They wouldn't have a male grade school art teacher." Indeed, in the previous twenty-two years, there had never been a male art teacher assigned to the Eastchester elementary schools. Pouring oil on the fire, the school district then filled Rodriguez's middle school position with a male high school art teacher with half her teaching experience in the district.

Rodriguez filed suit, alleging that the transfer was discriminatory and that it constituted a professional setback and stigma on her career. Later in the litigation, Rodriguez offered evidence showing that the art programs at the elementary school level were so profoundly different from those in the middle school as to render useless her twenty years' study and experience in developing programs for middle school children. Clearly, for Rodriguez, this was an undesirable transfer.

Rodriguez also submitted evidence showing that female teachers in the Eastchester system were relegated to lower grade levels. Even with this evidence, Rodriguez's case was dismissed on the trial court level, but on appeal the appellate court reversed the dismissal of her case:

> In her complaint, Dr. Rodriguez alleges that there has never been a male grade school art teacher in the Eastchester schools. . . . If substantiated . . . these allegations would prove nothing less than segregation, depriving female teachers of the opportunity to instruct older, more advanced pupils. Regardless of whether a higher wage-rate is at issue, female teachers have the statutory right to compete on an equal basis with their male counterparts throughout the entire school system. While this sort of sex stereotyping may once have been a virtually unquestioned feature of our national life, it will no longer be tolerated.[24]

CORPORATE REORGANIZATIONS

In the course of a corporate reorganization, executive personnel often target women for termination or other adverse treatment. In some instances, an employer has implemented a corporate reorganization primarily to deplete its workforce of female workers. A case in point involved a newly assigned plant manager who reorganized his employer's administrative structure, changing it from a traditional supervisory staff model to an administrative format that depended upon team leaders for supervisory guidance. Before the reorganization, twenty-five management and professional employees worked at the plant—twenty-one men and four women. After the plant manager eliminated eight of those jobs in the reorganization, only men were left serving in those positions. The plant manager then selected two team leaders, both of whom were men.

Two of the women affected by the reorganization filed charges of sex discrimination against the company, alleging that the plant manager had initiated the team leader concept with the intention of removing all the women from supervisory positions. They further argued that even if the plant manager had adopted the team leader concept for gender-neutral reasons, he had nonetheless targeted women in the reorganization for either demotion or termination. The court ruled that the charges were valid, and it held the company accountable for the women's damages, while enjoining the company and its officials from further discriminatory conduct. [25]

In an even more outrageously conceived plan of reorganization, the president of a company decided to permanently reduce the number of women employed on the company's production staff. To achieve that goal, he implemented a plan to create the appearance of a gender-neutral plan of reorganization. He ordered ten men and eleven women to be laid off, and during the next nine months, none of them was recalled to work and no new employees were hired. After nine months, however, when the workers' collective bargaining right of recall had expired, the company began hiring new workers, and the vacancies created by the layoffs were filled, all by men. Over the next four and a half years, the company hired sixty-four new production workers, sixty-three of whom were men. When one of the female laid-off workers filed sex discrimination charges, the court awarded her over $833,000 in punitive damages. [26]

TERMINATION

Some workers are formally terminated; others are forced to resign. A worker who is compelled by her employer to work under conditions so intolerable as to require her, or any reasonable worker, to abandon her position is considered to have been "constructively discharged." The distinction between a resignation and a constructive discharge is a significant factor in determining the amount of damages a victim of sex discrimination is entitled to receive, as the sex discrimination claimant who voluntarily resigns may be deprived of a full recovery of her damages, while the constructively discharged complainant will not.

Whether a particular set of working conditions is tolerable or intolerable is an issue often litigated. Claims of constructive discharge have generally failed in cases based on pay inequality and denial of a promotion, as the courts rarely find that disparities in compensation or refusals to promote create circumstances that a reasonable person would consider "intolerable."[27] The courts generally limit the application of the term "intolerable" to workplace conditions that fall far outside the scope of the ordinary and commonplace workplace events.

In one case, after a worker requested a transfer to another location, her employer at first denied her request, claiming that no positions were then open at that location. Later, it attempted to accommodate the worker by offering her the option of choosing one of several positions at that location, but apparently none of these positions were to her liking and she resigned. The court held that these circumstances failed to rise to the level of a constructive discharge.[28]

In another case involving a transfer, an employer ordered a female worker transferred to a distant facility that was scheduled to be closed within the year. If the worker had accepted the transfer, she would have had to remove her son from school and relocate her family, only to face job elimination when the facility closed. When the worker left the company to seek another position in the area in which she was then residing, a court ruled that she had been constructively discharged. But when the court's decision was appealed, an appellate court ruled that, although the complainant surely confronted a painful choice, the exercise of that choice did not render her situation intolerable and thus she was not constructively discharged.[29] I suspect that many readers will agree with me that the courts, on occasion, render really dumb decisions.

Stella Chertkova filed a successful claim against Connecticut General Life Insurance Company, for whom she had worked for several years in various computer-related positions. Immediately following a change in her department chief, two supervisory employees began a campaign of harassment calculated to force Chertkova from her job. They placed her on probation and ordered her to improve her job performance in such areas as "active listening skills." One of her supervisors held "coaching sessions," calling her into his office and screaming at her and criticizing her performance. At one session, he threatened her: "What do you hope for? Do you think you are going to outlive us? There is no chance. You are not going to be here."

Subsequently they again placed her on probation. When she completed her period of probation, her supervisor informed her that during the ensuing two years she would be dismissed if she failed to maintain satisfactory performance standards in all areas of her position, including her communication skills. Yet when Chertkova asked to attend a course on communication skills offered to all department employees, her supervisor denied her request.

Later, when Chertkova discovered that her supervisor was soliciting other company employees for negative information about her, she suffered a mental breakdown and was unable to continue on the job. These circumstances, the court ruled, were sufficient to establish a constructive discharge. [30]

What one judge considers intolerable, another considers it tolerable. Each case must stand on its own facts, and although each set of facts may be viewed from a different perspective, as a general rule, the greater the variance between an employer's conduct and that which is generally accepted as normal behavior, the more likely a worker will be successful in persuading a court that she has been subjected to a constructive discharge.

All kinds of other issues arise in connection with the termination of a worker's employment. In one case, an employer claimed that a worker was terminated because she was difficult to work with, but the court was convinced that these difficulties arose only after her employer had discriminated against her. "[N]othing in the law says that a person suffering discrimination must stand mute in the face of invidious treatment."[31] An employer cannot consider a worker's forceful response to discriminatory conduct as a basis for termination. Personality dysfunction induced by a hostile work environment cannot stand as justification for the discharge of a worker who negatively reacts to that environment. [32]

The battle for gender equality is not yet over. Women are still channeled into low-paying positions that offer little opportunity for advancement. Women higher on the income scale confront deliberate attempts to disrupt their careers and are barred from following career paths that men have followed without difficulty for decades. As in the past, employers intent upon acting adversely to the interests of female workers will strive to conceal their unlawful conduct with the appearance of propriety and lawfulness, while women, as in the past, will strive to unmask and expose such conduct.

Over 30,000 sex-based charges were filed with the EEOC in 2012. [33] Still, most employer acts of employment discrimination do not result in formal complaints. Those women who choose to fight face a difficult path. But the uncertainty, discomfort, and anxiety that inevitably follow upon the decision to sue may eventually be justified. In February 2013, a Boston female physician settled her sex discrimination claim against the hospital that employed her for $7,000,000. [34]

Chapter Twelve

Current Trends in the Law Prohibiting Discrimination of Pregnant Women

In 1978, Congress provided women with the means to contest employer-imposed limitations on their employment during pregnancy. The Pregnancy Discrimination Act, which in effect overruled a Supreme Court decision that excluded acts of pregnancy discrimination from the protections afforded by Title VII, amended the statute to require employers to treat pregnant women the same as any other temporarily disabled employee.[1] For example, if an employer allows temporarily disabled employees to perform alternative work assignments or take disability leave, it must treat a pregnant employee in the same manner. Since the enactment of the PDA, pregnant women have relied upon its provisions to combat employer restrictions on their continued participation in the workplace.

As noted in chapter 5, although the PDA requires an employer to treat pregnant workers in the same manner as it treats other workers temporarily disabled, it does not obligate employers to grant preferential treatment to pregnant women. Apparently, Mirtha Urbano and her attorney were unaware of this limitation.

Urbano worked for Continental Airlines as a ticketing sales agent, assisting travelers with ticket purchases and their baggage. When she became pregnant and began to suffer low-back pain, her physician ordered her to refrain, during the balance of her pregnancy, from lifting anything heavier than twenty pounds. Urbano then asked Continental to reassign her to a light-duty position that would not require her to lift passenger baggage. Because Continental's policy was to grant reassignments to light-duty positions only to employees who had suffered on-the-job injuries, it denied her request. Workers with nonoccupational injuries or illnesses did not have the right to reassignment but were assigned to light-duty positions in accordance with seniority. In these circumstances, Urbano was unable to obtain a reassignment and was forced to use her accrued sick leave and, ultimately, to take unpaid medical leave during the remainder of her pregnancy. Urbano then sued Continental for pregnancy discrimination.

Continental treated Urbano in the same manner as it treated other workers suffering from nonoccupational injuries and illnesses. Light-duty positions were at a premium; each of the forty-eight workers who had received light-duty assignments during the year previous to Urbano's application for reassignment had suffered on-the-job injuries.

Continental denied Urbano's application for a light-duty assignment only because she had not suffered a work-related injury. It was entitled to deny Urbano a light-duty assignment as long as it treated nonpregnant workers in the same manner. Since the PDA does not impose any duty on an employer to treat pregnant employees better than other employees, Urbano's discrimination claim was dismissed.[2]

An employer must treat its pregnant employees as well as it treats its other employees, but it may, if it chooses, treat them as badly as it treats its other employees. Holly-Anne Geier's discrimination claim is a case in point. Geier, a sales representative for Medtronic, Inc., was something less than a model employee. Her supervisors had given her several warning notices and on one occasion placed her on probation. Geier later became pregnant and soon thereafter was confined to bed due to pregnancy-related problems. Despite her problems, her supervisor called her at home once or twice a day, demanding that she continue to contact her sales accounts and threatened to relieve her of her position if she declined. Geier complied, working from her bed. When Geier was later hospitalized, her supervisor continued to harangue her about remaining in communication with her accounts. Geier then miscarried. While she was recovering at home, her supervisor directed her to get out of bed and start calling her sales accounts if she wanted to keep her job. Geier returned to work less than a week later.

Geier's performance deficiencies continued. Her supervisor again placed her on probation, and when her performance failed to improve he dismissed her. Geier then sued for pregnancy discrimination, but she faced a difficult evidentiary hurdle. She had to prove that the treatment she had been subjected to differed from that meted out to nonpregnant workers. But, she was unable to establish that her supervisor's haranguing telephone calls were motivated by her pregnancy rather than by reason of her absence from the workplace. The PDA requires an employer to ignore an employee's pregnancy, but it does not require it to ignore her absence from work, unless it also ignores absences from work of nonpregnant workers. Evidence of the supervisor's boorish behavior, in and of itself, did not establish a discriminatory intent, as he may very well have acted similarly with any employee, pregnant or not, who was absent from the office. Without evidence that her employer treated bedridden pregnant employees differently than bedridden nonpregnant employees, Geier's case could not succeed.

Geier's case illuminates the underlying philosophy of the PDA—pregnancy discrimination exists only in those situations in which pregnant women are treated less favorably than nonpregnant employees working in similar circumstances. Holly-Anne Geier was treated badly, but not unlawfully.[3]

The major hurdle facing a woman claiming pregnancy discrimination is the indispensable requirement that she prove that *on account of her pregnancy* her employer treated her differently and less favorably than other employees, that it failed to deal with the disability associated with pregnancy in the same manner as it dealt with other temporary disabilities. A California hotel made it easy for a group of female housekeepers to clear that hurdle when it admitted that it customarily fired all housekeepers when they became pregnant but did not terminate other employees who had temporary disabilities.[4] Most employers are not so accommodating as to admit their discriminatory practices.

Frequently, the evidence necessary to establish a pregnancy discrimination claim is not readily available to the complainant. One method of establishing differences in treatment is to show that the employer, while acting adversely to the interests of a pregnant worker, failed to follow its own policies and procedures. On the last day of her maternity leave, Margaret McLemore was notified by her employer, Continuity Programs, that due to a business downturn the company could no longer afford to pay her salary, and she was to be laid-off. Her supervisor could not predict how long the downturn would last, but he envisioned little opportunity for her to return to work during the ensuing six months.

Continuity's maternity leave policy stated that, as with the case of leave taken by other workers, the company would attempt to place a woman returning from maternity leave in the position she held before she left work to give birth. In the event a position was unavailable for a woman returning from maternity leave, the policy afforded her a preference for the next available position for which she was qualified. A short time after McLemore was laid-off, Continuity filled three positions for which McLemore was qualified. In each instance, however, Continuity failed to notify her of the vacancy and therefore failed to follow its own policy, thus denying McLemore a benefit the company provided nonpregnant employees returning from disability leaves. The court noted that an "employer's customary employment practices are relevant when considering pretext. . . . Here, defendant did not 'play by its own rules' with respect to McLemore." The company's violation of its own policy lent support to McLemore's claim that she had been discriminated against because of her pregnancy.[5]

Although women generally establish their claims of pregnancy discrimination by showing that pregnant workers are treated less advantageously than nonpregnant workers, a woman may also prove her claim by showing that she was treated less advantageously after she informed her employer of her pregnancy. Instead of comparing her treatment as a pregnant employee with the treatment afforded nonpregnant employees with temporary disabilities, she compared her treatment as a pregnant employee with the treatment she experienced before becoming pregnant. This was the approach Caroline Sanford used in her discrimination suit against Yenkin-Majestic Paint Corporation.

Yenkin-Majestic hired Sanford to work in its operations division to perform secretarial duties and other tasks related to the work performed by chemists in the company's paint laboratory. Some of her work was highly technical, as she was required to complete material safety data reports and type paint formulas and other documents containing technical data. A significant portion of Sanford's job functions involved the work she performed for the laboratory chemists.

About six months after she was hired, Sanford informed her supervisor she was pregnant. Four days later, her supervisor, for the first time, criticized her performance, claiming that she often overstayed her lunch hour and abused her personal telephone privileges. Not long after, the company was reorganized; the operations division in which Sanford worked was dissolved and a technical division was created. The newly hired manager of the technical division asked the company to assign to him a secretary with a technical background and experience with paint laboratory functions and who was familiar with chemical terminology. Although Sanford clearly met those criteria, the new manager was advised that the company did not currently employ any secretaries with that type of experience. Subsequently, the company fired Sanford, purportedly because of a lack of work, even though until the day of her departure from the company she remained involved in ongoing projects and was fully occupied.

On the day of Sanford's discharge, the company began interviewing candidates for the new technical secretarial position. The person hired possessed only a cursory knowledge of technical paint data, and after she resigned a few months later, the company replaced her with a worker having no training or experience with paint or chemicals.

Once she announced her pregnancy, Sanford's world was turned upside down, as the manner in which she was treated subsequently changed dramatically. Her supervisor criticized her performance, the company ignored the expertise she had gained working for the laboratory chemists, and, although she was constantly busy, she was terminated, purportedly for lack of work. The EEOC sued Yenkin-Majestic on Sanford's behalf, alleging that the company's actions following the advent of Sanford's pregnancy violated the Pregnancy Discrimination Act. After a trial, the court agreed with the EEOC and entered judgment against Yenkin-Majestic and in favor of Sanford.[6]

On occasion, comments uttered by management or supervisory personnel may lend support to a pregnancy discrimination claim. After a waitress announced her pregnancy, her working hours were reduced because, as her manager explained, "it doesn't look right" to have someone pregnant waiting on tables. The same manager later commented to another employee that "it looks tacky" for a pregnant woman to wait on tables." After, the EEOC sued the restaurant on the waitress's behalf, the court ordered the restaurant to reimburse her for lost wages, and it enjoined the restaurant from committing similar violations of the PDA against its other waitresses.[7]

In another pregnancy discrimination case, Regina Sheehan was five months pregnant with her third child when she was fired by her employer, the Donlen Corporation, and this led to a legal claim asserted by Sheehan under the Pregnancy Discrimination Act. Sheehan's first and second pregnancies also occurred while she was working for Donlen. Upon her return to work after her second maternity leave, Sheehan was assigned a greatly increased workload. She jokingly commented to her supervisor, "Maybe I should go home and have another baby." Her supervisor responded, "If you have another baby, I'll invite you to stay home." A year later, when notified of the third pregnancy, the supervisor said, "Oh my God, she's pregnant again," and a short time later she informed Sheehan, "you're not coming back after this baby." Three months later, after Sheehan's department head informed her that she was to be dismissed, he commented, "Hopefully, this will give you some time to spend at home with your children." Until that time, her department head had fired only one other worker. She too was pregnant at the time of her termination.

The remarks of the supervisor and the department head, both of whom participated in the decision to discharge Sheehan, provided the court with direct evidence of discrimination, and the jury awarded Sheehan $117,000 in damages. On appeal, Donlen argued that inasmuch as the department head did not explicitly say that Sheehan's termination was ordered because of her pregnancy, his statement did not rise to the level of direct evidence of discrimination. The appellate court rejected that position, noting that remarks that reflect a propensity to evaluate an employee on the basis of an illegal criterion constitute direct evidence of discrimination. In this case, pregnancy was the illegal criterion that Donlen used to determine whether Sheehan's employment would continue or not.[8]

After nearly thirty-five years of experience with the Pregnancy Discrimination Act, employers are far more likely to conceal rather than disclose any discriminatory aversions they may have to pregnant women in their employ. As a consequence, they are far less likely to engage in discussions with their workers that reveal those aversions. Since direct evidence of pregnancy discrimination, similar to that in the Sheehan case, is less often available to pregnant workers, they must rely on other types of evidence to establish their discrimination claims.

Currently, the most commonly used approach to proving pregnancy discrimination is through the use of indirect or circumstantial evidence, which was the route taken by Sondra Tamimi, a desk clerk at a Howard Johnson Motor Lodge in Montgomery, Alabama. When Tamimi was hired, her supervisor informed her that she had to comply with a dress code, but he did not advise her that she had to use makeup while working behind the front desk. This was important for Tamimi since, for religious reasons, she did not use makeup. Tamimi did not use cosmetics of any kind during her work hours, and although she was the only member of the staff working at the front desk without makeup, management did not complain about her appearance. However, later in her employment, after she announced her pregnancy, management initiated a new dress code requiring all employees working at the front desk to wear makeup. When Tamimi refused to comply with the new dress code, she was fired.

Management's discontent with Tamimi's appearance commenced on the day it became aware of her pregnancy. It then inaugurated a new dress code that affected only Tamimi, as all other female workers already used makeup. When Tamimi sued for pregnancy discrimination, the court ruled that management was aware that Tamimi would refuse to use makeup, and thus it proceeded to adopt a course of action that could only culminate in her discharge. The dress code was implemented for the purpose of getting rid of the pregnant Tamimi.

Although Tamimi did not have available to her any direct evidence of discrimination, she was able to offer the court indirect evidence of management's discriminatory intent—indirect evidence demonstrating that the mandatory makeup rule was conceived, implemented, and applied to Tamimi only because she was pregnant. Hence, the court awarded judgment in her favor.[9]

A rejected job applicant cannot successfully sue an employer for pregnancy discrimination unless she is able to prove that the employer was aware of her pregnancy and on that account rejected her. A job applicant's failure to reveal her pregnancy may lead to other unhappy events, as Margaret Ahmad found when she applied to the Loyal American Life Insurance Company to fill the position of medical claims examiner. She was told that the company's training process for that position usually lasted five to six months, but in view of her prior experience, it could be shortened. On her first day on the job, Ahmad informed Loyal personnel that she was four months pregnant. The company advised Ahmad that the timing of her anticipated maternity leave would significantly interfere with her training, and under the circumstances Loyal could not employ her. Ahmad then sued Loyal for pregnancy discrimination, but the court dismissed her claim. The evidence failed to establish that the company denied Ahmad employment on account of her pregnancy. Rather, the evidence confirmed that Loyal withdrew its offer of employment only because Ahmad's maternity leave would have adversely affected her training and thus materially reduce her value to the company. Since these circumstances constituted a legitimate business reason for rejecting Ahmad, the court refused to hold Loyal liable for pregnancy discrimination. [10]

Pregnant workers frequently find that once their employers learn of their pregnancies, promotions previously promised are instead given to other employees. In one case, a female worker, after receiving favorable performance evaluations, was offered a supervisory position. At the time, no other employees were even considered for the promotion. However, when her employer learned that the worker was pregnant, it withdrew the offer and awarded the supervisory position to a male worker instead. [11] Failures to promote, undesirable transfers, and objectionable job assignments, unfortunately, commonly occur following the announcement of a pregnancy.

In addition to pregnancy, the PDA bars discrimination "on the basis of . . . childbirth, or related medical conditions." What are related medical conditions? Does the PDA afford protection to a woman fired on the ground that her infertility treatments interfered with the performance of her job responsibilities? The argument has been made that the inability of a woman to become pregnant is not a pregnancy-related condition. A broader interpretation of the statute, however, would afford its protections to any condition that is related to the potential for pregnancy. The courts have generally assumed the broader view, holding that adverse acts directed against a female worker because she intends to become or is trying to become pregnant constitutes a form of discrimination barred by the statute. [12] Yet breast-feeding and other child-rearing concerns occurring after a pregnancy are not considered conditions related to pregnancy. [13] Similarly, claims of discrimination based on the status of being a new parent—or, as sometimes alleged, a "new mom"—are not cognizable under the provisions of the PDA. [14]

Because the statute has been broadly interpreted by the courts, its basic coverage has also been extended to women who choose to terminate their pregnancies. Thus, an employer may not refuse to hire, terminate, or otherwise treat a woman adversely simply because she has exercised her right to have an abortion. [15] Conversely, an employer may not discriminate against a woman because she refuses to have an abortion. [16]

Women filed more than 52,000 pregnancy discrimination claims with the EEOC during the ten-year period between 2001 and 2010. [17] Even these figures understate the problem. The full extent of the discrimination practiced against pregnant women cannot be accurately reflected in the compilation of claim filings since many, if not most, mothers are reluctant to initiate legal proceedings when caring for a newborn child. As a result, the full

extent of the workplace discrimination that confronts pregnant women may
never be known.

Chapter Thirteen

Current Trends in the Law Prohibiting Discrimination of Women with Children

Beginning with the first appearance of women in the American workplace, employers have singled out married women with children for treatment differing from that extended to other employees. In 1908, when the Supreme Court gave its approval to an Oregon statute limiting the working hours of women, its comments on motherhood and women's place in the workplace epitomized the stereotypical thinking that was then prevalent: "[Public opinion has produced] a widespread belief that women's physical structure and the functions she performs in consequence thereof, justify special legislation restricting or qualifying the conditions under which she should be permitted to toil. . . . That woman's physical structure and the performance of maternal functions place her at a disadvantage in the struggle for subsistence is obvious. This is especially true when the burdens of motherhood are upon her." [1]

At the end of World War II, the Edwin L. Wiegand Company initiated a policy of discharging female employees upon marriage and of refusing to hire women who were married. The policy was necessary, according to Wiegand's management, to provide jobs for male "bread winners" returning from the war. [2] At the time, the policy was lawful and it remained lawful until Congress enacted the 1964 Civil Rights Act. The EEOC later adopted regulations providing workplace protection specifically for married women: "The Commission has determined that an employer's rule which forbids or restricts the employment of married women and which is not applicable to married men is discrimination based on sex prohibited by Title VII of the Civil Rights Act. [3] An employer policy or practice, even if not directed against all female employees, is nevertheless discriminatory if a subgroup of

119

women, such as women who are married, are singled out for treatment different from that extended to male employees. In this chapter, we will examine
the various types of employer discriminatory conduct that still targets married women with children.

Over the last four decades, the number of married women with children
employed outside the home has increased significantly. In 1970, approximately 6 million married women with children—ages six to seventeen—
were employed in the workplace. By 2009 that number had grown to 10.2
million workers. The workplace participation of women with very young
children—under age six—also greatly increased, from 3.6 million to 6.8
million. In 1970, the labor force participation rate of married women with
children under six years of age was 30.3 percent, but by 2009 it had increased
to 61.6 percent. In that year, 76.7 percent of married women with children
between the ages of six and seventeen were gainfully employed.[4] These
statistical studies forecast the continued presence of working mothers in the
workplace, even while they continue to fulfill the role in the home as major
child-care giver.

This marked growth in the employment of married women with children
has been accompanied by an increased reliance of working mothers on Title
VII protections against workplace discriminatory conduct. Joann Trezza was
one of those working mothers.

Trezza, an attorney employed in the legal department of Hartford, Inc., an
insurance company with offices in New York City, was married and had two
children. Working alongside Trezza in the legal department was a female
attorney, unmarried and without children. When an opening occurred for a
management position in the legal department of one of Hartford's suburban
offices, Hartford elevated the unmarried attorney to the position, even though
Trezza was senior to her. When Trezza asked why Hartford had not considered her for the post, the managing attorney of the legal department told her
that it was assumed that she would not be interested in the position because
of her family obligations.

A year or so later, Trezza was in line for promotion to an assistant managing attorney position, but Hartford again rejected her in favor of a female
attorney who was unmarried and childless. At the time, Hartford also elevated a male attorney who was married and had children to an assistant manager
position. After Trezza complained to one of Hartford's senior vice presidents
that she felt she had been denied promotion solely because she was a married
woman with children, Hartford finally ordered her advancement to an assistant managing attorney position.

Four years later, the managing attorney of the legal department decided to
retire. Since Trezza was then the second most senior attorney in the office
and had been consistently awarded excellent performance evaluations, she
believed she was the logical choice to be named as the retiree's successor.

Rather than naming Trezza, however, Hartford appointed a female attorney who had no children. The appointee had considerably less experience than Trezza, had never practiced law in New York, and, in fact, was not admitted to practice law in the state. Trezza sued Hartford for sex discrimination.

When Hartford asked the court to dismiss Trezza's case, her attorneys submitted an abundance of evidence supporting Trezza's claim that during the course of her employment Hartford had discriminated against her merely because she was a married woman with children and that male employees with children were not similarly treated. First, they pointed to the fact that only seven of the forty-six managing attorneys employed by Hartford nationwide were women; of these seven, four were employed in East Coast offices, and none of the four had school-age children. On the other hand, many of the men serving in managing attorney positions had children. Second, on three occasions, Trezza's supervisor disparagingly commented on "the incompetence and laziness of women who are also working mothers." In addition, on another occasion, a senior vice president of the company declared that it was his opinion that working mothers could not simultaneously be both good mothers and good workers, remarking to Trezza, "I don't see how you can do either job well." Based on this evidence, the court denied Hartford's motion to dismiss Trezza's claims, and thus the parties to the suit were required to proceed to a trial of the ultimate issue: Did Hartford discriminate against Trezza because she was working mother?[5] A trial was avoided, however, when Hartford agreed to settle Trezza claims. If the matter had not been resolved prior to the trial, it appears likely that Trezza would have prevailed.

Trezza submitted evidence that her employer favored its male employees who had children over female employees with children. This evidence provided the basis that underlay all sex discrimination cases based on disparate treatment: that men and women, similarly situated, are not similarly treated. What would have been the result in this case if evidence of disparate treatment had not been available? We turn to Andrea Bass's sex discrimination claim against Chemical Bank for the answer.

Bass's responsibilities as assistant vice president and product manager at the bank included the development of marketing plans for new cash management products. Given the success she achieved in that position, Bass anticipated promotion to vice president. Chemical, however, declined to promote her. Subsequently, Bass gave birth to her first child, and on her return to work from maternity leave, Chemical relieved her of certain of her major responsibilities, making it less likely that thereafter she would be promoted. Three years later, Bass had her second child, and upon her return from maternity leave, Chemical reassigned to other workers virtually all of her remaining responsibilities as product manager. Not long after, Chemical promoted a single woman with no children to the vice presidency position that Bass had anticipated being awarded. At this juncture, Bass sued Chemical for

sex discrimination, claiming that she had been denied promotion only because of her status as a working mother.

Bass was passed over for promotion in favor of another woman, not a
man. She was unable to produce any evidence comparing the treatment afforded her by Chemical with the treatment afforded married men with children. Thus, the basic piece of evidence that would have established the
existence of an act of sex discrimination was missing; Bass could not prove
that Chemical's denial of the promotion was based on gender. The most that
Bass could show was that she was discriminated against because of her
parental status, but that type of discrimination is not prohibited by Title VII.
In the case previously examined, Joann Trezza showed that she was discriminated against, not only because of her parental status, but also because she
was a woman. Her claim was based upon sex *plus* parental status. Missing
from Bass's claim was any evidence that she was discriminated against by
reason of the fact that she was treated less favorably than similarly situated
male employees, and thus her claim was doomed to failure. [6]

Some working mothers, among them Susan McGrenaghan, have attempted to extend the scope of the protections of Title VII to smaller sub-
groups of married women with children. McGrenaghan charged the St. Denis
School in Philadelphia of discriminating against her because she was the
mother of a disabled child. After the birth of her son, the school transformed
McGrenaghan's full-time teaching position to one requiring her to work a
half day as a teacher and a half day as a resource aide. This constituted a
demotion, as it involved significantly diminished job responsibilities.
McGrenaghan alleged that the reduction in her job responsibilities was based
on unfounded stereotypes concerning the adequacy of the work performance
of mothers having disabled children and that a similar employment decision
would not have been made either for a woman without a disabled child or for
a father of a disabled child. In support of her claim, McGrenaghan offered
evidence that she was replaced in her full-time teaching position by a less
qualified woman who was not the mother of a disabled child. She also introduced testimony that the principal of the school had expressed animus
against working mothers of disabled children. Even though McGrenaghan's
claim extended only to a very small subclass of women, the court ruled that
she had a valid Title VII claim. [7]

We turn now to a different type of discrimination that is encountered by
married women with children. Title VII provides for a strict equal opportunity policy for women; women must be treated no less favorably than similarly situated men. But enforcement of this policy does not inevitably lead to
equality. Although men are now more likely than in the past to assume a
larger share of family and child-rearing responsibilities, women remain the
primary caregivers in the home. Many working mothers must fulfill their
family responsibilities while employed in a work environment designed by

men with far fewer family obligations. Since men have traditionally relied upon their wives to take on most child-rearing and other family responsibilities, they have found it possible to structure a work environment that demands nearly total commitment to the job, while ignoring in greater part the impact that such commitment has upon their families. But it is more difficult for a married woman with children to fulfill her familial responsibilities while working in such an environment. Thus, providing women with treatment equal to that extended to male workers fails to produce equality, as a strict equal opportunity policy holds mothers to a male model of workplace participation in which they cannot equally compete.[8]

The failure of employers to afford workplace equality for working mothers appears under many guises, one of which condemns the common practice of women who absent themselves from the workplace for relatively long periods of time to raise their children. Men who have made their jobs the central priority in their lives often find it difficult to accept on equal terms coworkers who have not accepted a similar set of priorities. These men—and on occasion, even some women—are unwilling to accommodate working mothers who, because of their responsibilities to their children, cannot and will not be guided by those priorities. The refusal to accommodate working mothers is an attitude that too often culminates in job-related decisions adverse to working mothers.

The courts have struggled with these workplace issues. On some occasions, courts have viewed charges of workplace inequality from the perspective of a working mother, but on other occasions they have been blind to that perspective, regarding it as irrelevant or inappropriate to its determination that the workplace in question is or is not infected with discriminatory animus. This restrictive perspective led to the demise of Cynthia Fisher's claim against her employer, Vassar College.

In her sex discrimination case against Vassar, Fisher claimed she had been denied tenure when Vassar discriminated against her because of her absence from academia for a period of eight years while she was engaged in raising her young children. Fisher won a resounding victory in the trial court, only to encounter total defeat on appeal.

At the time of the trial, Fisher was married with two adult daughters. She held a bachelor's degree from the University of Wisconsin and master's and doctoral degrees from Rutgers University. She also had engaged in postdoctoral studies at Rutgers Medical School and, after the eight-year hiatus, had taught biology at Marist College. At that point, Vassar hired Fisher as a member of its biology department faculty. After teaching nine years at Vassar, Fisher was denied tenure. She sued Vassar for sex discrimination.

In the thirty years prior to Fisher's tenure review, no married women had ever achieved tenure in Vassar's hard science departments, that is, in the biology, mathematics, physics, chemistry, geology, and computer science departments. All women tenured in the hard science departments during that thirty-year period had been unmarried when they were hired and remained unmarried at the time they were granted tenure. Evidence submitted to the trial court showed that while married women in the hard sciences were discouraged from advancing to tenure, single women without children were not. In fact, at the time of Fisher's denial of tenure, Dr. Pinina Norrod, an unmarried female, was granted tenure. But while Norrod had not experienced any breaks in her career, the biology professors reviewing Fisher's credentials and qualifications for tenure were very much aware that she had interrupted her career to raise her children. During the tenure review process, the biology department focused on this hiatus in Fisher's career, criticizing her for being "out of the field for [eight] years" and being "out of date." The "out of date" reference implied that Fisher's scholarship was obsolete as a result of the time spent at home with her children. But this accusation did not square with the facts. While Fisher was caring for her children, she kept abreast of developments in her field of study. At the time of her tenure review, seven of Fisher's papers had been accepted for publication in prestigious journals, and she also had written a book that was later published. Her record of publication was superior to that of three male assistant professors who had just been granted tenure. In addition, she had received several grants that would not have been awarded if her knowledge of her field was deficient or out of date.

In examining the evidence submitted in support of Fisher's claim, the trial court focused its attention on Vassar's grant of tenure to the unmarried Dr. Norrod, who, unlike Fisher, had not experienced a break in her career. Norrod had taught in the biology department six fewer years than Fisher, had a much lighter teaching load, and was considered for tenure after she had served as an assistant professor for two years while the normal period of service was seven years.

Ultimately, the court ruled that the biology department's apparent obsession with a married woman's family choices reflected its acceptance of the stereotype that a married woman with child-rearing responsibilities cannot be a productive member of its faculty: "The persistent fixation of the Biology Department's senior faculty on a married woman's pre-Vassar family choices reflects the acceptance of a stereotype and bias; that a married woman with an active and on-going family life cannot be a productive scientist and, therefore, is not one despite much evidence to the contrary." The court ruled, despite Vassar's protest that it had historically advanced the cause of women, that the college had consistently acted in a biased manner toward its married female faculty members. It awarded Fisher damages in the sum of $627,000 and directed Vassar to grant her tenure.[9]

On the appeal of the trial court's ruling, the appellate court noted that the trial evidence supported an inference that Fisher's eight-year absence from academia had diminished her chances for tenure and that, if the Vassar professors and administrators involved in the tenure process equated that absence with child-rearing, a sex-based animus may have underlain the entire process. But, for such a claim to succeed, the appellate court ruled, Fisher would have to submit evidence comparing the tenure experience of women who had taken extended leaves of absence from work with the tenure experience of men who had taken such leaves of absence. That is to say, Fisher would have to prove that women who absented themselves from the workplace to fulfill child-rearing responsibilities were treated differently and less favorably than men who took extended leaves of absence and that these men were more likely to be granted tenure than the women. This type of evidence, however, was unavailable to Fisher or, for that matter, anyone else, as men rarely absent themselves from the workplace for long periods of time, solely for the purpose of rearing their children. Nevertheless, from the perspective of the appellate court, Fisher's claim had to be rejected.[10]

This narrow-minded and parochial approach to the issue was highly criticized by three dissenting judges:

> [T]he predominant reason that working women take absences from work is to bear and raise children; there is no persuasively comparable reason for absences among working men, and it is fatuous . . . to suggest that Dr. Fisher is to be faulted for not producing evidence of the tenure experiences of men who took absences. . . . With rare exception, men do not take extended absences from work to raise children (or for any other reason). . . . [The trial court] was entirely correct: the Biology Department's "persistent fixation on [Dr. Fisher's] pre-Vassar family choices reflects the acceptance of a stereotype and bias."

It was clear to the dissenting judges that the majority's position called for an exercise in futility.

Vassar was entitled to deny Fisher tenure if her extended absence had left her deficient in knowledge of the developments in the field of biology. But, her publications and grant awards demonstrated the timeliness of her knowledge. The trial court was entirely justified in considering the biology department's adverse views of Fisher's hiatus as constituting evidence of bias against married women. Unfortunately, the appellate court's position prevailed.

Despite the sometimes unfavorable reception given by the courts to cases that raise these issues, some employers have altered their position regarding the workplace role of working mothers. In recognition that women with children confront problems in the workplace unique to them, some employer have initiated special career paths, commonly called "mommy tracks," designed specifically to accommodate working mothers. Flex-time, part-time, extended maternity leaves, and job sharing are some of the workplace variations that typical mommy track plans offer. Many women, however, object to special career paths designed for working mothers, since the acceptance of the mommy track as a normal workplace fixture stands as an acknowledgment that women with children require special consideration to succeed. Opponents of the mommy track fear that its existence will only buttress the stereotype that working mothers, regardless of the efforts they exert on behalf of their employers, are less committed to their jobs and their employers. Others fear that women who accept the mommy track remove themselves from the center of activity; they become second-string players, consigning themselves to lesser positions in the corporate hierarchy.

Progress has been made, but the elimination of the workplace problems that working mothers have long experienced does not appear to be close at hand. Sex bias will continue to corrupt the workplace whenever employers question the appropriateness of the presence of working mothers. Unhappily, the courts give increasing evidence that their view of the protections provided by Title VII for the protection of working women with children may not be sufficiently expansive to bring about a meaningful change in the work environment.

Chapter Fourteen

Sexual Harassment and the Sex Discrimination Prohibitions of Title VII

The sexual harassment of a woman by a man higher on the corporate ladder conveys the message that she is primarily perceived as a sexual object, not as a workplace colleague and valuable business asset. The sexual harassment of women expresses the age-old belief that women should be sexually available to men, and it simultaneously reminds women that they are neither respected nor viewed as workplace equals. [1]

Because sexual harassing acts generally evolve from an unequal status between a man and a woman, the harassment of a female worker usually involves a power relationship affecting the terms and conditions of the woman's employment. Since such acts generally culminate in a hostile and offensive work environment, the harassed woman must live and work under abusive and antagonistic conditions. Women, therefore, perceive sexual harassment as a reflection of a status that emphasizes their sex roles over their work roles and thus threatens their economic livelihood. [2]

Catharine A. MacKinnon, one of the first to argue that workplace sexual harassment constituted a major problem for women, stated in her seminal book *Sexual Harassment of Working Women* that "[s]exual harassment is seen to be one dynamic which reinforces and expresses women's traditional and inferior role in the labor workplace." From these circumstances, MacKinnon concluded and was one of the first to contend that sexual harassment in the workplace is a form of sex discrimination. [3] At first, most courts did not agree.

In chapter 5 we reviewed the early sexual harassment cases decided after the advent of Title VII. In one case, the complainant alleged that her supervisor had retaliated against her when she refused his request for an after-hours affair, but the court held that the substance of the complainant's allegations centered on her claim that she was discriminated against, not because she was a woman, but because she had declined to engage in a sexual affair with her supervisor. According to the court, this was not sex discrimination.[4]

Less than a year later, an Arizona federal court arrived at a similar conclusion. The court ordered the dismissal of the complaints of two women who alleged they had been verbally and physically harassed by their supervisor and that his sexual harassment continued unabated until they were compelled to resign their employment. The court stated that Title VII does not apply to the sexual advances of a supervisor.[5] Another judge remarked that if sexual harassment was covered by Title VII, "we would need 4,000 federal trial judges instead of 400."[6] If the rationale of these decisions had prevailed, no working woman would ever have successfully prosecuted a sexual harassment claim under Title VII. Fortunately, not all courts were as myopic.

One year later, a District of Columbia federal appellate court ruled that women subjected to acts of sexual harassment are discriminated against simply because they are women, not because of their refusal to engage in sexual acts demanded by a supervisor as the first court had held: "But for her womanhood . . . her participation in sexual activity would never have been solicited. To say, then, that she was victimized in her employment simply because she declined the invitation is to ignore the asserted fact that she was invited only because she was a woman."[7] Soon after, another federal appellate court ruled that if a supervisor, with the knowledge of his employer, made sexual demands of a subordinate female employee and conditioned her employment status on a favorable response to those demands, he and his employer acted in violation of Title VII.[8]

Following these cases, the EEOC entered the fray and issued guidelines based upon the assumption that sexually harassing conduct constituted a violation of Title VII. There the matter stood until 1986, when Mechelle Vinson's sexual harassment case against Meritor Savings Bank reached the Supreme Court, presenting it with its first opportunity to rule on issues involving allegations of sexual harassment in the workplace.

Vinson had worked for the bank for four years, first as a teller, next as a head teller, and then an assistant branch manager. Throughout the term of Vinson's employment, she worked under the supervision of Sidney Taylor. After Vinson was fired for taking excessive sick leave, she brought a legal action against the bank and Taylor, claiming that during her four years at the bank, Taylor had continuously subjected her to acts of sexual harassment.

Vinson alleged that soon after she began her employment with the bank, Taylor suggested to her that they have sexual relations. At first she refused, but when he persisted she agreed out of fear of losing her position. Thereafter, Taylor made repeated demands for sex, both during and after business hours, and they had intercourse on numerous occasions. Vinson also alleged that Taylor fondled her in the presence of other employees, followed her into the restroom, exposed himself to her, and even raped her on more than one occasion. Because she feared Taylor and was concerned for her job, Vinson neither reported Taylor's harassment to any of his supervisors nor attempted to use the bank's grievance procedures.

Vinson's case presented the Supreme Court with three basic issues for resolution:

- Is sexual harassment a form of sex discrimination barred by Title VII?
- Is an employer liable to a female worker for an offensive work environment created by her supervisor's acts of sexual misconduct?
- Does a Title VII violation occur when a sexual relationship between an employee and her supervisor is "voluntary"?

The court's responses to these questions proved to be of paramount importance in the development of the law barring sexual harassment in the workplace.

In holding that a woman may establish a Title VII violation by proving that her supervisor sexually harassed her, the court quoted from an earlier court of appeals opinion: "Sexual harassment which creates a hostile or offensive environment of one sex is every bit the arbitrary barrier to sexual equality at the workplace that racial harassment is to racial equality. Surely, a requirement that a man or woman run a gauntlet of sexual abuse in return for the privilege of being allowed to work and make a living can be as demeaning and disconcerting as the harshest of racial epithets."[9]

For sexually harassing conduct to violate Title VII, however, it must be sufficiently severe or pervasive to alter the terms and conditions of the harassed woman's employment, thus creating a hostile and abusive work environment. Without question, Taylor's conduct, as alleged, was sufficiently severe to alter the terms and conditions of Vinson's employment, and his behavior created an abusive and hostile work environment in which she was compelled to work. Thus Vinson's allegations of Taylor's harassing conduct, if proved, were sufficient to establish a claim of sexual harassment under Title VII.

On the issue of the bank's liability for Taylor's conduct, the bank argued that it could not be held liable for Taylor's behavior because it was unaware that he had engaged in the sexual harassment of Vinson. Vinson's attorneys, on the other hand, maintained that since Taylor had been placed in a supervisory role over Vinson, the bank was liable for Taylor's misconduct even if it had no knowledge of the harassment. They also maintained that when Vinson received direction from Taylor, she in effect received direction from the bank. That is to say, when Taylor acted in his supervisory capacity, he acted as the representative or agent of the bank; and since the bank is legally liable for the actions of its representatives and agents, it was liable for Taylor's acts of sexual harassment.

The Supreme Court essentially agreed with Vinson's attorneys. Since a supervisor is delegated authority by his employer, the supervisor generally acts as an agent of the bank when he exercises that authority, and thus the employer is liable for any misuse of that authority. Circumstances may arise, however, where a supervisor may not be acting as an agent of his employer. In each case, therefore, the court must determine whether—in light of the facts existent in that case—the harassing supervisor actually acted as an agent of his employer, thus rendering it liable for his harassment.

On the issue of Vinson's voluntarily consenting to a sexual relationship with Taylor, the court pointed out that the correct inquiry is not whether Vinson's participation in sexual intercourse with Taylor was voluntary but whether Taylor's conduct was "unwelcome" to her. The fact that Vinson was not forced to participate against her will in a sexual relationship with Taylor is not a valid defense to her sexual harassment claim. However, one of the elements of proof borne by the complainant in a sexual harassment suit may be sustained only with persuasive evidence that the harassing conduct was unwelcome to her. Since that issue had not been considered by the lower court, Vinson's case had to be remanded for further proceedings. Before these proceedings were conducted, however, Vinson and the bank agreed to a settlement of the case.[10]

Through its decision in this case, the Supreme Court established three principles to guide the courts in the adjudication of sexual harassment claims. First, to be actionable, an abusive or hostile environment claim must affect the terms and conditions of the claimant's working conditions. Second, the harassment must be "sufficiently severe or persuasive" to have been the cause of that change in working conditions. And, third, the harassing conduct must have been unwelcome to the victim of the harassment.

Subsequent to the court's ruling, lower courts categorized sexual harassment cases as falling into one of two distinct forms. First, it is the abusive treatment of a female employee that would not occur but for the fact that she is a woman, and it usually entails demands for sexual favors either in return for employment benefits or under threat of some adverse employment action. This type of sexual harassment is referred to as *quid pro quo* harassment. Under guidelines later adopted by the EEOC, quid pro quo sexual harassment exists when "submission to [sexual] conduct is made either explicitly or implicitly a term or condition of an individual's employment [or when] submission or rejection of such conduct by an individual is used as the basis for employment decisions affecting such individual."[11]

The second form of sexual harassment occurs when an employer encourages or tolerates the existence of a work environment that is replete with sexual innuendo, intimidation, or other form of harassing conduct that are sufficiently severe or pervasive to alter the terms and conditions of a woman's employment, This type of sexual harassment is referred to as *hostile work environment* harassment.

Recent sexual harassment cases, for the most part, have involved issues relating to the hostility of the woman's work environment. In these cases, the courts must consider the conditions under which the woman is compelled to work and then determine whether those conditions are sufficiently abusive or hostile to support a sexual harassment claim. A sexually hostile environment is one that is both objectively and subjectively hostile: objectively, in that any reasonable person would find it hostile or abusive; and subjectively, in that the victim of the harassment also perceives it to be so. As in cases of racial harassment (chapter 10), whether a work environment is sufficiently hostile or abusive to support a sexual harassment claim is determined by viewing all the circumstances, including

1. the frequency of the acts of sexual harassment
2. the severity of the offensive conduct
3. whether the offensive conduct was physically threatening or verbal
4. the extent to which the victim was humiliated by reason of the conduct
5. whether the harasser was a coworker or a supervisor
6. whether other workers joined in the harassment
7. whether the harassment was directed at more than one individual
8. whether the harassment unreasonably interfered with the victim's work performance, thus altering the terms and conditions of her employment [12]

The incidence of legal claims alleging sexual harassing conduct in the workplace increased substantially after October 1991. At that time, the Senate conducted confirmation hearings in connection with the nomination of Clarence Thomas as a justice of the Supreme Court. While viewing the nationally televised hearings conducted in connection with the nomination, the nation heard law professor Anita Hill's vivid testimony describing the sexual harassment she experienced while working under Thomas's supervision at the EEOC. The hearings greatly increased public awareness of the existence of sexual harassment in the workplace. Subsequently, the number of sexual harassment charges filed with the EEOC increased from 6,883 in 1991 to 10,532 in 1992, and these filings continued to increase each year until 1997, when they numbered 15,889. [13] By 2010, the number of EEOC filings had increased to more than 21,000 and they have remained at that level ever since. [14]

But even these figures fail to disclose the full extent of workplace harassment of women. Similar to other forms of sexual victimization, such as rape and domestic violence, the incidence of sexual harassment is generally underreported. Several studies have shown that the occurrence of sexual harassment in the workplace is far more common than annual EEOC charge filings portray.[15] One survey reported that 60 percent of women in management positions have experienced some form of sexual harassment during their work lives, but only 14 percent of these women have reported the harassment and less than 1 percent have filed a charge or commenced legal action.[16] If all of these women formally charged their employers with sexual harassment, the annual EEOC filings would number in the hundreds of thousands.

Women who decide to turn to the law are often richly rewarded, as juries have displayed little reluctance to huge damage verdicts. A jury awarded a female police officer employed by the Village of Sleepy Hollow, New York, damages of $2,200,000, after it heard testimony that she had been sexually harassed by her training officer, the police chief, and the village mayor.[17] A jury awarded a sexually harassed legal secretary compensatory damages of $50,000 and punitive damages of $7.1 million, even though she had worked for the defendant law firm for less than two months.[18] Still another jury awarded a female worker employed in a Daimler Chrysler factory the sum of $21 million for acts of sexual harassment she had been subjected to over a period of years.[19] Even though huge jury rewards of these proportions are often reduced by trial or appellate courts, still the recovery of damages in cases of this type may run into the millions.

Sexual harassment cases also are settled outside of court for immense sums. A family-owned importing firm in New Rochelle, New York, agreed to pay $2.6 million to 104 of its women workers who were sexually harassed by the 79-year-old owner and president of the company.[20] The EEOC reached a major settlement with the Ford Motor Company providing nearly $8 million in damages to be paid to female workers who were sexually and racially harassed.[21] After the Mitsubishi Company was accused of ignoring—and even encouraging—the sexual harassment of women working in its automobile assembly plant, it agreed to pay $34 million to the harassed women. This settlement followed upon an earlier settlement of a private lawsuit for $10 million.[22]

Whether a work environment is sufficiently hostile or offensive to support a sexual harassment case is a question a court can assess only after examining all of the circumstances. While the court will always consider as paramount the frequency, severity, and degree of pervasiveness of the harassing conduct, they will scrutinize other factors as well. Was the defendant's conduct physically threatening? Did it unreasonably interfere with the victim's work performance? Were there any other factors bearing on the degree of hostility and offensiveness of the harasser's behavior?

A lone instance of sexual harassment may appear at first glance to fail the test of frequency and degree of pervasiveness, but a single act of physical touching, or some other egregious act of harassment, may create a work environment as offensive and hostile as that resulting from a long-running pattern of harassment.

The EEOC guidelines state that an act of sexual harassment that "has the purpose or effect of substantially interfering with an individual's work performance or creating an intimidating, hostile, or offensive working environment" constitutes a violation of Title VII. The severity and pervasiveness of the offending conduct must be viewed objectively and subjectively, that is, from the perspective of a reasonable person and from that of the victim. [23]

Suppose a woman alleges that she perceived her work environment to be hostile and that a reasonable person would similarly view it. Furthermore, the totality of the circumstances appear to support her claim that her employer forced her to work in that environment. But, in spite of the abusive conduct she experienced, she was able to deal with it without suffering any psychological ill effects. She is unable to prove, therefore, that the hostility and offensiveness of her work environment seriously affected her psychological well-being. Is her inability to prove psychological harm fatal to her claim? This question arose in connection with Teresa Harris's sexual harassment claim against her employer.

Harris worked as a manager at Forklift Systems, and over several years the company's president subjected her repeatedly to offensive sexual remarks and disgusting behavior. But Harris was unable to prove that this conduct had caused her any psychological harm. Ultimately, her case reached the Supreme Court, where the primary issue to be decided was whether Harris could successfully sue Forklift for hostile environment sexual harassment in light of her inability to prove that the president's harassing conduct had psychologically damaged her.

Justice Sandra Day O'Connor succinctly imparted the court's stance on the issue: "Title VII comes into play before the harassing conduct leads to a nervous breakdown." Although an abusive work environment may not seriously affect a worker's psychological well-being, it may nevertheless detract from her job performance, interfere with the advancement of her career, or discourage her from remaining on the job. Thus, even if the harassment produced no tangible effect upon her mental well-being, a woman may still prevail in a hostile environment case if she proves that the harassing conduct was so severe or pervasive as to create an abusive work environment that altered the terms and conditions of her employment. [24]

A victim of harassment need not endure the harasser's conduct for an extended period of time before becoming entitled to the remedies provided by Title VII. This is especially the case when the objectionable behavior includes unwelcome touching. The offensiveness of the behavior complained of is the principal factor to be considered in determining whether it is sufficiently severe or pervasive to create an abusive work environment. As noted, even a single act may be sufficiently repugnant to be characterized as severe or pervasive.

Ordinarily, a worker has little difficulty in establishing subjective hostility. If she testifies that she found the defendant's conduct to be offensive, her testimony generally is sufficient. On occasion, however, the credibility of the plaintiff's testimony on this issue is questioned, as was the case with Lisa Ann Burns, who worked for McGregor Electronics Industries. The evidence admitted in her sexual harassment suit against McGregor painted a picture of a glaringly, hostile work environment. The owner of the company continuously barraged her with sexual propositions, asked her to attend pornographic movies with him, suggested oral sex, and stalked her at work. The trial court, however, questioned whether Burns considered any of the owner's behavior to be offensive, as she had posed nude for two national motorcycle magazines. The court reasoned that a woman who would allow her nude photograph to be distributed nationally would not be offended by the type of conduct engaged in by the company's owner, and thus she had exaggerated the severity and pervasiveness of the harassment and its effect on her.

When Burns appealed the trial court's adverse decision, the appellate court viewed the case differently. A worker's activities engaged in outside of the workplace are irrelevant to whether she considered her employer's conduct offensive. Evidence of her private life cannot be used to demonstrate a woman's acquiescence to sexual advances in the workplace.[25]

The worker may confront greater difficulty in demonstrating to the court that a reasonable person would view her workplace as hostile and offensive in the same way she views it. Since men are infrequently the victims of sexual assault, they generally view workplace sexual conduct from an entirely different perspective than that of women. In some circumstances, the perspective of a reasonable man may materially diverge from the perspective of a reasonable woman. Should a man's view of workplace hostility be a factor the court considers in determining the degree of hostility in the workplace? Is the "reasonable person" test appropriate if that test is colored by a man's point of view? When Kerry Ellison sued the Internal Revenue Service for sexual harassment, the court questioned the appropriateness of applying a "reasonable person" test rather than a "reasonable woman" test to the circumstances of her case.

Ellison worked as a revenue agent for the IRS in San Mateo, California. Sterling Gray worked at a desk located about twenty feet from hers. Revenue agents in the San Mateo office often lunched in groups, and on one occasion Ellison lunched with a group that included Gray. Ellison later claimed that subsequent to that lunch, Gray dawdled around her desk and pestered her with silly questions. About two months later, Gray asked her out for a drink after work, an invitation Ellison declined. A week later, Gray invited her out for lunch, and again Ellison was unwilling. A few days later, Gray handed her a handwritten note: "I cried over you last night and I'm totally drained today. I have never been in such constant term oil (sic). Thank you for talking with me. I could not stand to feel your hatred for another day."

Ellison was so shocked and frightened upon reading the note that she ran from the office. Gray followed her into the hallway and demanded that she talk to him, but she fled the building. Ellison later reported Gray's behavior to her supervisor who agreed that Gray was engaging in sexually harassing conduct.

Rather than file a formal complaint of harassment, Ellison decided to handle the matter herself. She then asked a male coworker to speak to Gray and inform him that she was not interested in him and that he should leave her alone.

The following week, after Ellison had started a four-week training session in St. Louis, Gray sent her a three-page love letter. Ellison notified her supervisor, who immediately confronted Gray and directed him to cease all contact with Ellison. Gray was then transferred to the San Francisco office, but after he filed a union grievance, he was ordered transferred back to San Mateo. Before returning to San Mateo, Gray wrote another letter to Ellison, intimating that they had some kind of relationship. At that point, to avoid Gray on his return to the San Mateo office, Ellison asked to be transferred to another IRS office, and she followed her request with the filing of a formal complaint alleging sexual harassment.

The court that heard Ellison's case had to decide whether Gray's conduct was sufficiently severe or pervasive to have altered the conditions of Ellison's employment. The court emphasized that the victim's view of the allegedly offensive conduct must first be considered and the nature of that perspective fully understood: "We therefore prefer to analyze harassment from the victim's perspective. A complete understanding of the victim's view requires, among other things, an analysis of the different perspectives of men and women. Conduct that many men consider unobjectionable may offend many women. . . . [M]any women share common concerns which men do not necessarily share." Men and women do not share the same perspective with regard to rape and sexual assault. Since women are far more often victims of criminal assault, they are much more concerned with any form of aberrant or aggressive sexual behavior. Even when confronted with a mild form of sexual harassment, a woman may be worried that a harasser's conduct is merely a prelude to a violent assault. A man, on the other hand, who probably has never been the subject of a sexual assault, may view the same conduct without a full appreciation of the underlying threat of violence that a woman perceives. Based on this rationale, the court concluded that the severity and pervasiveness of Gray's actions should be viewed from the perspective of a reasonable woman rather than that of a reasonable person: "We adopt the perspective of a reasonable woman primarily because we believe that a sex-blind reasonable person standard tends to be male-biased and tends to systematically ignore the experiences of women."[26]

Analyzing the facts of this case from Gray's point of view, he was only trying to woo Ellison. There was no evidence that he harbored any ill will toward her and thus, from his perspective, his actions were trivial and unintimidating. Ellison, however, was shocked and frightened by Gray's conduct. The court felt that a reasonable woman would have similarly reacted and would have considered Gray's conduct to be sufficiently severe and pervasive to alter the conditions of her employment and thus create a hostile work environment.

Few courts have adopted the "reasonable woman" test. The EEOC approach to the issue, however, appears to differ little from the *Ellison* court approach. In applying the "reasonable person" standard, the EEOC holds that the victim's perspective must also be considered, and all stereotypical notions of acceptable behavior must be discarded.[27] Stereotypical notions of acceptable workplace sexual behavior are notions advanced by men. The EEOC formula, therefore, is not far distant from the reasonable woman test.

In a hostile work environment case, a woman may recover damages for acts of sexual harassment only if the harassment is "sufficiently severe or pervasive to alter the conditions of the victim's employment."[28] In Mechelle Vinson's case against the Meritor Savings Bank, Vinson alleged that her supervisor repeatedly demanded sex of her, both during and after business hours, fondled her in the presence of other employees, followed her into the restroom and exposed himself, and raped her on several occasions. The Supreme Court ruled that Vinson's allegations "which include not only pervasive harassment but also criminal conduct of the most serious nature are plainly sufficient to state a claim for '"hostile environment' sexual harassment."[29] Flirtation, teasing, off-hand comments, vulgar language, and annoying isolated incidents are usually insufficiently serious or pervasive to support a sexual harassment charge. Similarly, differences in the ways men and women routinely interact with members of the opposite sex ordinarily do not rise to a level that would warrant classification as acts of sexual harassment. Many acts of sexual harassment, however, are less severe than the criminal conduct alleged in the Vinson case. In most cases, the severity of the harassing conduct lay somewhere between that classified as flirtation, teasing, and isolated incidents on the one hand and the conduct experienced by Vinson on the other.

A case in point involved Sheri Bishop and her employer, Interim Industrial Services. Shortly after she was hired, Bishop charged her supervisor, Armando Perez, with sexual harassment. She testified that Perez asked her out on a date, but she rejected his request. On another occasion, Perez followed her around the workplace, and on another he asked her why she did not wear looser clothing. He once asked her if she was involved with anyone and inquired as to why not. Although one of Perez's responsibilities as Bishop's supervisor was to observe her performance, she claimed that he watched her work while sitting in his office, with the lights off. The court ruled that Bishop had failed to show that Perez's conduct was severe or pervasive, categorizing it as ordinary workplace socializing and flirtation, conduct that should not be confused with sexual harassment that breeds discriminatory conditions of employment.[30] Perez's conduct was neither pervasive nor sufficiently severe to create a hostile work environment or to alter the conditions of Bishop's employment.

The conduct of one of Susan McKenzie's coworkers was somewhat more offensive than that experienced by Sheri Bishop, but McKenzie's claim of sexual harassment met a similar fate. As an employee of the Illinois Department of Transportation, McKenzie was responsible for training one of her coworkers, Donald Croft, in the use of a computerized inventory system. On one occasion during a training session, McKenzie became ill and vomited. At the time, Croft remarked to her that she had "screwed around" so much with one of her supervisors that she probably was pregnant. Some weeks later, Croft telephoned McKenzie in her office and said that he had heard that coffee induces sexual arousal, and since he was about to come to her office, he wanted to know if she was drinking coffee. Shortly after, when one of the workers mentioned to Croft that he had to collect some money from McKenzie for her participation in a baseball betting pool, Croft said that he should "take it out in trade."

Croft's remarks were made over a three-month period. When McKenzie sued for sexual harassment, the court held that a reasonable person would not perceive McKenzie's work environment to be hostile or abusive: "Title VII is not directed against unpleasantness per se but only . . . against discrimination in the conditions of employment. . . . Although Croft's comments were most certainly offensive, we cannot hold that the frequency or severity of the comments rose to the level of unreasonably interfering with Ms. McKenzie's working environment." Accordingly, the court dismissed McKenzie's claim.[31] A complainant requires more than three isolated instances of moderately offensive behavior to prove an alteration in the terms and conditions of her employment.

A case where the harasser's offensive behavior was described by a court as tending "toward the lower end of the spectrum" of sexually harassing conduct was brought by Brenda Borello, who worked as a bookkeeper for A. Sam & Sons Produce Company. Charles Sam, son of the president of the company, served as the company's vice president. Borello's work required her to have intermittent contact with Sam, such as delivering telephone messages and obtaining delivery authorizations. Five months into her employment, Borello left a delivery slip on Sam's desk for his authorization. The following morning, she found the slip on her desk with Sam's notation, "whore, what is the amount?" Later that day, Borello overheard a loud argument in which Sam shouted that all the women in the office were "whores and all [they] knew how to do [was] fuck." In the following week, while walking near Borello's office, Sam remarked, "nothing but a whore, nothing but a little whore, just a whore." A week later, while Borello was waiting to punch her time card, Sam said as he passed by, "why don't you stare at the time clock a little bit more ya whore." About a week later, when Borello called Sam to advise him that he had telephone messages, he shouted "go fuck yourself" and slammed down the receiver.

When Borello filed a sexual harassment claim, the company contended that since the incidents of Sam's conduct were sporadic and isolated, they were neither sufficiently severe nor pervasive to result in a hostile environment. The court, however, ruled otherwise. A female worker need not be subjected to an extended period of demeaning and degrading treatment before becoming entitled to the protections of Title VII. The offensiveness of the behavior complained of is a factor to be considered, and the greater the severity of the offensive conduct, the fewer the number of incidents needed for it to be characterized as severe or pervasive. For the court, the five incidents of harassment were sufficient to create a hostile work environment.[32]

Unwelcome touching, even a single, isolated occurrence, nearly always leads to a verdict for the harassed victim. James Pocrnick worked for the Professional Bank as senior vice president of consumer lending and in that capacity had the authority to hire and fire employees in his department. Pocrnick first met Rhonda Mallinson-Montague when he closed a consumer loan transaction for her at the bank. Despite Mallinson-Montague's lack of banking experience, Pocrnick offered her a loan officer position, paying a salary plus commissions based on the number of loans closed. Although Mallinson-Montague had reservations concerning the job, she accepted the offer after Pocrnick assured her that she would be properly trained and he would provide her with sufficient leads to earn commission income.

Almost immediately after Mallinson-Montague began work at the bank, Pocrnick began to sexually harass her. On one occasion, he instructed her to meet him at a nearby park to review some business matters, and when she arrived at the park, he pressed himself against her, kissed her, and asked her if she could feel his erection. When Mallinson-Montague rebuffed these advances, Pocrnick denied her the business leads he had previously promised and began to reject loans that she had originated. Apparently, Pocrnick had induced Mallinson-Montague to accept employment at the bank primarily for the purpose of facilitating his plans of sexual conquest. His acts of retaliation following Mallinson-Montague's rejection of his advances only added to the severity and pervasiveness of his harassing conduct.

Not long after, Mallinson-Montague retained an attorney who wrote to the bank's president disclosing Pocrnick's behavior, and the harassment subsequently ceased. Mallinson-Montague, however, felt her career at the bank had been compromised and she resigned. When she later sued Pocrnick and the bank for sexual harassment, the jury quickly rendered its verdict in her favor.[33]

In a similar case, Lynn Fall worked for the South Bend branch of the University of Indiana, and David Cohen served as its chancellor. Not long after Fall was hired, Cohen sent her an email message requesting her to see him regarding legislative issues that were important to the university. According to Fall's recollection, on the day of her meeting with Cohen, she entered his office and he closed the door behind her. After they had spent some time discussing matters then before the state legislature, Cohen told her that he had used the email message merely as a ruse to get her into his office. Fall rose from her chair to leave, but before she could make her exit, Cohen put his arms around her, started kissing her, and forced his hands down her blouse and groped her breasts. Fall broke from his grasp and fled the office, proceeding directly to a restroom where she vomited.

Fall filed suit against the university. The court focused its attention on whether Cohen's single act of harassment rose to the level of severity or pervasiveness required to support a hostile environment claim. First, the court noted Cohen's deception in luring Fall into his office, indicating that his attack upon her was calculated in advance, significantly adding to the degree of severity of his conduct. Second, the court observed that the social context in which the offensive behavior was committed was a factor to be considered. Cohen had not approached Fall in a social setting or out in the open where she could more readily have deterred or escaped his advances. Instead, Cohen's attack occurred behind closed doors within the confines of his office, concealed from public view. Third, and most important to the court, the physical nature of Cohen's harassment bore upon its severity. He grabbed and kissed Fall while groping her breasts. Although Fall alleged only a single act of sexual harassment, the court ruled that an incident involving physical assault, such as that experienced by Fall, may sufficiently alter the conditions of the victim's employment and create an abusive work environment.[34]

The EEOC adopted a similar position. Because an unwelcome physical advance can seriously corrupt a victim's work environment, the EEOC assumes that an unwelcome, intentional touching of a woman's intimate body areas is sufficiently offensive to alter her working conditions: "More so than in the case of verbal advances or remarks, a single unwelcome physical advance can seriously poison the victim's working environment. If an employee's supervisor sexually touches that employee, the Commission normally would find a violation [of Title VII]."[35]

The offensive conduct that forms the basis of a sexual harassment claim must be unwelcome in the sense that the victim of the harassment neither solicited nor incited the conduct and regarded it as undesirable and offensive.[36] If the complainant immediately protests the offensive behavior and advises a supervisor or higher authority in the company of its occurrence, her case will be considerably strengthened, since questions regarding the welcomeness and severity of the conduct are less likely to arise in the minds of the jurors and the court. On the other hand, a delay in protesting and reporting the harassment will only create doubt. If the complainant fails to protest the harassment and undertake measures to deter its reoccurrence, jurors may ask themselves whether the conduct was truly unwelcome and was it truly undesirable and offensive.

It has become evident over the years that nearly all women choose to wait before reporting acts of sexual harassment. Some women fear retaliation or other repercussions. Others, at least initially, believe they are capable of resolving the situation without the intervention of third parties, and still others are too embarrassed to disclose to anyone the particulars of the harassment. Since the credibility of the complainant is almost always placed in issue in a sexual harassment case, the defendant employer generally attempts to exploit the complainant's delay in reporting the harassment as a means of undermining and discrediting her testimony.

The unwelcomeness issue requires the victim of sexual harassment to immediately protest the harassment, thus apprising the harasser that she considers his behavior reprehensible and wholly unwelcome. If she fails to protest, not only will the harassment continue, but when the harasser is called to task, he will plead innocence, claiming that he understood the complainant was not offended by his actions since she never indicated otherwise. In such instances, the female worker usually insists that the very fact that she failed to respond to the harasser's conduct sufficiently communicated to him the unwelcomeness of his behavior.

At times, the harasser's actions are so degrading that the court will assume they were unwelcome, as any reasonable person would be offended by them.[37] In other instances, defendants have successfully used the welcomeness issue as a defense, especially when the evidence indicates that the complainant participated in the conduct she claims to have found offensive. In one case, the court described an employer's work environment as "very distasteful" and conducive to sexual harassment. The evidence showed, however, that the harassing conduct was substantially welcomed and, in fact, encouraged by the complainant. She regularly used crude and vulgar language and initiated sexually oriented conversations with her male and female coworkers. She frequently asked male employees about their marital sex lives and made her own marital sex relationship a topic of office conversation. Under these circumstances, she could not prove that similar conduct of other workers was unwelcome to her.[38]

The unwelcomeness issue has also frequently arisen when one of the workers involved in a consensual sexual relationship decides to end it. Feelings of betrayal may elicit unsubstantiated charges of harassment on the one hand or acts of actual harassment on the other. Shayne Kahn worked for Objective Solutions International as a senior executive recruiter. She had an exemplary work history, having been neither criticized nor disciplined at any time during her employment. Throughout her employment, she had a consensual sexual relationship with Steven Wolfe, the company's owner and president. Soon after Kahn's second anniversary with the company, Wolfe told her that because of his wife's objections, he was terminating their sexual relationship. Wolfe told her that, if he could not be intimate with her, he no longer wanted her present in the office. He then fired Kahn.

Kahn sued Wolfe and the company for sexual harassment, but the court dismissed her claim. In view of the fact that her relationship with Wolfe had been consensual and had not been a condition of her employment, the relationship could not be said to have been unwelcome. Nor could she claim that her termination had arisen out of a refusal on her part to submit to sexual requests. Rather, she could only allege that she was discharged in the wake of Wolfe's decision to terminate their sexual relationship. As observed by the court, these facts cannot support a claim of sexual harassment. Wolfe's decision to simultaneously terminate the sexual and the employment relationships may have been callous, but it was not sexually harassing conduct.[39]

On occasion, defendants have offered the court evidence of a claimant's sexual history to show she could not have considered the alleged harassing conduct to have been unwelcome. Most courts frown upon, if not reject outright, this type of evidence. Whether a victim welcomed the harassing conduct should not turn on her private sexual behavior. A woman's workplace rights should not be affected by the life she leads outside the workplace.[40] The workplace is one part of her life; the rest of her life remains separate and wholly apart.

When does an employer become liable for the harassing acts of its employees? That is the next issue to be examined.

Chapter Fifteen

Employer Liability for Employee Acts of Sexual Harassment

Title VII makes it unlawful for an *employer* to discriminate against a woman because of her sex. Although acts of sexual harassment are committed by individual employees, most courts have ruled that under Title VII individual workers are not liable for their acts of harassment. Liability for acts of sexual harassment is limited to employers.

An employer is liable to a victim of acts of sexual harassment committed by one of its workers if the employer knew—or the circumstances demonstrate that it should have known—of the harassment. An employer is also liable for acts of sexual harassment committed by nonemployees, such as customers or clients, if the employer knew or should have known of their harassing conduct and acquiesced in its continuance. That leaves for consideration, under what circumstances will an employer be held liable for the sexually harassing actions of one of its supervisors if it was unaware of his sexually harassing conduct?

In its *Vinson* decision,[1] the Supreme Court did not analyze in any detail the circumstances under which an employer should be held liable for the harassing acts of one of its supervisors. The court, however, did examine the issue in broad terms. Since a supervisor generally acts as an agent of his employer, his employer is liable for the supervisor's misuse of his power or authority. In each case, the court must determine whether—in light of the facts existent in that case—the harassing supervisor actually acted as an agent of his employer.

Kimberly Ellerth worked in the Chicago office of Burlington Industries, first as a merchandising assistant and later as a sales representative. After about a year on the job, Ellerth reported that she had been subjected throughout her employment to a series of sexually harassing actions by one of her supervisors. During her pre-employment interview, Theodore Slowik, who held a midlevel management position, asked her sexually suggestive questions and stared at her breasts and legs. After she was hired, Ellerth had intermittent contact with Slowik, and on nearly every occasion he told her offensive, off-color jokes and made other sexually inappropriate comments. While on a business trip, Slowik invited Ellerth to the hotel lounge. During the ensuing conversation, when Ellerth failed to respond to Slowik's remarks about her breasts, he told her to "loosen up" and warned her that "I could make your life very hard or very easy at Burlington."

Burlington later considered Ellerth for promotion. During her promotion interview Slowik expressed reservations concerning her prospects for promotion, commenting that she was not "loose enough" and at that point he reached over and rubbed her knee. When Slowik later called her to announce the promotion had been authorized, he said, "you're gonna be out there with men who work in factories, and they certainly like women with pretty butts/legs." During a subsequent telephone call, Slowik said, "I don't have time for you right now, Kim—unless you want to tell me what you're wearing." On another call, he asked if she was "wearing shorter skirts yet" as it "would make your job a whole heck of a lot easier." During her tenure at Burlington, Ellerth did not report any of Slowik's behavior, although she knew that Burlington had a sexual harassment policy in place. Ultimately, Ellerth resigned in response to criticism leveled against her by another supervisor.

Subsequently, Ellerth sued Burlington Industries for sexual harassment. When her case reached the Supreme Court in 1998, the court had to determine under what circumstances an employer may be held liable for a hostile working environment caused by the acts of sexual harassment committed by one of its supervisors. At the outset of its analysis, the court affirmed a major distinction between a hostile working environment that culminated in a "tangible employment action," adversely affecting the employment status of the victim of the harassment, and a hostile working environment that did not culminate in a tangible employment action. [2]

A *tangible employment action*, as defined by the court, causes a significant change in the employment status of the victim of the harassment, such as the denial of a promotion, a reassignment to a position with significantly different responsibilities, a decision causing a significant change in benefits, or the termination of employment. As a general proposition, only a supervisor, acting with the authority of his employer, has the power to effect a tangible employment action. A nonsupervisory employee can cause physical or psychological harm to a coworker as readily as a supervisor can, but a nonsupervisory employee is not empowered to fire, promote, demote, or increase or reduce another's pay. Tangible employment actions fall within the special province of a supervisor who has been empowered by his employer to make employment decisions affecting the status of workers under his control: "Tangible employment actions are the means by which the supervisor bring the official power of the enterprise to bear on subordinates. A tangible employment decision requires an official act of the enterprise, a company act. . . . For these reasons, a tangible employment action taken by the supervisor becomes for Title VII purposes the act of the employer."

Thus, the court ruled that when a supervisor harasses a subordinate female employee, and thereby creates a hostile working environment that culminates in a tangible employment action adversely affecting the victim's employment status, the employer is liable for the supervisor's conduct.

Ellerth, however, did not suffer the consequences of an adverse tangible employment action. In fact, she had been promoted and had later resigned from the company without ever having complained of Slowik's harassment. Under these circumstances, could Burlington be held liable to Ellerth for Slowik's harassing conduct? The Supreme Court answered in the affirmative; Burlington could be held liable for Slowik's acts of sexual harassment, even if those acts did not culminate in a tangible employment action affecting the Ellerth's employment status. In those circumstances, however, Burlington had available to it a defense it could elect to assert that, if established, would insulate itself from liability to Ellerth. To establish that defense, Burlington would be required to prove that (1) Burlington exercised reasonable care to prevent and correct promptly any sexually harassing behavior occurring in its workplace, and (2) Ellerth unreasonably failed to take advantage of preventive or corrective opportunities provided by Burlington to avoid harm from sexual harassment, such as reporting the harassment in accordance with Burlington's sexual harassment policy.[3]

The court emphasized that this defense was available to employers only where no tangible employment action had been taken by the supervisor during the course of the harassment. In other cases, where a tangible employment action had been implemented, employers were strictly liable for the harassing conduct of its supervisors.

Because this ruling essentially constituted a new statement of the law, the court remanded the case for further proceedings, thus providing Ellerth with another opportunity to establish Burlington's liability and providing Burlington with the opportunity to plead and prove the newly fashioned defense.

The Supreme Court's ruling not only affirmed an old standard of liability for employers but also established a new one. As we have just seen, the court reaffirmed an employer's liability for a hostile work environment caused by a supervisor's acts of sexual harassment that culminate in tangible employment decisions adversely affecting the victim of the harassment. It established a new criterion for liability in those circumstances where the hostile environment does not result in tangible employment actions adverse to the harassment victim, but it also provided the employer with an affirmative defense that it could assert in those circumstances. The court placed the burden of proving the essential elements of this new defense squarely upon the employer. Because the court allocated to the defendant employer the burden of proving this defense, it afforded the plaintiff employee with an enormous advantage in relation to issues involving the employer's liability for supervisory harassment.

Since employer liability for the sexually harassing acts of a supervisor is established under a standard different from that used to establish employer liability for acts of nonsupervisory harassment, determining who is a supervisor and who is not constitutes a significant issue for the courts, one they frequently have had to address following the *Ellerth* decision.

A supervisor generally is defined as one who has immediate or successively higher authority over an employee. An individual qualifies as a supervisor if he is authorized to recommend or take tangible employment actions affecting a worker, such as hiring, firing, promoting, demoting, and reassigning. An individual who is authorized to direct an employee's day-to-day activities also qualifies as a supervisor. A person that meets these criteria possesses the power of a supervisor and as a consequence his ability to commit acts of harassment is enhanced by his authority to adversely affect an employee's employment status and her daily work life.[4]

While the Supreme Court defined a tangible employment action as a "significant change in employment status, such as hiring, firing, failing to promote, reassignment with significantly different responsibilities, or a decision causing a significant change in benefits," the EEOC has defined it in somewhat more expansive terms. It included in its definition a significant change in a worker's duties, with or without a change in salary or benefits. As an example, a change in duties that blocks an opportunity for promotion would qualify as a tangible employment action under the EEOC definition. But a change in job title probably would not, unless the change signaled a demotion or some other downward change in employment status.[5]

A series of adverse actions taken against the victim of harassment may in combination amount to a tangible employment action. That was the case with Dianne Evans, a successful life insurance salesperson employed by the Durham Life Insurance Co. After she had been working for Durham for about two years, the company was acquired by another insurance company. Subsequently, new management appeared on the scene, and from that point forward Evans's career proceeded downhill.

When new management assumed control of Durham, Evans was the only full-time female sales agent in an office of thirty agents. Apparently resenting the success she had achieved as a woman, certain male members of new management set out to undermine her position by depriving her of the staff and other support provided by previous management. Two members of new management told Evans that she did not fit the company profile for sales agents; her clothes were too expensive, she dressed too well for the job, and she "made too much money for a goddamn woman." Thereafter, Evans was continually humiliated with sexist remarks and crude sexual and physical touching. She suffered repeated slights from new management. At an awards dinner, her sales accomplishments were unrecognized. At a training session, she was publicly mocked on account of her speech and the way she carried herself when she walked. She was not furnished the legal assistance she had requested, and as a result she lost an important account. She was assigned more than her share of work with lapsed policies—a thankless job, generally distributed proportionately among the sales agents—thus reducing her commission income. Her secretary was fired and not replaced. She was forced out of her private office, and at the time some of her critical files unexplainably disappeared. The result again was a diminution in commission income. After patiently enduring this harassment for several months and ultimately concluding that she no longer had a future at Durham, Evans resigned and sued Durham for sexual harassment.

After Evans was successful in gaining a favorable trial verdict, Durham appealed, arguing that the trial court had erred in aggregating sexual-related and nonsexual-related events in its determination that a hostile environment had existed at Durham. The appellate court disagreed: "Some of these events were apparently triggered by sexual desire, some were sexually hostile, some were non-sexual but gender based, and others were facially neutral. . . . Title VII may be applied to all of these types of conduct."[6]

None of the actions taken against Evans falls within any one of those specified in the Supreme Court definition of a tangible employment action, but in combination they resulted in a significant change in employment status. Thus the court held that the affirmative defense—available to a defendant in cases not involving a tangible employment action—could not be utilized by Durham.

On occasion, the courts have proved quite flexible when confronted with issues involving the liability of an employer for the acts of a harasser. The East Chicago Community School employed Lisetta Molnar as an intern to teach art. Molnar hoped, at the conclusion of her internship, to qualify for a license as a full-fledged art teacher. Beginning with her first day at the school, her principal, Lloyd Booth, made sexual advances she found offensive. Booth told her he could secure various benefits for her, such as a permanent art room and art supplies and benefits other interns were not granted. Molnar perceived this as a sexual advance, making her very uncomfortable. The unwelcome behavior continued during succeeding weeks, but Molnar rejected each of Booth's advances. After Molnar had spurned him, Booth ordered the return of all art supplies previously furnished Molnar, and all discussion of a permanent art room ceased. At the end of the school year, Booth issued Molnar a negative performance evaluation, making it far less likely she would be granted a teacher license.

After Molnar sued the school for sexual harassment, the court ruled that Booth's conduct in dealing with Molnar culminated in tangible employment actions and that the affirmative defense was thus unavailable to the school. The clearest tangible employment action, in the court's estimation, was Booth's confiscation of art supplies he had instructed to be furnished to Molnar, supplies she required to perform her functions as an art teacher. The negative performance evaluation also fell into that category of employment action, and even though the school board later reversed Booth's negative evaluation, the fact that Molnar's career had been temporarily derailed was sufficient to render the original evaluation a tangible employment action. With the affirmative defense unavailable to the school, the jury rendered a verdict in Molnar's favor.[7]

In those instances in which the plaintiff fails to prove she suffered a tangible employment action, employers generally attempt to take advantage of the Supreme Court's newly created affirmative defense. As noted, that defense requires the defendant employer to prove that it was unaware that the harassment had occurred, that it had exercised "reasonable care" in preventing acts of sexual harassment from occurring in its workplace, and that upon discovering the presence of such conduct, it promptly enacted measures to eliminate it. The EEOC has suggested that "reasonable care" generally requires an employer "to establish, disseminate, and enforce an anti-harassment policy and complaint procedure and to take other reasonable steps to prevent and correct harassment."[8] However, even the best formulated sexual harassment policy and complaint procedure will not satisfy the employer's burden of proving reasonable care unless the employer effectively implements, maintains, and enforces the policy and the complaint procedure.

Smaller employers may be able to effectively use informal means to fulfill its responsibilities in this regard, while larger employers may need to institute more formal procedures.[9] The failure to implement, maintain, and enforce an antiharassment policy and complaint procedure will render it far more difficult for an employer to prove that it exercised reasonable care in preventing sexual harassment from occurring in its workplace or eliminating it when it did occur.

Plaintiff employees often charge their employers with ineffective enforcement of their antiharassment policies. Employers, of course, vigorously defend their enforcement efforts. In one such case, the employer was able to establish that immediately after the plaintiff employee asserted a complaint of harassment, management assured her that sexual harassment would not be tolerated in its workplace and it initiated an investigation of the alleged harasser, who was suspended during the investigation and later demoted. The court ruled that the employer had exercised reasonable care in eliminating the harassment and preventing its reoccurrence.[10]

In another case, a female worker's supervisor periodically subjected her to offensive sexual advances, and on two occasions she filed formal complaints with her manager. The manager verbally warned the supervisor but failed to make a written record of the complaints or of any efforts to prevent further harassment. To no one's surprise, the harassment continued. The worker then complained to another supervisor who advised her that nothing further could or would be done to stop the harassment. Although this employer had a sexual harassment policy in place, clearly, it failed to enforce it.[11]

One other issue is relevant to the employer's reliance upon the affirmative defense. The second prong of the defense requires the employer to show that the plaintiff employee unreasonably failed to take advantage of preventive or corrective opportunities provided by the employer to avoid harm from sexual harassment. If an employer has instituted an antiharassment policy having an adequate complaint procedure, the plaintiff worker is required to report the harassment. If the worker fails to comply with the complaint procedure and later sues her employer for sexual harassment, will her case be dismissed? A court provided Kelly Scrivner with the answer.

Shortly after Scrivner started teaching at the Socorro Independent School District in Texas, Kelly Scrivner's principal began to harass her with lewd and offensive remarks. Subsequently, the school district superintendent received an anonymous letter—not written by Scrivner—complaining of the principal's sexual harassment of teachers and his use of vulgar language in the presence of staff and parents. The school district immediately undertook an investigation, interviewing sixty-four teachers and staff members, three of whom stated that the principal had engaged in sexually harassing conduct. However, when Scrivner was interviewed, she denied the principal had sexually harassed her. Based on the investigation, the school district found insufficient evidence of sexual harassment to discipline the principal, but it warned him in a memorandum to refrain from unprofessional jokes and comments.

Six months later, the principal's harassment of Scrivner intensified. She filed a complaint with the school district, and a second investigation was promptly initiated. Eventually, the school district officials concluded that the principal's conduct could have created the perception of a hostile environment at the school, and it ordered his removal from his position. Scrivner then filed suit against the school district.

Scrivner's sexual harassment claim rose or fell on the validity of the affirmative defense asserted by the school district. Because Scrivner had not sustained a tangible employment action, the school district could escape liability for the principal's acts of sexual harassment if it were able to prove (1) that it had exercised reasonable care in preventing sexual harassment and in acting quickly to eliminate sexual harassing conduct when it appeared in its workplace, and (2) that Scrivner had unreasonably failed to take advantage of preventive or corrective opportunities provided by the school district, including its procedures for reporting acts of sexual harassment.

By relying on its two investigations of the principal's conduct, the school district easily established that it had exercised reasonable care in preventing and eliminating sexual harassment from its workplace. The evidence also showed that Scrivner had declined to avail herself of the school district's preventive and corrective policies. She did not complain of the principal's behavior until nearly two years after she first began to experience it. Even when she was presented with an opportunity to disclose the harassment during the first investigation, she chose to lie and report that she had not witnessed any harassing conduct by the principal. By failing to inform the school district of the principal's behavior when given the opportunity, Scrivner acted unreasonably. The court concluded that Scrivner's complaint should be dismissed. [12]

A female worker should not be expected to complain immediately following the initial incident of harassment. Often, she may ignore the first few incidents, provided they are minor, with the hope that they will cease before she has to file a formal complaint. Then again, she may elect to resolve the issue herself by advising her harasser that his conduct is unwelcome and should cease. If the harassment persists, however, she must report it in accordance with her employer's sexual harassment complaint reporting procedure. The failure to act in accordance with that procedure will undoubtedly doom any future sexual harassment claim.

Scrivner faced different circumstances. Two complaints of harassment were filed, and the school district undertook two investigations. It could reasonably be argued that Scrivner was subjected to two separate and distinct series of harassing acts. The fact that Scrivner declined to confirm the harassment during the first investigation should not have undermined the claim she later filed that initiated the second investigation. Since at that point she acted promptly in reporting the second series of harassing acts, in accordance with school district procedures, it can reasonably be argued that the court should have concluded that the school district's assertion of the affirmative defense had failed and, as a consequence, Scrivner's claim should not have been dismissed. The court's ruling, therefore, appears to have been erroneous.

Even if a defendant employer is held liable to a plaintiff worker for acts of sexual harassment, the worker's damages may be substantially limited if she elects to resign from her employment rather than continue to work in what she considers a hostile environment.

As discussed in chapter 11, if a worker resigns and later charges her employer with Title VII violations, her damages may be materially reduced, unless she is able to demonstrate that she resigned involuntarily, a resignation commonly referred to as a *constructive discharge*. Unless a worker's resignation is considered to be a constructive discharge, her back pay and other damages will be limited to those that accrued prior to her departure from the company. Since back pay and other damages generally continue to accrue after she resigns and accumulate until she finds comparable employment, the damages she may recover will be substantially reduced.

A worker's resignation will be considered a constructive discharge if the employer requires the worker to perform her job functions under conditions so difficult that any reasonable person laboring under those conditions would feel compelled to resign. Thus a worker is constructively discharged if she is forced to quit because of the intolerable working conditions. If the court determines that a worker resigned under circumstances the court considers less than intolerable, damages that accrue after her resignation may be denied the worker, even if the employer is found guilty of sexual harassment. Conversely, a worker who is constructively discharged may be eligible for the entire panoply of damages and other relief available to any worker unlawfully discharged.

Even if a worker establishes that her working conditions were intolerable, the court will sustain her constructive discharge claim only if she also proves that the harassment was the primary cause of her resignation. In other words, she must establish a causal link between the harassment and her resignation. Generally, the causal link is established by considering the amount of time that elapses between the harassment and the resignation; the shorter the passage of time, the greater the likelihood the court will determine that the worker resigned because of the harassment and not on account of some other reason.

Michelle McCrackin filed a constructive discharge claim against LabOne, alleging that her supervisor in the company's message center department subjected her to lewd and sexually suggestive leers, unwanted physical touching, and stalking and that he refused to alter his conduct despite her repeated expressions of discomfort and disapproval. Although management was aware of her supervisor's behavior, it took no action to discipline him or control his behavior. After enduring this treatment for six months, McCrackin complained to two company officials, including the vice president of its human resources department. Other than to suggest that she change her desk location so as to make it easier to avoid her supervisor, no remedial or preventative action was undertaken. Firmly of the belief that the company would not act to alleviate her situation, McCrackin resigned. Her fears that the company would not act to eliminate the harassment were confirmed when she picked up her final pay check and the human resources vice president commented, "It's not as if you were raped."

McCrackin sued LabOne, alleging that she had been forced to work in an offensive and hostile work environment, ultimately culminating in her constructive discharge. Later in the litigation, LabOne asked the court to dismiss

McCrackin's constructive discharge claim, but the court ruled that McCrackin had alleged facts sufficient to show that a reasonable person in her circumstances would have felt compelled to resign. If McCrackin had been subjected to a pattern of leers, touching, and unwelcome advances as she alleged, then management should have done more than merely suggest ways that McCrackin might mitigate her supervisor's offensive behavior. It should have taken action to eliminate the harassment. Rather than continue to work in such an environment, McCrackin could reasonably and justifiably have felt that she had no alternative but to resign. Her belief that management would do nothing to improve her working conditions was heightened and reinforced by management's indifference to the hostility and offensiveness of her work environment and was buttressed by the human resources vice president's comment concerning rape. The court denied LabOne's motion to dismiss McCrackin's constructive discharge claim.[13]

If the supervisor's conduct had been the sole element in the case, the court might very well have arrived at a different conclusion. A six-month lapse between the first acts of offensive behavior and McCrackin's resignation suggested that her working conditions may have been less than intolerable. But they became intolerable once she learned that management had no intention of changing them. Immediately after learning that her working conditions would not improve, McCrackin resigned, thus establishing the requisite causal link.

In another case, the court rejected a constructive discharge claim because the worker's resignation did not occur until six months after the harassment had ended.[14] If a worker intends to claim a constructive discharge, she must act expeditiously, lest an element of uncertainty be introduced about how intolerable her working conditions were. Delay may also create doubt about the causal linkage between the harassment and her resignation. But, on the other hand, if she resigns before her employer has had a reasonable opportunity to implement measures to halt the harassment and eliminate a hostile work environment, the court may conclude that the employer, given ample time, would have resolved these problems. In those circumstances, a court would probably rule that the worker had failed to establish that her working conditions were intolerable. Whether to resign and when to resign are decisions requiring the advice of an attorney well versed in sexual harassment law.

This area of the law has often been litigated, and as a result its guiding legal principles have been well defined. But the Supreme Court was unable to resist an urge to interfere, and its most recent decision materially increased plaintiffs' burden of proof in cases of this type. As previously noted, under Title VII, an employer's liability for workplace harassment may depend on the status of the harasser. If the harassing employee is the victim's coworker, the employer is liable only if it was negligent in controlling working conditions. The complainant must show that the employer knew or should have known of the coworker's offensive conduct but failed to take appropriate corrective action. Proving negligence in these circumstances often proves to be a daunting task. The Supreme Court, in a case decided in 2013, enlarged the role of the coworker, while diminishing the role of the supervisor, thus making it even more difficult for the plaintiff to prevail.

Within a year of the Court's decisions in the *Ellerth* case, the EEOC defined "supervisor" to include any employee with "authority to undertake or recommend tangible employment decisions" or with "authority to direct [another] employee's daily work activities."[15] In its 2013 decision, however, the Court held that an employee is a "supervisor" for purposes of vicarious liability under Title VII only if he or she is empowered by the employer to take tangible employment actions against the victim. The court rejected the "vagueness" of the EEOC's standard as, in the opinion of the majority, it would impede the resolution of the issue. The dissenting justices accused the court of disregarding its previous decisions:

> Exhibiting remarkable resistance to the thrust of our prior decisions, workplace realities, and the EEOC's Guidance, the Court embraces a position that relieves scores of employers of responsibility for the behavior of the supervisors they employ. Trumpeting the virtues of simplicity and administrability, the Court restricts supervisor status to those with power to take tangible employment actions. In so restricting the definition of supervisor, the Court once again shuts from sight the "robust protection against workplace discrimination" Congress intended Title VII to secure. [Citing *Ledbetter v. Goodyear Tire & Rubber Co.*] [16]

Justice Ginsburg, author of the dissenting opinion, concluded that the Court's decision in this case should prompt Congress to overturn yet another of its restrictive rulings.

Chapter Sixteen

Current Trends in the Law Prohibiting National Origin Discrimination Issues

About 10 percent of Americans are foreign-born, with the largest numbers of recent immigrants coming from Asia, including China, India, and Vietnam, and from Latin America, including Mexico and El Salvador. As the American workforce has continued to diversify, Title VII's prohibition against national origin discrimination has become increasingly more significant in efforts to protect and preserve the workplace rights of these peoples.

The Equal Employment Opportunity Commission's *Compliance Manual*[1] notes that Title VII prohibits employers from imposing more restrictive workplace policies on some national origin groups than on others. For example, an employer may not require Hispanic workers to wear business attire while permitting non-Hispanic workers in similar positions to wear more casual clothing. However, an employer may impose the same dress code on all workers in similar jobs, regardless of their national origin, as long as the policy is not adopted for discriminatory reasons and is enforced evenhandedly.

Another issue that has drawn the attention of the EEOC is the presence of a foreign language in the workplace. An employer may have a legitimate business reason for basing an employment decision on linguistic characteristics. However, linguistic characteristics are often closely associated with national origin. Therefore, employers must ensure that the business reason for reliance on a linguistic characteristic justifies any burdens placed on individuals because of their national origin.

An employment decision based on foreign accent does not violate Title VII if an individual's accent materially interferes with the worker's ability to perform job duties. This assessment depends upon the specific duties of the position in question and the extent to which the individual's accent affects his ability to perform the functions of his position. Generally, an employer may only base an employment decision on accent if effective oral communication in English is required to perform job duties and the individual's foreign accent materially interferes with his or her ability to communicate orally in English. Positions for which effective oral communication in English may be required include teaching, customer service, and telemarketing. Even for these positions, the EEOC notes that an employer must still determine whether the particular individual's accent interferes with the ability to perform job duties.

Generally, a fluency requirement is permissible only if required for the effective performance of the position for which it is imposed. Because the degree of fluency that may be lawfully required varies from one position to the next, employers should avoid fluency requirements that apply uniformly to a broad range of dissimilar positions. As with a foreign accent, an individual's lack of proficiency in English may interfere with a worker's job performance in some circumstances but not in others.

Some employers have instituted workplace policies restricting communication in languages other than English, often called *English-only rules*. Title VII permits employers to adopt English-only rules under certain circumstances. As with any other workplace policy, an English-only rule must be adopted for nondiscriminatory reasons, and thus an English-only rule would be unlawful if it were adopted with the intent to discriminate on the basis of national origin. Likewise, a policy that prohibits some but not all of the foreign languages spoken in a workplace, such as a no-Spanish rule, would be unlawful.

Albert Estrada and Francisco Gracia, and the members of the class of workers for whom they sought relief, were of Hispanic national origin—they or their parents were born in Mexico or another country in which Spanish is the primary or predominant language. The class members were bilingual, typically having learned English through the US school system. Nevertheless, their primary language or language of national origin was Spanish.

The class members worked as telephone operators for Premier Operator Services, Inc., located in DeSoto, Texas. The recruitment and hiring of workers was based or conditioned upon their bilingual ability and, in particular, their ability to speak Spanish because Premier served many Spanish-speaking customers. The ability to speak Spanish was viewed by Premier as an asset in conducting its business. In fact, class members were tested at the time of hire to ensure their ability to speak and understand Spanish.

Premier enacted an English-only policy prohibiting the speaking of Spanish on the company premises except when speaking to Spanish-speaking customers. The policy was posted on the door at the entrance of the building in which Premier was located:

> *Absolutely* No Guns, Knives or Weapons of any kind are allowed on these Premises at any time! *English* is the official language of Premier Operator Services, Inc. All conversations on these premises are to be in English. Other languages may be spoken to customers who cannot speak English.

The sign, conspicuously coupling the English-only policy with a warning about carrying guns and other weapons while on company premises, implied a concern about the conduct of those persons who spoke languages other than English.

This policy prohibited the speaking of Spanish during the free moments operators had between calls—during lunch periods, while present in the employee break room, when making personal telephone calls, and before and after work while present inside the building. Under Premier's policy, the only time it was acceptable to speak Spanish was when a worker was assisting a Spanish-speaking customer. Working shoulder to shoulder, workers experiencing free time between calls were required to speak to their Hispanic colleagues in English or face discipline or dismissal. Lunchroom conversations—even between a Hispanic husband and wife—could not include Spanish words or phrases.

After Estrada and Gracia sued Premier, asking the court to order the company to withdraw the English-only policy, the court held that Premier had failed to present sufficient evidence to show a business necessity for the policy, as it was neither job-related nor necessary for the performance of the operators' duties and functions:

> To the contrary, the evidence is clear that the speaking of Spanish was a job requirement. Even if the Court were to assume that office "harmony" was properly considered to be a business necessity that would justify an English-only policy, there is no credible or persuasive evidence that there was "discord" amongst Defendant's employees which required harmonization in this manner. Further, there is no evidence that the subject policy and its enforcement promoted "harmony" in the workplace. Quite the opposite, the evidence shows that the policy served to create a disruption in the work place and feelings of alienation and inadequacy by Hispanic employees who had, up until that time, been proven performers for the company. Likewise, there is no evidence sufficient to establish that there was any inability of the employees, all of whom were bilingual, to communicate with their supervisors . . . in carrying out their job duties and responsibilities.

The evidence showed that the English-only policy, as implemented and enforced by Premier, was a tool to discriminate against its employees on the basis of their national origin.

The court ruled that Premier's enactment and implementation of the English-only policy constituted disparate treatment of Hispanic employees based upon their national origin, in violation of Title VII. "A blanket policy or practice prohibiting the speaking of a language other than English on an employer's premises at all times, except when speaking to a non-English speaking customer, violates Title VII's prohibition against discrimination based on national origin."[2]

Irma Rivera, a former saleswoman for the Baccarat store on Madison Avenue in New York City, testified at the trial of her national origin suit against Baccarat that the company president had complained about her Puerto Rican accent, barred her from speaking Spanish to a coworker, and finally dismissed her because of her ethnic origins.

Rivera, the mother of five children, had an exemplary record at the store and had never prompted a complaint from a customer in her nine years on the sales force. A Baccarat official acknowledged that Rivera was ordered to refrain from speaking Spanish to a coworker in the presence of customers. He said the policy was instituted after a customer complained. "It's just a matter of common sense," he said. "If the customer is not Spanish-speaking, don't talk another language. That's rude." The jury apparently disagreed with that analysis as it found that the company discriminated against Rivera and awarded her $125,000 in compensatory damages and $375,000 in punitive damages.[3]

Firing Hispanics because of their national origin clearly violates Title VII. Recently, the EEOC charged an Illinois company with having fired a group of Hispanic janitors after subjecting them to discriminatory working conditions, such as requiring them to perform more difficult work assignments than those required of non-Hispanic coworkers. The company agreed to a consent decree that ordered them to pay $360,000 to ten of the Hispanic janitors.[4]

Title VII's prohibition against national origin discrimination often overlaps with the statute's prohibitions against discrimination based on religion or race. The same set of facts may state a claim of national origin discrimination and religious discrimination when a particular religion is strongly associated, or perceived to be associated, with a specific national origin. If a claim presents overlapping bases of discrimination prohibited, the EEOC recommends that a claimant assert each of the pertinent bases in an employment discrimination charge filed with that agency.

Complaints of workplace discrimination against individuals perceived to be Arab and Muslim soared after the September 11, 2001, attacks. In effect, a new category of discrimination came into being—discrimination against workers who are or who are perceived to be Arab and Muslim. Record numbers of Muslim and Arab workers have complained of employer and coworker acts of workplace discrimination.

The EEOC charged Rugo Stone, a Virginia-based stone contracting company, with having violated Title VII by subjecting a male employee to harassment based on his national origin, religion, and color. According to the

EEOC's complaint, Shazad Buksh, an estimator and assistant project manager for Rugo Stone, was subjected to derogatory comments from his supervisors, project manager, and the company's owner on the basis of his national origin (Pakistani), religion (Islam), and color (brown). These comments occurred almost daily. Buksh was called a "Paki-princess"; he was told he was the same color as human feces, that his religion was "backwards" and "crazy," and that Muslims were "monkeys." On one occasion, Buksh was shown a video of a man being hanged in Iran and was told that the activity depicted on the video was "cool" and that Buksh's "country and religion does it this way." The EEOC complaint alleged that Buksh complained about the conduct and comments, but the harassment continued. Rugo Stone settled the case soon after it was filed.[5]

Foreign-born Americans often find themselves the object of national origin discrimination at the hiring stage of the employment relationship. Professor Maivan Lam found herself in those circumstances. Professor Lam sued the University of Hawaii's Richardson School of Law, alleging that when she applied for the position of director of the law school's Pacific Asian legal studies program, she was discriminated against on the basis of her race, sex, and national origin. Born in Vietnam, Lam was fluent in several languages, including French, English, Vietnamese, and Thai. After college, she received a master's degree in Southeast Asian studies at Yale and later was awarded a Ford Foundation Fellowship. After several years as a full-time mother, Lam taught anthropology courses at Hawaii Loa College and then obtained a second master's degree from Yale. Lam then changed direction and attended the Richardson School of Law. After graduation from law school, Lam taught courses at Hawaii Loa College, served as a lecturer at the University of Hawaii, and presented guest lectures at the law school.

Lam and approximately 100 other persons applied for the position of director of the law school's Pacific Asian legal studies program. A committee designated to review the credentials of the applicants recommended a list of ten finalists for review by the full faculty. Lam was among the finalists. Five of the ten finalists were women, three were Asians, and, of these, two were women. The candidate list was eventually reduced to four, but a consensus did not form around any of the candidates, and the faculty voted to cancel its search to find an appropriate person to fill the position.

When Lam was not awarded the directorship position, she claimed she had been discriminated against as an Asian woman. The law school, however, argued that its dean had supported the application of an Asian male and that the committee subsequently offered another position to a white female. These two factors, the law school insisted, showed a lack of bias toward Asians as well as women. The court criticized this separate treatment of national origin, race, and sex discrimination because "they cannot be neatly reduced to distinct components." An attempt, the court continued, to bisect a person's identity at the intersection of race and sex or national origin and sex, ignores, if not distorts, the nature of the person's experiences.

Like other subclasses under Title VII, Asian women may be subjected to a set of assumptions shared neither by Asian men nor white women. In consequence, they may be targeted for discriminatory conduct even in the absence of acts of discrimination against Asian men or white women.[6]

An economy that employs workers of all races, nationalities, and colors, male and female, requires a body of law capable of acknowledging and responding to workplace experiences that may be unique to particular groups of workers. Fortunately, the employment discrimination laws have been developed to a degree that they are now capable of providing protection to specific groups of workers by removing workplace disadvantages only those groups may encounter.

Chapter Seventeen

Current Trends in the Law Prohibiting Religious Discrimination

Several factors have caused a sharp increase in the desire of workers to express their religious convictions while at work. Surveys show that as people grow older, religion becomes a matter of greater significance in their lives and thus plays a more extensive role in many aspects of the later years of their lives. Since many workers do not become religiously observant until later in life, expression of their religious beliefs less often creates workplace conflicts until the later stages of their lives.[1] As the workforce has grown older—as it has in recent decades—the presence of religious practices and beliefs in the workplace has intensified.

The increased incidence of religious expression in the workplace also is a product of a more diversified workforce. A large foreign-born population has joined the American workforce, and these workers have introduced disparate worldviews and religious customs wholly alien to most native-born American workers.[2] These views and customs often clash with more traditional views and customs, as divergent groups of employees attempt to adjust to rapidly changing work environments. Employees holding competing worldviews vary not only in their spiritual, religious, or moral perspectives but also in the way they choose to express those perspectives in the workplace.[3]

The expanded public role of personal religious experience has greatly altered popular perceptions regarding the rightful place the discussion of religious matters has in the workplace. Contrasting opinions regarding the appropriate place of religion in the workplace have led to a dramatic increase in filings of Title VII religious discrimination charges levied against employers by their employees. The filing of religious discrimination charges doubled between 1997 and 2011.[4] This increase reflects, in part, workers' belief that they should be free to observe their religious convictions while at work. Employer interference with that expression is looked upon as religious bias. In a recent survey, 20 percent of the workers interviewed reported that they had either experienced religious prejudice while at work or knew of a co-worker who had been subjected to some form of religious discriminatory conduct. Regardless of their religion, 55 percent of the workers surveyed believed that religious bias and discrimination commonly occur in the work-place.[5]

Record numbers of Muslim workers have filed employment discrimination charges since 2005. Although Muslims comprise less than 2 percent of the US population, they accounted for 25 percent of the religious claims filed with the EEOC in 2009, exceeding even those filed by Muslims during the year following the September 11 terrorist attacks.[6]

One of the more persistent causes of workplace religious disputes arises out of efforts of workers to convert fellow workers. Most people tend to keep their religious beliefs to themselves, refraining from open discussions of matters they consider wholly private. Others are less inhibited and at times freely engage in open discussions of religious beliefs and practices. Still others feel obligated to express their deeply held religious beliefs to those with whom they come in contact during the work day. This is especially the case with those evangelical Christians who, dedicated to the concept of converting one's neighbor, are frequently cited as likely to engage their cowork-ers in religious discussion.[7]

Title VII requires an employer to reasonably accommodate its workers' religious observances and practices, unless such accommodation imposes an undue hardship upon the conduct of its business. An employer must try to balance the religious commitments of its workers with its normal business needs; and although it can often accommodate a worker's religious practices without inconveniencing or unduly burdening other employees, on occasion this is a difficult feat to achieve, as executive personnel of the Tulon Company of Richmond discovered.

Tulon, a manufacturer of drill bits and routers used in the printed circuit board industry, maintained several service centers throughout the United States, including one in Richmond, Virginia. Charita Chalmers, a star employee in the Richmond office, rapidly rose through the employee ranks to the top management position in that office. Her immediate supervisor, Richard LaMantia, was in charge of all of Tulon's sales in the eastern part of the United States and customarily visited Richmond only occasionally. In LaMantia's absence, Chalmers was responsible for the office's operations.

Chalmers was a lifelong member of the Baptist Church. During the course of her employment with Tulon, she also adopted the beliefs held by evangelical Christians and thereafter felt compelled to share the gospel and her beliefs with others. She became convinced that the time had come for LaMantia "to accept God," as she believed he had been guilty of misrepresenting delivery times to certain of Tulon's customers. Accordingly, she wrote to him at his home:

> Dear Rich,
>
> The reason I'm writing you is because the Lord wanted me to share somethings [sic] with you. After reading this letter you do not have to give me a call, but talk to God about everything. One thing the Lord wants you to do is get your life right with him. The Bible says in Roman 10:9 that if you confess with your mouth the Lord Jesus and believe in your heart that God hath raised him from the dead, thou shalt be saved—vs 10—for with the heart man believeth unto righteousness, and with the mouth confession is made unto salvation. The two verse are [sic] saying for you to get right with God now.
> The last thing is, you are doing somethings [sic] in your life that God is not please [sic] with and He wants you to stop. All you have to do is go to God and ask for forgiveness before it is too late. . . . I have to answer to God just like you do, so that's why I wrote you this letter. Please take heed before its [sic] too late. In his name,
>
> Charita Chalmers

After receiving the letter, LaMantia advised the company's vice president of administration that he could no longer work with Chalmers, and he recommended her termination. While investigating LaMantia's complaint, company officials discovered that Chalmers, on the same day that she had written to LaMantia, had sent a second letter to another Tulon employee, Brenda Combs, who was convalescing at her home, suffering from an undiagnosed illness after giving birth to a child out of wedlock. The letter read as follows:

> Brenda,
>
> You probably do not want to hear this at this time, but you need the Lord Jesus in your life right now. One thing about God, He doesn't like when people commit adultery. You know what you did was wrong, so now you need to go to God and ask for forgiveness. Let me explain something about God. He's a God of Love and a God of wrath. When people sin against Him, He will allow things to happen to them or their family until they open their eyes and except [sic] Him. God can put a sickness on you that no doctor could ever find out what it is. . . . All I'm saying is you need to invite God into your heart and live a life for him and things in your life will get better. . . . Please take this letter in love and be obedient to God. In his name,
>
> Charita Chalmers

Combs later told company officials she felt the letter was cruel and that she had been crushed by its tone, as she believed Chalmers had implied that an immoral lifestyle had caused her illness.

After being apprised of these occurrences, upper management concluded that the letters had inappropriately invaded the privacy of LaMantia and Combs and negatively impacted the working relationships in the Richmond office. They ordered Chalmers's dismissal. She responded by filing suit, alleging that Tulon had discriminated against her by failing to accommodate her religious beliefs. In effect, she claimed that Tulon was required to accommodate her belief that God wanted her to convince her coworkers to live without sin.

The court that ruled on Chalmers's case noted that a worker forces her employer into a difficult position when she attempts to impose her religious beliefs upon her fellow employees. If Tulon were to allow a worker to act freely in that manner, her co-employees could claim that the company had allowed a coworker to engage in religious harassment. On the other hand, Title VII required Tulon to endeavor to accommodate that worker's religious beliefs and practices.

To effectively operate its Richmond office, Tulon had to assure its staff that management would not tolerate a coworker's actions that adversely impacted the religious beliefs of others and that the privacy of its employees would be protected from the meddling of a coworker professing religious beliefs generally unacceptable to other employees. Concluding that Tulon could not accommodate Chalmers's religious beliefs and practices without incurring undue hardship in the conduct of its business, the court dismissed her suit. [8]

Employee proselytization of other employees often requires the employer to engage in a delicate balancing act. As the *Chalmers* case demonstrates, while Title VII requires an employer to attempt to accommodate the religious beliefs of an employee committed to persuading other workers to adopt his or her religious beliefs, it must also endeavor to accommodate the religious beliefs of the workers targeted by the proselytizer. Thus the employer may be confronted with demands for accommodation by both the proselytizer and the targeted employees, and if it accedes to the demands of one, it may face harassment charges asserted by the other.

Not all employee proselytization is unlawful; it is only unlawful if it is unwelcome. If the fellow workers of an employee bent on converting them to his system of religious beliefs do not resist his efforts, the employer need not intervene. But if a single worker objects to religious conduct he considers as unwelcome proselytizing, the employer must intercede.

The line demarcating the division between acceptable and unacceptable workplace religious practices may not always be clear. As a general rule, however, conduct that intrudes less directly upon the workplace environment is more likely to be found acceptable than conduct that directly clashes with that environment, and thus highly provocative behavior is unlikely to attain court approval. Two cases, each involving workers who insisted upon using religious greetings when communicating with others in their workplaces, illustrate the point.

In accordance with its contract with General Motors, the Service America Corporation operated a cafeteria at GM's plant in Kansas City, Kansas. This operation represented a significant portion of Service America's business, and thus it took pains to make certain that GM and its workers remained satisfied with its operation. It employed eighteen workers to serve daily meals to approximately 3,000 GM workers, and they were trained to greet cafeteria customers in a friendly fashion. But two of its food service employees—Lee Ray Banks and Marcus Horton—on occasion greeted their customers with such phrases as "God Bless You" or "Praise the Lord"; at times when they claimed to have been moved by the Holy Spirit, they greeted all their customers in that fashion.

Because they believed God had introduced joy into their lives, Banks and Horton were convinced they were obligated to greet others in a positive, uplifting, and inspiring manner. Although they were always careful in conveying these greetings in a polite, pleasant, and nonconfrontational manner, some GM workers complained about them. Service America warned Banks and Horton that unless they ceased greeting cafeteria customers in that manner, they would be terminated. The two refused to comply, stating that honoring God through their speech, such as in their greetings to GM employees, was a deep-seated religious belief they could not abandon. When they were later discharged, they filed a Title VII lawsuit against Service America.

Service America made no attempt to accommodate Banks's and Horton's religious practices, arguing that their religious greetings were incompatible with the proper performance of their food service jobs, that the only possible accommodation would have involved keeping Banks and Horton separate from cafeteria customers, but that would have left the company shorthanded or have required it to hire other employees to replace them on the food line. Moreover, it argued, if it had not removed Banks and Horton from the cafeteria, it confronted a possible boycott by the GM workers, and that could have led to a material diminishment in the profitability of its business.

The court was unmoved. It observed that Service America had failed to establish the loss of any business by reason of Banks's and Horton's religious practices. The fear of a GM worker boycott was groundless, since complaining GM workers could easily avoid Banks or Horton by choosing another of the eighteen Service America food servers. The court further noted that Banks and Horton had not been attempting to proselytize GM workers or impose their beliefs on them. In these circumstances, it was compelled to rule in their favor.[9]

In the second case, an employee of a retail business in Missouri often prefaced her greetings to customers with the phrase "In the name of Jesus of Nazareth." Her employer was fearful that this language would offend some of his customers, thus undermining his business. Although he attempted to accommodate the employee's religious practice, she refused to make any effort to cooperate in resolving the problems confronted by her employer. A court later ruled that the employer could not accommodate her religious practices without incurring undue hardship, and it dismissed her religious discrimination claims. [10]

The religiously oriented language used by this employee was more likely to offend her customers than the phrases used by Banks and Horton, since "God bless you" and "Praise the Lord" are clearly less likely to offend non-Christians than the phrase "In the name of Jesus of Nazareth." It is not surprising, then, that the first court ruled that greetings such as "God bless you" and "Praise the Lord" were acceptable, whereas the second court held that "In the name of Jesus of Nazareth" was inappropriate and should be barred.

The *Banks* case points up another matter that the courts focus on in determining whether an employee's religious practices amount to unlawful proselytization and should be barred from the workplace. The court ruled that the evidence submitted in that case did not compel a finding that Banks and Horton were attempting to proselytize or impose their religious views on the GM employees. The daily encounter between them and the cafeteria customers was at best fleeting, and these religious greetings did not adversely affect the job performance of any GM worker. These religious practices may have been bothersome to some, but they did not constitute an undue hardship for Service America. [11]

As the preceding cases demonstrate, it is impossible to formulate universal guidelines definitively establishing the acceptability or non-acceptability of particular workplace religious practices. When unlawful proselytization is defined too broadly, the curtailment of lawful religious expression may follow; when it is defined too narrowly, the rights of targeted employees may remain unprotected. For those working at the side of a fellow worker who, as a central tenet of his identity, believes that he is compelled to share his faith with others, the problem will persist.

On occasion, employers have engaged in proselytizing, targeting their employees for religious conversion. An employer's proselytization of its employees may constitute a particularly egregious violation of Title VII because workers who find themselves in those circumstances are more likely to endure repeated violations of their rights rather than risk losing their jobs by reacting negatively to efforts to convert them. Similarly, a job applicant made aware of the religious beliefs and practices of an employer may decide to refrain from opposing its proselytization endeavors, hoping thereby to gain employment.

Fundamentalist Christians and others who openly center their daily lives on their religious beliefs, firmly believing that all persons should similarly direct their lives, frequently find themselves in violation of antidiscrimination laws. Although they honor and respect what they perceive to be God's law, they often demonstrate a lack of respect for human law, always granting greater priority to the former while rejecting the latter whenever they view it as conflicting with or standing in opposition to their religious beliefs. Those charged with the responsibility of enforcing the antidiscrimination laws must then act to make certain that those who purport to follow God's law also fulfill the responsibilities required of them by laws designed by human beings to govern the workplace. Those purporting to act in accordance with God's law, however, at times strongly resist efforts to bring them within the confines of those workplace laws.

Such were the founders of the Townley Manufacturing Company. When Jake and Helen Townley first organized their company in Florida to manufacture mining equipment, they covenanted with God to make certain that the company would always stand as a "Christian faith-operated business." They ran their company in accordance with what they perceived to be God's law while ignoring the proscriptions of Title VII. The Townleys were "born again believers in the Lord Jesus Christ," convinced that they were wholly unable to separate God from any portion of their daily lives, including the activities of their manufacturing company. As the company flourished, it expanded its activities to other states, including Arizona, where a plant was established in the town of Eloy.

In keeping with its covenant with God, the company enclosed a gospel tract in every piece of its outgoing mail and printed biblical verses on all company invoices, purchase orders, and other commercial documents. It gave financial support to various churches and missionaries and initiated a weekly devotional service for its employees, a move that became particularly significant in later years.

From its inception, the company's Florida plant conducted these weekly services. Typically lasting from thirty to forty-five minutes, the services included prayer, singing, giving testimony, and scripture readings as well as discussion of business matters. Failure to attend a weekly service was regarded as equivalent to missing work.

These devotional services had not yet been inaugurated at the Arizona plant at the time that Louis Pelvas was hired, but subsequently the company required all employees to attend weekly nondenominational devotional services. At first Pelvas attended those services without complaint, but later he asked to be excused from attendance because he was an atheist. His supervisor advised him that attendance was mandatory, regardless of his religious beliefs or lack of such beliefs; however, if he wished, he could read his newspaper or sleep through the service. This was not good enough for Pelvas. He filed a religious discrimination charge with the EEOC and resigned his position with the company.

In the litigation that followed, Pelvas argued that the Townleys should have accommodated his atheist beliefs by relieving him of the obligation to attend the devotional meetings. The Townleys responded that their covenant with God required them to share the gospel with all their employees, and the accommodation sought by Pelvas would have caused them "spiritual hardship." The court rejected this argument, noting that Title VII states that the employer must show undue hardship in "the conduct of [its] business." The mere assertion that excusing Pelvas from devotional services would have inflicted spiritual costs on the company or on the Townleys was not enough: "Townley's attempts to link the alleged spiritual hardship to the conduct of the business must fail. It is not enough to argue that Townley was founded to 'share with all of its employees the spiritual aspects of the company,' . . . and that the proposed accommodation would have a 'chilling effect' on that purpose. To 'chill' its purpose has no effect on its economic well-being."

While the court did not question the Townleys' assertion that their covenant with God compelled them to share the teachings of the Bible with all their employees, it observed that the strength of the government's interest in eradicating discrimination through the application of the principles of Title VII was clear: "Congress' purpose to end discrimination is equally if not more compelling than other interests that have been held to justify legislation that burdened the exercise of religious convictions. . . . Protecting an employee's right to be free from forced observance of the religion of his employer is at the heart of Title VII's prohibition against religious discrimination."

The court refused to allow the Townleys to override a worker's objections to forced attendance at devotional services solely on the basis of their assertion that their covenant with God obligated them to share their faith with all their employees. The Townleys had to accept Title VII's proscriptions over their covenant with God.[12]

Title VII did not require the Townleys to suspend their religious beliefs when they opened their Arizona plant, but it prohibited them from forcing those religious beliefs upon their workers. They were free to operate their company in accordance with their covenant with God, but they were not free to compel unwilling employees to accede to the terms of the covenant. Attendance at the devotional services should have been made optional, and adverse consequences should not have been levied against workers who opted not to participate in them.

An employer set on proselytizing to its employees may succeed in its purposes without adopting the extreme measures utilized by Townley Manufacturing Company. A more reasoned approach, using less intrusive methods, may elicit a more positive response from it's workers. As long as an employee does not object to an employer's efforts at proselytization, the employer may proceed. Once an objection is asserted, however, the employer must desist. The employer is always skating on thin ice when it engages in workplace religious activities, and therefore its management must remain constantly on guard that it not pass over the line separating activities that are condoned by Title VII from those that are not.

Another issue has frequently been litigated in the courts. First Amendment principles do not allow the federal courts to exercise jurisdiction over the internal affairs of religious organizations, especially over issues pertaining to church governance and to matters of faith and doctrine. Since the selection of members of the clergy is central to the internal governance of the church, the courts must refrain from becoming involved or entangled in legal disputes emanating from church decisions regarding its personnel who exercise ministerial or pastoral functions. Thus, religious organizations, in some circumstances, are exempt from the proscriptions of Title VII.

When the Civil Rights Act of 1964 was enacted, Congress exempted religious organizations from much of Title VII's prohibition against employment discrimination on the basis of religion. The exemption reads:

> [Title VII] shall not apply . . . to a religious corporation, association, educational institution, or society with respect to the employment of individuals of a particular religion to perform work connected with the carrying on by such corporation, association, educational institution, or society of its activities.[13]

Schools operated by religious organizations were granted their own exemption:

> It shall not be an unlawful employment practice for a school . . . to hire . . . employees of a particular religion if such school . . . is, in whole or substantial part owned, supported, controlled, or managed by a particular religion . . . or if the curriculum of such school . . . is directed toward the propagation of a particular religion.[14]

Thus Title VII authorizes religious organizations and schools to adopt religious preferences that would otherwise be discriminatory. For example, a religious organization may limit its staff to members of a particular religious denomination, and religious schools may impose religious requirements in the hiring of their teachers and other workers.

Although the language of these two sections of Title VII is clear, legal disputes relating to their application have been many. Is the institution in question a religious organization within the meaning of the statute? Is it barred for any reason from relying upon Title VII exemptions? May religious organizations and religiously affiliated schools require their employees to subscribe to a code of conduct demanded by church doctrine? Do the Title VII exemptions allow a school, established to teach a specified religious faith, to discriminate against an employee of another faith solely because her conduct fails to conform to the mores of the faith taught by the school?

If the court rules that the employer is entitled to rely on one of the exemptions, the case is over, the employer wins, and the plaintiff employee is barred from proceeding with the case. On the other hand, if the court denies application of the exemption, the case continues to follow its normal litigation path, but with the exemption no longer looming as a barrier to the litigation of the claims of the Title VII plaintiff. Although the employer has been denied the exemption, it still retains the right to defend against the claims asserted by its employee. Thus, for the employer, issues relating to the availability of the exemptions present a win-win situation. Either it is granted the exemption and wins the litigation outright, or it retains the right to contest the employee's case.

We turn to a case in which church officials denied a woman's application for a pastoral position, raising significant issues relating to the appropriate role of the Title VII exemptions. Carole Rayburn, a member of the Seventh-Day Adventist Church, held a Master of Divinity and a PhD in psychology. She applied to an administrative body within the church for a position as an associate in pastoral care and at about the same time also applied for a vacancy on the pastoral staff of the Sligo Seventh-Day Adventist Church, one of the denomination's largest churches. When she was denied both positions, she filed charges with the EEOC alleging that the church had discriminated against her because of her sex as well as on account of her association with African Americans and her membership in black-oriented religious organizations.

The appellate court that examined the charges she had levied against the church observed that the application of Title VII in a matter of this nature raised serious constitutional issues. While Title VII grants religious institutions a narrow exemption—that they may base hiring decisions upon religious preferences—it does not confer upon them a license to make those decisions on the basis of race, color, sex, or national origin. The exemption applies only to one particular reason for an employment decision—religious preference.

In determining whether the church could rightfully rely upon the Title VII exemption to defeat Rayburn's sex and race charges, the court focused on the doctrine of the separation of church and state:

> Each person's right to believe as he wishes and to practice that belief according to the dictates of his conscience, so long as he does not violate the personal rights of others, is fundamental to our system. . . . This basic freedom is guaranteed not only to individuals but also to churches in their collective

> capacities which must have power to decide for themselves, free from interference, matters of church governance as well as those of faith and doctrine. . . . Ecclesiastical decisions are generally inviolate; civil courts are bound to accept the decisions . . . of a religious organization . . . on matters of discipline, faith, internal organization, or ecclesiastical rule.

The court ruled that if it were to subject the church's actions relating to its employees to Title VII scrutiny, the court's decision would give rise to concerns of "excessive government entanglement" with the internal affairs of that institution, an act prohibited by the Constitution's Establishment Clause. The court thus declined to examine the church's decision not to hire Rayburn and instead dismissed her claims.

The court noted in passing that churches are not above the law. The employment decisions of a religious organization are subject to Title VII scrutiny where they do not involve the church's spiritual functions. Even though the Title VII exemptions generally do not apply to cases involving claims of sex and race discrimination, the court was constrained from adjudicating Rayburn's charges.[15]

A Catholic school may hire Catholics in preference to non-Catholics, but does the Title VII exemption allow a Catholic school to discriminate against a non-Catholic employee because her conduct fails to conform to Catholic principles? This distinction was considered in the case of Susan Little, a Protestant, who was employed as a teacher in a Catholic elementary school located in the Pittsburgh diocese. School authorities refrained from giving her any responsibilities for teaching religion, but she nonetheless attended Catholic ceremonies with her students and participated in teachers' programs designed to strengthen their ability to impart Catholic values to their students. Included in the terms of her contract with the school was a provision stating that the failure of a teacher to perform in accordance with the terms and conditions of the teachers' handbook would be considered a cause for termination. One of the handbook's provisions, referred to as the "Cardinal's Clause," read as follows: "One example of termination for just cause is a violation of what is understood to be the Cardinal's Clause [which] requires the dismissal of the teacher for serious public immorality, public scandal or public rejection of the official teachings, doctrine or laws of the Catholic Church. Examples of the violation of this clause would be the entry by a teacher into a marriage . . . not recognized by the Catholic Church."

When first hired, Little was married, but she later divorced. Subsequently she married a man who had been baptized in the Catholic Church but was no longer a practicing participant in any religion. The Catholic Church considers that all baptized Catholics remain Catholics for life, but it recognizes the legitimacy of a marriage of a Catholic performed by a member of another denomination, provided the parties have not been previously married. Thus, in the eyes of the Catholic Church, before Little and her second husband married each other, she should have first applied for and obtained an annulment of her first marriage.

At the end of the school year following Little's second marriage, school authorities refused to renew her contract, purportedly because she had remarried without pursuing the proper canonical process to obtain validation of her second marriage. Little then filed a religious discrimination charge against the school.

The court that subsequently considered Little's discrimination claim noted that Congress obviously intended Title VII to free individual workers from religious prejudice, and Susan Little had every right to expect her Catholic school employer to respect her rights as an individual to freely exercise her religious beliefs and practices. But Congress also intended to explicitly exempt religious organizations from the proscriptions of Title VII so as to allow them to create and maintain communities composed solely of individuals faithful to their doctrinal practices. The court, clearly of a mind to broadly interpret the Title VII exemption, ruled in favor of the school: "It does not violate Title VII's prohibition of religious discrimination for a parochial school to discharge a Catholic or a non-Catholic teacher who has publicly engaged in conduct regarded by the school as inconsistent with its religious principles. We therefore hold that the exemptions to Title VII cover [the school's] decision not to rehire Little because of her remarriage."[16]

In addition to schools, business organizations affiliated with a church or religious institution have on occasion claimed the exemption. The *Christian Science Monitor,* a highly regarded secular newspaper, claimed the exemption when Mark Feldstein sued it for religious discrimination.

The *Monitor* is published by the Publishing Society, an organ of the Christian Science Church. Both the Publishing Society and the *Monitor* were established by Mary Baker Eddy, the founder of the church. The deed of trust of the Publishing Society declared its purpose as "more effectually promoting and extending the religion of Christian Science," and, according to the church's bylaws, it was the "privilege and duty" of every member to subscribe to periodicals published by the Church, including the *Monitor.* The board of trustees was directed to conduct the business of the Publishing Society "on a strictly Christian basis, for the promotion of the interests of Christian Science." It is beyond dispute that the church was intimately involved in the management and day-to-day operations and financial affairs of the *Monitor.*

Feldstein, intent on pursuing a career in journalism, inquired at the offices of the *Monitor* about a possible job opening on its news reporting staff. He was directed to the church's personnel department, where he was advised that the newspaper hired only Christian Scientists except in that rare circumstance where no qualified member of the church was available and that, since he was not a member, he had little chance of being hired. Nonetheless, Feldstein submitted his application for employment.

The application used throughout the church contained several questions relating to the applicant's religious practices:

- Are you a member of the Mother Church or branch church?
- Are you free from the use of liquor, tobacco, drugs, and medicine?
- Do you subscribe to the Christian Science periodicals?
- Are you a daily student of the lesson-sermon?
- Have you ever been or are you now affiliated with any other church or religion?

The applicant was also required to submit references from two members of the Christian Science Church, which were to include comments on the applicant's character and his practice of the Christian Science religion.

One month after Feldstein submitted his application, he was notified that it had been rejected because he was not a member of the Christian Science Church. Feldstein then commenced Title VII religious discrimination litigation against the church, the Publishing Society, and the *Monitor*.

Although the court recognized that the *Monitor* held itself out as an objective and unbiased reporter of world news, it could not ignore the close relationship between the Church, the Publishing Society, and the *Monitor* nor the newspaper's declared purpose to promulgate the tenets of Christian Science. Even with its established reputation in the secular world, the *Monitor* was itself a religious activity conducted by a religious organization. As such, it was entitled to apply a religious affiliation requirement to candidates for employment. The court dismissed Feldstein's Title VII suit.[17]

Title VII provides for still another exemption from its provisions barring discrimination based on religion. The bona fide occupational qualification (the BFOQ exemption) provides, "It shall not be an unlawful employment practice for an employer to hire employees . . . on the basis of [their] religion . . . where religion . . . is a bona fide occupational qualification reasonably necessary to the normal operation of that particular business or enterprise."[18]

This exemption, as with the others previously discussed, has been the subject of frequent interpretation by the courts. May a nonsectarian employer make religion a bona fide occupational qualification for employment? Does this exemption apply when religion is only an incidental aspect of the job in question?

The Society of Jesus, commonly known as the Jesuits, is a religious order of the Catholic Church. Composed primarily of priests, the order has for many years been engaged in education in the United States, establishing and maintaining twenty-eight universities throughout the country. One of those, Loyola University of Chicago, has a long Jesuit tradition dating from 1909.

Jerrold Pime, who was Jewish, held a part-time lecturer position in Loyola's philosophy department. He expressed interest in a tenure-track position but was advised that he would not be considered for any of the three vacant tenure-track positions in the department. He then resigned and filed religious discrimination charges against the university.

At the time, seven of thirty-one tenure-track positions in the philosophy department were held by Jesuits, and each of the three positions about to be filled had formerly been held by a Jesuit. The department chairman decided that Jesuits should be assigned to all three positions, reasoning that the philosophy department, as a segment of a university with a long Jesuit tradition, required an adequate Jesuit presence. Because of that tradition, philosophy held a place of special significance in the education of Loyola students, and the chairman believed it was necessary to acknowledge that tradition by maintaining a strong Jesuit influence. Faculty members of the philosophy department agreed, and they subsequently voted to fill each of the three positions with a professionally competent Jesuit philosopher.

There was no hint of invidious action against Pime on account of his religion; the faculty resolution merely excluded every non-Jesuit from consideration, whether of the Catholic or any other faith. In defending against Pime's religious discrimination charge, the university argued that membership in the Jesuit order was a bona fide occupational qualification for each of the three philosophy department positions. The court agreed: "It appears to be significant to the educational tradition and character of the institution that students be assured a degree of contact with teachers who have received the training and accepted the obligations which are essential to membership in the Society of Jesus. It requires more to be a Jesuit than just adherence to the Catholic faith, and it seems wholly reasonable to believe that the educational experience at Loyola would be different if a Jesuit presence were not maintained."

The court ruled that being a Jesuit was a legitimate requirement of those selected to fill the three vacancies. This was a bona fide occupational qualification for each position. As stated by one of the judges on the appellate court that reviewed the case, Pime was rejected not because he was a Jew or a non-Catholic but only because he was not a Jesuit. Every person of every faith faced that same hurdle. The court dismissed Pime's discrimination suit. [19]

Courts often confront difficult decisions in applying Title VII religious exemptions. Disputes involving sincere parties, each advancing significant issues of public concern, weigh heavily upon judges called to rule on these disputes. In addition to these exemptions, a church is also exempt from the proscriptions of Title VII with respect to one other group of employees—its clergy. This exemption will be examined in the following chapter.

Chapter Eighteen

The Ministerial Exception

The cases reviewed in this chapter record sharp clashes between interests of the highest order—the interest of government to eradicate discrimination from the workplace versus the interest of religious institutions to manage their own affairs without governmental interference. In these cases, the Constitution's Free Exercise Clause of the First Amendment comes into play when the government encroaches upon the church's management of its internal affairs, since a religious organization possesses the right to decide for itself, free of governmental involvement, matters of church governance. In that regard, the right to select members of the clergy falls wholly within the domain of the church.

Historically the courts have held that church decisions relating to the selection of clergy are exempt from the proscriptions of Title VII and the Age Discrimination in Employment Act. The courts are barred from adjudicating Title VII and ADEA claims asserted by members of the clergy against the religious organizations that employ them. This exception to the antidiscrimination statutes is referred to as the "ministerial exemption" or "ministerial exception."

The courts have applied the ministerial exception to claims advanced by members of the clergy as well as to claims made by church employees who fulfill the functional equivalent of a minister's duties. More specifically, the ministerial exception comes into play when an employee whose position is central to the spiritual and pastoral mission of a religious institution asserts a discrimination claim against that institution. The courts are constitutionally barred from adjudicating these claims. The courts may not interfere with decisions made by a religious organization on matters of faith, employee discipline, ecclesiastical law, and other matters involving the internal governance of the organization. This rule of law has in most cases strengthened the wall separating church and state but in other cases has led to bizarre and often unjust outcomes.

Early in the history of Title VII, the courts assumed that the ministerial exception would need to be broadly applied if the wall separating church and state were to be preserved. In a 1972 case, a federal appellate court ruled:

> Though that "wall of separation" between permissible and impermissible in-trusion of the State into matters of religion may blur, or become indistinct, or vary, it does and must remain high and impregnable. Only in rare instances where a "compelling state interest" . . . is shown can a court uphold state action which imposes even an "incidental burden" on the free exercise of religion. In this highly sensitive constitutional area "only the gravest abuses, endangering paramount interests give occasion for permissible limitation."[1]

Having set the stage for a broad application of the ministerial exception, the court wasted little effort in justifying the use of the exception in the case pending before it. In that case Billie McClure brought suit under Title VII claiming that her former employer, the Salvation Army, had discriminated against her on account of her gender. It was apparent from the opening paragraph of the court's decision that McClure was headed for defeat: "The Salvation Army is a church and Mrs. Billie B. McClure is one of its ordained Ministers." Once it is determined that the parties to Title VII litigation are a church and an ordained minister, the court will refuse to adjudicate the dispute.

Under what circumstances will the exception apply where the employee-claimant is not an ordained minister? To what extent must the job functions of a lay employee involve the exercise of pastoral or spiritual duties for the exception to apply? What job functions fall within the sphere of the pastoral and spiritual? We turn to cases that have considered these issues.

Sister Elizabeth McDonough charged the Catholic University of America with sex discrimination in violation of Title VII. After her profession of vows to the Dominican order, Sister McDonough taught mathematics, science, and religion in high schools in Connecticut and later in Ohio. Subsequently, her superior suggested that she pursue a degree in canon law, a field of study that the Catholic Church had only recently made available to women. She then enrolled in the School of Religious Studies at Catholic University, later trans-ferring to the University's Department of Canon Law. After the university awarded her a doctorate in canon law, she applied for a position in the department and became the first woman to be admitted to its faculty with a tenure-track appointment.

In due course McDonough applied for tenure, but after a lengthy process the university denied her application. While recognizing her contributions to canon law, it maintained that these failed to counterbalance her marginal performance in teaching and submissions to scholarly publications. McDonough responded by filing a sex discrimination claim against the University. In opposing that claim, the school officials argued that McDonough's primary role in the Department of Canon Law had been the functional equivalent of a minister, and thus the Free Exercise Clause precluded judicial review of the decision to deny her tenure.

The court began its review of the case by summarizing previous judicial rulings relating to the scope and application of the ministerial exception. It noted that the Supreme Court had recognized that government action may unlawfully burden the free exercise of religion in two respects: (1) by interfering with a believer's ability to observe the commands and practices of his or her faith and (2) by encroaching on the ability of a church to manage its internal affairs. With respect to the second, the Supreme Court had shown a particular reluctance to interfere with a religious organization's selection of its clergy, and other courts had ruled that the Free Exercise Clause exempted the process of selecting clergy from the proscriptions of Title VII and other antidiscrimination statutes. Thus it was clear that courts were precluded from adjudicating employment discrimination suits initiated by ministers against the religious institutions that employed them. But it also was clear that this restriction was not limited to members of the clergy. Rather, it applied also to a religious organization's lay employees "whose primary duties consist of teaching, spreading the faith, church governance, supervision of a religious order, or supervision or participation in religious ritual and worship"[2] when those positions were essential to the spiritual and pastoral mission of the church. Thus the court in the *McDonough* case had to determine whether her position in the Department of Canon Law fell within the ministerial exception. Did her primary duties consist of teaching and spreading the faith, and were they central to the spiritual and pastoral mission of Catholic University?

Sister McDonough was a member of an ecclesiastical faculty whose stated mission was to "foster and teach sacred doctrine and disciplines related to it." As a member of that faculty she was entrusted with (1) instructing students in the laws that governed the church's sacramental life and (2) defining the rights and duties of its faithful and the responsibilities of their pastors. It could not be reasonably denied that the role of this faculty was vital to the spiritual and pastoral mission of the Catholic Church. Because McDonough's employment in the Department of Canon Law clearly met the ministerial function test, the court dismissed her claims on the basis of the Free Exercise Clause.[3]

Departing from the world of academia, we turn to the world of public relations. Gloria Alicea-Hernandez worked for the Catholic Diocese of Chicago as its Hispanic communications manager, a position requiring her to perform a number of tasks—to compose media releases for the Hispanic community, to develop a working arrangement with local Hispanics aimed at promoting church activities, and to compose articles for church publications.

She encountered difficulties in fulfilling these duties because of what she considered poor office conditions. When she attempted to rectify those conditions, she was opposed by her supervisors, denied the resources necessary to perform her functions, and excluded from management meetings. Ultimately she resigned, and the diocese replaced her with a less qualified male and paid him a higher salary. Alicea-Hernandez then filed sex and national origin discrimination charges against the diocese. The question for the court was whether her position as Hispanic communications manager could be classified as functionally equivalent to a position held by a member of the clergy.

Alicea-Hernandez served in part as a press secretary. In that capacity she was responsible for conveying her employer's message, serving as the primary communications link to the general populace. Her role was critical in disseminating the church's message to the Hispanic community, and in fact she served as the church's liaison with that community. In that capacity, she served a role that was functionally equivalent to that of a minister or member of the clergy. The court barred her Title VII claims. [4]

Alicea-Hernandez's employment role clearly was not that of a minister, but her role placed her close to the center of the church's mission. Thus the court did not hesitate to extend the ministerial exception to cover her position as a communications manager.

We have yet to review a case where a court declined to apply the ministerial exception. Are there any such cases? The Southwestern Baptist Theological Seminary was owned and operated by the Southern Baptist Convention, an association of Southern Baptist churches. The seminary's mission was "to provide theological education, with the Bible as the center of the curriculum for God-called men and women to meet the need for trained leadership in the work of the churches." The degrees it offered were limited to those relating to theology, religious education, and church music.

The seminary's employees fell into three groups—faculty, administrative staff, and support personnel. Members of the faculty and the administrative staff were considered ministers and were hired, assigned, promoted, tenured, evaluated, and terminated on religious criteria. Support personnel were not considered ministers but nevertheless performed some religious and educational functions.

A conflict arose between the seminary and the EEOC when the seminary refused to file reports required by the EEOC. Pursuant to the authority granted it by Congress, the EEOC had promulgated regulations that required private institutions of higher education to biennially file a Higher Education Staff Information Report EEO-6. This report called for detailed data relating to each employee's job description, length of employment contract, salary bracket, gender, race, and national origin. When the seminary refused to file the EEO-6 report, the EEOC initiated legal action asking the court to compel the filing.

The seminary defended its refusal to file on the ground that the application of EEOC regulations to any aspect of the employment relationship between the seminary and its employees would lead to excessive governmental entanglement with religion and would infringe its rights under the Free Exercise Clause. That position would have carried the day if all its employees had either been ministers or served ministerial functions; but did all its employees serve such functions?

Surely members of the faculty belonged under that umbrella. Decisions regarding faculty were largely made according to religious criteria, as the level of personal religious commitment of faculty members was considered of greater significance than their devotion to the Baptist Church or their academic abilities. They modeled the ministerial role for their students.

Some members of the administrative staff served the seminary in a capacity similar to that of the faculty. The president and executive vice president, the chaplain, the deans of men and women, and other personnel who supervised faculty were considered ministers since they, without question, served ministerial functions, thus entitling them to stand next to the faculty. But that could not be said of administrators whose functions related exclusively to the seminary's finance, maintenance, and other nonacademic departments. They were not charged with ministerial functions and thus could not be considered ministers or members of the clergy any more than could the support personnel. Ruling in favor of the EEOC, the court stated that when churches and religious organizations expand their operations beyond the functions traditionally held essential to the propagation of their beliefs and practices, those employed in the performance of services traditionally thought of as nonreligious may not be considered ministers.[5] Imprecise as this definition is, it is the best that our study has yet offered.

John Bollard claimed that while he was a novice in training to become a Jesuit priest he was sexually harassed by superiors at two Jesuit schools. He alleged that they had sent him pornographic materials, made unwelcome sexual advances, and engaged him in inappropriate sexual discussions. Although he reported the harassment to Jesuit officials, they took no corrective action. Bollard claimed that the harassing conduct was so severe that he was forced to leave the Jesuit order before taking his vows. When he sued, the primary issue before the court was whether the ministerial exception precluded him from pursuing his claim.

Evidence in support of the ministerial exception defense was clearly lacking. Rather than offering a religious justification for the alleged acts of harassment, the Jesuits condemned all types of harassment as inconsistent with their religious values and beliefs. Their disavowal of the harassment assured the court that application of Title VII to Bollard's charges would have no significant impact on their religious beliefs or doctrines. Thus there was no danger that the court would be thrust into an untenable position of being required to pass on questions of religious faith or doctrine.

The central issue in the case related to Bollard's charge that the Jesuit authorities had failed to intervene to halt the sexual harassment. If the court were to reject application of the ministerial exception—thus allowing the case to proceed—the court would not then be required to intrude upon church autonomy in any greater degree than if it allowed a suit against a church for negligent supervision of a minister charged with inappropriate sexual behavior with a parishioner.

If the court permitted the case to proceed, ultimately it would have to determine whether Bollard had been victimized by acts of sexual harassment sufficiently severe or persuasive to be actionable under Title VII. As the trial proceeded, the Jesuits would undoubtedly assert that they had exercised reasonable care to prevent and correct the harassing conduct that Bollard alleged had occurred and that he had failed to take advantage of opportunities offered to him to avoid the harassment. Nothing in the character of that defense would require an evaluation of religious doctrine or religious practices followed by the Jesuit order. Instead, the judicial inquiry would involve secular judgments concerning the nature and severity of the harassment and the measures undertaken by the Jesuits to stop it. Since the limited nature of this inquiry would prevent a broad-based intrusion into sensitive religious matters, the court concluded that the ministerial exception was inapplicable, thus allowing Bollard to proceed with his case.[6]

A 2006 *New York Times* article was headlined "Where Faith Abides, Employees Have Few Rights." The article began with the story of a nun, a member of a Catholic religious order in Toledo, who was dismissed from her order after being diagnosed with breast cancer. The nun subsequently sued the religious order, claiming that it had violated the Americans with Disabilities Act (ADA) when it dismissed her solely because of the state of her health. Her lawsuit did not long survive because the court ruled that the ministerial exception required the judiciary to remove itself from the case.[7] The nun lost her home (the convent), her occupation and vocation (that of a contemplative nun), and her health insurance.

The nun's name was Mary Rosati.[8] In middle age she had joined the Contemplative Order of the Sisters of the Visitation of Toledo, Ohio, a religious order affiliated with the Catholic Church. Members of the Sisters of the Visitation are contemplative nuns, living lives of prayer and contemplation. They lead a cloistered life, rarely leaving their convent.

The affairs of the order are regulated by the mother superior with her council, composed of several other nuns living in the convent. A candidate for the order enters the convent as a postulant. The postulancy, lasting from six to twelve months, is a time of transition from the secular life to life in the cloister. Following that period the postulant may be admitted to the novitiate, a period of initiation into the evangelical life of the religious order and the church. At the end of the novitiate, generally lasting two years, the novice is admitted to a status referred to as "temporary profession," normally lasting three years, and at the end of that time she may take her perpetual vows, thus becoming a permanent member of the order.

When Rosati joined the convent, she passed a physical examination and was enrolled in the Toledo diocese's employee health insurance program. After fulfilling the requirements of the postulancy, she passed to the novice stage of her preparation for taking her permanent vows. Until that point, no concerns had been expressed by any of the sisters regarding her vocation as a contemplative nun.

A year and a half after entering the convent, Rosati discovered a lump in her breast. She was examined by Dr. Candilee Butler, a Toledo surgeon specializing in the diagnosis and treatment of breast cancer. After a series of tests, including a biopsy, Butler determined that Rosati had a slow-growing form of breast cancer. She asked Rosati to schedule an appointment at her office to discuss the treatment options available to her. Accompanied by Sister Jane Frances, the mother superior of the convent, and Sister Mary Bernard, an assistant to the mother superior and Rosati's immediate superior, Rosati met with Dr. Butler, who explained that further tests would be necessary—bone scan, chest examination, and liver and other tests—but the best treatment option appeared to be surgery to remove the lump, followed by six weeks of daily radiation therapy. At that point the mother superior stated, "We will discuss this at home." Rosati then asked the mother superior if she had her permission to schedule the next appointment in the process recommended by Dr. Butler. When the mother superior failed to respond, the doctor asked her directly whether Rosati could proceed to the next step in the process. This time she did respond: "We will have to let her go. I don't think we can take care of her."

The court records do not reveal how Rosati reacted to the mother superior's revelation, but she must have been stunned, barely comprehending what had just occurred. Dr. Butler immediately asked the mother superior to re-evaluate her position, that she take into account that Rosati was about to begin long-term treatment for a life-threatening illness. If she were to be dismissed from the order, she would lose her health insurance and it would be extremely difficult, if not impossible, for her to obtain new coverage. Again the mother superior failed to respond. The three sisters then left the office without scheduling the next step in the treatment of Rosati's cancerous condition.

Later that day, after their return to the convent, Sister Mary Bernard took Rosati aside and said to her, "Maybe God is trying to tell you something. Perhaps you don't have a vocation [as a nun]." This was the first time since she had entered the convent that anyone had even hinted at the possibility that Rosati did not have a vocation to the religious life.

The following day Sister Mary Bernard reversed course, stating that the question of Rosati's vocation was not then an issue, that the convent's council would be voting on that matter sometime in the future, but that in her opinion it would be ridiculous to dismiss Rosati from the convent. She added that the sisters would walk Rosati through her illness and recovery process. Rosati was relieved.

Her relief was short-lived. As she pursued the treatment process recommended by Dr. Butler, she began to experience other medical problems, the most serious of which was numbness in her arms and neck, a condition apparently unrelated to her cancer. Ultimately it was determined that she would require neurosurgery for a herniated disc in her neck. Shortly after this new health issue was revealed, Sister Mary Bernard commented to Rosati that in light of all these health issues, "Don't you think God is trying to tell you something?"

Some months later, Sister Mary Bernard advised Rosati that although she had always acted properly during her life at the convent, the council had nevertheless voted to dismiss her from the order. She believed that with all her health problems, Rosati would be better off outside the convent. Among the other issues Rosati had to confront following her dismissal from the order was the loss of her health insurance coverage.

After recovering from the shock of what she had experienced at the Sisters of the Visitation convent, Rosati turned to the law, asking the court to award her damages for the humiliation, loss of self-esteem, and severe emotional distress she had suffered as a consequence of her dismissal from the convent, a dismissal she claimed had occurred only because of her health issues. In the complaint she filed with the court, Rosati alleged that the Sisters of the Visitation had dismissed her because of her health problems, thus violating the Americans with Disabilities Act, a federal statute that bars an employer from rendering workplace decisions, such as termination of employment, based on an employee's state of health.[9]

The attorneys for the order immediately asked the court to dismiss Rosati's claim, contending that the Free Exercise Clause of the First Amendment protects the power of a religious organization to decide for itself, free from state interference, all matters of internal management, particularly in the selection of their religious personnel. In other words, they claimed that the ministerial exception barred Rosati's ADA claim.

The Sisters of the Visitation informed the court that they had concluded that Rosati was not suited for their way of life and thus was not an appropriate candidate for permanent membership in their religious order. Because she would be unable to take her permanent vows, Rosati had to leave the convent. Their attorneys argued that if the court were to second-guess the sisters' decision, it would be guilty of committing an act of impermissible interference with the internal ecclesiastical affairs of a church organization in violation of the Free Exercise Clause. [10]

Rosati's attorneys, arguing in opposition to the contention that the ministerial exception required dismissal of her ADA claim, relied heavily on the *Bollard* case decision cited in the previous chapter. The *Bollard* case did not concern a religious organization's choice of clergy. Rather, the court had to determine whether the Jesuit authorities had intervened to halt the alleged sexual harassment. If the court allowed the case to proceed, it would not need to intrude upon church autonomy in deciding that issue. Rosati's attorneys argued that her case was similar. The Sisters of the Visitation could not conceivably take the position that they supported acts in violation of the ADA or that the proscriptions of that statute were inconsistent with their beliefs and values. If Rosati's suit were allowed to proceed, they argued, there was no danger that the court would immerse itself in questions of religious faith or doctrine or intrude upon the order's autonomy.

Rosati's attorneys also argued that the sisters were using the ministerial exception simply to shield themselves from liability under the statute. The sisters did not deny that the decision to exclude Rosati from the convent had been made because of her disabilities; they simply stated that she was not suitable for their way of life. But that statement appeared inconsistent with earlier comments made by Sister Mary Bernard that Rosati's health problems, not her suitability for the religious life, raised questions concerning her future with the order. It also appeared to be inconsistent with the fact that prior to the occurrence of Rosati's health issues her vocation to the contemplative life had not been questioned.

Rosati's attorneys also maintained that the court should not apply the ministerial exception merely because the individual in question may have served in a quasi minister-equivalent role, that the ministerial exception should not be applied automatically in religious organization cases but rather on a case-by-case basis. In short, the court should follow the rule applied by the *Bollard* court. [11]

The attorneys for the sisters were quick to point out that Bollard had not been asked to leave the Jesuit order. On the contrary, the Jesuits had encouraged him to pursue his vocation to the priesthood while remaining in the order. Thus the court in that case did not need to involve itself in issues relating to the selection of religious personnel. In contrast, the sisters' decision not to allow Rosati to remain in the convent had been made in the course of a selection process instituted to choose those who would remain as permanent members of the order. If the court were to permit Rosati to litigate her ADA claim, it would of necessity involve itself in that selection process. Thus the sisters' attorneys concluded:

[W]hen a case—like the present case—involves a [religious organization's] selection or rejection of ministerial personnel, the First Amendment bars inquiry regardless of the motivation attributed to the decision maker. There is no need to determine whether . . . religious doctrine is involved in the decision making process in order to gain the protection of the First Amendment. In fact, to start down that road would ultimately require the court (or a jury) to decide the contours of the [sisters'] religious doctrine in order to determine whether the rationale proffered was grounded on that doctrine. This the First Amendment forbids. [12]

In the end the court adopted that reasoning. The *Bollard* decision turned on the fact that the principal issue in the case did not involve the ministerial selection process. In the *Rosati* case, in contrast, the sisters' determination that Rosati was unsuitable for permanent membership in the order emanated from a selection process utilized to determine their membership, and that process fell within the ministerial exception. [13]

The problem with this ruling is obvious. A religious organization may cut off judicial inquiry into its motives in terminating one of its members by categorizing it as an employment decision made with respect to the selection of its ministerial personnel. But the position taken by the sisters was open to serious doubt. Prior to the appearance of her health issues, Rosati's vocation to the religious life had never been questioned. It was only after those problems arose that her vocation became a subject of discussion. When Sister Mary Bernard informed Rosati that the council had voted to remove her from the convent, she reported that the council members were of the opinion that with all her health problems Rosati would be better off living outside the convent. She did not say that Rosati was unsuitable for the religious life. She did not denigrate her vocation as a nun. She referenced only health problems as the reason for requiring Rosati to leave. Thus it appears that the sisters were not engaged in making a decision regarding the selection of religious personnel. Rather, the evidence tended to show that they made an employment decision that terminated an employee for reasons of health.

Delving into these matters, however, would have required the court to involve itself in the religious affairs of the Sisters of the Visitation. Was Rosati asked to leave the convent because she was unsuited to the religious life or because of her health problems? That was an inquiry the court could not make without violating the Free Exercise Clause. It was an ecclesiastical issue regarding church governance and administration, beyond the reach of the court as the First Amendment bars governmental intervention in religious matters of that nature.

Strictly adhering to the law as it has developed in this area, the court appears to have made the correct decision in dismissing Rosati's claims. But did justice prevail? When the underlying facts of a case cry out for further investigation, should that investigation always be curtailed? Should a religious organization be allowed to avoid the application of federal discrimination laws by misstating the basis for an employment action taken against one of its employees? Is not the enforcement of those discrimination laws of such great importance as to allow a court to determine whether a religious organization is using the ministerial exception for invalid purposes? Should laws requiring employers to desist from acts of workplace discrimination at all times fall victim to demands that religious organizations be free to hire and discharge religious personnel without governmental interference?

The Supreme Court had not considered the ministerial exception in the context of an employment discrimination case until Cheryl Perich lost her job at the Hosanna Evangelical Lutheran Church and School, a member of the Lutheran Church–Missouri Synod. The synod classified its teachers as either "called" or "lay." Called teachers were regarded as having been called to their vocation by God. Once called, a teacher received the formal title "minister of religion, commissioned."

Perich was a called teacher. In addition to teaching secular subjects, she taught a religion class, led her students in daily prayer and devotional exercises, and accompanied her students to weekly schoolwide chapel services. During the course of her employment, Perich developed narcolepsy and began the school year on disability leave. Five months later, she notified the principal that she would be able to return to work in the month following. The school, however, had already hired her replacement. Subsequently, the school offered to pay a portion of Perich's health insurance premiums if she would agree to resign. But Perich declined the offer. Instead, she presented herself at the school and refused to leave until she received written acknowledgement that she had reported for work. She also advised the principal that she intended to assert her legal rights. The church then rescinded Perich's call and terminated her for "insubordination and disruptive behavior."

The EEOC brought suit against Hosanna, alleging that Perich had been discharged in retaliation for threatening to file an ADA lawsuit. Hosanna invoked the ministerial exception, arguing that the lawsuit was barred by the First Amendment's Free Exercise Clause because it involved the employment relationship between a religious institution and one of its ministers. Thus the stage was set for the Supreme Court to examine the application of the ministerial exception. A writer for the *New York Times*, who apparently was in the courtroom when the case was orally argued before the Court, caught perfectly the conflicting positions of the parties:

> Is Religion Above the Law? . . . If the ministerial exception is to have any bite, there must be a way of distinguishing employees central to a religious association's core activities from employees who play only a supporting role. . . . But if the line marking the distinction is drawn by the state, the state is setting itself up as the arbitrator of ecclesiastical organization and thus falling afoul of the

establishment clause. And if the line is drawn by the religious association, the religious association is being granted the power to deprive as many of its employees as it likes of the constitutional protections supposedly afforded to every citizen. It is these equally unpalatable alternatives—this Scylla and Charybdis—that the Justices find themselves between in oral argument. What a mess! [14]

Chief Justice Roberts, speaking for the court, stated that the court was reluctant to adopt "a rigid formula for deciding when an employee qualifies as a minister." Accordingly, the court limited its decision to the circumstances of Perich's employment. Hosanna held her out as a minister. When it extended her a "call," it issued her a "diploma of vocation" according to her title: minister of religion. Perich was charged with performing the office of the minister of religion "according to the Word of God and the confessional standards of the Evangelical Lutheran Church as drawn from the Sacred Scriptures." The congregation prayed that God "bless her ministrations," and it also undertook to periodically review her "skills of ministry" and "ministerial responsibilities" and to provide for her "continuing education as a professional person in the ministry of the Gospel."

Perich held herself out as a minister of the church by accepting the formal call to religious service. Her job duties reflected a role in conveying the church's message and in carrying out its mission. She taught her students religion, led them in prayer, and accompanied them to chapel services.

In light of these factors—the formal title given to her by the Church and her own use of that title in the religious functions that she performed—the court ruled that Perich was a minister covered by the ministerial exception. [15]

How would Ms. Rosati have fared if the Supreme Court ruling had been in effect at the time her case was litigated? Inasmuch as the court limited its ruling to the facts of the Perich case, little has changed. True, the court did not issue a blanket rule barring all employees of a religious organization from relying upon Title VII or other employment discrimination laws to contest a termination of employment, but the court provided little guidance for the adjudication of cases where the claimant's role in the activities of her church is other than clearly obvious.

As one commentator expressed it, "People who wish to serve their God should not have to choose between their calling and their civil rights." [16] One can only hope that the courts in the future may find a solution to their quandary.

Chapter Nineteen

Accommodating Employee Religious Beliefs and Practices

Early in the history of Title VII, the Supreme Court set the limits of an employer's responsibility to accommodate its employees' religious beliefs and practices. An employer may refuse to accommodate only in those circumstances where undue hardship will result from all available forms of accommodation, and the court defined "undue hardship" as that which would require it to bear more than a "de minimus cost."[1]

Justices Marshall and Brennan dissented from the decision on the ground that from that point onward the courts need not grant even the most minor accommodation to religious observers to enable them to follow their religious beliefs and practices (chapter 7). Justice Marshall concluded that despite Congress's enactment of Title VII, one of this country's "pillars of strength—our hospitality to religious diversity—has been seriously eroded."[2] We will look to the cases that follow to determine whether Justice Marshall was correct in that assessment.

The Supreme Court and the guidelines established by the EEOC[3] call for the employer and the employee to fulfill certain responsibilities while engaged in the process of finding an appropriate accommodation. The employer is solely responsible for initiating a good-faith discussion to determine whether the employee's religious observances and practices can be accommodated, while the employee is required to make a good-faith attempt to satisfy her needs through the means offered by her employer. In endeavoring to work out a solution, the employer and the worker have a duty to cooperate with each other.

If an employer is to adequately perform its obligation to accommodate the religious observances of its employees, it had better understand fully what that obligation entails. Executive personnel managing Consolidated Freightways failed to properly educate themselves in that regard and ultimately the court had to call them to account.

Consolidated hired Corine Proctor as a payroll clerk and later assigned her to various other positions, including that of data input clerk and balancing clerk. During her employment Proctor became a member of the Seventh-Day Adventist Church and began to observe the Sabbath from Friday sundown to Saturday sundown. Prior to that time, she had occasionally been required to work on Saturdays. On the first such occasion after joining her new church, she notified her supervisors that her religious beliefs now precluded her from working on Saturdays. When she failed to appear at work on the designated Saturday, she was placed on five-day suspension. But Consolidated's manager of labor relations then directed Proctor's supervisors to accommodate her religious practices by not requiring her to work on Saturdays, and over the next three years, other employees were substituted for her when Saturday work was necessary.

After seven years on the job, Proctor bid for a balancing clerk position. She was asked to sign a statement acknowledging that if given the job she would be required to work Saturdays. Even though she refused to sign the statement, Consolidated awarded her the position. For the next several months, the company was able to honor Proctor's request not to work on Saturdays by arranging for volunteers to work on those days instead. That state of affairs came to an end when Proctor's supervisor insisted that she work, as others did, on certain Saturdays. When she failed to appear for work on the first of those days, she was suspended for three days without pay. When these circumstances occurred again the following week, Consolidated terminated her employment.

Proctor filed a grievance, but an arbitrator ruled against her, finding that she had caused her own problem by requesting and then accepting a job that obligated her to work on Saturdays. She then filed discrimination charges against Consolidated, alleging that after her assignment to the balancing clerk position, the company failed to accommodate her religious practices. The company's defense was in large part based on the efforts it had made to accommodate Proctor in her position as a data input clerk. But the court held that Consolidated's obligation to accommodate continued after she left the data input clerk position and assumed the duties of the balancing clerk position, even though at the time she applied for that job she was fully aware that Saturday work would be necessary:

> It is clear that Consolidated had an obligation to initiate good faith efforts to accommodate Proctor's religious beliefs after she assumed her new position as a balancing clerk. [Title VII] makes it an unfair labor practice to refuse to hire an individual because of her religion. A refusal to hire Proctor because she was unable to work on Saturdays would have been a violation of Title VII in

absence of good faith efforts to accommodate her religious beliefs. The fact that Proctor applied for a position which she knew required Saturday work thus does not exempt Consolidated from its statutory duty to initiate a good faith effort to accommodate her in that position. [4]

Despite the fact that Consolidated could point to a long history of having accommodated Proctor during the time she worked as a data input clerk, its obligation to accommodate her religious practices did not end when she changed positions. Its obligation to accommodate continued even after she accepted a new position, knowing that its requirements would interfere with her Sabbath observance.

The employee's responsibility to cooperate in finding a reasonable accommodation frequently becomes a subject of contention. Elizabeth Anderson, a believer and follower of the Christian Methodist Episcopal faith, was accustomed to expressing her faith by concluding her conversations and correspondence with the phrase "Have a Blessed Day." After working for over three years for U.S.F. Logistics, she was promoted to office coordinator, a position in which she acted as liaison between U.S.F. and its customers and vendors. In her new position Anderson continued to use the phrase "Have a Blessed Day" with coworkers and customers. Her use of the phrase, however, drew a complaint from an employee working for Microsoft, U.S.F.'s largest customer. In response to the complaint, U.S.F. instructed Anderson to cease using the phrase on all documents sent to Microsoft. But Anderson refused to obey, and she continued to use the phrase in her emails to Microsoft. When Microsoft again complained, Anderson's supervisor instructed her to refrain from using the phrase in all her daily interactions with Microsoft. Anderson then notified her supervisor that the "Have a Blessed Day" phrase constituted an essential aspect of her religious practices. She offered, as an accommodation, to cease the use of that phrase with all persons her supervisor identified as offended by it. Her supervisor did not respond.

Anderson's persistence in using the phrase culminated in a reprimand and notification that continued use would be considered grounds for termination. U.S.F. then issued a policy statement to its employees requiring them to refrain from using "religious, personal, or political statements" in their closing remarks in verbal or written communications with customers and fellow employees. Despite the policy statement, U.S.F. permitted Anderson to continue the use of the phrase with her coworkers.

At first, Anderson stopped using the phrase with Microsoft personnel, but subsequently sent an email to Microsoft with the phrase in all capitals and set off with quotation remarks—"HAVE A BLESSED DAY." Again she was reprimanded, but Anderson was not one to acquiesce without a fight. She filed legal action against U.S.F., alleging that it had violated Title VII by reason of its repeated failures to accommodate an essential element of her religious practices. The court ruled, however, that U.S.F. had reasonably accommodated Anderson by allowing her to freely use the phrase with her coworkers while restricting its use only with regard to the company's primary customer. Despite this reasonable accommodation, Anderson refused to be moved, declining to compromise in any respect. The court ruled against her.[5]

Workers are not placed under any burden to propose specific forms of accommodation. The search for reasonable accommodation requires bilateral cooperation, a joint effort to find an accommodation of the worker's religious needs without unduly upsetting the employer's business practices. Although the statutory burden to accommodate rests squarely with the employer, the employee is nonetheless charged with a correlative duty to attempt to satisfy her religious needs through the means offered by her employer. Compromise is nearly always an element of a successful search for a reasonable accommodation.[6]

Nine years after its ruling on accommodation, the Supreme Court again had an occasion to consider a case presenting accommodation issues. It involved a high school teacher, Ronald Philbrook, who taught business and typing classes in Ansonia, Connecticut. Philbrook was a member of the Worldwide Church of God. The tenets of the church obliged members to refrain from work on designated holy days, causing Philbrook to miss six school days each year. The school board's collective bargaining agreement with its teachers provided for three days of annual leave for the observance of religious holidays. It also provided for three days of personal leave, but this leave could not be used for religious purposes. That left Philbrook in a position where he was forced to take unauthorized leave to cover three of his church's six holy days. On each of those occasions his pay was reduced accordingly.

After following this agenda for a number of years, Philbrook decided to change it. Instead of taking unauthorized leave on the three holy days, he scheduled medical visits on those days. When the school board found this unsatisfactory, he asked the board to adopt one of two alternatives. His preferred alternative would have allowed him to use three days of personal leave for religious observance, effectively giving him six days of annual leave for the observance of religious holidays. Alternatively, he offered to pay the cost of a substitute teacher if he were paid for the three additional days of leave. The school board rejected both proposals.

Philbrook then filed suit against the school board, charging it with violations of Title VII by reason of its refusal to permit use of personal leave for religious observance. After Philbrook lost in the trial court but later won on appeal, the case moved to the Supreme Court, where the court was called on to answer the following question: Is an employer obliged to accept its employee's preferred proposal for accommodation if that accommodation does not cause undue hardship in the conduct of its business? The court responded in the negative—nothing in Title VII requires an employer to choose any particular reasonable accommodation. *Any* reasonable accommodation is sufficient to satisfy the employer's obligation. Where an employer has already reasonably accommodated an employee's religious practices, as it did in this case, it need do nothing more. Thus the school board was not obligated to show that alternative accommodations suggested by Philbrook would result in undue hardship because hardship becomes an issue only when the employer claims that it is unable to offer *any* reasonable accommodation without incurring such hardship. The school board did not act improperly in rejecting Philbrook's suggestions for alternative means of accommodation.[7]

As one commentator noted, both of the Supreme Court rulings—this one and the decision noted at the beginning of this chapter—present serious difficulties for an employee seeking an accommodation of his or her religious practices. "The message sent by the [Supreme Court] is that the 'reasonable accommodation' standard mandated by Title VII need not be all that accommodating." Despite the presence of more accommodating alternatives, an employer may fulfill its statutory duty by offering a far less extensive accommodation.[8] Another commentator put it more starkly: "After these cases, the religiously observant employee in the secular corporation is left with very little [Title VII] protection for religious practices and observances."[9] Justice Marshall's assessment that the Supreme Court's stand on accommodation would prove to be overly restrictive appears to have been clairvoyant.

Despite the Supreme Court opinions, the lower courts continued to view the employer's duty of accommodation less restrictively. A good example of how far the courts have extended the employer's responsibility to formulate an appropriate accommodation appears in a case involving a coal miner.

Pyro Mining Company operated a coal mine in Kentucky, employing over 1,000 underground workers and 150 surface workers. Danny Smith worked as an underground mechanic. As a member of a local Baptist church, Smith held the offices of treasurer and trustee and served as a Sunday school teacher. Church doctrine precluded all officers and teachers of the church from working on Sundays, and Smith personally believed it morally wrong, in the absence of a life-threatening situation, to work on Sundays.

During the first year of his employment, Smith was not called upon to work on any Sunday. But Pyro Mining then instituted a new work schedule that required each worker to work approximately twenty-six Sundays per year. A worker who objected to working on Sundays was authorized to trade shifts with a worker who did not object. Smith decided that it was morally wrong of him to ask another worker to swap shifts with him since, in effect, he would be inducing that person to sin by working on Sunday. On the first Sunday that Smith was scheduled to work, he advised his supervisor that because of his religious convictions he would be unable to appear at the mine on that day. When he did not arrive for work as scheduled, the company charged him with an unauthorized absence. On the next Sunday that he was scheduled to work, he was again sanctioned for his absence. After his third unauthorized absence, Pyro terminated him in accordance with longstanding policy.

On the day of his termination, Smith appealed his discharge, suggesting to the mine superintendent that he be allowed to work additional days without overtime pay to make up for Sunday absences. Alternatively, he proposed a transfer to a surface job that did not require Sunday work. Pyro rejected both suggestions. Smith then filed suit, alleging that Pyro had violated the religious discrimination provisions of Title VII by discharging him on account of his religious beliefs.

The company alleged that Smith's refusal to solicit a replacement constituted a failure on his part to cooperate with efforts to accommodate him. As the courts have repeatedly made clear, although the burden is on the employer to accommodate the employee's religious needs, the employee must make some effort to cooperate with the employer's attempt to accommodate. Where an employee refuses to engage in any effort to accommodate his own beliefs or refuses to cooperate with his employer's endeavor to reach a reasonable accommodation, he may render it impossible to find one. But the cooperation that Pyro suggested—that Smith himself arrange for a shift swap—was an act that he considered sinful. If he had no religious qualms about asking others to work on Sunday, then the company's proposed accommodation might have been considered reasonable. But that was not the case. Where an employee sincerely believes that working on Sunday is morally wrong and that it is sinful to induce another to work in his place, a proposed accommodation that forces the employee to seek his own replacement is not reasonable.

Since the accommodation proposed by mining company officials was unreasonable, Pyro Mining should have made further attempts at accommodating Smith. It would not have constituted an undue hardship for the company to arrange a shift swap. In fact, before instituting the new work schedule, Pyro Mining had had a long-existing policy of informing its employees of the need of a worker for a shift trade, and it took an active role in contacting employees willing to participate in shift trades. Moreover, the company had in place a mechanism for soliciting replacements. It could have accommodated Smith simply by placing a notice in its monthly newspaper or on its bulletin boards that a replacement was needed for him on a designated Sunday. No undue hardship was involved. The court ruled in favor of Smith.[10]

The federal district courts and the circuit courts of appeal have been more inclined than the Supreme Court to search out the truth lying beneath facades erected by some employers to obscure their opposition to involvement in the accommodation process. But at the same time, these courts rarely exhibit empathy for workers who refuse to compromise and thus block efforts to accommodate their religious needs. The failure to pursue an acceptable accommodation undermines the cooperative approach and is universally condemned by the courts. Yvonne Shelton learned this the hard way.

Shelton worked as a staff nurse in the labor and delivery department of the University of Medicine and Dentistry of New Jersey. Employees of that department performed routine vaginal and cesarean-section deliveries. They did not perform elective abortions but on occasion were required to perform emergency procedures that resulted in the termination of a pregnancy. As part of their responsibilities, nurses working in that department were obligated to assist in such emergencies.

Shelton, a member of a Pentecostal church, was forbidden by her beliefs from participating in any medical procedure that directly or indirectly resulted in the ending of a life. Of course, that included abortion. When possible, the hospital allowed Shelton to trade assignments with other nurses rather than participate in emergency procedures involving what she considered to be abortions. But trading assignments was not always a viable alternative.

In two incidents, Shelton's religious beliefs clashed with the emergency treatment of patients with life-threatening conditions. In the first, she refused to participate in the treatment of a pregnant patient suffering from a ruptured membrane, as the hospital planned to induce labor, thus terminating the pregnancy. After the incident, Shelton's supervisor asked her to provide a note from her pastor specifying her religious beliefs. Instead, Shelton submitted her own note: "Before the foundations of the earth, God called me to be Holy. For this cause I must be obedient to the word of God. From his own mouth he said 'Thou shalt not kill.' Therefore, regardless of the situation, I will not participate directly or indirectly in ending a life."

In the second incident, Shelton refused to participate in the treatment of a patient standing in a pool of blood who was diagnosed with placenta previa. The situation was life-threatening and the attending physician ordered an emergency cesarean-section delivery. Because this procedure would terminate the pregnancy, Shelton refused to assist or participate in the delivery. This refusal required the hospital to locate another nurse before the attending physician could begin the procedure, thus causing a delay of thirty minutes.

After hospital officials had closely reviewed the details of the two incidents, they determined that Shelton's refusal to assist at these emergency procedures had risked patient safety. Because of her refusal to assist in "medical procedures necessary to save the life of the mother and/or child," the hospital removed her from the labor and delivery department. Instead of terminating her, however, it offered her a lateral transfer to a staff nurse position in the newborn intensive care unit, and if she found that assignment unsatisfactory, she was invited to contact the human resources department to help her identify other available nursing positions.

Shelton contacted nurses working in newborn ICU and later claimed she had been told that "extremely compromised" infants who were not expected to survive were "set aside" and allowed to die. She declined to contact the human resources department to investigate other available positions.

The hospital then gave Shelton thirty days to either accept the newborn ICU position or apply for another nursing position. Shelton did neither. Instead, she wrote to her supervisor: "The ultimatum given me . . . doesn't align with the response I am [allowed by God] to submit. The decision is not ours to make but the Lord's. The Living God is in control of that which concerns my life and job. 'Many are the plans in a man's heart but it's God's plan/purpose that will prevail.'" At that point, the hospital terminated Shelton.

Shelton sued, claiming the hospital was guilty of violations of Title VII. The primary issue before the court was whether the hospital had reasonably accommodated Shelton by offering her a transfer to the newborn ICU. She argued that the offer was not reasonable because in that position she would again be asked to undertake religiously untenable nursing actions. The hospital responded with testimony showing that severely compromised infants were not denied medical treatment, were not taken off life support, and were not denied nourishment. Shelton had no evidence to counter that testimony and thus was unable to support her position that she would confront religious conflicts if assigned to that department.

The court then turned to the hospital's suggestion that Shelton confer with its human resources department about other available nursing positions. Once that proposal had been placed on the table, Shelton was obligated to determine whether it was reasonable. This she failed to do, even though, as she later admitted, nursing positions to which she could have transferred were open at the time. She claimed that her duty to cooperate in finding an accommodation never arose because any transfer would have required her to give up eight years of specialized training and would have compelled her to undertake extensive retraining for a new position. Again, the evidence failed to support her contentions. Some retraining would have been necessary, but it would not have been burdensome, and there was no evidence she would have lost pay or benefits by transferring to a new position. In short, Shelton's failure to cooperate with the hospital in searching for a reasonable accommodation was unjustified. By failing to cooperate, she undermined the cooperative approach to resolving religious accommodation issues. The court dismissed her lawsuit against the hospital.[11]

A Title VII claimant must be prepared to support each of her claims with admissible evidence establishing the truth of the matters asserted. A claim that the employee knows cannot be established should be abandoned, as a claim that remains unproven undermines the entire case. Shelton claimed that a nurse in the newborn ICU had told her that extremely compromised infants who were not expected to survive were set aside and allowed to die, but she could not recall the name of that nurse. When she advised the court that she could not remember the nurse's name, her credibility was destroyed. That was her first mistake, one having deadly consequences for her case.

Mistake number two occurred in connection with Shelton's assertion that a transfer to any other nursing position would have made it necessary for her to undertake a course of retraining for the new position. Again, she made a factual assertion she was unprepared to support with admissible evidence. When hospital witnesses showed that any required retraining would not have been burdensome and that Shelton would not have suffered any diminution in pay or benefits in consequence of making the transfer, the weakness of her case immediately became apparent.

It was clear to the court that Shelton did not have the slightest intention of cooperating with the hospital in searching out a reasonable accommodation. A noncooperative stance ends in defeat. Allegations that are not supported by evidence also end in defeat.

In another case, a court refused to order an employer to compel one of its employees to switch from a daytime to a nighttime shift so as to accommodate Sabbath observance of another employee.[12] Where the employer is able to accommodate a worker's religious beliefs only by undertaking an action that adversely affects one or more other employees, the courts most often rule that such an action involves more than a de minimis cost to the employer, thus constituting an undue hardship.

Precisely what is a de minimis cost? When does an employer's cost constitute an undue hardship? In determining whether a cost is more than de minimis, EEOC guidelines provide that the cost of the accommodation should be considered in relation to the size of the employer, its operating costs, and the number of employees who will need such an accommodation.[13] These issues were confronted by a federal district court when Volkswagen of America dismissed Angeline Protos because she refused to work on her Sabbath.

Hired by Volkswagen to work on its assembly line, Protos was assigned to the trim department as an assembler. Her task was to connect four color-coded wires to four connectors and to attach a ground screw. Initially her work schedule did not conflict with her religious principles, but three months after she was hired, Volkswagen announced new work schedules that included mandatory overtime work on a significant number of Saturdays. Protos's church prohibited her from working on Saturdays, and her failure to observe the Sabbath commitments constituted grounds for excommunication. She duly advised her supervisor that she would be unable to comply with the demands of the new work schedule, and when she persisted upon not working on Saturdays, Volkswagen discharged her.

Protos sued Volkswagen, alleging religious discrimination. The principal issue presented to the trial court was the degree of hardship that would have been imposed on Volkswagen if it had accommodated Protos' request to be relieved of Saturday work. The court ruled that Volkswagen would have suffered no economic loss because of her absence on the Saturdays in question because the "efficiency, production, quality, and morale" of the trim department remained intact. The court concluded that Volkswagen could have accommodated Protos without undue hardship and at no cost, not even a de minimis cost. Unsatisfied with this outcome, Volkswagen appealed the trial court's decision.

In reviewing the case, the appellate court considered the evidence showing that Volkswagen regularly maintained a crew of roving absentee relief operators to be deployed as substitutes for absent employees. Since the requirements of Protos's job were easily learned by an absentee relief operator, the efficiency of the assembly line did not suffer by reason of her absence. The appellate court affirmed the lower court's ruling in favor of Protos.[14]

An employer may argue that if it were to accommodate the religious beliefs of one of its workers, other workers would seek a similar accommodation, thus multiplying the costs of accommodation. The difficulty with this argument is that more often than not it is based on speculation. This was the case with the defense of the Watertown School District in South Dakota against discrimination claims asserted by one of its teachers.

Orley Wangsness was hired by the school district as its junior high school industrial arts teacher. He taught five classes daily involving approximately 125 students. As a member of the Worldwide Church of God, he was required by one of its tenets to attend a religious festival known as the Feast of Tabernacles, an event observed each fall over a period of seven days at several places around the world, including locations in the United States. Wangsness submitted a written request to the principal of the junior high school for a one-week leave of absence to attend the Feast of Tabernacles in Missouri, but his request was denied, first by the principal, then by the superintendent of schools, and finally by the board of education. Wangsness was warned that if he attended the festival, he would be discharged. He attended and was fired.

When he filed a Title VII action against the school district, it proffered a defense described by the courts as the "multiplier" effect. It maintained that if it had approved Wangsness' request for a leave of absence, it would have set a precedent, which would have led to requests by other teachers for other types of absences, thus seriously affecting the discipline of the school system. As the court noted, references to future hardships, wholly speculative in nature, are irrelevant. Because the school district had failed to make any attempt at accommodation and had not established that it had suffered undue hardship, the court ruled in favor of Wangsness.[15]

If an employer intends to assert undue hardship as the reason for its failure to accommodate a worker's religious practices, it had better have at hand detailed evidence of the hardship it claims to have suffered. Otherwise, the court will surely rule against it.

The import of recent lower court rulings on accommodation issues may be summarized as follows:

1. A worker's discrimination suit will almost certainly fail if it is shown that he refused to cooperate with his employer in its efforts to find a suitable accommodation of his religious practices. In those circumstances, courts nearly always side with the employer.
2. When an employer establishes the non-availability of any appropriate form of accommodation, the courts have no alternative but to rule in its favor.
3. The courts will not order an accommodation of a claimant's religious practices if that accommodation adversely affects coworkers.
4. The courts reject all accommodations that require the employer to violate the terms of a collective bargaining agreement.
5. An employer pleading undue hardship must support its position with actual—not speculative—evidence of the hardship.
6. An employer's reliance upon unsubstantiated predictions of requests for accommodation by other employees is generally considered by the courts to be speculative and thus must be rejected.

History reveals that Justice Marshall correctly assessed the negative consequences that would result from the role played by the Supreme Court in adopting a restrictive stance on issues relating to employer obligations to accommodate worker religious beliefs and practices. But it also shows that he failed to anticipate the corrective role the lower courts would later play, as these courts have advanced a far more expansive view of the employer's obligation to accommodate the religious beliefs and practices of their employees. Undoubtedly, this view, rather than the restrictive views of the Supreme Court, more closely reflects the intent of those in Congress who acted to adopt the 1964 Civil Rights Act and Title VII.

Chapter Twenty

Current Trends in the Law Prohibiting Age Discrimination

The refusal of employers to hire older workers remains as serious a concern today as in 1967 when the Age Discrimination in Employment Act was enacted. The ADEA has accomplished little if anything of consequence in resolving that concern. At one point, more than 75 percent of all ADEA claims filed with the EEOC involved the terminations of employment and a mere 9 percent dealt with failures-to-hire.[1] Even fewer failure-to-hire claims ever got to the courts.

Various reasons have been offered to explain the dearth of failure-to-hire lawsuits. One is based on the lack of relevant information generally available to the job applicant. Terminated workers usually have a fair amount of information at hand concerning the circumstances existing at their job site at the time of their terminations. Even after being discharged, a worker may have a source of information in the friends left behind at the workplace. If a newly hired, younger employee appears on the scene to perform the job responsibilities of an older worker terminated a few weeks earlier, purportedly because his job was eliminated, the older worker will soon learn of these circumstances. A job applicant, on the other hand, has none of these advantages. Thus, an employer's discriminatory conduct may be more readily concealed from the job applicant than from one of its terminated workers.

It is especially difficult to prove that age discrimination has affected the hiring process. Little evidence of discrimination is generally available in the first instance, and, unfortunately, little additional evidence becomes available during the discovery phase of the litigation process. Consequently, some lawyers are reluctant to take on these cases.

The employer's defense, invariably offered in response to a failure-to-hire claim, is based upon its contention that "the person hired was better qualified, and the older job applicant was less qualified, for the vacant position." A myriad of factors may be included in the decision to hire Ms. X rather than Mr. Y, many of which are wholly subjective. Indeed, the hiring decision is generally a product of a highly subjective process. Subjective employer decisions are rarely upset by the courts as, historically, judges have been extremely reluctant to substitute their judgment for that of the business person. In these circumstances, it is readily apparent that an employer bent on discriminating against an older worker job applicant need exert little effort to conceal its illegal intentions.

Even when a job applicant suspects that age bias may have played a role in her rejection, she may be reluctant to file a discrimination claim with the EEOC and even more hesitant to become later involved in litigation. Obtaining a job is the primary interest of the unemployed worker, and, in most instances, she will not allow the mere suspicion of unlawful employer behavior to deflect her from the job search. Also, the bitterness suffered by the wrongfully discharged, long-term worker is less often experienced by the unsuccessful job applicant, and thus the latter's motivation to become involved in allegations of age discrimination is less compelling. And, as many of us have experienced, the employer's rejection of a job candidate is invariably accompanied by the promise that the applicant's resume will remain on file in the event another position opens up. It almost never does, but hope springs eternal. Why charge a company with discrimination when, if you don't, it may offer you another position next week?

The reluctance of the older worker to file a failure-to-hire suit, combined with the difficulties ordinarily endured in prosecuting such a suit, tend to insulate the employer from liability for rejecting the older worker. Since employers are clearly aware that the prospect of a discrimination charge is remote, they are less inclined to concern themselves with compliance with the ADEA. The employer, obviously aware that an older worker not hired cannot later initiate a termination suit, as can an older worker who is hired, has still another reason not to hire the older worker. Therefore, in deciding whether to hire an older worker, the employer may take into account its anticipated cost of defending against a future termination suit, and then the odds in favor of the hiring of an older worker decrease dramatically. By some estimates, the probability that an employer will have to defend itself against an age discrimination suit arising out of a termination of employment is thirty times greater than the likelihood that it will have to defend itself against a suit arising out of a failure-to-hire.[2] Thus, the employer is strongly motivated *not* to hire an older employee. Not only has the ADEA failed to afford the older worker with protection from acts by an employer bent upon denying him employment because of his age, it actually may move the employer to engage in such unlawful conduct.

From the employer's perspective, the rejection of the older worker applicant may be justifiable, even if the applicant appears eminently qualified for the open position. The older worker's work experience may be too closely allied with that of her former employer, and some employee skills simply are not readily transferable from one position to another or may even prove to be obsolescent. Some employers may experience difficulty in placing an older worker in a position subordinate to a younger supervisor. And then there is the question of the proximity of retirement. Is the older worker likely to remain on the job long enough to justify the cost of any retraining that may be required?

In most instances, a failure-to-hire age discrimination case is destined for failure unless the rejected applicant is able to provide the court with direct evidence of age bias. Such evidence, however, is generally unavailable. If it is unavailable, the older worker will be required to introduce very persuasive circumstantial evidence pointing to the presence of age bias in the employer's decision-making process.

Isaac Punahele was fortunate in that regard. After Punahele submitted an application to United Airlines for a ramp service position, United hired thirty-eight people for the positions, all of whom were younger and had less experience than he had. In these circumstances, an employer, even with the advantages it has in a hiring case, will be hard pressed to persuade a jury that age discrimination did not play a prominent role in the worker's rejection.[3]

Whether direct or indirect, evidence of age discrimination in the hiring process must be nearly overwhelming to achieve a successful outcome. Without such evidence, the older worker and his attorney are well advised to consider whether litigation should be pursued. The wrong decision can lead to a costly defeat.

George Reed worked for Signode Corporation as general manager and vice president of its electrical division. When he was fifty-eight, Reed experienced serious health problems and requested a one-year leave of absence. Signode advised him that company policy precluded such leave, and Reed was left with the choice of continuing to work with his illness or resigning. He chose to resign, and Signode replaced him with a newly hired Canadian citizen.

Six months later, Reed's health improved, and he wrote to Signode expressing his desire to return to work in a suitable position. Soon after, Signode transferred the Canadian replacement to another position, leaving Reed's former general manager position again vacant. Despite Reed's availability, Signode actively sought another replacement for that position.

Reed persisted. His letters to Signode, requesting a managerial position, were met with the response that no positions were available, even though Reed's former position was yet to be filled. Ultimately, Signode considered three candidates for that position, each much younger than Reed, and hired one of these. Signode declined to hire Reed for any other position.

In Reed's subsequent suit for age discrimination, Signode argued that Reed was not rehired because of his weak sales and marketing orientation. This was a strange position to assert since Reed had extensive sales and marketing experience, both before being initially hired by the company and while working for Signode, and the person Signode hired for Reed's former position had limited sales experience.

Given the difficulties confronting the older worker in a hiring case, it is remarkable that Reed was able to assemble such an array of evidence tending to show that he had, in fact, been a victim of age discrimination. The presence of this type of evidence made it relatively easy for Reed to decide in favor of proceeding to litigation. [4]

Gary Senner was not so fortunate. He was fifty-four when he applied for a position as a psychology instructor at Northcentral Technical College in Wausaw, Wisconsin. There were forty-eight applicants for the position, but after the college eliminated those not qualified and those who had submitted incomplete or defective applications, nine applicants remained under consideration for the position. Two males, one over forty (Senner), and seven females, one over forty, were given numerical ratings based on academic credentials and experience. Of these nine, the three with the highest numerical ratings were granted interviews. Even though Senner was the only one of the nine who had a doctorate, the college did not select him for an interview. All three to whom the college granted interviews were women younger than forty, and one of them was eventually hired.

The successful candidate previously had not taught full time but had taught psychology courses part time on the college level. Senner's doctorate was in education, but he had taken courses in psychology. Although Senner had never previously held a full-time teaching position, he had taught as an adjunct professor in nearby universities in Wisconsin. Believing that he was the better-qualified candidate, Senner filed suit charging age and sex discrimination. He did not prevail on either count. [5]

In his suit, Senner argued that the college's numerical rating system was overly subjective and that many of his attributes could have been better assessed on an interview, which he had been denied. But he could offer no evidence that the college's denial of an interview was discriminatory. Even if the college had unfairly evaluated or underevaluated his credentials, Senner could establish only that the college's criteria were subjective but not that they were discriminatory. Even though the evidence suggested that Senner may have been treated unfairly, it was insufficient to persuade the court that he had been was a victim of discrimination. As Senner discovered, absent direct or highly persuasive circumstantial evidence of age bias, a failure-to-hire suit rarely succeeds.

Ann Hertz had very persuasive evidence of age bias to offer the court in her age discrimination case against The Gap. At the age of sixty-one, Hertz submitted by mail an application for a sales or office position with The Gap store located in Bayside, New York. In the application, Hertz indicated that she was available to work between the hours of 9:00 a.m. and 5:00 p.m., on Mondays, Tuesdays, and Fridays. Hertz later testified that she listed these hours on the application because she felt it was more likely she would be selected for a part-time position, that perhaps would subsequently develop into a full-time position. After Hertz submitted her application, The Gap's store manager contacted her and they agreed on a date and time for an interview. The following account of the interview was reported by Hertz at her deposition taken some time later.

On the day of the interview, Hertz arrived at the store and was asked by the associate manager, "May I help you?" Hertz responded that she was to be interviewed by the store manager. The associate manager informed the store manager, who at the time was standing on a ladder shelving merchandise. As you visualize this scene, you should be aware that Hertz had not listed her age on her application, and thus the first knowledge the store manager had that Hertz was a woman in her sixties was when she looked down from the ladder and viewed Hertz for the first time. The store manager immediately said to the associate manager, "I'm busy now. You handle it."

The associate manager then beckoned Hertz to follow her, and she preceded Hertz out of the store where they sat down on a park bench. "Why do you want to work for the Gap?" Hertz was asked. This was followed by a question about her experience. At that point, after asking Hertz two questions, the associate manager looked at Hertz's application and said, "Well, we really want someone to work nights and weekends." Hertz then asked, "Why did you call me then?" The associate manager then stood up and said, "That's the way it is. If we need someone around holiday time . . . we'll get in touch." The associate manager then walked back into the store, leaving Hertz on the park bench. End of interview.

Hertz filed a suit for age discrimination, alleging that when the store manager discovered that she was an older woman, she was given only a perfunctory interview and then falsely informed that the open position required work hours different from those stated in her application. The Gap asked the court to dismiss Hertz's case on the ground that insufficient evidence existed showing that the decision not to hire Hertz was based upon her age. The court disagreed.

The court first observed that The Gap store manager had screened Hertz's application before scheduling an interview, and thus the manager was aware of Hertz's listed hours of availability. In addition, the associate manager refrained from asking Hertz at the interview whether she was available to work at times other than those listed in her application. Nor did she ask Hertz whether she was willing to work nights and weekends. The associate manager abruptly ended the interview after just two questions and then left Hertz sitting on the bench outside the store. At the very least, this occurrence raised an inference of discrimination, thus permitting Hertz to continue with the case. Her case was later settled.[6]

When the store manager looked down from her ladder and saw below an elderly lady seeking a job, her first thoughts probably were negative—I don't want an old woman like that working in my store. She reacted without thinking and may not have been fully aware that what followed was in violation of the law. A store manager more attuned to the discrimination laws would have carried out the interview in ordinary fashion and then found some excuse, such as lack of relevant experience, to reject Hertz's application. If the manager had proceeded in that manner, it is likely that Hertz never would have been able to show even a trace of discriminatory conduct. She was successful because the evidence showed that she had been treated shabbily, and these circumstances undoubtedly motivated the court to examine her allegations of discriminatory conduct more closely. Less egregious conduct may have produced a different result. The lesson to be learned from this case is that if an age claimant has any thoughts about filing a failure-to-hire age discrimination lawsuit, it would be to her advantage if she were able to show that she had been grossly mistreated or humiliated by her prospective employer.

Clearly, the ADEA has not worked well in failure-to-hire cases. The litigation process that has developed over the last fifty years simply does not lend itself to hiring cases. Except in unusual circumstances, such as those confronting George Reed and Ann Hertz, the unemployed older worker will receive little help from the ADEA.

The profile of the average age discrimination claimant has changed. Women are now far more likely than in the past to be found in the courtroom prosecuting age claims. In previous years, the small number of female claimants may have been attributable, at least in part, to the common employer practice of channeling women into lower-paying positions. Having less at stake, women were less enthusiastic about becoming embroiled in litigious discrimination proceedings. But women now appear more inclined than men to initiate legal action once they have been victimized on the job. Long subjected to sex discrimination in the workplace, women are extremely sensitive to any form of animus exhibited by their supervisors and are more apt to attribute adverse job actions to the bias of their managers and supervisors. Middle-aged and older women identify that bias as associated with age as well as with gender.

Men ordinarily do not experience the effects of age discrimination until they reach their mid-fifties. Women, however, first become aware of age-biased actions by the time they reach their mid- to late forties. In the workplace, women get "old" at a younger age than men, because youth is considered a more important qualification for women than for men. The combination of sex *and* age may culminate in a job loss for a woman but not a man.

Joan Palmiero worked as a manufacturing supervisor for Weston Controls, a division of Schlumberger, Ltd. At age fifty-four, after thirty years on the job, Palmiero was fired. When she asked her supervisors the reason for her dismissal, they told her that her duties were to be assumed by two male workers, both of whom were much younger than she.

Subsequently, Palmiero sued Weston for both age and sex discrimination. At the trial, the testimony of Weston's executives proved damaging to the company's defense. They described how they had set out to replenish Weston's work force, that they had maintained statistics on the average age of the workers on staff, and in the hiring of new personnel, they had closely followed Schlumberger's directive to recruit individuals "fresh out of college." Their goal was to keep the organization "lean and mean." They described Palmiero's male replacements as "young comers." This testimony left little doubt that age and sex discrimination paved the way for Palmiero's termination, and the jury awarded her more than half a million dollars in damages.[7]

Merced Community College, located in California, employed Edyna Sischo-Nownejad for the faculty of its art department. The college generally based the assignment and scheduling of classes on the input of its faculty members, who customarily were consulted for their preferences. Senior faculty members who had developed particular courses were normally selected to teach them. The college followed these practices in connection with all faculty members other than Sischo-Nownejad, who was the only female member of the art department faculty and, moreover, one of its oldest members. The college not only declined to consult with Sischo-Nownejad concerning the courses she was assigned to teach, it assigned courses to her she would rather not have taught, and it failed to select her to teach the courses she had developed. Although other faculty members received all the supplies they requested, she received none. If all this were not enough for her to endure, for three years she was singled out among the art department faculty to have her classes closely monitored by her fellow male teachers.

For six years, Sischo-Nownejad was subjected to biased age and gender comments. She was referred to as "an old warhorse," and her students were characterized as "little old ladies." Her division chairperson sarcastically referred to her as a "women's libber," and on at least two occasions he urged her to retire.

Sischo-Nownejad alleged that the college had discriminated against her on the basis of sex, in violation of Title VII, and on the basis of age, in violation of the ADEA. The college asked the court to dismiss her claims, but the court refused, ruling that she had introduced sufficient evidence to give rise to inferences of both age and sex discrimination. As the only female and one of the oldest art department faculty members, she was subjected to treatment that differed substantially from that accorded all other faculty members. At the same time that her superiors were subjecting her to less favorable working conditions, she was made the butt of ageist and sexist stereotypical remarks. Sischo-Nownejad presented a strong case of age as well as sex discrimination. [8]

What Sischo-Nownejad experienced in an academic community, Verna Turner encountered in the world of the blue-collar worker. Turner worked for Independent Stave Company (ISC), a manufacturer of wooden barrel staves. ISC purchased white oak logs, debarked them, and then formed them into barrel staves and headings. ISC hired Turner to work in its mill in Bunker, Missouri, and it assigned her the jobs of "strip catcher, stacker, and second edger." Turner, however, was unable to keep up with the mill's production demands, and ISC reassigned her to the position of "grader," a position she remained in for several years.

When the demand for barrels diminished, ISC merged some of the Bunker mill positions as a means of reducing its operating costs. It combined the jobs of grader and stacker and assigned the new position to Turner, but again she was unable to keep up with production. Not long after, ISC halted operations at the Bunker mill and shut it down, and nine of the mill's thirteen workers, including Turner, were laid off. At the time the mill ceased operations, Turner was the only woman working at the mill and, at the age of fifty-four, was next to the oldest of the mill's workers. About seven months later, ISC recalled all the workers who had been laid off, except for Turner, who was notified that she had been permanently laid off because the position she had previously held had been eliminated.

After the mill was reopened, the positions of grader and stacker were again combined, and several men, each younger than Turner, attempted to perform the operations of the combined positions. None, however, was successful, because none could keep up with production. Ultimately, ISC separated the positions of grader and stacker, as they had been when Turner filled the grader position, but Turner was not recalled to fill the reconstituted grader position. Turner then filed suit for age and sex discrimination.

Turner's case was tried before a court, without a jury, and the court found in her favor, ruling that she had met her burden of proving that sex and age were determining factors in ISC's decision not to recall her after the mill reopened. The court was persuaded by the fact the Turner was the only female worker employed at the mill, that she was the oldest worker but for one, and that she had satisfactorily filled the grader position for several years. The court was of the opinion that, except for her age and sex, ISC, upon reopening the mill, would have recalled Turner to fill the grader position. [9]

Older women often face circumstances at the work site men never have to confront. Some employers prefer attractive women on their staffs, and they largely equate attractiveness with youth. If older women are held to a standard of attractiveness that differs from that for men and the basis of that standard is youth, then an employer implementing that standard is guilty of both age and sex discrimination.

Before she was fired, Carolyn Proffitt worked as a salesperson for Anacomp, Inc., in Ohio. One of the reasons given the forty-one-year-old Proffitt for her discharge was that in order for women to do well in sales, they had to be sexually attractive and that Proffitt would not do well because, as she was told, she was no longer sexually attractive. After Proffitt was terminated, her accounts were assigned to a thirty-four-year-old female trainee, whom management apparently found to be more sexually attractive than Proffitt.[10] Waitresses and other workers whose positions require them to deal with the public are frequently held to this standard of attractiveness that clearly violates the ADEA. Older men are spared that indignity.

Even though their life expectancy exceeds that of men by seven years, women are expected to retire at the same age as men. But continuing in the workforce may be a matter of necessity for a self-supporting widow, as it is for an increasing number of older divorced women who seek to hold on to their jobs well beyond the normal retirement age of 65. Many other women enter the workplace later in life, and still others interrupt their work life during childbearing years.[11] These women, if self-supporting, will opt to remain in the workforce long after the retirement dates suggested by their employers. Inevitably, the increasing tension between these women and youth-oriented employers will force greater numbers of women to assert their rights under the ADEA.

As they grow older, men also wish to remain in the workforce, especially those holding professional or managerial positions. They prefer being active, deferring their retirement until long after reaching the normal retirement age. Moreover, many older workers, regardless of their positions, are motivated to remain on the job when they discover that their savings and Social Security benefits will be inadequate to maintain their accustomed lifestyle.

Employers, for a number of reasons, tend to prefer younger workers. Their salaries are generally much lower than those of the older folk. The desire of the older worker to continue working clashes with the bottom-lined intentions of his employer. The most likely result—an age discrimination claim. Age claim disputants will remain active in our courts for some time to come.

IV

Proving Employment Discrimination

Chapter Twenty-One

Later Developments in Proving Discrimination in Title VII Cases

The application of the 1973 *McDonnell Douglas*[1] rule has proved trouble-some for the lower courts, and thus the Supreme Court has had to return to the issue on several occasions. Until 1993, the court did not deviate from its rule that evidence of the falsity of an employer's explanation for an adverse action taken against the claimant was sufficient to compel judgment in favor of that claimant. But in that year, the court added to the claimant's burden. It declared that the claimant must also show that the employer's decision was discriminatory.[2]

In addition to *McDonnell Douglas* issues (discussed later in this chapter), the court has ruled on other significant evidentiary issues in recent years.

"ME TOO" EVIDENCE

Ellen Mendelsohn had been working for Sprint/United Management Company for thirteen years when Sprint terminated her as part of a companywide reduction in force. She sued Sprint under the ADEA, alleging disparate treatment based on her age.[3] Although this was an age discrimination case, the principles announced by the court are applicable to Title VII cases.

In support of her claim, Mendelsohn sought to introduce testimony of five other former Sprint employees who also claimed their supervisors had discriminated against them on account of age. Sprint asked the trial court to exclude their testimony because the five witnesses had not worked in the same department or under the same supervisors as Mendelsohn. The court agreed with Sprint that the testimony would be relevant only if the five witnesses were similarly situated to Mendelsohn in that they worked under the same supervisors. The appellate court that reviewed that ruling thought otherwise, and it reversed the lower court ruling. The Supreme Court decided to review the case to determine whether the testimony of fellow employees, alleging discriminatory acts of other supervisors who played no role in the adverse action challenged by the claimant, was relevant. Ultimately, rather than answer that question, the court remanded the case to the trial court on procedural grounds, thus declining to clarify a rule of evidence holding great significance for employment discrimination litigants, not only in ADEA cases, but also in Title VII litigation.

Establishing an employment discrimination claim is very difficult. Attorneys who represent claimants often feel as if litigation procedures were designed to defeat their clients' causes. In the first Title VII cases that appeared on the Supreme Court docket, the court appeared to have recognized the evidentiary hurdles claimants confront, and it acted to ease their plight. The *McDonnell Douglas* ruling is a case in point. The court set forth a reasonable approach for claimants to pursue in their endeavor to establish an employer discriminatory motive. The pretext doctrine has stood the test of time, and, but for this approach to proving discrimination, many more discrimination claims would have ended in defeat for the claimants.

The court missed a similar opportunity in the *Sprint* case. Prior to this case, the federal courts of appeal and district courts were split on whether the type of testimony Mendelsohn sought to introduce was relevant and thus admissible in a Title VII case. Evidentiary rulings rarely reach the Supreme Court level, and, therefore, the court may not be presented with another opportunity to rule on this issue. The court had an opportunity to clarify the application of a rule of evidence that could have significantly leveled the playing field by assisting claimants in establishing their claims, but the court declined to act. The court should have rejected Sprint's argument that the testimony of supervisors having no authority over Mendelsohn was irrelevant. Mendelsohn was dismissed in a *companywide* reduction in force. Sprint's supervisors implemented that reduction in force pursuant to a plan put in place for that purpose. Since all supervisors were acting under a companywide plan, the testimony of each of them was relevant to the action taken against any one employee, including Mendelsohn. The court ignored those facts. If it had considered them, its decision undoubtedly would have led to a holding favoring the admissibility of all evidence bearing on the issue of workplace discrimination. To successfully litigate their claims, claimants must have available to them all of the evidence that bears on matters in issue.

MIXED-MOTIVE CASES

Recent applications of the mixed-motive doctrine have been subjected to close judicial scrutiny, both in Title VII cases and in age discrimination cases (chapter 22). The Supreme Court first approved the application of the mixed-motive doctrine in the 1989 case of *Price Waterhouse v. Hopkins* (chapter 9).[4] In essence, the mixed-motive doctrine provides that a defendant may offer, as an affirmative defense, evidence showing that even if it had not acted unlawfully in dealing with the claimant, it would have made the same decision regarding the plaintiff. Although Price Waterhouse unlawfully discriminated against Hopkins by employing an evaluation process corrupted by sexual stereotyping criteria, it also articulated legitimate reasons for rejecting her for partnership. By showing that sex discrimination played a role in the firm's decision, the burden of proof shifted to Price Waterhouse, requiring it to show that Hopkins would have been rejected for partnership even if the firm had not utilized illicit criteria to reject her.

In rendering this decision, the court assigned consideration of the mixed-motive aspects of the case to the violation, rather than to the remedy, stage of the case. Thus, in the court's view, if a defendant employer establishes a mixed-motive defense, the plaintiff employee cannot be declared the prevailing party, even though he showed that his employer had acted unlawfully, and thus the plaintiff must be denied all relief, including prospective injunctive relief and attorney fees.

Congress was not happy with the court's ruling. When it enacted the Civil Rights Act of 1991, Congress rejected the court's rationale, declaring that once the plaintiff proves that an illicit reason motivated the employer's decision, he has established a Title VII violation, and the employer's proof that it would have made the same decision in absence of the illicit reason cannot alter that fact. Congress removed the mixed-motive defense from the violation stage of a Title VII case and assigned it to the remedy stage. Proof of defendant's mixed motive may affect the remedy available to a prevailing plaintiff, but it cannot render the defendant a prevailing party. Congress denied compensatory relief to a plaintiff worker if the defendant employer proved that it would have taken the same action even if it also acted unlawfully, but even in those circumstances the worker may still be awarded declaratory and injunctive relief as well as attorneys' fees.

The *Price Waterhouse* case and the 1991 amendments to Title VII left an evidentiary issue unresolved. Are plaintiffs required to introduce direct evidence of discriminatory bias before they are entitled to take advantage of the mixed-motive approach? The court considered the issue in 2003 after Catharina Costa sued her former employer, Caesars Palace in Las Vegas, for sex discrimination.

Caesars Palace employed Costa as a warehouse worker and heavy equipment operator. She was the only woman employed in those positions. Costa experienced a number of problems with management and her coworkers that led to an escalating series of disciplinary sanctions, including the denial of privileges and suspension. Following her involvement in a physical altercation with a coworker, she was terminated. At the trial of her sex discrimination case against Caesars, she presented evidence that (1) one of her supervisors singled her out for "intense stalking," (2) she received harsher discipline than men for the same conduct, (3) she was treated less favorably than men in the assignment of overtime, (4) supervisors repeatedly falsified her disciplinary record, and (5) her supervisors tolerated coworker use of sex-based slurs against her character.

At the conclusion of the testimony, the trial court presented to the jury a mixed-motive instruction: "You have heard evidence that the defendant's treatment of the plaintiff was motivated by the plaintiff's sex and also by lawful reasons. If you find that the plaintiff's sex was a motivating factor in the defendant's treatment of the plaintiff, the plaintiff is entitled to your verdict, even if you find that the defendant's conduct was also motivated by a lawful reason."

The attorneys for Caesars Palace objected to this instruction on the ground that Costa had failed to adduce "direct evidence" that sex was a motivating factor in her dismissal or other adverse employment actions taken against her. The court denied the objection, and the jury proceeded to rule for Costa, awarding her back pay and compensatory and punitive damages as well.

The Supreme Court upheld the trial court's ruling. Direct evidence of discrimination is not required in a mixed-motive case. In order to obtain a mixed-motive instruction to the jury, the plaintiff need only present sufficient evidence for a jury to conclude that "race, color, religion, sex, or national origin was a motivating factor in the employer's unlawful employment practice." The court affirmed the jury's verdict in favor of Costa.[5]

This ruling constituted a significant victory for employment discrimination plaintiffs. Since direct evidence of discrimination is rarely available, a contrary ruling would have all but eliminated the mixed-motive method of establishing a Title VII claim.

EVOLUTION OF THE PRETEXT DOCTRINE

In a disparate treatment case, the *McDonnell Douglas* rule requires the plaintiff to prove, by a preponderance of the evidence, that he applied for an available position for which he was qualified but was rejected under circumstances that give rise to an inference of unlawful discrimination.[6]

The burden of production then shifts to the employer to articulate a non-discriminatory reason for the alleged adverse employment action. The plaintiff then may show that the employer's reason is unworthy of credence or, in other words, a pretext for unlawful discrimination. As initially conceived by the Supreme Court, pretext was the central issue in a disparate treatment case. It is in the pretext stage of the process that the plaintiff endeavors to establish the employer's discriminatory animus. But it is here that ambiguity and uncertainty have been introduced to the process, as the courts have differed widely in application of the pretext doctrine.

Three competing rules relating to pretext have been developed. Under the *pretext-only rule*, if the plaintiff successfully shows that the reasons proffered by the employer for her discharge are factually false, then she is automatically entitled to a judgment in her favor. According to the courts favoring this rule, a finding by the district court that the employer's proffered justification is false is itself equivalent to a finding that the employer intentionally discriminated.

The second approach is a weakened version of the pretext-only rule. Under this rule, if the employer offers a pretext for why it fired an employee, the court or jury is permitted, *but not compelled,* to infer that the real reason was a discriminatory motive.

The courts have designated the third variation "pretext-plus." The pretext-plus courts require more than a simple showing that the employer's proffered reasons are false. These courts require both a showing that the employer's reasons are false and direct evidence that the employer's real reasons are discriminatory. A plaintiff must do more than simply refute or cast doubt on the company's rationale for the adverse action. He must also show a discriminatory animus.[7]

In 1993, the Supreme Court addressed the issue when it examined the three rules. In that case, Melvin Hicks, an African American, brought a Title VII action against St. Mary's Honor Center alleging that he was illegally discharged because of his race. The district court found that Hicks had established a prima facie case and that St. Mary's had offered a nondiscriminatory reason for Hicks's discharge. However, the district court also ruled that the reasons St. Mary's gave were not the real reasons for Hicks's discharge. The district court nonetheless held that Hicks had failed to meet his ultimate burden of proving that race was the determining factor in St. Mary's decision to discharge him. On appeal, the appellate court reversed the lower court's ruling, holding that once the district court determined that St. Mary's proffered reasons for Hicks's discharge were false, and thus pretextual, Hicks was entitled to a judgment as a matter of law. Clearly, the court of appeals adopted the pretext-only rule.

The Supreme Court then reversed the court of appeals, granting its approval to the weakened version of the pretext-only rule. The court held that a plaintiff is not entitled to judgment as a matter of law simply because he proves a prima facie case and shows that the employer's proffered reasons for his discharge are false. Those circumstances, however, will permit a judge or jury to infer the ultimate fact of intentional misconduct, and no additional proof of discrimination is required. Proof of pretext *permits* the judge or jury to infer that the employer engaged in discriminatory conduct, but it does not *compel* that finding.[8]

The *Hicks* ruling failed to settle the matter. Some lower courts continued to use the pretext-plus standard in evaluating plaintiffs' evidence and often found such evidence insufficient to prove discriminatory animus. In 2000, once again, the court was required to define the role of pretext in a disparate treatment case. In *Reeves v. Sanderson Plumbing Products, Inc.*, the court held that "[a] plaintiff's prima facie case, combined with sufficient evidence to find that the employer's asserted justification is false, *may* permit the [judge or jury] to conclude that the employer unlawfully discriminated." Justice O'Connor set forth the rationale supporting this rule:

> In appropriate circumstances, the trier of fact can reasonably infer from the falsity of the explanation that the employer is dissembling to cover up a discriminatory purpose. Such an inference is consistent with the general principle of evidence law that the fact finder is entitled to consider a party's dishonesty about a material fact as "affirmative evidence of guilt." Moreover, once the employer's justification is eliminated, discrimination may well be the most likely explanation, especially since the employer is in the best position to put forth the actual reason for its decision.[9]

The court in *Reeves* reaffirmed its holding in *Hicks*. The days when a claimant could rely upon court rulings that proof of pretext compelled a verdict in her favor may be gone forever.

DISPARATE IMPACT

A *New York Times* op-ed nicely distinguished disparate treatment from disparate impact: "It is disparate treatment when . . . you and I apply for a job and I am selected because I am white or black or male or female or Christian or Jewish. It is disparate impact when an action is taken without reference to race, gender or religion, but has the effect of disproportionately favoring one group over another."[10]

Disparate impact has led a tortuous life. Given birth by the Supreme Court in 1971, it has been altered in some respects on several occasions, both by the court and by Congress, but has continued to stand as a significant tool in eliminating unconscious or unintentional employment discrimination from the workplace.

In the 1971 case *Griggs v. Duke Power Co.*, the Supreme Court, rejecting the view that Title VII prohibited only intentional discrimination, ruled that the statute also proscribed "practices that are fair in form, but discriminatory in operation"[11] (chapter 4). Central to a disparate impact claim is the assertion that a particular employment practice, although apparently neutral, falls more harshly upon one group of workers than another. The employer can justify these circumstances only by showing that they were required by the nature of its business. The "business necessity" rule presents two issues: (1) Does a substantial relationship exist between the neutral employment practice and the employer's professed need for it in the operation of its business? and (2) Is the employer's interest in maintaining that employment practice warranted in light of its adverse effects on a specified group of workers?

In the 1988 case of *Watson v. Fort Worth Bank & Trust*, the court ruled that to prove a disparate impact case, the plaintiff had to (1) to identify "the specific employment practice that is challenged," and (2) proffer statistical evidence sufficient to show that the employment practice in question disparately affected the plaintiff group of workers. To avoid liability, the employer could then produce evidence demonstrating that its employment practices were based on legitimate business reasons. If the employer succeeds, the plaintiff could still prevail by showing that the employer could have used other practices that impacted the plaintiff group less adversely.[12]

A year later, in *Wards Cove Packing Co.*,[13] the court shifted the burden of proving business necessity from the employer to the plaintiff workers. At that point Congress interceded and basically returned the law to that in effect prior to the *Watson* and *Wards Cove* cases (chapter 9). That was the state of disparate impact law when in 2009 the Supreme Court was again presented with a significant issue in this area of Title VII law.

The City of New Haven, Connecticut, used a written examination to identify firefighters best qualified for promotion to lieutenant and captain positions. When the results of the examination disclosed that white candidates had outperformed African Americans, a rancorous public debate ensued. Confronted with arguments for and against certifying the results—and threats of lawsuits in either case—the city decided that the statistical racial disparity compelled it to reject the test results. The white firefighters who had passed the examination but were denied promotions by reason of the city's refusal to certify the results sued, alleging that the act of discarding the test results discriminated against them on account of race in violation of Title VII.

The Supreme Court, in an opinion written by Justice Kennedy, began its analysis of the case by stating, succinctly, the difference between disparate treatment and disparate impact. Title VII prohibits both intentional acts of employment discrimination based on race, color, religion, sex, and national origin (disparate treatment) as well as policies or practices that are not intended to discriminate but in fact have a disproportionately adverse effect on minority groups (disparate impact). Once a plaintiff has established a prima facie case of disparate impact, the employer may defend its business policies and practices by demonstrating that those policies and practices are job related for the position in question and consistent with business necessity. If the employer meets that burden, the plaintiff may succeed by showing that the employer refused to adopt an available alternative practice that had less disparate impact and still served the employer's legitimate business needs.

The New Haven case presented several issues, but one issue in particular underlay the others. May an employer engage in an intentionally discriminatory practice for the asserted purpose of avoiding an unintentional, disparate impact? Yes, the court responded; but before the city of New Haven could intentionally discriminate against its white firefighters by rejecting the test results, it would have to have a strong basis to believe it would be subject to disparate impact liability if it failed to take such a race-conscious discriminatory action.

New Haven's rejection of the test results would clearly violate Title VII's disparate treatment prohibition unless it had a valid reason for that action. The evidence demonstrated that the city rejected the test results because higher-scoring candidates were white. Without some other justification— such as the intent to avoid disparate impact liability—this express, race-based decision making was prohibited. Did the city's expressed purpose of avoiding disparate impact liability excuse what otherwise would be prohibited disparate treatment discrimination?

The Supreme Court had considered similar cases but in the context of the Fourteenth Amendment's Equal Protection Clause; in those cases, the court had held that certain governmental actions designed to remedy past racial discrimination were constitutional only where there was a strong basis in evidence that the remedial actions were necessary. Applying the strong basis-in-evidence standard to Title VII allows the disparate impact prohibition to work in a manner that is consistent with other Title VII provisions. The court, therefore, adopted that standard to resolve conflicts between the disparate treatment and disparate impact provisions of Title VII.

In applying that standard, the court first noted that the racial adverse impact was significant, but it did not follow that the city would have been liable under Title VII had it certified the test results. It could be held liable for disparate impact discrimination only if the tests were not job related and were inconsistent with business necessity; but there was no evidence that the tests were deficient in that respect.

The court then rejected the notion that fear of litigation alone could justify the city's reliance on race to the detriment of the white firefighters who passed the test. The court ruled in favor of the white firefighters. [14]

The four liberal justices on the Court, in an opinion written by Justice Ginsburg, dissented. She began her analysis with the observation that in assessing claims of race discrimination, context matters. In this case, the court had to consider that race discrimination was once prevalent in fire departments across the country. In 1972, Congress extended Title VII of the Civil Rights Act of 1964 to cover public employment. At that time, municipal fire departments across the country, including New Haven's, pervasively discriminated against minorities. The extension of Title VII to cover jobs in firefighting effected no overnight change. It took decades of persistent effort, advanced by Title VII litigation, to open firefighting posts to members of racial minorities. It is in this context that the action taken by the city of New Haven must be measured.

Justice Ginsburg noted the white firefighters who scored high on New Haven's promotional exams had no vested right to promotion. The city maintained that it refused to certify the test results because it believed that it would be vulnerable to a Title VII disparate-impact suit if it relied on those results. "By order of this Court, New Haven, a city in which African-Americans and Hispanics account for nearly 60 percent of the population, must today be served—as it was in the days of undisguised discrimination— by a fire department in which members of racial and ethnic minorities are rarely seen in command positions." The city made a judgment that a result so dramatically at odds with the demographic fact of a population 60 percent African American and Hispanic made it vulnerable to Title VII litigation. To protect itself, the city opted for an alternative process that would not have the effect of screening out minority candidates. The dissenting justices, therefore, would have ruled in favor of the city.

Justice Ginsburg stated in her dissenting opinion that disparate treatment and disparate impact must be read as complementary. "Standing on equal footing, these twin pillars of Title VII advance the same objectives: ending workplace discrimination and promoting genuinely equal opportunity."

Chapter Twenty-Two

Later Developments in Proving Discrimination in ADEA Cases

As in the case of Title VII claimants, older workers have endeavored to establish discrimination claims through the use of indirect and circumstantial evidence of an employer's discriminatory conduct. Although Title VII and the ADEA are in most respects the same, they are not identical. The differences have allowed the Supreme Court to distinguish the ADEA from Title VII in some respects that, for the most part, have resulted in making it more difficult for age discrimination plaintiffs to prove their claims.

Even with congressional adoption of the 1991 amendments (chapter 9), the Supreme Court, dominated by conservative justices, on several occasions has made it more difficult for workers to prevail against employers who have discriminated against them. Two Supreme Court decisions, *St. Mary's Honor Center v. Hicks* and *Hazen Paper Company v. Biggins*, have made it substantially more difficult for workers to establish employer liability for their acts of age discrimination.

THE HICKS CASE

As was seen in chapter 21, in 1993, the Supreme Court abandoned its long established procedures for establishing a discrimination claim. Prior to the Hicks decision,[1] the Supreme Court held fast to the rule that the falsity of the employer's explanation was alone sufficient to compel judgment for the worker. If the worker carried the burden of showing the employer lied, the court was required to decide in the worker's favor. Proof of falsity was equated with proof of discrimination. But in the Hicks decision, the Supreme Court discarded that rule and instead held that "pretext" really means "pretext for discrimination." Merely proving the falsity of the employer's reasons is not sufficient. The worker still must prove that the employer's decision was discriminatory.

The Hicks decision, applicable to both Title VII and ADEA cases, greatly disfavors the worker who has no direct evidence of discrimination to present to the court. In most instances, the worker must rely upon evidence that his employer has fabricated a defense to cover up its illicit motives, and prior to the Hicks case, workers were able to rely upon the presumption that the employer who lied about its reasons for acting adversely to a worker was simply trying to cover up the illegality of its conduct as alleged by the worker. The Hicks decision, by placing an additional burden upon the worker, has made it substantially more difficult for an age claimant to prove that an employer's decision was motivated by a discriminatory intent.

Although the Court held that proof of pretext does not *compel* a verdict for the worker, the jury *may* nevertheless infer a discriminatory motive from the fact that the employer resorted to lying. Thus, if the only evidence offered in support of the worker's case is the falsity of the employer's position, a jury may decide that the employer's conduct was discriminatory; but it is no longer compelled to rule in that fashion.

THE *HAZEN* CASE

While the ADEA affords workers protection against age-biased conduct, it also recognizes the reasonable business concerns of employers. In the *Hazen* case,[2] also decided in 1993, the Supreme Court considered one of those employer concerns. Does the ADEA permit an employer to terminate an older worker in order to reduce its operating costs?

Before analyzing the action taken by the Supreme Court in the *Hazen* case, we first must review the law as it developed prior to 1993. The prior law is best exemplified by the age discrimination suit brought by Wayne Metz against his former employer, Transit Mix, Inc. of Plymouth, Indiana.

At age fifty-four, Metz was discharged after twenty-seven years of employment with Transit Mix, a company engaged in selling concrete to local construction contractors. At the time of his termination, Metz was the manager of Transit Mix's plant in Knox, Indiana. During the years just prior to his termination, Transit Mix experienced financial problems due to a decline in the local construction business. In November 1983, Will Lawrence, president of Transit Mix, closed the Knox plant for the winter, and Metz was laid off. Early in 1984, Lawrence sent Donald Burzloff, assistant manager of one of Transit Mix's other plants, to inspect the plant at Knox and arrange for any necessary repairs prior to the plant's reopening. Burzloff, who was forty-three and had been employed by Transit Mix for seventeen years, later requested that he be appointed manager of the Knox facility. Lawrence acceded to this request and then fired Metz, who in turn sued for age discrimination.

At the time of his layoff, Metz was Transit Mix's second most senior employee and one of its highest paid, a product of his many years of employment with the company when he received salary increases each year, even in those years when Transit Mix's operations were unprofitable. As Burzloff's salary was nearly one-half that paid Metz, Transit Mix relied upon the cost saving as justification for Metz's termination. The trial court ruled that the reduction in its payroll was the determining factor in Transit Mix's decision to replace Metz with Burzloff; and although this cost-savings factor "bore a relationship to Metz's age," Transit Mix had not violated the ADEA, because its decision was motivated by cost savings rather than by Metz's age. Transit Mix, according to the court, had been motivated by financial reasons to terminate Metz, and thus it had acted on the basis of a reasonable factor other than age. In other words, Transit Mix had made a business decision, unaffected by age bias. However, the appellate court that reviewed the lower court's decision rejected that reasoning.

The reviewing court first noted that Congress enacted the ADEA in response to the difficulties experienced by older workers in the job market, particularly the obstacles that long-term workers encounter when terminated at an older age. Long-term, older workers develop firm-specific skills, not readily transferrable to other job settings. In fact, the long-term, older worker's higher salary may lead to the very problem that ADEA was intended to address: the likelihood that the terminated older worker will be unemployable if forced into the job market. For this reason, the appellate court ruled, the ADEA must be interpreted to prohibit an employer from replacing higher-paid older workers with lower-paid younger workers, solely to effect a cost savings. Because of the high correlation between age and salary, it would undermine the goals of the ADEA to denominate cost cutting, achieved through the termination of older workers, as a nondiscriminatory justification for an employment decision.

The court relied heavily upon the fact that Metz's high salary resulted from a long series of annual increases, uninterrupted even in those years when the company suffered operating losses. Metz's salary reflected twenty-seven years of service; his salary directly correlated with his years of service, and his years of service directly correlated with his age. Thus, in these circumstances, salary may be considered as a proxy for age, and a decision to terminate Metz because of his high salary was really a decision to terminate him because of his age.[3]

Anticipating that its rationale might be criticized on the ground that the court was interfering with an employer's legitimate business judgment, the court quoted one of its earlier decisions:

Although the ADEA does not hand federal courts a roving commission to review business judgments, the ADEA does create a [legal] cause of action against business decisions that merge with age discrimination. Congress enacted the ADEA precisely because many employers . . . act as if they believe that there are good business reasons for discriminating against older employees. Retention of senior employees who can be replaced by younger, lower-paid persons frequently competes with other values, such as profits or conceptions of economic efficiency. The ADEA represents a choice among these values. It stands for the proposition that this is a better country for its willingness to pay the costs for treating older employees fairly. [4]

Regardless of his performance, Metz received a salary increase every year of his employment. In fact, no evidence was offered the court showing that he had ever been awarded a merit increase. Would the outcome have differed if his high salary were a consequence of merit increases and promotions? Would a worker's salary that reflected merit as well as longevity still be considered a proxy for age? We turn to Richard Holt's age discrimination case against Gamewell Corporation for the answer.

Due to large operating losses, Gamewell decided to reduce its payroll by $500,000, and Holt, the purchasing manager of Gamewell, was one of those selected for termination. Holt alleged that he was terminated because he was highly compensated, and since his rate of compensation was related to his seniority, he argued that his salary was actually a function of his age. But in contrast to Metz, Holt's salary had increased primarily as the result of promotions and merit raises, following upon excellent performance evaluations. Under these circumstances, the court rejected his contention that his high salary was a function of his age. [5]

Prior to the Supreme Court's *Hazen* decision, many federal courts across the country adopted the reasoning of the *Metz* decision as well as the limitations of the *Holt* ruling, recognizing that an employer's decision, based upon certain age-correlated factors, may constitute the functional equivalent of an age-based decision. Among the factors the courts considered as age proxies were years of service and retirement eligibility; but most often the issue was raised by those workers who contended their dismissals were directly related to their high rates of compensation. But not all courts considered a high salary as an age proxy, as Eugene Bay sadly discovered when he sued his former employer, Times Mirror Magazines, for age discrimination.

In 1975, Bay accepted the position of national marketing director for *Field & Stream* magazine, then owned by CBS Magazines. Four years later, he was promoted to associate publisher and, two years after that, to vice president and publisher. In 1986, Diamandis Communications acquired CBS Magazines, and the following year it sold *Field & Stream* and three other magazines—*Yachting, Home Mechanix,* and *Skiing*—to Times Mirror. Times Mirror already owned four magazines—*Ski, Golf, Popular Science,* and *Out-*

door Life—and after the acquisition of the four publications from Diamandis, Times Mirror restructured its operations so that its eight magazines were organized into two groups based upon reader demographics, advertising compatibility, and size of circulation. As a consequence of the restructuring, Bay's responsibility and authority were greatly diminished. At that point, Bay, who was fifty-four and earning nearly $200,000 a year, was replaced by a thirty-five-year-old earning $85,000 a year.

Bay's age discrimination suit was dismissed on Times Mirror's motion for summary judgment. In contrast to the reasoning of the Metz decision, the court ruled that "there is nothing in the ADEA that prohibits an employer from making employment decisions that relate an employee's salary to contemporaneous market conditions and the responsibilities entailed in particular positions and concluding that a particular employee's salary is too high. To be sure, high salary and age may be related, but so long as the employer's decisions view each employee individually on the merits . . . and are based solely on financial considerations, its actions are not barred by the ADEA."[6]

Thus, the stage was set for the Supreme Court's consideration of the issue, and this occurred in the *Hazen* case.

The Hazen Paper Company, owned by cousins Robert and Thomas Hazen, sold coated, laminated, and printed paper as well as paperboard. The company hired Walter Biggins as its technical director in 1977 but fired him in 1986, when he was sixty-two years old. The company's pension plan had a ten-year vesting period, and if Biggins had worked another few weeks he would have reached the ten-year mark. Biggins claimed that the Hazen cousins were guilty of age discrimination when they fired him so as to prevent his vesting in the pension plan. The issue presented to the court was whether an employer violates the ADEA by acting on a factor that correlates with a worker's age, such as pension status.

The Supreme Court began its analysis of the issue by first reiterating and emphasizing that the ADEA requires an employer to evaluate an older worker on the basis of his capabilities and not his age. An employer cannot rely on age as a proxy for evaluating a worker's capacity, such as assuming that a reduction in productivity necessarily occurs with age; rather the employer must focus on each individual worker's capacity to perform adequately. Stigmatizing stereotypes must be rejected; each worker's characteristics must be examined and evaluated individually. But the court pointed out that inaccurate age stereotypes do not come into play when the employer is wholly motivated by factors other than age, and this is true even if the motivating factors correlate with age. Generally, an older worker like Biggins has had more years in the workforce than a younger worker, and he may have accumulated more years of service with a particular employer: "Yet an employee's age is analytically distinct from his years of service. An employee who is younger than 40 . . . may have worked for a particular employer his entire career, while an older worker may have been newly-hired. Because age and years of service are analytically distinct, an employer can take account of one while ignoring the other, and thus it is incorrect to say that a decision based on years of service is necessarily 'age-based.'"

The court then applied this analysis to the situation confronting Biggins. Under the Hazen Paper pension plan, benefits vested after ten years of service. Although older workers are more likely to be close to vesting than younger workers, a decision by the company to fire Biggins solely because he had nine plus years of service and therefore was close to vesting does not constitute discriminatory treatment on the basis of age. The decision to terminate him was not made on the basis of inaccurate and denigrating generalizations about age but rather upon an accurate judgment about Biggins, that he indeed was close to vesting. The court did not preclude the possibility that an employer engages in age discrimination if it assumes that employees having a particular pension status are likely to be older and it then targets those employees for termination: "Pension status may be a proxy for age, not in the sense that the ADEA makes the two factors equivalent, . . . but in the sense that the employer may suppose a correlation between the two factors and act accordingly."[7]

The Supreme Court thus reaffirmed prior court holdings that an employer who targets a worker for dismissal by using age-correlated characteristics violates the statute. Therefore, if an employer uses salary as a basis for eliminating its older workers, or if it is motivated to dismiss workers both on account of their ages and an age-correlated factor such as high salary, it would be guilty of age discrimination. But, on the other hand, if an employer is motivated to reduce its staff solely by reason of cost, without regard to the ages of its workers, it would not be guilty of age discrimination.

Although the Supreme Court concluded that age is "analytically distinct" from years of service and other age-correlated factors, the typical employer decision makers sitting in the board room are not likely to make that fine a distinction. Within the confines of the board room, the decision to cut payroll costs is less likely to be distinct from a decision to fire higher-paid, older workers.

Under the *Hazen* reasoning, Wayne Metz's age discrimination case against Transit Mix would have failed, since Metz now would be unable to rely solely upon evidence that his termination was a product of his high salary and many years of service. Rather, he would have to prove that Transit Mix had been motivated to terminate him because of his age and not merely because of his high salary. The *Hazen* ruling has made the courts far less friendly to workers' cases cast in the age-proxy mold. Harold Johnson's travails with the Francis W. Parker School demonstrate the point.

Francis W. Parker School, a private school located in Chicago, established teacher salaries in accordance with a step system that linked salary to teaching experience, with the salaries of newly hired teachers credited with prior teaching experience. When an opening occurred in Parker's drama department, its principal established a salary of no more than $28,000 for the replacement to be hired. Harold Johnson, sixty-three years old with thirty years of teaching experience, applied for the position but was rejected in favor of a much younger teacher whose experience qualified her for a $22,000 salary under the step system. One of the reasons given for Johnson's rejection was that he qualified for a salary that Parker could not afford.

The EEOC filed suit on Johnson's behalf against the school. The school later filed a motion with the court to dismiss the suit, but its motion was denied. In the meantime, the Supreme Court decided the *Hazen* case, and after that decision was published, school officials renewed the motion to dismiss. This time the court decided in the school's favor.

The EEOC position in the case was based on the premise that the school's step system excluded a disproportionate number of older teacher applicants from consideration for teaching positions. Their longer experience placed these applicants higher up in the step system, but the school tended to hire those who placed lower in the system, and these were more likely to be younger applicants.

Because the school had not offered any business justification for maintaining the step system, the EEOC contended it violated the ADEA. On Parker's second attempt at dismissal, the court ruled that a compensation policy such as the step system, which linked salary to experience, is economically defensible, and even though it may be age-correlated, it is not barred by the ADEA, solely for that reason: "Though years of service may be age-correlated, *Hazen Paper* holds that it is incorrect to say that a decision based on years of service is necessarily age-based, unless [the EEOC] can demonstrate that the reason given was a pretext for a stereotype-based rationale. . . . Ultimately, the EEOC must show that [the school's] rationale is pretextual and that the salary system is predicated on some stereotype, conscious or unconscious."[8]

The existence of an age-correlated system of compensation was of no assistance to the EEOC in proving age discrimination in Parker's failure to hire Johnson. The EEOC could not prove pretext; it could not prove that Parker's step system was a subterfuge to conceal its belief that older teachers are less effective than younger teachers. Case dismissed.

THE AFTERMATH OF THE *HICKS* AND *HAZEN* DECISIONS

As in the *Hicks* case, the Supreme Court's decision in the *Hazen* case has made it substantially more difficult for the older worker to establish an age discrimination claim. The *Hicks* decision fundamentally altered the direction the courts had followed from the outset of the employment discrimination laws. As we have seen, the Supreme Court early on recognized the difficulties that confront a worker trying to prove that her employer intentionally engaged in discriminatory conduct, and thus it devised a system of proof whereby a court will assume that an employer who lies about its reasons for treating a worker adversely is covering up illicit conduct.

Even prior to the *Hicks* case, some courts exhibited hostility to this approach of proving discrimination, and as a consequence, in those courts it became increasingly less likely that a worker would prevail, absent the submission of some direct evidence of discrimination. With the *Hicks* decision, the Supreme Court decided that a jury *could* assume an employer lied so as to cover up its discriminatory conduct but that the jury was not *compelled* to make that assumption.

Having made it more difficult through the *Hicks* ruling to establish pretext, the Supreme Court in the *Hazen* case materially narrowed the scope of the age-proxy doctrine. Proof of age-correlated conduct is now generally insufficient to prove age discrimination. A worker is required to prove conscious or unconscious stereotype-based employer conduct, and without such proof, age-correlated conduct is of no relevance.

Underlying the rationale of the *Hazen* case is the formative language of the ADEA that eliminated "reasonable factors other than age" (RFOA) from that conduct defined as unlawful. The RFOA defense bars liability where employer action is taken for reasons other than age. Employers frequently assert the RFOA defense, but at times the proffered defense correlates so closely with age that it is little more than a thinly veiled cover for age discrimination. The ADEA cannot serve the purpose for which it was enacted if the courts allow employers to use age-correlative criteria—such as higher position, greater salary, or retirement status—to justify the termination of its older employees.

Law professor Judith J. Johnson sees the problem clearly: "The problem is that the courts, including the Supreme Court, have not come to grips with what 'reasonable' means for RFOA purposes. At this point, the courts seem to be interpreting 'reasonable' to be whatever the employer wants it to mean, without reference to the effect on [older workers]."[9] Subsequent Supreme Court cases have not resolved the problem,[10] and lower courts continue to reject age claims even though the employers' proffered defenses closely correlate with age. This is precisely what the ADEA was intended to prevent. The more difficult the courts make it for discrimination complainants to prove their claims, the more likely it is that the discrimination laws will continue to be flouted.

DISPARATE IMPACT

The disparate impact approach has proved a significant legal tool for older workers primarily because it challenges systemic impediments to the hiring, advancement, and extension of employment of older workers. But early in the history of the ADEA, the appropriateness of this approach to proving age discrimination came under attack, as several federal appellate courts cast doubt on the viability of disparate impact claims in age discrimination cases. It was argued that the domain of the ADEA is confined to employment policies and practices based upon inaccurate stereotyping of older workers. In a disparate impact case, however, the employer's policy in question is not motivated by unlawful stereotypes or by the ages of the workers. Neither an illicit motivation nor a discriminatory intent plays a role in those cases. Thus, some authorities concluded that the disparate impact approach falls outside the purview of the age statute. [11]

It was not until 2005 that the Supreme Court had occasion to rule on the matter. The city of Jackson, Mississippi, enacted a plan to make the salaries of its employees competitive with other public employees in neighboring towns and cities. The plan granted police officers having up to five years of service proportionately higher salary increases than those who had served longer. As a result, 66 percent of the police officers under age forty received a pay increase of more than 10 percent, while only 45 percent of the officers over forty received increases of that amount.

Jackson police officers over the age of forty filed suit alleging that under the city's plan they were disparately impacted in violation of the ADEA. Whether the disparate impact approach is available under the ADEA was directly in issue, and when the case reached the Supreme Court, it had to respond to that issue. The court noted differences between the ADEA and Title VII, differences the court thought made clear that the scope of the disparate impact doctrine is narrower under the ADEA than under Title VII. In an age discrimination case, the employer may assert any "reasonable factor other than age" as a defense to a disparate impact claim. Put more starkly, an employer's reliance upon any factor other than age is sufficient to defeat such a claim. "Any factor" might well include cost savings. [12]

In 2008, the court revisited the issue and ruled that in a disparate impact case, an employer who relies on a reasonable factor other than age to justify an employment decision bears the burden of establishing that defense. [13] Although this clarification may be helpful to age discrimination claimants, it did not alter the court's earlier ruling limiting the scope of the disparate impact theory in age discrimination cases. [14]

MIXED-MOTIVE CASES

If during the course of a trial, the plaintiff presents substantial proof of an illicit motivating factor—in other words, the evidence strongly suggests that the employer has been guilty of age bias—the employer, in anticipation that it is about to lose the case, may try to demonstrate that it would have made the same decision regardless of its age bias. That is to say, the employer argues that even if it harbored an unlawful motive, it would have fired the worker in any event because it also had a legitimate reason to fire him. The burden of proving this argument shifts to the employer, and if the employer succeeds in sustaining this burden of proof, the worker will be unable to claim that he was damaged as a consequence of the discriminatory conduct.

In a mixed-motive case, the burden of proving that the employer would have made the same decision even if it had not taken the worker's age into account may be a burden the employer is incapable of sustaining. In such a case, it could lead to disastrous end for the employer's case. As an example, Bethlehem Steel Corporation's failure to sustain its burden of proof in a mixed-motive case resulted in a large verdict for one of its former workers.

Alvin Joel Tyler began working for Bethlehem Steel when he was twenty-two. After twenty-six years of service, he was laid off when, for financial reasons, Bethlehem closed its Buffalo office. Prior to his layoff, Tyler had been serving as a general products salesman in Bethlehem's Buffalo office and also worked one week each month in the company's Pittsburgh office. When advised that he was to be laid off, Tyler asked about a transfer to the Pittsburgh office but was informed there were no transfer possibilities. Two months after Tyler's termination, Bethlehem filled a sales position in its Pittsburgh office with a twenty-six-year-old having only four years of service with the company. This young worker had previously resigned from Bethlehem and had been rehired but was generally dissatisfied with his position. Thus, Bethlehem terminated Tyler after denying his request for a transfer to a position in the Pittsburgh office, a position it then assigned to a much less experienced, discontented salesman, barely half Tyler's age. A disgruntled Tyler then sued Bethlehem for age discrimination.

During the fifteen months following Tyler's termination, Bethlehem transferred thirteen sales people, each younger than Tyler. In fact, the youth of the transferees was cited as one of the factors in their selection for transfer. One of those transferred, who was twenty-five at the time, was described in glowing terms: "All indications point to a 'Young Tiger' classification. We will continue to follow closely; feel we have a future 'High Potential' individual here." Bethlehem also hired twelve new sales representatives, ten of whom were recruited directly from college campuses. Bethlehem's manager of sales and marketing administration testified that it was necessary to recruit from the colleges because the sales force was getting too old.

With this type of evidence available to him, it appeared as if Tyler would have little difficulty in showing that age had been a substantial motivating factor in Bethlehem's decision to fire him rather transfer him to the Pittsburgh office. But Bethlehem argued that it would have terminated Tyler in any event, as tightening economic conditions required it to make that decision. As the law then existed, the burden of proving that defense shifted to Bethlehem, but it failed in that regard, as the jury was not persuaded that Bethlehem would have fired Tyler without the age bias. The jury then ruled against Bethlehem and in favor of Tyler.

Tyler established much more than a pretext case. The plaintiff showed compelling evidence that age had been a substantial factor in Bethlehem's decision to deny him a transfer and terminate his employment. As the appellate court that reviewed the case commented, "If there is no 'smoking gun' in Tyler's case . . . there is at the very least a thick cloud of smoke, which is certainly enough to require Bethlehem to [show] that, despite the smoke, there is no fire." This, Bethlehem was unable to do, and the jury awarded Tyler damages totaling $995,000.[15]

A mixed-motive case does not come into play unless the worker is first able to offer evidence sufficient to show that the worker's age was a substantial factor in the employer's decision that adversely affected that worker. With that type of evidence available, the worker is more than likely to succeed in establishing that any other reason offered by the employer for the adverse decision is merely pretextual. The worker's evidence, therefore, probably will lead to a verdict for the worker. But if the employer steps in at that point and argues that it would have made the same decision even without age bias, the employer will be provided with a second opportunity to defeat the worker's case. Although the burden of proof shifts to the employer, thus making it more difficult for it to obtain a jury verdict, the employer has nothing to lose, as it was facing defeat in any event. The shifting of the burden of proof, in effect, provides the employer with another opportunity to undermine the worker's case and avoid liability.

This was the law until 2009 when the Supreme Court considered Jack Gross's age discrimination case against FBL Financial Services. Gross began working for FBL in 1971, and thirty years later he held the position of claims administration director. In 2003, when he was fifty-four years old, he was reassigned, and many of his job responsibilities were transferred to a newly created position filled by a young woman who had formerly worked under Gross's supervision. Gross considered the reassignment a demotion and sued the company for age discrimination. The case proceeded to trial, where Gross introduced evidence that his reassignment was based, at least in part, upon his age. FBL countered with evidence that Gross's reassignment was part of a corporate restructuring and his new position was better suited to his skills. The jury returned a verdict for Gross, and FBL appealed.

When the case reached the Supreme Court, the issue the court was asked to decide was whether a plaintiff in an age discrimination case was required to present direct evidence of discrimination in order to obtain a mixed-motive instruction. But the court did not respond to that question, focusing its attention instead on another issue: Does the burden of proof ever shift to the defendant in a mixed-motive age discrimination case? The court's response: No, the burden of proof remains with the plaintiff.

Before the Supreme Court decided this case, an older worker could establish an age discrimination claim by proving that age was a substantial factor motivating an adverse employment action. The burden of proof then shifted to the employer to show that it would have taken the same action regardless of the worker's age. But the Supreme Court now abolished that approach. The only way an older worker can establish an age discrimination claim is to prove that but for the discriminatory motive, the employer would not have taken the adverse action. In effect, the court required age discrimination plaintiffs to prove that age was the *sole* cause of the adverse action. Thus, the age discrimination plaintiff is now charged with a much higher burden of proof than that required of Title VII plaintiffs.

Four justices—Stevens, Souter, Ginsburg, and Breyer—dissented. Observing that the relevant language in Title VII and the ADEA is identical, the dissenters pointed out that the court had long recognized that its interpretations of Title VII's language applied with equal force in the context of age discrimination, for the substantive provisions of the ADEA were derived from Title VII.[16]

Congress made clear in 1967 that it wanted to protect older workers from employer discriminatory conduct, but in the *Gross* case the Supreme Court interfered with that effort. Legislation was immediately introduced in the Senate and in the House of Representatives to reverse this ruling and place age discrimination cases on an equal footing with Title VII cases.[17] As of the writing of this book, conservative forces in the Congress have prevented this from occurring. The *New York Times* took up the issue in 2012:

> In a 2009 ruling, the Supreme Court disregarded longstanding legal procedure and made it much harder for older workers who are victims of age discrimination to win in court. The 5-to-4 decision shifted the burden of proof under the [ADEA] so that older workers have to show that their age was the deciding factor in an adverse employment decision—an unfairly hard standard to meet. Previously, if a worker had showed that age bias was one of the factors in a dismissal or demotion, the employer would then have to demonstrate that it had acted for valid and nondiscriminatory reasons. [Two Senators] recently introduced a bill to reverse the court's age-bias ruling and restore older workers' rights. This is a matter of some urgency. Since the Supreme Court ruled three years ago, lower courts have applied its onerous standard of proof to

deny thousands of age-discrimination claims. . . . [Passing this legislation] would be a good start toward fairness for older workers.[18]

The Supreme Court went out of its way to establish a more difficult burden of proof for older workers litigating age discrimination claims. In time, the old rule will have to be restored if the ADEA is to serve the purpose for which it was enacted.

STRAY REMARKS

The federal judiciary has created a host of problems for older workers who strive to establish an age discrimination claim. One of the most troublesome positions adopted by some judges requires the rejection of age-biased remarks by an employer as evidence of age discrimination.

Some, but not all, age-biased or age-stereotypical comments or remarks are admissible as evidence in support of a worker's age discrimination claim. The rule of admissibility for these types of remarks and comments, as announced by the Supreme Court, is restrictive. The comment must have been made by a person who either made the decision adversely affecting the older worker or by a person who was in some way involved in making that decision. Remarks made by non-decision-makers or persons not involved in the decision-making process are classified as *stray remarks*, and remarks assigned to that category are not admissible as evidence against the employer.[19]

One court excluded the ageist comments of a company CEO because he was not personally involved in the decision affecting the worker.[20] In another case, a senior vice president greeted a worker, just prior to his discharge, with the remark, "You've been around since the dinosaurs roamed the earth." The court excluded the remark because the decision to fire the worker was made by a managing director of the company and not by the senior vice president.[21]

To be admissible in evidence, the age-biased remark must have been made fairly close in time to the adverse decision. An appellate court, in reversing a jury verdict in favor of an older worker, ruled that the trial court should have excluded evidence of age-biased remarks of the employer's president. Three or four years prior to the worker's termination, the president had referred to some of his older employees as "old ladies with balls." Even though the president made the decision to fire the worker, the court said his ageist comment was made too far in the past to be relevant.[22] Some courts have limited the admissibility of these types of statements to those made within one year of the adverse decision.[23]

Abstract comments are generally inadmissible. Facetious remarks, comments reflecting a favorable opinion of younger workers, and statements susceptible to both innocent and invidious interpretations are usually labeled *abstract* and thus incapable of raising an inference of discrimination. Comments that are merely condescending or inappropriate in the circumstances also are generally rejected by the courts.

The negative attitude of certain members of the federal judiciary toward age discrimination cases has led them to even more restrictive rulings, culminating in the rejection of nearly all ageist remarks on the grounds that they are irrelevant and not probative. In the courts of these judges, an age-related comment rarely sees the light of day before it is banned from the courtroom. Proving discrimination is always difficult; proving it under conditions where evidence of age bias of this type is rejected as irrelevant makes it nearly impossible.

A court's more liberal approach to the admissibility of ageist comments involved John Ryder and Westinghouse Electric Corporation. Ryder, employed for eleven years as a staff assistant to the controller group for Westinghouse's Power Systems Group, was terminated at the age of fifty-two. When his age discrimination claim reached the trial stage, a jury verdict in his favor was challenged by Westinghouse on the ground that the trial court should not have admitted into evidence a memorandum written by Westinghouse's CEO. The memorandum referred to ageist comments by unidentified Westinghouse executives. These comments were made at a series of meetings that occurred *after* Ryder had been terminated. The memorandum recording the minutes of these meetings included these remarks:

> 1. In many of our businesses we have an older workforce. As a result, that workforce gets a higher salary. Additionally, our low growth business can strain opportunities for younger workers. Somehow we must provide those opportunities. We have to get the 'blockers' out of the way.
> 2. Westinghouse has been pretty paternalistic in the past and we've ended up with too much dead wood in the organization.
> 3. We don't have enough people in the organization ages 30 to 40.
> 4. What we need to do . . . is force ourselves to those standards so that the best persons get into the right positions. An eager high-energy person will get more done in a month than someone who has retired in place will do in one year.
> 5. We seem to be missing the people in the middle of the age range.

Westinghouse argued that the memorandum was largely irrelevant and highly prejudicial, and on those accounts the trial court should have prohibited it from passing into evidence. Ryder's lawyers, on the other hand, argued that the memorandum was properly admitted as reflecting the corporate culture as it existed at Westinghouse at the time Ryder was terminated.

The appellate court that examined the issue noted that it is appropriate for a court to consider circumstantial proof of age discrimination, particularly if it is in the form of a supervisor's statements relating to managerial attitudes held by corporate executives. Such evidence becomes even more critical as sophisticated discriminators render their actions increasingly more subtle in circumventing the law.

After adopting Ryder's position that ageist statements of corporate executives are relevant to the company's culture and managerial policies, the court proceeded to set forth guidelines for evaluating such statements: "[T]he court must . . . evaluate factors pertaining to the declarant's [that is, the person making the ageist remark] involvement in recognizing a formal or informal managerial attitude, including the declarant's position in the corporate hierarchy, the purpose and content of the statement, and the temporal connection between the statement and the challenged employment action."

Although the comments quoted in the memorandum did not relate directly to Ryder's termination and, in fact, were made about one year after his discharge and by persons not involved in making the termination decision, the court still held that the comments were relevant to that decision. These comments reflected past managerial viewpoints, and a jury might very well have concluded that they also reflected a managerial attitude toward older workers at the time of Ryder's discharge. The appellate court then affirmed the jury's verdict in favor of Ryder.[24]

All too often, courts have failed fully to realize the very heavy burden of proof imposed on workers who exercise their rights to sue their employers for age discrimination. Unless workers are given free rein to present all the evidence they are able to muster, it is unlikely they will be able to sustain the heavy burdens required of them and acts of age discrimination will remain unaddressed. But the distressing number of unfriendly and overly restrictive courts continues to undermine the enforcement of the age discrimination laws. In fact, these courts may actually encourage acts of discrimination, since an employer, perceiving that courts are unsympathetic to age discrimination complaints, may be more willing to risk litigation and consequently will focus less attention on adhering to the precepts of the ADEA.

V

More Recent Developments

Chapter Twenty-Three

The Gender Pay Gap and the Lilly Ledbetter Case

Lilly Ledbetter, a native of Possum Trot, Alabama, began work in 1979 at the Alabama plant of the Goodyear Tire and Rubber Company. During the nineteen years of her employment, she served as a supervisor and then as an area manager, a position largely filled by men. Initially, Ledbetter's salary was in line with the salaries of men performing substantially similar work, but over time her pay slipped in comparison to the pay of male area managers with equal or less seniority. By the end of 1997, Ledbetter was the only woman working as an area manager and the pay discrepancy between her and her fifteen male counterparts was stark: She was paid $3,727 per month, while the lowest-paid male area manager received $4,286 per month and the highest was paid $5,236.

After Ledbetter retired in 1998, she filed a discrimination claim with the EEOC and subsequently filed suit against Goodyear, asserting, among other things, a Title VII sex discrimination claim. Her case proceeded to trial where she produced evidence showing that several supervisors had discriminated against her by giving her poor performance evaluations. As a result, (1) her pay had not increased as much as it would have if she had been evaluated fairly; (2) those past pay decisions affected the amount of her pay throughout her employment; and (3) by the end of her employment, she was earning significantly less than her male colleagues. Goodyear maintained that the performance evaluations had been nondiscriminatory, but the jury found for Ledbetter, awarding her back pay and damages.

The Court of Appeals for the Eleventh Circuit reversed the finding for Ledbetter. Relying on Goodyear's system of annual merit-based pay increases, the court held that Ledbetter's claim, in relevant part, was time barred, as she had failed to comply with Title VII's provision that a charge of discrimination "shall be filed within [180] days after the alleged unlawful employment practice occurred."[1] Ledbetter charged, and proved at trial, that within the 180-day period preceding the filing of her EEOC claim, her pay was substantially less than that paid men doing the same work. Further, she introduced evidence sufficient to establish that discrimination against female managers at the Goodyear plant, not performance inadequacies on her part, accounted for the pay differential. That evidence was unavailing, the Eleventh Circuit held that it had been incumbent on Ledbetter to file charges year by year, each time Goodyear failed to increase her salary commensurate with the salaries of male peers. Any annual pay decision not contested within 180 days could not later be resurrected.

The Supreme Court agreed with the court of appeals, ruling that Ledbetter's claim was untimely. Ledbetter's position—that the paychecks that she received violated Title VII and triggered a new EEOC charging period— failed because, as the court ruled, that would require the court to jettison the defining element of any disparate treatment claim, namely, proof of discriminatory intent with regard to each alleged discriminatory act. In the court's view, Ledbetter should have filed an EEOC charge within 180 days of each paycheck.[2]

The dissenting justices took another view. They pointed out that the court's insistence on an EEOC filing following each paycheck overlooked common characteristics of pay discrimination. Pay disparities often occur, as they did in Ledbetter's case, in small increments, and thus the suspicion that discrimination is at work develops over time. Comparative pay information, moreover, is often hidden from the employee's view, as employers conceal pay differentials as well as the reasons for those differentials. Moreover, small initial pay discrepancies may not be perceived as justifying litigation, particularly when the employee, trying to succeed in a nontraditional environment as was the case with Ledbetter, is averse to making waves.

The dissenting justices noted that pay disparities are significantly different from adverse employment actions such as terminations, failures to promote, or refusals to hire, all involving fully communicated discrete acts, readily identifiable as discriminatory. It is only when the disparity becomes apparent and sizable that an employee in Ledbetter's situation is likely to comprehend her plight and, therefore, to complain. Her initial readiness to give her employer the benefit of the doubt should not preclude her from later challenging the continuing payment of a wage depressed on account of her sex.

Ledbetter's claim presented a question important to the sound application of Title VII in compensation cases: What activity qualifies as an unlawful employment practice in cases of discrimination with respect to compensation? One answer identifies the pay-setting decision, and that decision alone, as the unlawful practice. Under this view, each particular salary-setting decision is discrete from prior and subsequent decisions and must be challenged within 180 days on pain of forfeiture. Another response counts both the pay-setting decision and the actual payment of a discriminatory wage as unlawful practices. Under this approach, each payment of a wage or salary infected by sex-based discrimination constitutes an unlawful employment practice. The court adopted the first view, but in the eyes of the dissenting justices, the second is "more faithful to precedent, more in tune with the realities of the workplace, and more respectful of Title VII's remedial purpose:"

> Specifically, Ledbetter's evidence demonstrated that her current pay was discriminatorily low due to a long series of decisions reflecting Goodyear's pervasive discrimination against women managers in general and Ledbetter in particular. Ledbetter's former supervisor, for example, admitted to the jury that Ledbetter's pay, during a particular one year period, fell below Goodyear's minimum threshold for her position. Although Goodyear claimed the pay disparity was due to poor performance, the supervisor acknowledged that Ledbetter received a "Top Performance Award" in 1996. The jury also heard testimony that another supervisor—who evaluated Ledbetter in 1997 and whose evaluation led to her most recent raise denial—was openly biased against women. And two women who had previously worked as managers at the plant told the jury they had been subject to pervasive discrimination and were paid less than their male counterparts. One was paid less than the men she supervised. Ledbetter herself testified about the discriminatory animus conveyed to her by plant officials. Toward the end of her career, for instance, the plant manager told Ledbetter that the "plant did not need women, that [women] didn't help it, [and] caused problems." After weighing all the evidence, the jury found for Ledbetter, concluding that the pay disparity was due to intentional discrimination.
>
> Yet, under the Court's decision, the discrimination Ledbetter proved is not redressable under Title VII. Each and every pay decision she did not immediately challenge wiped the slate clean. Consideration may not be given to the cumulative effect of a series of decisions that, together, set her pay well below that of every male area manager. Knowingly carrying past pay discrimination forward must be treated as lawful conduct. Ledbetter may not be compensated for the lower pay she was in fact receiving when she complained to the EEOC. Nor, were she still employed by Goodyear, could she gain, on the proof she presented at trial, injunctive relief requiring, prospectively, her receipt of the same compensation men receive for substantially similar work. The Court's approbation of these consequences is totally at odds with the robust protection against workplace discrimination Congress intended Title VII to secure. [Citations omitted][3]

The dissenting justices noted that this was not the first time the court had ordered a cramped interpretation of Title VII, incompatible with the statute's broad remedial purpose. A spate of court decisions in the late 1980s drew congressional fire and resulted in demands for legislative change that culminated in the 1991 Civil Rights Act. The dissenters noted that "Once again, the ball is in Congress' court. As in 1991, the Legislature may act to correct this Court's parsimonious reading of Title VII."

Reaction to the decision was swift and highly critical. A *New York Times* op-ed, titled "Injustice 5, Justice 4" in reference the court's split decision, stated that "The Supreme Court struck a blow for discrimination this week by stripping [Title VII] of much of its potency. The majority opinion . . . forced an unreasonable reading on the law, and tossed aside longstanding precedents to rule in favor of an Alabama employer that had underpaid a female employee for years. The ruling is the latest indication that a court that once proudly stood up for the disadvantaged is increasingly protective of the powerful."[4]

Other major newspapers across the nation joined in criticizing the court. Congress moved quickly to draft legislation providing that in cases like Ledbetter's, each paycheck would constitute an act of discrimination, thus extending the period within which a worker would be able to file a claim with the EEOC. Within two weeks of the court's decision, Ledbetter testified before the House Education and Labor Committee in relation to the proposed legislation.[5] The bill passed in the House of Representatives, but in April of 2008 it died in the Senate when Republican senators threatened to filibuster. In January 2009, a new Congress passed the "Lilly Ledbetter Fair Pay Act,"[6] and it was immediately signed by newly elected President Obama, the first bill he signed as president.

As in 1991, Congress took a very dim view of the Supreme Court's restrictive interpretation of Title VII and acted promptly to reverse the consequences of a myopic act of the judiciary.

Chapter Twenty-Four

Same-Sex Sexual Harassment

Donald Wright, an employee of Methodist Youth Services, alleged in 1981 that his male supervisor directed overt homosexual advances toward him and that, when he resisted those advances, he was terminated. Prior to this case, no litigant had proposed the notion that same-sex sexual harassment violated Title VII precepts. Without any direct precedent to rely on, the court turned for guidance to female harassment claims, where adverse employment actions followed the rejection of sexual advances of a male supervisor. Resolution of those cases had been predicated on the premise that a male supervisor's sexual demands on a female employee were demands that would not have been made on a male employee and thus were sex discriminatory and actionable under Title VII. The court reasoned in the *Wright* case that since the supervisor's homosexual demands on Wright would not have been made on a female worker, Wright's claim also was based on discrimination on account of sex and thus actionable under Title VII.[1]

Following the *Wright* case, the federal courts seized on wildly divergent positions regarding the viability of same-sex harassment claims. Some courts rejected the rationale of the *Wright* ruling, holding that same-sex sexual harassment claims are never cognizable under Title VII, while other courts held that those claims are actionable only if the plaintiff proves that the harasser is homosexual. Still other courts required the plaintiff to prove that the harassment was motivated by sexual desire, and others expressed the opinion that workplace sexual harassment is always actionable, regardless of the harasser's sexual orientation or motivation. It remained for the Supreme Court to sort this out, but an opportunity for it to do so did not arise until 1998, when a case involving same-sex harassment claims asserted by Joseph Oncale against his employer, Sundowner Offshore Services, came before the Court.

Oncale worked as a member of an eight-man crew on an oil platform in the Gulf of Mexico. He alleged that on several occasions, in the presence of the rest of the crew, he was forcibly subjected to sex-related, humiliating actions by a coworker and two supervisors and that they sexually assaulted him and threatened him with rape. When Oncale's complaints to supervisory personnel failed to produce remedial action, he resigned.

The lower courts' "bewildering variety of stances" offered little assistance to the Supreme Court in determining whether same-sex sexual harassment violated Title VII. The Court began its analysis with the wording of the statute, that it "shall be an unlawful employment practice for an employer . . . to discriminate against any individual . . . because of such individual's . . . sex."[2] This language, the Court had previously held, demonstrated a congressional intent to strike at the entire spectrum of discriminatory acts against men and women in employment.[3] Consequently, the courts may not exclude from Title VII coverage any workplace conduct based on sex. Since same-sex harassment claims may be based on sex, Congress must have intended Title VII to encompass those claims.

But, Title VII comes into play only in instances of discriminatory conduct. Can it be said that Title VII even recognizes the possibility that a man may discriminate against another man or that a woman may discriminate against another woman? In responding to those queries, the Court noted that just as one may not presume an employer will not discriminate against members of his or her own race, one may not presume men will refrain from discriminating against other men or women against other women.

The Court concluded that there was no justification in the statutory language to categorically exclude same-sex harassment claims from Title VII coverage. The Court emphasized, however, that the plaintiff who asserts a same-sex harassment claim must always prove the harassment occurred because of his or her sex.

A plaintiff alleging same-sex harassment must always prove that the conduct at issue was not merely tinged with offensive sexual connotation but actually constituted discrimination on account of sex. The Court emphasized that point, and it cannot be overly emphasized here, as the issue appears time and again in same-sex harassment cases.

The Court also issued a caveat: Its recognition of employer liability for same-sex harassment was not intended to transform Title VII into a "general civility code for the American workplace." Title VII does not address genuine but innocent differences in the ways men and women routinely interact with members of the same and opposite sex:

> The prohibition of harassment on the basis of sex requires neither asexuality nor androgyny in the workplace; it forbids only behavior so objectively offensive as to alter the "conditions" of the victim's employment. "Conduct that is

not severe or pervasive enough to create an objectively hostile or abusive work environment . . . is beyond Title VII's purview . . . ." We have always regarded that requirement as crucial, and as sufficient to ensure that courts and juries do not mistake ordinary socializing in the workplace—such as male-on-male horseplay, or intersexual flirtation—for discriminatory "conditions of employment.

The court further noted that common sense and an appropriate sensitivity to social context will enable the courts and juries to distinguish between simple teasing or roughhousing among members of the same sex and conduct that a reasonable person would find severely hostile or abusive.[4]

Following the Supreme Court's *Oncale* decision, several other issues arose in same-sex sexual harassment cases. May sexual commentary provide the basis for a same-sex harassment claim? Can obscene expressions or anatomical references, uttered by men while conversing with one another, rise to a level that it could be said that one of the men was engaged in same-sex harassment?[5]

May sexual stereotypes provide the basis for a same-sex claim? Antonio Sanchez worked for Azteca Restaurant Enterprises, an operator of restaurants in Washington and Oregon. Throughout his tenure at Azteca, Sanchez was subjected to a relentless campaign of insults, name-calling, and vulgarities. Male coworkers and a male supervisor referred to Sanchez as "she" and "her," called him a "faggot" and a "female whore," mocked him for walking "like a woman," and derided him for not having sexual intercourse with a waitress he had befriended. The issue presented to the court was whether Sanchez was harassed because of sex.

Sanchez maintained that the verbal abuse he suffered was based on the perception that he was effeminate and failed to conform to male stereotypes. Thus, he argued, the source of the harassing conduct was his gender. The court agreed. The vulgar name-calling was cast in female terms, and the systematic abuse directed at him reflected coworker belief that he failed to act as a man should act. The court concluded that this verbal abuse was closely linked to gender, and thus the harassing conduct occurred because of sex.[6]

Does the harassment of a worker on account of his or her sexual orientation violate Title VII? In its *Oncale* decision, the Supreme Court did not suggest that male harassment of other males or female harassment of other females *always* violated Title VII. Rather, as has been stressed here, the court insisted that every alleged victim of same-sex harassment must demonstrate he or she was harassed because of his or her sex. A critical issue in these cases is whether the members of one sex are exposed to disadvantageous terms or conditions of employment to which members of the other sex are not exposed. This seems to eliminate claims alleging harassment because of sexual orientation. At first, the courts distinguished harassment on account of sex and harassment because of sexual orientation and dismissed those cases falling into the latter category. In 2002, however, the 9th Circuit Court of Appeals ruled to the contrary. The issue arose in litigation involving Medina Rene and his employer, the MGM Grand Hotel in Las Vegas.

Rene, who was openly gay, worked for the hotel as a butler, serving wealthy, high-profile, and famous guests. Rene provided evidence that his supervisor and several of his fellow butlers harassed him by blowing kisses at him, calling him "sweetheart," telling him crude jokes, and forcing him to view pictures of naked men having sex. They also caressed and hugged him and grabbed his crouch. When asked what motivated this harassing behavior, Rene responded, "because I am gay."

The 9th Circuit Court ruled that Rene's sexual orientation was irrelevant. The offensive conduct was clearly sexual and discriminatory.[7] Other courts have ruled that claims asserted by gays and lesbians, alleging that they were sexually harassed because of their sexual orientation, may be cognizable under Title VII but only if they are able to establish that they were subjected to conduct of a sexual nature that was offensive and discriminatory. It appears that the courts will continue to reject harassment claims based solely upon sexual orientation.

Chapter Twenty-Five

Retaliation

The reaction of an employer to a worker's discrimination charge, whether based on race, color, sex, national origin, religion, or age, does not differ greatly from its reaction to allegations of fraud or criminal activity. Employers are all too prone to strike back at any worker who even utters the word "discrimination." Once a worker accuses a supervisor or other company official of committing a discriminatory act, his life may be made extremely difficult. The victim of discrimination then also becomes a victim of retaliation.

Workers exercising the rights granted them by Title VII and the ADEA are protected from acts of employer retaliation. When Congress enacted Title VII, it decreed it unlawful for an employer to retaliate against a worker who charges it with a discriminatory policy or practice or who participates in a legal or administrative proceeding relating to the company's employment policies or practices. Once a worker has engaged in a protected activity—defined as (1) an action opposing an act of discrimination, such as the filing of a charge of discrimination; (2) testifying on behalf of a fellow worker who has asserted a claim of discrimination; or (3) participating in an investigation of alleged discriminatory conduct—an employer is barred from retaliating against that worker on account of her participation in that protected activity.[1] The ADEA similarly protects workers against retaliatory acts.[2]

A retaliation claim consists of four components, each of which must be established by the claimant:

1. The worker participated in a protected activity.
2. At the time, the worker was performing his or her job functions in accordance with the employer's legitimate expectations.

3. Subsequently the worker was subjected to an adverse employment action.
4. A causal connection existed between the worker's participation in the protected activity and the adverse action.

An employer who ignores its legal duty to refrain from retaliatory acts subjects itself to liability for damages suffered by the worker as a consequence of those acts. Charges alleging retaliation in violation of Title VII precepts, filed annually with the EEOC, steadily increased from just over 18,000 in 1997 to nearly 38,000 in 2012. This steady rise in the filings of retaliation charges reflects an increased tendency on the part of employers to react negatively and irresponsibly to charges of discriminatory conduct as well as an increased willingness on the part of workers to call their employers to task for their acts of retaliatory conduct.

Prior to 2006, the courts held that an employer action directed against a worker engaged in a protected activity, if it resulted in a material adverse change in that worker's terms and conditions of employment, could provide the basis for a retaliation charge. In that year, the Supreme Court broadened the concept of retaliatory conduct, ruling that Title VII's ban on retaliation is not limited to actions adversely affecting a worker's terms and conditions of employment. Although the court's decision in *Burlington Northern & Santa Fe Railway Co. v. White* involved claims of sex discrimination, the court made it clear that its newly formulated definition of retaliatory conduct applied to cases involving all categories of discrimination.

In the *Burlington* case, Sheila White, the only woman working in the maintenance of way department of the Burlington Northern & Santa Fe Railway, operated a forklift. Her supervisor was not happy with her in that position, and he repeatedly told her that the department was no place for a woman. He also made insulting and inappropriate remarks to her in the presence of her male coworkers. White complained, and after company officials conducted an internal investigation, Burlington suspended the supervisor and ordered him to attend sexual harassment training sessions. Immediately afterward, Marvin Brown, another member of Burlington's supervisory staff, removed White from forklift duty and assigned her to track laborer tasks, explaining that her reassignment reflected coworker complaints that "a more senior man" should have the "less arduous and cleaner job" of forklift operator. White then filed a charge with the EEOC, claiming that her reassignment amounted to sex discrimination and retaliation for having complained about her supervisor. A few days later, White had an argument with another supervisor, and later that day Brown charged her with insubordination and suspended her without pay. White invoked internal grievance procedures, and these led to her reinstatement with back pay for the thirty-seven day period of her suspension.

Subsequently, she filed another retaliation charge with the EEOC and later commenced litigation against Burlington on the ground that its decisions to change her job responsibilities and suspend her without pay constituted acts of retaliation in violation of Title VII. A jury found in her favor, and that verdict was affirmed on appeal. When the case reached the Supreme Court, Burlington argued that employment actions prohibited by the antiretaliation provisions of Title VII should be limited to those that affect an employee's "compensation, terms, conditions, or privileges of employment" and that, since White's wages and hours were not affected by her reassignment, she did not suffer an adverse employment action as that term is understood in the law. The court did not agree and ruled that acts of retaliation extend beyond those that affected her compensation and other terms of her employment, since an employer can effectively retaliate against an employee by taking actions not directly related to her employment, even by causing her harm outside the workplace.

A reassignment to a more difficult, dirtier, and less prestigious job is no less retaliatory because it does not result in a diminishment in pay or benefits. Similarly, a thirty-seven-day suspension without compensation is no less retaliatory because in the end the worker is fully compensated, since many employees would find a five-week period without a paycheck to be a material hardship.

How much harm need be done before an employer's conduct is considered retaliatory? Not much, responded the Supreme Court. The action against the worker must be sufficiently severe to dissuade a reasonable worker from charging the employer with discriminatory conduct. In other words, the retaliatory act must be of such severity as to deter the worker from filing a complaint against the employer because of the fear that such an act would likely motivate the employer to undertake additional retaliatory measures against the worker. The court deliberately phrased this standard in general terms, since the significance of any given act of retaliation often depends upon particular circumstances:

> The real social impact of workplace behavior often depends on a constellation of surrounding circumstances, expectations, and relationships which are not fully captured by a single recitation of the words used or the physical acts performed. . . . A schedule change in an employee's work schedule may make little difference to many workers, but may matter enormously to a young mother with school age children. . . . A supervisor's refusal to invite an employee to lunch is normally trivial, a non-actionable petty slight. But to retaliate by excluding an employee from a weekly training lunch that contributes significantly to the employee's professional advancement might well deter a reasonable employee from complaining about discrimination.

Justice Breyer, writing for the court, stated that the standard that the court was adopting would not impose a "general civility code" on the workplace. Rather, it would "screen out trivial conduct while effectively capturing those acts that are likely to dissuade employees from complaining."

White's new job was less prestigious and its duties more arduous and dirtier than those of a forklift operator. Such a reassignment of responsibilities would have been considered materially adverse to a reasonable worker, sufficient to dissuade her from charging the employer with discriminatory conduct. White's suspension without pay led the court to the same conclusion. She and her family had to live thirty-seven days without income, not knowing whether she would ever be allowed to return to work. An employee facing a choice between retaining her job and filing a discrimination complaint might well decline to charge her employer with discriminatory conduct, since the prospect of an indefinite suspension without pay could very well act as a deterrent to taking action against her employer that might add to her problems.

White chose to charge Burlington with discriminatory conduct and retaliation. In allowing her to do both, the Supreme Court greatly expanded those circumstances in which workers may charge their employers with retaliation.[3]

This was the first of three recent Supreme Court cases in which the court ruled in favor of workers who charged their employers with retaliatory conduct. These decisions widely expand the concept of retaliation and its role in the enforcement of Title VII's and the ADEA's ban on antidiscriminatory conduct.

The question in the second of these cases required the court to determine whether the protection against retaliation extended to an employee who spoke out about discrimination, not on her own initiative but in response to questions during an employer's internal investigation. In 2002, the Metropolitan Government of Nashville and Davidson County, Tennessee (Metro), began looking into rumors of sexual harassment by the Metro School District's employee relations director, Gene Hughes. When a Metro human resources officer asked Vicky Crawford, a thirty-year Metro employee, whether she had witnessed "inappropriate behavior" on the part of Hughes, Crawford described several instances of sexually harassing behavior. Although Metro took no action against Hughes, it fired Crawford and the two other accusers. In Crawford's case, she was charged with embezzlement. Crawford then claimed Metro had retaliated against her because she had reported Hughes's behavior. She then filed a charge with the EEOC and later a lawsuit against Metro.

As noted, the Title VII antiretaliation provision makes it an unlawful employment practice for an employer to discriminate against any of its employees because (1) she has opposed an unlawful employment practice or

(2) she has made a charge, testified, assisted, or participated in any manner in an investigation, proceeding, or hearing.[4] The first is known as the *opposition clause*, the other as the *participation clause*, and Crawford accused Metro of violating both.

But the lower court that considered Crawford's claims rejected that position on the ground that Crawford had merely answered the questions of the investigator, and since she had not yet initiated a claim, neither clause protected her against acts of retaliation. The Supreme Court refused to accept that limitation on the retaliation protections and ruled in favor of Crawford.[5]

The third retaliation case decided by the Supreme Court related to discrimination and retaliation charges filed by an engaged couple. Eric Thompson and his fiancée, Miriam Regalado, both worked for North American Stainless (NAS).Three weeks after Regalado filed charges against NAS alleging sex discrimination, NAS fired Thompson. Thompson then filed his own charge, claiming that NAS fired him so as to retaliate against Regalado for filing her sex discrimination charge. When Thompson sued NAS, the district court dismissed his case on the ground that third-party retaliation claims were not permitted by Title VII, which prohibits discrimination against an employee "because he has made a [Title VII] charge."[6] The court of appeals affirmed, reasoning that Thompson was not entitled to sue NAS for retaliation because he had not engaged in any activity protected by the statute.

When the Supreme Court considered the case, it first referred to its decision in the *Burlington Northern & Santa Fe Railway Co.* case where it ruled that Title VII's antiretaliation provisions are not limited to employer conduct that affects the terms and conditions of employment. "Rather, Title VII's anti-retaliation provision prohibits any employer action that 'well might have dissuaded a reasonable worker from making or supporting a charge of discrimination.'"[7] The court thought it was "obvious" that a worker might be dissuaded from filing an EEOC charge if she knew her fiancé would be fired.

The more difficult question for the court was whether Thompson could sue NAS for its alleged violation of Title VII. The statute provides that "a civil action may be brought . . . by the person claiming to be aggrieved."[8] It is arguable that the aggrievement referred to is nothing more than the minimal standing requirement, and Thompson's claim undoubtedly met that requirement. NAS took a position at the other extreme from the position that "person aggrieved" merely means standing to sue, arguing that it is a term of art that refers only to the employee who engaged in the protected activity. But the court rejected this reasoning, stating that if Congress had intended that result, it would more naturally have said "person claiming to have been discriminated against" rather than "person claiming to be aggrieved." The court concluded that it saw "no basis in text or prior practice for limiting the latter phrase to the person who was the subject of unlawful retaliation":

[W]e conclude that Thompson falls within the zone of interests protected by Title VII. Thompson was an employee of NAS, and the purpose of Title VII is to protect employees from their employers' unlawful actions. Moreover, accepting the facts as alleged, Thompson is not an accidental victim of the retaliation—collateral damage, so to speak, of the employer's unlawful act. To the contrary, injuring him was the employer's intended means of harming Regalado. Hurting him was the unlawful act by which the employer punished her. In those circumstances, we think Thompson well within the zone of interests sought to be protected by Title VII. He is a person aggrieved with standing to sue.[9]

The Supreme Court has often adopted a negative approach in interpreting the antidiscrimination statutes (chapter 27). Its pro-business stance has led to the defeat of many discrimination claims, and its cramped interpretations of the scope of those statutes has made it materially more difficult for plaintiff workers to prevail. On the other hand, it was generally believed that the court would consistently expand the scope of the retaliation provisions of those statutes, rendering it significantly more likely that workers would be able to obtain adequate relief in cases where their employers have turned to retaliatory conduct. But on June 24, 2013, the court reversed course.

On that day, the court ruled that a retaliation case requires a more rigorous standard of proof than an ordinary Title VII discrimination case. Instead of holding a defendant liable upon proof that a discriminatory reason was a motivating factor for an employer's decision alleged to have been discriminatory, the court declared that liability would attach in a retaliation case only if the plaintiff proved that the desire to retaliate was the *but-for cause* of the challenged employment action.

Writing in dissent, Justice Ginsburg said the tougher "but-for causation standard" would undercut efforts to fight employment discrimination:

Similarly worded, the ban on discrimination and the ban on retaliation . . . have traveled together. . . . Today's decision, however, drives a wedge between the twin safeguards in . . . mixed motive cases. To establish discrimination, all agree, the complaining party need show only that race, color, religion, sex, or national origin was a 'motivating factor' in an employer's adverse action; an employer's proof that 'other factors also motivated the action' will not defeat the discrimination claim. . . . But a retaliation claim, the court insists, must meet a stricter standard: the claim will fail unless the complainant shows 'but-for' causation, i.e., that the employer would not have taken the adverse employment action but for a design to retaliate. In so reining in retaliation claims, the Court misapprehends what our decisions teach: Retaliation for complaining about discrimination is tightly bonded to core prohibition and cannot be disassociated from it.

Justice Ginsburg concluded that this decision should prompt Congress to act to reverse this ruling.[10]

Chapter Twenty-Six

Arbitration

An employer being sued by one of its workers for employment discrimination will do nearly anything to avoid trial before a jury. Workers who successfully litigate their cases before a jury can reasonably expect to attain a significant measure of relief. At times, they are made the recipients of huge damages awards. Thus, it is not surprising that employers abhor jury trials and do everything within their power to avoid them. On the other hand, attorneys who customarily represent workers, recognizing the advantages to be attained, nearly always insist on trial by jury for their clients.

The fear of a jury trial has prompted management to alter its approach to preparing a discrimination case for trial. This fear has left its mark on the litigation process itself, profoundly influencing the strategies of lawyers for the employers as well as lawyers for the workers. The worker's counsel engages in pretrial discovery with the aim of developing a record of testimony and documentary evidence that will be viewed favorably by the jurors. Lawyers for the employer, on the other hand, as a consequence of their disdain for the jury trial, devote the greater part of their attention to developing a record that will enhance the prospect of a dismissal of the worker's case before it reaches the jury. The motion for summary judgment is a powerful weapon used by the defendant's counsel to avoid a trial before a jury.

Employers, however, have available an even more effective means of evading a jury trial. In fact, they possess the means of barring the judicial system from adjudicating any discrimination claims that are asserted against them. Securities brokerage firms were among the first to master this approach.

These securities firms required each newly hired worker to sign an employment form that required the worker to submit all future employment disputes to arbitration. Lawyers for these securities brokerage firms argued that a worker who signed such a form waived her right to a judicial forum and a trial by jury of any claims made by the worker against the firm; that the worker waived her right to sue the employer for employment discrimination; and that, as a consequence, the worker may be compelled to arbitrate any discrimination claim later alleged against the firm. If the worker violates this covenant not to sue and initiates litigation against the firm, the securities firm, with the signed form in hand, may obtain a court order compelling the worker to move her discrimination claim to the arbitral forum, thus assuring the firm that a jury will never hear the worker's case.

Workers argued that a compulsory or pre-dispute agreement to arbitrate discrimination claims is inconsistent with the statutory scheme contemplated by Congress when it enacted Title VII and the ADEA. These statutes provide for a two-step resolution of discrimination claims: the first, an administrative process conducted by the EEOC, and the second, a judicial process conducted before the courts. From the workers' viewpoint, arbitration should play no role in this process.

Prior to 1991, the courts generally held that a worker could not waive the right to litigate employment discrimination claims. But in 1991, in the age discrimination case *Gilmer v. Interstate/Johnson Lane Corp.*, the Supreme Court declared that no inconsistency existed between the social issues fostered by antidiscrimination statutes and pre-dispute agreements to arbitrate age disputes:

> Gilmer also argues that compulsory arbitration is improper because it deprives claimants of the judicial forum provided for by the ADEA. Congress, however, did not explicitly preclude arbitration or other non-judicial resolution of claims, even in its recent amendments to the ADEA . . . Gilmer's argument ignores the ADEA's flexible approach to resolution of claims. The EOC, for example, is directed to pursue "informal methods of conciliation, conference, and persuasion" . . . which suggests that out-of-court dispute resolution, such as arbitration, is consistent with the statutory scheme established by Congress.[1]

Once given Supreme Court approval, pre-dispute arbitration agreements spread to other industries, and the arbitration of employment discrimination claims quickly became the employers' most favored method of resolving these disputes. Despite the many difficulties workers and their counsel have experienced with the courts (chapter 28) arbitration is not a viable alternative to judicial resolution of discrimination complaints. Compulsory, pre-dispute arbitration is unacceptable for a number of reasons.

THE WORKER IS NOT FREE TO REJECT ARBITRATION

A pre-dispute arbitration agreement is basically nonnegotiable. The worker is required, as a condition of employment, or as a condition to remaining employed, to consent to the arbitration of all future employment disputes. These agreements appear in employment agreements, employment application forms, and employee handbooks. In all events, the worker is presented with a take-it-or-leave-it situation: "Agree to arbitration, or you don't get the job."

By agreeing to arbitration, the worker waives his statutory right to a judicial determination of any discrimination claim that the worker may later assert. But a waiver of a statutory right will be considered valid only if made voluntarily and knowingly. When the worker's choice is between the acceptance of arbitration as a method of resolving future disputes or the relinquishment of a desirable position, the worker's agreement to arbitrate cannot be considered voluntary. An agreement to arbitrate disputes that have not yet occurred, the nature and identity of which are purely conjectural, cannot be considered to have been made knowingly. Yet these agreements to arbitrate future disputes are routinely enforced by the courts.

Experience and common sense tells us that an unemployed job applicant cannot afford to be overly concerned about problems that may never occur in the employment relationship. First and foremost, the worker needs a job and will agree to almost anything to get that job. Freedom of contract in these circumstances is a fiction. Employers cannot justify the enforcement of an arbitration agreement imposed upon workers as a condition of employment simply by arguing that the worker voluntarily and knowingly agreed to arbitration. Nonetheless, employers, aided by the Supreme Court, have found a near fail-proof method of avoiding jury trials of discrimination claims.

ARBITRAL FORUMS LACK THE BENEFITS AND PROTECTIONS OF THE COURT SYSTEM

In a lifetime, a worker may be involved in a single employment dispute requiring resolution by a third party, such as a court or a panel of arbitrators. Employers, who require their workers to submit disputes to arbitration, appear before the same panel of arbitrators time and again. While the worker typically has only one experience with these arbitrators, the employer and the arbitrators may know each other well. Because they are paid for their services, the arbitrators want to be selected for future arbitrations, and an employer is far more likely to select arbitrators who have previously decided in its favor. Furthermore, inasmuch as it is unlikely that the worker will again appear before these particular arbitrators, the arbitrators have no concern about the worker's failure to select them in the future. One study showed that while 22 percent of race discrimination claimants won their cases in court, only 5 percent were successful in arbitration.[2] In these circumstances, the worker is justifiably concerned that the arbitrators may be biased in favor of the employer.

Even with the hostility exhibited by some members of the federal bench toward discrimination cases (chapter 27), workers and their attorneys favor judges over arbitrators, because judges have a great deal of experience in dealing with employment discrimination cases while arbitrators do not. Some years ago, when arbitration was first offered as an alternative to judicial resolution of disputes, the business community favored arbitration, primarily because it was commonly believed that business disputes could be more readily resolved by arbitrators who were familiar with the particular business giving rise to the dispute. At that time, the knowledge and experience of the arbitrator was the driving force behind the arbitral concept. But arbitrators are totally inexperienced in the nuances of the antidiscrimination laws. The underlying reason that could possibly justify the arbitration of discrimination complaints is missing.

When an arbitrator makes a mistake, the mistake probably will remain uncorrected, as the judicial review of arbitration decisions is severely limited by law. Recently, a panel of arbitrators ruled in favor of a worker but then failed to provide in their award for the payment of the worker's attorney's fees. When the worker complained to the court, the court refused to intervene to correct the mistake, even though the law clearly provides that a worker who prevails on a discrimination claim is entitled to recover his attorney's fees.[3]

Arbitration favors the employer in another respect. Pre-hearing discovery in arbitral proceedings is considerably more limited than the pre-trial discovery available in court cases. Arbitral procedures generally allow only minimal discovery, while the Federal Rules of Civil Procedure call for very broad discovery. Although employers are often guilty of discovery abuse in court cases, the worker would rather suffer that abuse than be denied the discovery needed to develop the evidence required to support the worker's case. To the extent that the worker's discovery is limited, the worker's chance of success is reduced.

Limited discovery that denies the worker access to the employer's documents and records may materially undermine the development of the worker's case. Under such circumstances, the employer will be free to use its own documents to its own advantage while preventing the worker from obtaining its documents that may support her position. For example, personnel records of other employees may provide evidence of widespread disparate treatment. In a judicial proceeding, the court would order these records be made available to the worker; but in an arbitral proceeding, their availability to the worker is far less likely.

In the federal court system, the appointment of magistrate judges to oversee pre-trial discovery assures both the worker and the employer that the discovery process will be conducted fairly, while affording both parties discovery broad enough in scope to develop their cases. Nothing of a similar nature exists in the arbitral system. Arbitrators, inexperienced in the area of employment discrimination, not having the slightest inkling of what it takes in the way of discovery to construct a case around circumstantial evidence, are totally at sea when it comes to the discovery process. The inability of the arbitrator to serve a meaningful role in this process serves to benefit the employer and materially undermines the worker's ability to present a viable case.

These objections to the arbitral process were considered by the Supreme Court in the *Gilmer* case, but in each instance the court rejected them.

ARBITRATION DOES NOT ADEQUATELY FURTHER THE PURPOSES OF TITLE VII AND THE ADEA

Civil rights cases involving major public policy issues, which require the analysis of complex legal questions, are best left to the courts. A federal judge in Massachusetts said it best: "[W]hatever the competence of arbitrators to resolve disputes in a commercial setting . . . the litigation of civil rights claims require[s] different sensibilities. Civil rights litigation . . . not only calls for 'dispute resolution,' but require[s] the articulation of public rights and obligations."[4]

A judge decides a case by writing an opinion, explaining his decision and citing the precedents he relied upon in support of the decision. An appellate court reviewing the determination of a lower court also writes an opinion, detailing its reasons for upholding or reversing the lower court's decision. Arbitrators generally do not write opinions. The arbitration of discrimination claims, therefore, retards development of the law inasmuch as it deprives courts the opportunity of interpreting the statute in the light of differing factual situations. Court decisions, and the precedents that develop through the judicial process, guide employers with respect to distinguishing permissible conduct from the impermissible. Unpublished, one-line decisions of an arbitrator accomplish nothing in that regard.

Five years after the Supreme Court decision in the *Gilmer* case, a prominent employer's lawyer surveyed decisions rendered in employment-related disputes by arbitrators sitting on New York Stock Exchange (NYSE) and the National Association of Securities Dealers (NASD) arbitration panels. His survey disclosed that the securities firms prevailed in 76 percent of the cases heard by NASD arbitrators and in 59 percent of the cases heard by NYSE arbitrators. He concluded that employers experienced greater success in arbitration than in the courts, and even in those cases where the employers lost in arbitration, the size of the damage awards levied against the employers was smaller.[5]

Following the 1991 Supreme Court decision in *Gilmer*, the use of pre-dispute arbitration agreements by employers spread from the securities industry to other areas of the business world, with the securities firm employment form serving as a stepping stone to a variety of documents incorporating pre-dispute arbitration provisions.

One of the types of documents employers have used that requires workers to resort to arbitration for the resolution of employment disputes is the employee handbook. The employee handbook loomed large in the litigation involving Sharon Kinnebrew and her employer. After Kinnebrew had begun working for Gulf Insurance Company in Texas, the company instituted a pre-dispute arbitration policy, and it mailed copies of its arbitration policy to all its workers, along with an explanatory memorandum. Gulf also outlined the arbitration policy in its employee handbook, which included this provision: "Arbitration is an essential element of your employment relationship and is a condition of your employment. This policy makes arbitration required, and exclusive, for the resolution of all employment disputes which may arise."

Kinnebrew, a claims administrative manager, discovered she was being paid substantially less than the male manager who held the position before her, and she decided to file a claim against Gulf for sex discrimination. Rather than submitting her sex discrimination claim to arbitration, Kinnebrew filed a discrimination claim with the EEOC and thereafter filed suit with the federal court.

When Gulf argued before the court that Kinnebrew's claim should be dismissed, for the reason that she had agreed to the arbitration of all future employment disputes, Kinnebrew countered that she had never agreed to arbitration, that Gulf had unilaterally distributed copies of the new policy to its workers without adequately explaining the effect of the policy and without obtaining their acceptance or express agreement to the policy. The court rejected Kinnebrew's position, pointing out that she had received a copy of the newly initiated policy and had continued her employment with Gulf. In other words, according to the court, Kinnebrew had the option either of accepting the policy or quitting. Because she did not quit, she waived her statutory right to have her sex discrimination claims tried before a jury of her peers.

No evidence was submitted to the court showing that Kinnebrew understood the implications of the arbitration policy, that she specifically formulated an intent to accept the new policy, or that she consciously waived her statutory right to a jury trial of future disputes. No evidence of any kind was submitted showing that Kinnebrew actually agreed to arbitration. But the court simply ignored this lack of evidence and concluded that she must have assented to the new policy, or else she would have resigned. The court ignored the legal requirement that a waiver of a statutory right must be made voluntarily and knowingly.[6]

Peter Nghiem was required to submit his employment discrimination claim to arbitration even though he had signed an employment contract that did not contain any provision for arbitration. Nghiem worked for NEC Electronics in California for nine years before being fired. At the outset of his employment, Nghiem and NEC entered into a written employment agreement that provided, among other things, that it could not be varied or modified except by another written agreement signed by both parties.

NEC's employee handbook provided for a "Problem Resolution Process," a process that culminated in arbitration. After he was dismissed, Nghiem abided by the terms of this process, including the arbitration. When the arbitrator ruled against him, Nghiem filed suit in court against NEC, arguing that the arbitrator's adverse decision was not binding on him since he had never signed an agreement to arbitrate. The court rejected Nghiem's position, holding that his participation in the arbitral process constituted his agreement to arbitrate. Thus, the court ruled that his participation served as a modification of his employment agreement, even though the agreement itself stated that it could not be modified except by another written agreement signed by both parties.[7]

In 1997, the EEOC announced that it was firmly opposed to the enforcement of arbitration agreements imposed upon workers as a condition of employment. It felt compelled to announce this policy, publicly and formally, since it noted an increasing number of employers were requiring workers, as a condition of gaining employment, to give up their rights to pursue employment discrimination claims in court and to agree instead to the resolution of these disputes through arbitration. The use of these agreements, according to the EEOC, was no longer primarily limited to the securities industry; the practice had spread to retail, restaurant and hotel, health care, broadcasting, security services, and other areas of the business sector.

The EEOC prefaced its policy statement by reminding the public that federal civil rights laws, including the laws prohibiting discrimination in employment, have played a unique role in American jurisprudence: "They flow directly from core Constitutional principles, and this nation's history testifies to their necessity and profound importance." The EEOC then stated that any analysis of mandatory arbitration of rights guaranteed by these laws must "be squarely based in an understanding of the history and purpose of these laws." While the EEOC is the primary federal agency responsible for enforcing the employment discrimination laws, the courts have been vested with the final responsibility for statutory enforcement through the interpretation of the statutes while adjudicating claims. The EEOC then proceeded to enumerate the reasons why that responsibility must remain with the courts:

1. Many of the legal principles governing the application of these laws have been developed through judicial interpretations and case precedents. Without the courts, doctrines essential to free the workplace of unlawful discrimination would not have been developed.
2. The courts are public bodies; the exercise of judicial authority is subject to public scrutiny. When courts fail to apply these laws in accordance with public values, they are subject to correction by higher courts and by Congress.
3. The courts also play a critical role in preventing violations of the law. Court decisions give guidance to those covered by the laws, thus enhancing voluntary compliance with them. By issuing orders and decisions, later made known to the public, the courts identify violators of the law and their conduct. "As has been illustrated time and again, the risks of negative publicity and blemished business reputation can be powerful influences on behavior."
4. The courts cannot fulfill their enforcement responsibilities if workers do not have access to the courts. Individual workers act as "private attorneys general" in bringing claims to the courts, serving not only their own private interest, but also as instruments of deterrence of would-be violators of the statutes.

The EEOC expressed its concern that pre-dispute arbitration "privatizes" the enforcement of the employment discrimination laws, thus undermining public enforcement of those laws. The nature of the arbitral process allows for minimal public accountability of arbitrators, as arbitrators answer only to the private parties to the dispute but not to the public. The arbitrator is part of a system of self-government created by and for the private parties. Because arbitrators' decisions are private, employers are not held publicly accountable for their violations of the law, and this lack of public disclosure weakens deterrence of further violations.

The EEOC also observed that the arbitral process does not allow for the development of the law. Arbitration decisions are usually not written and in any event are not made public. As a result, there is virtually no opportunity for the courts to correct errors of statutory interpretation.

The EEOC confirmed the long-held concerns of employment lawyers. Arbitrators are often biased in favor of the employer, discovery is overly limited, and arbitration is imposed upon the worker simply because the employers stand a greater chance of success in arbitration than in a court before a jury.

The EEOC concluded that further use of arbitration agreements as a condition of employment should be barred because it harms both the civil rights of the claimant and the public interest in eradicating discrimination: "Those whom the law seeks to regulate should not be permitted to exempt themselves from federal enforcement of civil rights laws. No one should be permitted to deprive civil rights claimants of the choice to vindicate their statutory rights in the courts—an avenue of redress determined by Congress to be essential to enforcement."[8]

That was where the matter stood when the Supreme Court had another occasion to examine the matter. In 1995, Saint Clair Adams applied for a job with Circuit City Stores and signed an employment application that included this provision:

> I agree that I will settle any and all previously asserted claims, disputes, or controversies arising out of my application or candidacy for employment, employment and/or cessation of employment with Circuit City, exclusively by final and binding arbitration before a neutral Arbitrator. By way of example only, such claims include claims under federal, state, and local statutory or common law, such as the Age Discrimination in Employment Act, Title VII of the Civil Rights Act of 1964, as amended, including the amendments of the Civil Rights Act of 1991, the American Disabilities Act, the law of contract and the law of tort.

Circuit City hired Adams and assigned him to its store in Santa Rosa, California. Two years later, Adams filed an employment discrimination against the company. Circuit City in turn sued Adams, seeking to enjoin his suit and compel arbitration of his claims. When the case reached the Supreme Court in 2000, the primary issue before the court related to the scope of the Federal Arbitration Act. Section 1 of the FAA excludes from its coverage "contracts of employment of seamen, railroad employees, or any other class of workers engaged in foreign or interstate commerce." Was Adams' agreement to arbitrate claims against Circuit City excluded from FAA coverage, thus freeing him to litigate his employment discrimination claims against Circuit City in the courts?

To the supporters of America's antidiscrimination laws, Adams's agreement to arbitrate his claims against Circuit City appeared to fall within the scope of the FAA provision that excluded from arbitration "contracts . . . of workers engaged in . . . interstate commerce." But when the court decided the case in 2001, it held to the contrary—those words applied only to "transportation workers" such as seamen and railroad workers.[9] Thus the court chose not to change course. The restrictions placed on employment discrimination claimants by the court in its *Gilmer* decision would continue to block their efforts to litigate their Title VII and ADEA claims in the courts.

Senator Patrick Leahy, US Senator from Vermont and chairman of the Senate Judiciary Committee, subsequently chaired a hearing of the committee called to consider the question: Has the Supreme Court misinterpreted laws designed to protect American workers? Senator Leahy commented on the issue at some length:

> The Supreme Court's recent decisions make it more difficult for victims of
> employment discrimination to seek relief in court, and more difficult for those
> victims to get their day in court to vindicate their rights. . . . The Supreme
> Court's misinterpretation of the Federal Arbitration Act in the *Circuit City*
> case threatens to undermine the effective enforcement of our civil rights
> laws. . . . Congress never intended this law to become a hammer for corpora-
> tions to use against their employees. But in *Circuit City*, the Supreme Court
> allowed for just that when it extended the scope and force of the arbitration act
> by judicial fiat, so as to make employment arbitrations provisions enforce-
> able. . . . Now, after the *Circuit City* decision, employers are able to unilateral-
> ly strip employees of their civil rights by including arbitration clauses in every
> employment contract they draft. Countless large corporations have done
> so. . . . There is no rule of law in arbitration. There are no juries . . . . There is
> no transparency. And . . . there is no justice. [10]

Obviously, employers cannot require their employees to sign contracts of
employment that violate or dilute the protections of Title VII or the ADEA.
But pre-dispute agreements to arbitrate discrimination claims accomplish
that result. Some judges sitting in the lower courts—the federal courts of
appeal and the district courts—understand that this has occurred and have
undertaken steps to limit the application of the *Gilmer* rule, while holding to
its basic commands.

Susan Rosenberg signed a standard securities industry form agreeing to
arbitrate certain claims after being hired by Merrill Lynch, Pierce, Fenner &
Smith as a trainee financial consultant. The form itself did not state which
claims were to be arbitrated. When her employment was later terminated,
Rosenberg filed suit alleging age and gender discrimination and related
claims. Merrill Lynch moved to enforce the agreement and compel arbitration in the arbitration system of the New York Stock Exchange. The court
refused to enforce the agreement because it did not state that it covered all
employment disputes including those arising under Title VII and the ADEA.
"Had Merrill Lynch taken the modest effort required to make relevant information regarding the arbitrability of employment disputes available to Rosenberg, as it committed itself to do, it would have been able to compel
Rosenberg to arbitration." Thus on very limited grounds, the court denied
Merrill Lynch's application to compel Rosenberg to arbitrate her age and
gender claims. [11]

Another court invalidated an arbitration agreement because it was "egre-
giously unfair" to the company's employees. Under its rules, the company
was free to name as arbitrators those who had existing relationships, financial
or familial, with management. In fact, the rules did not even prohibit the
company from placing members of management on the list of arbitrators.
Further, nothing in the rules restricted the company from punishing arbitrators who ruled against the company by removing them from the list. "Given

the unrestricted control that [the company] has over the panel, the selection of an impartial decision maker would be a surprising result." By promulgating this system of warped rules, the company so skewed the process in its favor that its employees were denied arbitration in any meaningful sense of the word. "To uphold the promulgation of this aberrational scheme under the heading of arbitration would undermine, not advance, the federal policy favoring alternative dispute resolution. This we refuse to do." [12]

The DC Court of Appeals listed what it would require before giving approval to arbitration as an adequate substitute for a judicial forum:

1. The arbitration agreement must provide for neutral arbitrators.
2. That agreement must require more than minimal discovery.
3. The arbitrator's award must be promulgated in written form.
4. All types of relief that would otherwise be available in a court proceeding must also be available, under the terms of the arbitration agreement, to the arbitrator.
5. The employee has access to the arbitral forum without cost or obligation to pay the expenses of the arbitration or the arbitrator's fee.

Thus minimal standards of procedural fairness must be satisfied before a civil action may be stayed and arbitration ordered. [13]

The Supreme Court took up the subject again in 2009, reaffirming its commitment to the arbitral rather than the judicial forum. The court held that a collective bargaining agreement requiring union members to submit age discrimination claims against their employers to arbitration was binding upon and enforceable against individual members who filed ADEA claims against their employers. [14] This ruling reversed the court's position on the issue that had remained unaltered for thirty-five years. [15] One commentator expressed his frustration with the path the court was following: "Arbitration is the 'darling' of the Supreme Court of the United States. Milton Friedman lived not only in the flesh, but continues to live in the way that the Supreme Court embraces arbitration." [16] There exists little doubt that the court, if again confronted with the issue, will continue to support arbitration over judicial proceedings.

The court's broad endorsement of arbitration has motivated increasing numbers of employers to make it a condition of employment for newly hired workers to agree to submit all employment discrimination issues to arbitration. The court has simply ignored the fact that the difference in the bargaining power inherent to the hire of a new employee makes such agreements inherently coercive and unfair.

The Arbitration Fairness Act of 2013, introduced in both houses of Congress, would ban pre-dispute forced arbitration of employment and civil rights claims. [17] Congressional adoption of the AFA is necessary to end the expanding practice of employers to force workers to give up their rights to litigate employment and civil rights disputes as a condition of their employment.

This practice must be halted.

VI

The EEOC and the Private Attorney

Chapter Twenty-Seven

Political and Judicial Opposition to the Employment Discrimination Laws

The support for the employment discrimination laws, extended by presidents serving since 1964, has varied widely. President Johnson, following in President Kennedy's footsteps, was the driving force behind enactment of the 1964 Civil Rights Act and also the 1967 Age Discrimination in Employment Act. The Nixon administration was generally supportive of efforts to strengthen and expand civil rights, and Nixon's Justice Department joined in the battle to persuade the Supreme Court to adopt the disparate impact concept (chapter 4).

When the Supreme Court restrictively interpreted Title VII's sex discrimination provisions by ruling that discrimination on the basis of pregnancy was not sex discrimination, the Carter administration responded with the Pregnancy Discrimination Act of 1978 (chapters 5 and 9). President Carter also expanded the powers and functions of the EEOC and gave the agency responsibility for enforcing the ADEA.

With the arrival of the Reagan administration, presidential support for Title VII and the ADEA declined precipitously. Reagan administrative officials, determined to radically alter civil rights enforcement promoted by previous administrations, sought to refocus civil rights enforcement on blatant, intentional violations of the law, while de-emphasizing the disparate impact concept. Overall, the Reagan administration was unsuccessful in effecting fundamental changes in the enforcement of Title VII and the ADEA.[1] Nonetheless, as noted by an attorney for the Justice Department at the time, President Reagan's policies left their mark: "Although the basic structure of [Title VII] has remained sound, federal enforcement agencies have been hard hit by the policies and decisions of the recent past, . . . by the Reagan administration's advocacy of the rights and interests of white males and employers; and by the widespread perception both within and without the government that the Reagan administration would have been pleased if it did not have to confront the problems that follow from vigorous enforcement of the law."[2]

President George H. W. Bush signed into law the Civil Rights Act of 1991 (chapter 9), despite the fact that he had vetoed a similar act the previous year. As noted earlier, the 1991 act provided for jury trials and for compensatory and punitive damages in cases involving intentional discrimination, but it also placed caps on the amounts of damages that could be awarded.

The Clinton administration was generally supportive of efforts to expand civil rights but appeared to concentrate its efforts outside the area of employment discrimination. The George W. Bush administration, on the other hand, assumed a negative stance toward employment discrimination issues that arose during its two terms. It opposed the broad retaliation concepts espoused by the EEOC and later adopted by the Supreme Court. It rejected the EEOC position on the issues raised in the Ledbetter lawsuit against Goodyear and entered the case on behalf of the company. President Obama, in contrast, demonstrated strong support for Title VII when he signed the Lilly Ledbetter Fair Pay Act, the first piece of legislation to cross his desk after he assumed the presidency (chapter 23).

Conservative presidents appoint conservatives as justices to the Supreme Court and judges of the courts of appeal and the district courts. Over time, conservative justices and judges have clearly shown that they are far less supportive of the employment discrimination laws than their liberal brethren. It is not surprising, therefore, that Reagan and both of the Bush administration appointees to the federal bench tend to be more conservative, are generally less sympathetic to the objectives of the employment discrimination laws, and appear less receptive to the positions asserted by workers suing their employers than the judges appointed by earlier administrations and by the Clinton and Obama administrations.[3]

Some judges are well known to favor employers over workers. A federal judge once told me that when she is confronted with a serious employment discrimination legal issue, she refrains from considering the written opinions of certain of her judicial brethren because their perception of the rights of workers is much narrower than what she thought was appropriate. Those judges advocating this narrower perception are well known to lawyers who represent workers, since their success record before these judges is low to nonexistent. For example, a review of the decisions rendered in employment discrimination cases by one federal judge sitting in New York, over a period of one year, showed that he ruled in favor of the employer in twelve of thirteen cases. Another judge's record is fourteen of sixteen cases in favor of the employer. This antipathy toward discrimination complainants is not concealed. One federal judge, highly critical of the number of age discrimination cases on his calendar, expressed the opinion that older workers are able to file these cases with no more evidence of age discrimination at hand "than a birth certificate and a pink slip."[4] Another judge stated that "no Federal District Court can ignore the wave of dubious and potentially extortionate discrimination cases currently flooding the Federal docket."[5]

This negative attitude may result from the massive wave of discrimination case filings that in recent years has at times clogged court dockets. Absent those cases, a judge's life would undoubtedly be a lot simpler. Judges appear, however, not to be aware of the role private attorneys play in preventing even greater numbers of filings of cases of questionable merit. A very high percentage of discrimination claims do not survive an attorney's initial investigation of the facts of the case, and thus these cases do not advance to the point where a formal complaint is filed with the court. Attorneys routinely advise prospective claimants not to sue, knowing they will be unable to sustain their burden of proving discrimination. In fact, some attorneys estimate that 90 percent or more of the workers conferring with them do not proceed beyond the initial investigation of their claims. My own experience confirms this.

Judges also appear to be unaware that the most meritorious discrimination cases are rarely seen in the trial courts, since these are the cases more often settled by employers before trial. Thus, judges normally see only the weaker of the workers' cases in their courtrooms. One study showed that only 8 percent of employment discrimination cases filed in the federal courts actually proceed to the trial stage.[6] If 90 percent of potential discrimination cases do not proceed beyond the lawyers' offices, then the courts actually are confronted with trying only .008 percent of all potential employment discrimination cases.

Some judges also appear unconvinced that older workers should be afforded protection from acts of age discrimination, and others appear less committed to ending age discrimination than to eradicating race and sex discrimination. These negative attitudes may explain the outcome of a review of jury verdicts in age discrimination cases in 1996. This study disclosed that 42 percent of jury verdicts in favor of age discrimination plaintiffs were subsequently overturned by the trial court or an appellate court.[7]

The negative attitude of the lower court judiciary toward employment discrimination cases in general reflects the negative attitude of a majority of the justices of the Supreme Court. Professor William P. Murphy of the University of North Carolina School of Law has noted in 1994 that not since the New Deal days had the Supreme Court given laws passed by Congress such hostile treatment. He pointed to the court's 1988–1989 term, in which the court decided fourteen employment law cases, thirteen of which were decided in favor of the employer. In all fourteen cases, Justices Rehnquist and Kennedy adopted positions advanced by the employer, and they were joined in thirteen of those cases by Justices White, O'Connor, and Scalia. Justices

Brennan and Marshall, on the other hand, most frequently supported the worker's position. As Professor Murphy observed, "It seems obvious that the determinant in employment law cases is something other than dispassionate and objective application of neutral principles. The majority and minority were clearly marching to different drummers."[8] It does not appear as if Professor Murphy would evaluate present justices of the court any differently.

Professor Murphy is one critic among many. Professor Charles Craver of the George Washington National Law Center also harshly criticized the positions taken by the court during the 1988–1989 term: "Shortly after Justice Kennedy's elevation to the Supreme Court, a five-Justice conservative bloc coalesced, consisting of Chief Justice Rehnquist and Justices White, O'Connor, Scalia, and Kennedy, and was intent on restructuring the employment discrimination laws. They evidenced a clear willingness to ignore both established Court precedent and previously acknowledged congressional intentions. . . . [They] took it upon themselves to engage in a wholly unprincipled rewriting of the basic civil rights statutes."[9]

When Justice White left the court, Justice Thomas joined the conservative bloc, thus guaranteeing additional problems for plaintiff workers. It was not long before the newly established bloc made it much more difficult for workers to prevail, even in typical disparate treatment cases (chapters 21 and 22). By 1991, Congress had had enough. It enacted the Civil Rights Act of 1991, basically restoring Title VII to its form as it existed before the conservative bloc had done its work (chapter 9).

In more recent years, three trends have dominated Supreme Court decisions:

1. In retaliation cases, the court has generally acted to expand the concept of retaliation and its role in the enforcement of Title VII and ADEA precepts (chapter 25). However, in its most recent decision in this area, the court reversed course and made it more difficult for workers to prevail in cases alleging retaliation in mixed-motive cases.[10]
2. The court persists in favoring the arbitration of employment discrimination disputes. The court's stand on this issue is particularly troublesome in those cases where provisions for the arbitration of employment disputes are contained in compulsory, pre-dispute worker waivers of the right to have discrimination complaints heard in a court of law (chapter 26).
3. Workers have prevailed more frequently than in the past, but most often in less significant and less contentious cases.

Despite these trends, another factor may have far greater significance in determining the path the present court currently follows on any given day. According to a *New York Times* study, this Court is far friendlier to business than any court since at least World War II:[11]

> In the eight years since chief Justice Roberts joined the court, it has allowed corporations to spend freely in elections . . ., has shielded them from class actions and human rights suits, and has made arbitration the favored way to resolve many disputes. Business groups say the Roberts court decisions have helped combat frivolous lawsuits, while plaintiffs' lawyers say the rulings have destroyed legitimate claims for harm from faulty products, discriminatory practices, and fraud.

The *Times* analysis referred to a study reported in the *Minnesota Law Review* that ranked thirty-six justices who served on the court between 1946 and 2011 by the proportion of their pro-business votes. Each of the five current conservative bloc justices was ranked in the top ten, with Justices Roberts and Alito ranked one and two.[12] This shows that the Roberts court is indeed highly pro-business and is much friendlier to business than were either the Burger or Rehnquist Courts that preceded it.

The *Times* study also revealed that after the appointment of Justices Roberts and Alito, the other three conservative justices became more favorable to business. The authors of the study conjecture that the three may not have been as interested in business as Roberts and Alito but decided to go along with them to forge a more solid conservative majority.

Until such time that the conservative bloc's control on the court's decision making is broken, it appears highly likely that workers will continue to experience rough sledding in the days ahead.

Chapter Twenty-Eight

The Roles of the EEOC and the Private Attorney

The reduction in the incidence of acts of employment discrimination, and ultimately their eradication, depends upon the vigorous and effective enforcement of the antidiscrimination statutes. When Congress adopted the Civil Rights Act of 1964, barring discrimination in employment by reason of race, color, sex, national origin, and religion, it assigned enforcement of the statute to the newly created Equal Employment Opportunity Commission. From the outset of its existence, the EEOC has been burdened with a complaint load far in excess of that anticipated. By the time Congress adopted the ADEA in 1967, the EEOC had already experienced difficulty in performing its functions adequately, and a burgeoning backlog of race and sex discrimination cases threatened to undermine its effectiveness in enforcing the 1964 act. Congressional concern that this backlog would result in the subordination of age claims to race and sex discrimination claims moved Congress to assign the enforcement of the ADEA to the Wage and Hour Division of the Department of Labor, an administrative agency that was particularly efficient in performing its functions. The Carter administration, however, later concluded that all the employment discrimination laws should by administered by a single federal agency, and in 1978 the enforcement of the ADEA was transferred to the EEOC. Since that time, the EEOC has been responsible for the enforcement of all federal employment discrimination laws.

Once a worker files a discrimination charge pursuant to the provisions of Title VII or the ADEA, the EEOC is required to seek to eliminate unlawful employment practices while acting in accordance with informal methods of conciliation, conference, and persuasion. EEOC procedures call for it to investigate the allegations of the charge before engaging in the conciliation process; but, historically, a vast majority of these discrimination charges are dismissed by the EEOC before they reach the conciliation stage of the proceedings. Here lies the basic problem with the EEOC's efforts to enforce the employment discrimination statutes.

An EEOC investigation of a discrimination charge generally culminates in one of two findings: (1) a determination that reason exists to believe the worker has been subjected to discriminatory conduct (a *for-cause finding*), or (2) a determination that no reason exists to believe the employer has engaged in such conduct (a *no-cause finding*). A no-cause finding effectively terminates the EEOC's involvement in the charge. Conversely, a for-cause finding leads to further EEOC action, such as efforts to conciliate or settle the claimant's allegations set forth in the charge. However, in any one year, between 60 and 75 percent of all charges filed with the EEOC are disposed of with a no-cause finding, and a large portion of the remainder of the charges are dismissed for other reasons or are withdrawn by workers grown weary with EEOC delays in completing its investigation. Thus, a relatively small number of charges reach the point where the EEOC ventures to conciliate or settle the worker's claim against the employer. Of the charges resolved by the EEOC in 2012 (that is, charges dismissed, withdrawn, and those settled or conciliated) only 8 percent of the race charges and 10 percent of the sex charges were settled, while only 1 percent of the race charges and less than 2 percent of the sex charges were successfully conciliated. [1]

A matter of greater concern than the small number of settlements and conciliations is the EEOC's apparent reluctance to conclude its investigations with affirmative for-cause findings. Of the nearly 38,500 race charges resolved by the EEOC in 2012, approximately 1,200 received a for-cause finding, representing approximately 3 percent of the case resolutions that year. About 4.4 percent of the sex discrimination charges resolved that year received a for-cause finding. [2]

Between 1997 and 2012, EEOC's annual for-cause findings in race discrimination charges varied from a high of 7.5 percent to a low of 2.5 percent of the charges resolved during those years. [3] Typically, the EEOC's no-reasonable-cause findings amounted to more than 65 percent of the race charges resolved, thus creating the impression that the EEOC was engaged in discovering where discrimination does not exist rather than where it does exist.

From its inception, the EEOC has been underfunded and understaffed, resulting in a huge backlog of cases that existed for many years. An underfunded and overworked staff cannot competently and efficiently investigate the thousands of charges filed each year, and many no-cause determinations are attributable to inadequate EEOC investigations. One of my cases graphically demonstrates the shortcoming of a typical EEOC investigation.

Dr. Samuel Song studied medicine in his native Korea, came to this country while still a young man, became a US citizen, and, after several years in medical research, began employment with a pharmaceutical division of

American Home Products (AHP). After several years with AHP, Song was fired, supposedly because of interpersonal problems with staff members. But Song blamed his termination on his supervisor, who Song claimed was anti-Korean. After his termination, Song filed a discrimination charge with the EEOC, alleging national origin discrimination. Following a time-consuming investigation, the EEOC found no cause to believe that Song had been subjected to any discriminatory actions. At that point, Song asked me to assume control of his case and to file a discrimination suit against AHP in the federal court.

My own investigation of the events related by Song quickly led to the impression that something had gone amiss at the EEOC, since it appeared that the no-cause determination was not warranted by the facts in the record. Eventually, after an extended period of discovery, the case came to trial before a jury in the federal court in New York City. After we presented our evidence of discrimination, AHP offered its defense, including the testimony of the EEOC investigator who had recommended the no-cause finding. Obviously, AHP hoped to persuade the jury that since the EEOC had found no reason to believe Song had been subjected to discriminatory acts, the jury should arrive at a similar conclusion.

At the point in the trial when the EEOC investigator took the witness stand, the jury had already heard a great deal of testimony that appeared to substantiate Song's position. In fact, one of Song's witnesses had testified to being present at a meeting where Song's supervisor had made scurrilous anti-Korean comments about Song. On her direct examination, the EEOC investigator related the steps she had undertaken to investigate Song's charge and said that ultimately she had concluded that he had not been subjected to any discriminatory conduct by his supervisors. On her cross-examination, I asked her whether she had uncovered any of the evidence that the jury had heard at the trial, and she responded that she had not. More particularly, her investigation failed to disclose the anti-Korean comments of Song's supervisor. By the time she left the witness stand, it was apparent that the EEOC had issued a no-cause finding without uncovering any of the evidence of anti-Korean bias that the jury had heard from other witnesses. The jury was thus made aware of the inadequacy of the EEOC investigation and its failure to discover evidence supporting Song's charge. At the conclusion of the trial, the jury rendered its verdict in favor of Dr. Song.[4]

When an attorney is first introduced to a case, evidence of discrimination may not be immediately apparent, and a lengthy period of discovery may be necessary before it can be determined whether sufficient evidence exists to support the charge. If an attorney is required to make that kind of effort before he can decide whether his client has a viable claim, how is it possible for the EEOC to make such a determination after a wholly inadequate investigation? True, at times an attorney having little information available must make a less-than-informed decision whether to proceed with a case. But if he decides not to proceed with the case, he makes that decision knowing that even if he has erred, there are other lawyers with whom the worker may consult, and another lawyer may view the claim from a different perspective and agree to proceed with the case. When the EEOC rejects a worker's claim, however, no other governmental agency exists for further consultation. When the EEOC dismisses a charge, the opportunity to resolve the charge administratively ceases at that moment.

Although Congress intended that the majority of employment discrimination claims were to be resolved administratively, it also granted the EEOC the right to initiate judicial proceedings. Thus, the EEOC has the option of filing suit on behalf of a claimant, but it rarely does. Of the 210 cases cited in this work, the EEOC appears as a party in only 13 of them. Of the 55 Supreme Court cases cited in this book—the most significant case holdings in the history of Title VII and the ADEA—the EEOC did not appear in any of them. In recent years, however, the EEOC has increased its involvement in the litigation of discrimination claims. In 2012 it filed 122 lawsuits across the country, resolved 254 pending lawsuits, and recovered $44.2 million for plaintiff workers.[5]

If the EEOC elects not to proceed in the courts, a Title VII claimant has the right to demand from the EEOC a right-to-sue notice, a document that provides the worker with entry to the judicial system. Upon the worker's demand, the EEOC must issue the right-to-sue notice, even if it has not completed its investigation or even if it has concluded its investigation with a no-cause determination.

As a practical matter, a worker who believes herself to be a victim of discrimination will have to pursue the matter on her own behalf, with little or no assistance from the EEOC. More than 95 percent of the employment discrimination cases adjudicated in the federal courts are shepherded through the court system not by the EEOC but by private attorneys retained by individual workers.[6]

The most far-reaching innovation of the 1964 Civil Rights Act was the introduction of the individual right to sue. Previous state antidiscrimination statutes had failed to provide an effective means of enforcing those laws, and thus they remained mostly ineffective. The individual right to sue, established under Title VII, became the driving force behind the enforcement of the statute, thus resolving the difficulties previously encountered by the state agencies.

Private attorneys have assumed a major role in protecting American workers from discrimination in employment, and in the years to come, their role will grow in parallel with increased numbers of employment discrimination complaints. As private attorneys have in the past been successful in providing American workers with broad protection against discrimination in the workplace, they will likely continue in the future to play a significant role in the continuing development of employment discrimination law and in the protection of workers from workplace discriminatory conduct.[7]

Because the EEOC has been less successful in obtaining relief for discrimination claimants, it has failed to attain the status of a major deterrent to discriminatory conduct. A pending EEOC administrative proceeding is generally not a matter of great concern for corporate directors, while a pending lawsuit may threaten corporate tranquility. On balance, the cost to an employer of defending against a discrimination claim litigated in the courts and the substantial risk of an adverse jury determination are far more likely to deter future unlawful employer conduct than an EEOC ruling. The private attorney is the instrument of the greater threat, and although employers and their attorneys may deny it, the deterrence value of the private attorney far exceeds that of the EEOC.

Even before enactment of the statutes requiring employers to pay the attorney's fees of prevailing discrimination complainants, a small group of dedicated lawyers assumed lead roles in protecting the American worker from employer discrimination. One of the effects of the fee statutes has been to advance the growth in the number of lawyers willing to specialize in this area of the law. Most of the attorneys representing workers are either members of small law firms or solo practitioners, and their litigation contests with major corporations and their mammoth law firms are frequently fought in David and Goliath circumstances. To gain mutual support, lawyers representing workers have banded together to form the National Employment Lawyers Association (NELA), the only professional organization in the country exclusively comprised of lawyers dedicated to representing workers in discrimination and other employment cases. Today, its membership numbers nearly 3,000, located in all fifty states and the District of Columbia.[8]

There are far easier ways to make a living than as a lawyer for discrimination complainants. The David and Goliath description is not an exaggeration; it exists in nearly every employment discrimination litigation. Employers take discrimination claims seriously, and in defending against these claims, they rely on the best and most experienced counsel available, usually found in the country's largest law firms. It is not uncommon for attorneys who represent plaintiffs claiming to have been discriminated against to confront the largest law firms in the country; and although they have grown accustomed to practicing law in these circumstances, it does not get any easier with the passage of time. The constant struggle against the vast resources brought to the litigation by employers and their counsel creates stress that the worker's lawyer must live with throughout his or her career.

Litigation is certainly not the ideal way of coping with a hostile and offensive work environment, but it is the best means currently available. The fear of public disclosure in a legal forum undoubtedly deters employers from engaging in discriminatory conduct and encourages them to adopt measures assuring a discrimination-free workplace. More litigation today may diminish its need tomorrow.

Undoubtedly, discriminatory conduct in the workplace will continue. Absent a dramatic change in employer conduct, the private attorney will continue to play an increasingly greater role in protecting workers from the scourge of employment discrimination.

VII

The Future of the Employment Discrimination Laws

Chapter Twenty-Nine

What Lays Ahead for the Employment Discrimination Laws

Most trials of employment discrimination cases turn on a single issue—has the plaintiff proved that the defendant company intentionally discriminated against her? Whether the defendant acted intentionally is a question of fact. It is the responsibility of the jury—not the judge—to decide issues of fact. If the jury finds that the defendant acted intentionally, one would expect that in most instances the plaintiff's victory at trial would be affirmed on appeal, as the role of the appellate court is to decide questions of law, not questions of fact. Yet one study revealed that on defendants' appeals of jury verdicts in favor of the plaintiff, the appellate courts have reversed 41 percent of those rulings. In contrast, when plaintiffs have appealed adverse jury rulings, they have succeeded only in 9 percent of those occasions.[1] Defendant companies, in contrast to plaintiff workers, emerge from the appellate court in much better position than when they left the trial court.[2] Two highly respected and frequently cited Cornell University law professors find this disturbing:

> The vulnerability on appeal of jobs plaintiffs' relatively few trial victories is more startling in light of the nature of these cases and the applicable standard of review. The bulk of employment discrimination cases turn on intent, and not on disparate impact. The subtle question of the defendant's intent is likely to be the key issue in a non-frivolous employment discrimination case that reaches trial, putting the credibility of witnesses into play. When the plaintiff has convinced the [jury] of the defendant's wrongful intent, that finding should be largely immune from appellate reversal, just as defendant's trial victories are. Reversal of plaintiffs' trial victories in employment cases should be un-usually uncommon. Yet we find the opposite.[3]

During the period 1979 through 2006, employment discrimination plaintiffs won approximately 15 percent of their cases litigated in the federal courts, whereas plaintiffs suing for other causes won 51 percent of their cases.[4] What explains this vast difference in the win rates between the two groups of plaintiffs?

Employers are less likely to settle employment discrimination claims than they are to settle other claims, thus compelling plaintiff workers to proceed to trial. Is it possible that employers are less willing to settle discrimination cases because they know that even if they lose at trial, they are likely to win on appeal? The Cornell law professors believe that is the case: "The antiplaintiff effect on appeal raises the specter that federal appellate courts have a double standard for employment discrimination cases, scrutinizing employees' victories [in the trial courts] while gazing benignly at employers' victories."[5]

The Cornell law professors do not stand alone. Other observers have also concluded that the low win rate experienced by employment discrimination plaintiffs results from the bias that judges bring to their courtrooms:[6]

> Judges exercise enormous discretion in civil litigation in general, a discretion that has only increased with recent decisions of the Supreme Court. The Court has directed that judges, when considering motions to dismiss, should exercise "common sense" in evaluating the plaintiff's claim in light of other "plausible" explanations for a defendant's conduct. The trial court's "common sense" view of what is or is not "plausible" affects employment litigation perhaps more than any other type of litigation. Studies have shown that judicial biases significantly influence summary judgment outcomes in discrimination cases. Indeed, many commentators have noted that employment discrimination plaintiffs face an unusually uphill battle. As a general matter, doctrinal developments in the past two decades have quite consistently made it more difficult for plaintiffs to establish their discrimination claims. In addition, many of these doctrines have increased the role of judicial judgment—and the role of judicial bias—in the life cycle of an employment discrimination case.[7]

Two other law professors studied thousands of votes of federal appellate judges who sit on three-judge panels and render decisions by majority vote. Not surprisingly, they found that judges appointed by Republican presidents were more conservative, while Democratic appointees were more liberal. Their study showed that that the effect of their political ideology was reflected in their decision making. They showed that in a case of an appeal of a trial court decision of an employment discrimination matter, the likely outcome depended upon the identity of the judges sitting on the panel:

- Before a panel of three Democratic appointees, plaintiffs win 75 percent of the time.

- Before a panel of two Democratic and one Republican appointees, plaintiffs win 49 percent of the time.
- Before a panel of one Democratic and two Republican appointees, plaintiff s' win rate is 38 percent.
- Before a panel of three Republican appointees, plaintiffs' win rate is 31 percent.[8]

More than a political bias is at play here—a bias that evolves from a way of perceiving and evaluating everyday life events. For example, some judges approach race discrimination cases with deep skepticism, while others view sex discrimination cases with jaundiced eye, and still others approach age discrimination cases with considerable impatience and disdain (chapter 27). Other judges seem to have concluded that employment discrimination plays a diminished role in contemporary America and they are unwilling to find discrimination in the absence of overwhelming evidence.[9]

As earlier noted, the Supreme Court appears to be biased in favor of business (chapter 27). The primary purpose of the National Litigation Center of the US Chamber of Commerce is to represent business interests before the courts. The chamber's board of directors includes officers of the nation's largest companies, including Ford, Verizon, Lockheed Martin, Viacom, and GlaxoSmith Kline. According to one of its lead attorneys, "Except for the Solicitor General representing the United States, no single entity has more influence on what cases the Supreme Court decides and how it decides them than the Chamber's National Litigation Center."[10] In the Supreme Court's 2009–2010 term, parties supported by the Chamber of Commerce won in thirteen of sixteen cases.

The existence of judicial bias cannot be established with certainty, as other forces may be at work leading to conditions that appear to owe their existence to judicial bias. As an example, some judges may fully accept the concepts embraced by Title VII and the ADEA yet feel that the enforcement of these concepts has gone too far, that those committed to enforcing these statutes have become radicalized and they should be compelled to moderate their actions.

In either event, the result has been the same—over the years, the task of establishing an employment discrimination claim in a court of law has become increasingly more onerous. Consequently, victims of employment discrimination have frequently failed in their endeavor to establish valid claims and thus have been denied the just result that should have been theirs. Some of the court decisions that have made life more difficult for employment discrimination plaintiffs have previously been discussed in this book. It remains for us to establish a list of the more significant of those decisions that remain matters of significant concern.

ESTABLISHING A DISPARATE TREATMENT CLAIM

Early in the history of the employment discrimination laws, the Supreme Court established what became known as the *McDonnell Douglas* rule (chapter 3). As thus sanctioned by the court, one method of proving intentional discrimination is through the disclosure, by indirect evidence, that an employer offered a false or pretextual explanation for its decision adversely affecting the worker. A court or jury may infer from the falsity of the explanation that the employer has disassembled or misrepresented the facts in order to cover up a discriminatory purpose. Thus, a court or jury may infer the ultimate fact of discrimination from the falsity of the employer's explanation.[11]

The *McDonnell Douglas* rule worked well for twenty years. Then in *St. Mary's Honor Center v. Hicks*,[12] the Supreme Court reversed course, ruling that "pretext" really means "pretext for discrimination." Merely proving the falsity of the employer's reasons was no longer sufficient. The worker still must prove that the employer's decision was discriminatory (chapter 21). This turned the concept of pretext on its head. What advantage does the worker gain by proving the employer lied if he still is required to prove that the employer's conduct was discriminatory (chapter 21)?

The allocation of the burden of proof may determine the outcome of any litigation, and this is particularly the case in employment discrimination cases. Allocating a heavy burden to the employee permits an employer to continue to freely discriminate without paying any penalty for its discriminatory conduct. The *Hicks* decision materially increased the employee's burden of proof. This decision, applicable to both Title VII and ADEA cases, greatly disfavors the worker who has no direct evidence of discrimination to present to the court. It rejects the Court's previous commonsense approach and makes it substantially more difficult to prove discriminatory intent.

Although the Court ruled that proof of the falsity of the employer's position does not compel a verdict for the worker, the jury may nevertheless infer a discriminatory motive from the fact that the employer resorted to lying. Thus, if the only evidence offered in support of the worker's case is the falsity of the employer's position, a jury may decide that the employer's conduct was discriminatory, but it is no longer compelled to rule in that fashion.

Why did the Court make it more difficult to prove an employer's discriminatory intent? Why did the Court scuttle a rule of evidence that had worked well for twenty years? The Court is not talking. We may never know. More importantly, can the Court be persuaded to return to the *McDonnell Douglas* rule? Not as it is currently comprised. Thus, this is a matter that should be added to the list of actions Congress should undertake to force the Court back on the right track.

ARBITRATION

Only a lawyer, charged with representing an employment discrimination plaintiff, can fully appreciate the perniciousness of arbitration as a means of resolving his client's discrimination claim. Pre-hearing discovery in arbitral proceedings is considerably more limited than the pre-trial discovery available in court cases. Limited discovery, denying the worker access to the employer's documents and records, almost certainly will materially undermine the development of the worker's case. Arbitrators, inexperienced in the law of employment discrimination and not having the slightest inkling of what it takes in the way of discovery to construct a case supported by circumstantial evidence, are wholly unprepared to rule on discovery issues. The inability of the arbitrator to serve a meaningful role in this process serves to benefit the employer and disadvantage the worker by materially weakening the worker's ability to present a viable case.

The arguments against the use of arbitration in Title VII and ADEA disputes have been spelled out in chapter 26. At this point, we must add "arbitration" to Congress's "to do" list.

PROVING AGE DISCRIMINATION

The Supreme Court has exhibited an especially unfriendly attitude toward age discrimination claimants. Two of its decisions—*Hazen Paper Co. v. Biggins* and *Gross v. FBL Financial Services, Inc.*[13] —were aimed at the hearts of aged claimants (cChapter 22).

Underlying the rationale of the *Hazen* case is the formative language of the ADEA that eliminated "reasonable factors other than age" (RFOA) from that conduct defined as unlawful. Employers frequently assert the RFOA defense, but at times the proffered defense correlates so closely with age that it is little more than a thinly veiled cover for age discrimination. The ADEA cannot serve the purposed for which it was enacted if the courts allow employers to use age-correlative criteria—such as higher position, greater salary, or retirement status—to justify the termination of its older employees.

The Court used the *Gross* case to increase the plaintiff's burden of proof in age cases. It held that an age discrimination claimant must prove that age was the "*but-for*" cause of the challenged employer action. Despite its contrary rulings, the Court held in the *Gross* case that age discrimination plaintiffs must prove that age was the sole cause of the employer's adverse action. The ruling constituted a major change in ADEA procedure, threatening the viability of the ADEA as a major deterrent to age-related employment actions.[14]

Congress should overturn both decisions.

STRAY REMARKS

One of the most troublesome problems for older workers striving to prove age discrimination is the rejection of employer-uttered age-biased remarks as evidence of age discrimination (chapter 22). The negative attitude of certain members of the federal judiciary toward age discrimination cases has led to ever more restrictive rulings, leading to the rejection of nearly all ageist remarks on the ground they are irrelevant and not probative. Proving discrimination is always difficult; proving it under conditions where evidence of age bias of this type is rejected as irrelevant makes it nearly impossible.

THE HIRING OF OLDER WORKERS

For the older worker who has lost his or her job and has sought substitute employment, the ADEA has been pretty much a total failure. In fact, the ADEA may actually exacerbate the plight of unemployed older workers by discouraging employers from hiring them. Since a newly-hired older worker may later be fired and, as a consequence, file an age suit, an employer may decide to avoid that risk in the first instance by not hiring the older worker. The anticipated costs of defending against an age claim may be a factor the employer considers before hiring an older worker. For this reason, the very existence of the ADEA stands as a barrier to the hiring of older workers.

Except for the expenditures incurred in defending against a failure-to-hire lawsuit, an employer has little reason to fear a claim made by a rejected, older job applicant, since the pattern of proof devised by the courts for establishing an act of discrimination does not readily lend itself to a hiring case. The nature of the hiring process is highly subjective, thus allowing the employer to conceal its discriminatory motives behind its protestations that, for this particular position, another applicant was better qualified than the rejected older worker. As a consequence, most rejected older job applicants do not sue, and those who do sue generally lose. If an employer is unlikely to find itself in court on account of its hiring practices and, if it is sued, it is more apt to prevail, then the employer, when it comes to the hiring of older workers, will be far less inclined to comply with the provisions of the ADEA.

Other than easing the proof requirements of the *Hicks*, *Hazen*, and *Gross* cases, there may be little else the Supreme Court or Congress can do to resolve this problem. Opening the hiring process to greater public scrutiny, however, may induce the employer to be more compliant. Broader record-keeping requirements, including the maintenance of hiring records for public inspection, would constitute a step in the right direction. The EEOC should require employers to file annual reports, identifying by age category the number of persons who applied for a position, the number of applicants in each age category that were interviewed, and the number in each age category hired. A review of these data may disclose the rejection, either for interview or for hire, of a disproportionate number of older workers. But even if these data fail to establish age-discriminatory conduct, the public scrutiny of employer hiring records would strongly motivate employers to remain more alert to the appropriateness of their hiring procedures and their treatment of older job applicants.

It is highly unlikely that the Supreme Court's conservative majority will reverse the decisions that have given rise to the problems that currently confront employment discrimination plaintiffs. If the Court fails to act, civil rights advocates must turn to Congress for legislative relief.

Can Americans eradicate discrimination from the workplace? This remains an unanswered question. Certainly, we have seen immense progress in the past fifty years. We should celebrate that progress, but not ignore the fact that workplace discrimination remains with us. It is inconceivable that we would ever move backwards, return to the times of open hostility to African American and foreign-born workers, to the denigration of women, the aged, and members of certain religions; but will we move forward? Is a workplace entirely devoid of discriminatory animus even conceivable?

Whether a workplace free of discrimination can be transformed from an ideal to a reality is a question for the future. We must believe that such a workplace is possible. And we must work to achieve it.

Table of Cases

Notes

INTRODUCTION

1. John F. Kennedy: "Radio and Television Report to the American People on Civil Rights," June 11, 1963.
2. EEOC Report No. 1, referred to by Alfred W. Blumrosen, *Black Employment and the Law* (New Brunswick, NJ: Rutgers University Press, 1971), 102–33.

1. EMPLOYMENT DISCRIMINATION PRIOR TO 1964

1. Plessy v. Ferguson, 163 U.S. 537 (1896).
2. Alfred W. Blumrosen, *Black Employment and the Law* (New Brunswick, NJ: Rutgers University Press,1971), 104.
3. David L. Rose, "Twenty-Five Years Later: Where Do We Stand on Equal Employment Opportunity Law Enforcement," *Vanderbilt Law Review* 42, no. 4 (1989): 1121, 1127.
4. Bradwell v. Illinois, 83 U.S. 130 (1872).
5. Goesaert v. Cleary, 335 U.S. 464 (1948).
6. James MacGregor Burns, *The Crosswinds of Freedom* (New York: Knopf, 1989), 81, 188.
7. Michael I. Sovern, *Legal Restraints on Racial Discrimination in Employment* (New York: Twentieth Century Fund, 1966), 9.
8. Executive Order No. 8802, 6 Fed. Reg. 3109 (1941).
9. Mona Harrington, *Women Lawyers: Rewriting the Rules* (New York: Plume, 1993), 19.
10. Cynthia Fuchs Epstein, *Women in Law* (Urbana: University of Illinois Press, 1993), 84–85.
11. Executive Order No. 9980, 146 Fed. Reg. 4311 (1948).
12. Executive Order No. 96,646, 10 Fed. Reg. 15,301 (1945).
13. Executive Order No. 10,479, 18 Fed. Reg. 4899 (1953).
14. New York Executive Law, Sections 290 et seq.
15. New Jersey (1945), Massachusetts (1946), Connecticut (1947), Rhode Island (1949), New Mexico (1949), Oregon (1949), Washington (1949), Alaska (1953), Michigan (1955), Minnesota (1955), Pennsylvania (1955), Colorado (1957), Wisconsin (1957), California

(1959), Ohio (1959), Delaware (1960), Illinois (1961), Kansas (1961), Missouri (1961), Idaho (1961), Indiana (1963), Hawaii (1963), Iowa (1963), and Vermont (1963).

2. ENACTMENT OF THE CIVIL RIGHTS ACT OF 1964 AND THE AGE DISCRIMINATION IN EMPLOYMENT ACT OF 1967

1. John F. Kennedy, "Radio and Television Report to the American People on Civil Rights," June 11, 1963.
2. Chapter 1, note 15.
3. Arthur Larson, *Employment Discrimination*, vol. 1 (Newark, NJ: Matthew Bender, 1974), 2–37.
4. Brown v. Board of Education, 347 U.S. 483 (1954).
5. Alfred W. Blumrosen, *Modern Law: The Law Transmission System and Equal Opportunity Employment* (Madison: University of Wisconsin Press, 1993), 40.
6. Lyndon B. Johnson, Address to Joint Session of Congress, November 27, 1963.
7. Charles and Barbara Whalen, *The Longest Debate: A Legislative History of the 1964 Civil Rights Act* (Washington, DC: Seven Locks Press, 1985), 84, 116–17.
8. U.S. Department of Labor, *The Older American Worker: Age Discrimination in Employment*, Report of the Secretary of Labor (1965).
9. McKennon v. Nashville Banner Publishing Co., 513 U.S. 352 (1995).
10. Kevin Stainback and Donald Tomaskovic-Dewey, *Documenting Desegregation: Racial and Gender Segregation in Private Sector Employment since the Civil Rights Act* (New York: Russell Sage Foundation, 2012), xxi.
11. David L. Rose, "Twenty-Five Years Later: Where Do We Stand on Equal Employment Opportunity Law Enforcement," *Vanderbilt Law Review* 42, no. 4 (1989): 1122.
12. Title VII, § 703, 42 U.S.C. § 2000e-2(a).
13. Age Discrimination in Employment (ADEA), 4(a), 29 U.S.C. § 623(a).
14. Alfred W. Blumrosen, *Black Employment and the Law* (New Brunswick, NJ: Rutgers University Press, 1971), 4.
15. Rose, "Twenty-Five Years Later," 1123.

3. PROVING EMPLOYMENT DISCRIMINATION

1. John Herbers, "Problems Face Job Rights Unit As Roosevelt Assumes Office," *New York Times*, June 3, 1965.
2. Deborah L. Rhode, "Perspectives on Professional Women," *Stanford Law Review* 40 (1988): 1163, 1178.
3. William B. Gould, *Black Workers in White Unions: Job Discrimination in the United States* (Ithaca, NY: Cornell University Press, 1977), 39.
4. Michael I. Sovern, *Legal Restraints on Racial Discrimination in Employment* (New York: Twentieth Century Fund, 1966), 205.
5. David L. Rose, "Twenty-Five Years Later: Where Do We Stand on Equal Employment Opportunity Law Enforcement," *Vanderbilt Law Review* 42, no. 4 (1989): 1136–37.
6. Gould, *Black Workers in White Unions*, 39–40.
7. Gould, *Black Workers in White Unions*, 39–40.
8. See comments made by the Supreme Court in U.S. Postal Service Board of Governors v. Aikens, 460 U.S. 711 (1983).
9. Rhode, "Perspectives on Professional Women," 1195.
10. Rhode, "Perspectives on Professional Women," 1193.
11. Moore v. Alabama State University, 980 F. Supp. 426 (M.D. Ala. 1997).

12. McDonnell Douglas Corp. v. Green, 411 U.S. 792 (1973).
13. Furnco Construction Corp. v. Waters, 438 U.S. 567 (1978).
14. Reeves v. Sanderson Plumbing Products, Inc., 530 U.S. 133 (2000).
15. Binder v. Long Island Lighting Co., 57 F.3d 193 (2d Cir. 1995).

4. EARLY RACE DISCRIMINATION CASES

1. Michael I. Sovern, *Legal Restraints on Racial Discrimination in Employment* (New York: Twentieth Century Fund, 1966), 16.
2. Drew S. Days, III, "The Court's Response to the Reagan Civil Rights Agenda," *Vanderbilt Law Review* 42, no. 4 (1989): 1003,1006
3. Griggs v. Duke Power Co., 401 U.S. 424 (1971).
4. EEOC v. Joe's Stone Crab, Inc., 220 F.3d 1263 (11th Cir. 2000).
5. Griggs v. Duke Power Co., 401 U.S. 424 (1971).
6. Albemarle Paper Co. v. Moody, 422 U.S. 405 (1975).
7. Griggs v. Duke Power Co., 401 U.S. 424 (1971).
8. DeGraffenreid v. General Motors Assembly Division, St. Louis, 413 F. Supp. 142 (E.D. Mo. 1976).
9. Kimberle Crenshaw, "Demarginalizing the Intersection of Race and Sex: A Black Feminist Critique of Antidiscrimination Doctrine, Feminist Theory and Antiracist Politics," *University of Chicago Legal Forum* (1989): 139.
10. Jefferies v. Harris County Community Act Association, 615 F.2d 1025 (5th Cir. 1980).
11. Jefferies v. Harris County Community Act Association, 615 F.2d 1025 (5th Cir. 1980).

5. EARLY SEX DISCRIMINATION CASES

1. Alfred W. Blumrosen, *Black Employment and the Law* (New Brunswick, NJ: Rutgers University Press, 1971), 112.
2. David L. Rose, "Twenty-Five Years Later: Where Do We Stand on Equal Employment Opportunity Law Enforcement," *Vanderbilt Law Review* 42, no. 4 (1989): 1121, 1136.
3. Phillips v. Martin Marietta Corp., 400 U.S. 542 (1971).
4. Title VII, 42 U.S.C. § 2000e-2(e).
5. Dothard v. Rawlinson, 433 U.S. 321 (1977).
6. *Dothard.*
7. City of Los Angeles Department of Water and Power v. Manhart, 435 U.S. 702 (1978).
8. Sprogis v. United Air Lines, Inc., 444 F.2d 1194 (7th Cir. 1971).
9. Title VII, Civil Rights Act of 1964, 42 U.S.C. § 2000e-2.
10. See, e.g., Communication Workers v. American Telephone & Telegraph, 513 F.2d 1024 (2d Cir. 1975).
11. General Electric Co. v. Gilbert, 429 U.S. 125 (1976).
12. Mona Harrington, *Women Lawyers: Rewriting the Rules* (New York: Plume, 1995), 97–98, 105, 115–16.
13. Barbara A. Gutek, *Sex and the Workplace* (San Francisco: Jossey-Bass, 1985), 8–9.
14. Catherine A. MacKinnon, *Sexual Harassment of Working Women* (New Haven, CT: Yale University Press, 1979), 4.
15. Barnes v. Train, 13 FEP Cases 123 (D. D.C. 1974).
16. Corne v. Bausch and Lomb, Inc., 390 F. Supp. 161 (D.C. Ariz. 1975), reversed on other grounds 562 F.2d 55 (9th Cir. 1977).
17. Tomkins v. Public Service Electric & Gas Company, 568 F.2d 1044 (3rd Cir. 1977).
18. Barnes v. Costle, 561 F.2d 983 (D.C. Cir. 1977).

6. EARLY NATIONAL ORIGIN DISCRIMINATION CASES

1. Korematsu v. United States, 323 U.S. 214 (1944).
2. Alfred W. Blumrosen, *Black Employment and the Law* (New Brunswick, NJ: Rutgers University Press, 1971), 111.
3. 29 C.F.R. 1606.1 (d) (1972).
4. Espinoza v. Farah Manufacturing Co., 414 U.S. 86 (1973).
5. U.S. Equal Employment Opportunity Commission Fact Sheet. Available at eeoc.gov/publications/index.cfm.
6. EEOC website, eeoc.gov//laws/types/nationalorigin.cfm.
7. Arthur Larson, *Employment Discrimination,* vol. 1 (Newark, NJ: Matthew Bender, 1974), 2–19, n9.

7. EARLY RELIGIOUS DISCRIMINATION CASES

1. 29 C.F.R. Part 1605 (1967), 45 Fed. Reg. 72610 and 72611.
2. Frazee v. Illinois Employment Security Department, 489 U.S. 829 (1989).
3. Citron v. Jackson State University, 456 F. Supp. 3 (S.D. Miss. 1977).
4. Young v. Southwestern Savings and Loan Association, 509 F.2d 140 (5th Cir. 1975).
5. Weiss v. United States, 595 Fed. Supp. 1050 (E.D. Va. 1984).
6. EEOC Guidelines on Discrimination Because of Religion, 29 C.F.R. § 1605.1 (1967).
7. Title VII, § 701(j), 42 U.S.C. § 2000e-(j).
8. Trans World Airlines, Inc. (TWA) v. Hardison, 432 U.S. 63 (1977).
9. *Trans World Airlines* (Marshall, J., dissenting).
10. EEOC Guidelines on Discrimination Because of Religion, 29 C. F. R. 1605 (1980).

8. EARLY AGE DISCRIMINATION CASES

1. Lawrence M. Friedman, *Your Time Will Come: The Law of Age Discrimination and Mandatory Retirement* (New York: Russell Sage Foundation,1984), 11.
2. U.S. Department of Labor, *The Older American Worker: Age Discrimination in Employment,* Report of the Secretary of Labor (1965).
3. Daniel P. O'Meara, *Protecting the Growing Number of Older Workers: The Age Discrimination in Employment Act* (Philadelphia: University of Pennsylvania, The Wharton School, Industrial Research Unit, 1989), 13.
4. *Hearings on H.R. 3651, H.R. 3768, and H.R. 4221, before the General Subcommittee on Labor of the House Committee on Education and Labor,* 90th Cong. 7 (1967), referred to by Samuel Issacharoff and Erica Worth Harris, "Is Age Discrimination Really Age Discrimination? The ADEA's Unnatural Solution," *New York University Law Review* 72, no. 4 (1997): 781–85.
5. Age Discrimination in Employment Act (ADEA), 29 U.S.C. § 623.
6. O'Meara, *Protecting the Growing Number of Older Workers,* 24–26.
7. McDermott v. Lehman, 594 F. Supp. 1315 (D.C. Me. 1984).
8. Richard A. Posner, *Aging and Old Age* (Chicago: University of Chicago Press, 1995), 45.
9. George v. Mobil Oil Corp., 739 F. Supp. 1577 (S.D.N.Y.1990).
10. Spence v. Maryland Casualty Co., 995 F.2d 1147 (2d Cir. 1993).
11. Geller v. Markham, 635 F.2d 1027 (2d Cir. 1980).
12. Lowe v. Commack Union School District, 886 F.2d 1364 (2d Cir. 1989).

13. Graffam v. Scott Paper Co., 848 F. Supp. 1 (D.C. Me, 1994).

14. Age Discrimination in Employment Act of 1967 (Pub. L. 90-202) (ADEA), 29 U.S.C. § 626(b).

15. Wise v. Olan Mills Incorporated of Texas., 485 F. Supp. 542 (D.C. Colo.1980).

16. The Hall case was reported along with Hodgson v. First Federal Savings & Loan Association of Broward County, Florida, 455 F. 2d 818 (5th Cir. 1972).

17. Trans World Airlines, Inc. v. Thurston, 469 U.S. 111 (1985).

9. CONGRESSIONAL AMENDMENTS OF TITLE VII AND THE ADEA

1. EEOC Guidelines, 29 C. F. R. 1605.1.

2. 29 C.F.R. 1605.1(a) (2) (1967). See chapter 7.

3. Communication Workers v. American Telephone & Telegraph, 513 F.2d 1024 (2d Cir. 1975).

4. General Electric Co. v. Gilbert, 429 U.S. 125 (1976).

5. Pregnancy Discrimination Act of 1978, 42 U.S.C. § 2000e(k).

6. The statute's provisions are summarized and described at greater length in Maldonado v. U.S. Bank and Manufacturers Bank, 186 F.3d 759 (7th Cir. 1999).

7. EEOC Title VII Regulations, 29 C.F.R. 1604.10; Appendix—Questions on the Pregnancy Discrimination Act

8. Michael Selmi, "The Supreme Court's Surprising and Strategic Response to the Civil Rights Act of 1991," *Wake Forest Law Review* 46 (2011): 281, 283.

9. Wards Cove Packing Co. v. Atonio, 490 U.S. 642 (1989).

10. Michael Selmi, "The Supreme Court's Surprising and Strategic Response to the Civil Rights Act of 1991," 185.

11. William P. Murphy, "Meandering Musings about Discrimination Law," *The Labor Lawyer* 10, no. 4 (1994): 649.

12. The statute overturned parts or all of five of the Supreme Court's major 1989 employment discrimination decisions: Patterson v. McLean Credit Union, 491 U.S. 164 (1989); Lorrance v. AT&T Techs, Inc., 490 U.S. 900 (1989); Wards Cove Packing Co. v. Atonio, 490 U.S. 642 (1989); Martin v. Wilks, 490 U.S. 744 (1989); and Price Waterhouse v. Hopkins, 490 U.S. 228 (1989).

13. *Price Waterhouse.*

14. 42 U.S.C. § 2000e-5(g)(2)(B)(i).

15. Swanson v. Elmhurst Chrysler Plymouth, Inc., 882 F, 2d 1235 (7th Cir. 1989).

16. Robinson v. Jacksonville Shipyards, Inc., 760 F. Supp. 1532 (M.D. Fla. 1991).

17. 42 U.S.C. § 1981a.

18. Senate Special Committee on Aging; Improving the Age Discrimination Law, 93rd Cong., 1st Sess., 14 Legislative History 215 (1973).

19. A Louis Harris poll conducted for the National Council on Aging showed that 90 percent of those interviewed in the survey felt that workers should not be forced into retirement if they were capable of performing on the job. Reported by Arthur Larson, *Employment Discrimination,* vol. 1 (Newark, NJ: Matthew Bender, 1974).

20. George Rutherglen, *Employment Discrimination Law: Visions of Equality In Theory and Doctrine,* 3rd ed. (New York: Foundation Press, 2010), 214.

10. CURRENT TRENDS IN THE LAW PROHIBITING RACE DISCRIMINATION

1. U.S. Department of Labor, *Labor Force Characteristics by Race and Ethnicity, 2010*, U.S. Bureau of Labor Statistics Report 1032.

2. U.S. Department of Labor, *Labor Force Characteristics by Race and Ethnicity, 2010*, table 16.

3. EEOC, 2011 Job Patterns for Minorities and Women in Private Industry, available from http://www.eeoc.gov/eeoc/statistics/employment/jobpat-eeo1/.

4. U.S. Census Bureau, *2012 Statistical Abstract of the United States*, Section 12: Labor Force, Employment, and Earnings, table 622, p. 401.

5. Michael Luo, "In Job Hunt, College Degree Can't Close Racial Gap," *New York Times*, December 1, 2009.

6. Pat K. Chew, "Arbitral and Judicial Proceedings: Indistinguishable Justice or Justice Denied?" *Wake Forest Law Review* 46 (2011): 185, 201.

7. Steven Greenhouse, "E.E.O.C. Finds Race Bias in Firing at Wet Seal Store," *New York Times*, December 3, 2012.

8. Ash v. Tyson Foods, Inc., 546 U.S. 454 (2006).

9. St. Mary's Honor Center v. Hicks ,756 F. Supp. 1244 (E.D. Mo. 1991).

10. Texas Department of Community Affairs v. Burdine, 450 U.S. 248 (1973); McDonnell Douglas Corp. v. Green, 411 U.S. 792 (1973).

11. *Texas Department of Community Affairs* at 255–56.

12. St. Mary's Honor Center v. Hicks, 509 U.S. 502 (1993).

13. Daniels v. Essex Group, Inc., 937 F. 2d 1264 (7th Cir. 1991).

14. Meritor Savings Bank v. Vinson, 477 U.S. 57 (1986). While in this case the Supreme Court recognized a cause of action for sexual harassment, the Court also implicitly approved claims for racial harassment. The Court reiterated that view in Patterson v. McLean Credit Union, 491 U.S. 164 (1988).

15. *Daniels*.

16. Williams v. New York City Housing Authority, 154 F. Supp. 2d 820 (S.D.N.Y. 2001). This opinion was written by Hon. Robert L. Carter, himself an African American, who, before he was appointed to the federal bench, was a civil rights activist and later counsel in more than twenty civil rights cases argued before the Supreme Court.

17. EEOC Compliance Manual, Section 15: Race and Color Discrimination, 19–20 http://www.eeoc.gov/policy/docs/race-color.html (2006).

18. Graham v. Bendix Corp., 585 F. Supp. 1036 (N.D. Ind. 1984).

19. Hicks v. Gates Rubber Co., 833 F.2d. 1406 (10th Cir. 1987).

20. Kathryn Abrams, "Title VII and the Complex Female Subject," *Michigan Law Review* 92 (1994): 2479, 2501.

21. Cruz v. Coach Stores, Inc., 202 F.3d. 560 (2d Cir. 2000).

11. CURRENT TRENDS IN THE LAW PROHIBITING SEX DISCRIMINATION

1. Diana Furchtgott-Roth and Christine Stolba, *Women's Figures: An Illustrated Guide to the Economic Progress of Women in America* (Washington, DC: AEI Press, 1999), 4–15.

2. Luciano v. Olsten Corp., 912 F. Supp. 663 (E.D.N.Y. 1995), affirmed 110 F.3d 210 (2nd Cir. 1997).

3. Glass Ceiling Act of 1991, Title II of the Civil Rights Act of 1991, Pub. L. 102–166, which amends Title VII of the Civil Rights Act of 1964.

4. This study was referred to in U.S. Department of Labor, Federal Glass Ceiling Commission, "The Environmental Scan," in *Good for Business: Making Use of the Nation's Human Capital* (Washington, DC: U.S. Department of Labor, 1995), 148.

5. EEOC Title VII Regulations, 29 C.F.R. § 1604.5.

6. King v. Trans World Airlines, 738 F.2d 255 (8th Cir. 1984).

7. Barbano v. Madison County, 922 F.2d 139 (2nd Cir. 1990).

8. Bruno v. City of Crown Point, 950 F.2d 355 (7th Cir. 1991).

9. Corning Glass Works v. Brennan, 417 U.S. 188 (1995).

10. McMillan v. Massachusetts Society for the Prevention of Cruelty to Animals, 140 F.3d 288 (1st Cir. 1998).

11. Houck v. Virginia Polytechnic Institute and State University, 10 F.3d 204 (4th Cir. 1993).

12. Cherrey v. Thompson Steel Co., Inc., 805 F. Supp. 1257 (D.C. Md. 1992).

13. U.S. Census Bureau, *Statistical Abstract of the United States* (1998), table 696.

14. U.S. Census Bureau, *Statistical Abstract of the United States* (2012), table 648.

15. David Leonhardt, "Gender Pay Gap, Once Narrowing, Is Stuck in Place," *New York Times,* December 24, 2006.

16. Rubin v. Regents of the University of California, 114 F.R.D. 1 (N.D. Cal. 1988).

17. Flucker v. Fox Chapel Area School District, 461 F. Supp. 1203 (W.D. Pa. 1978).

18. Bishop v. Wood, 426 U.S. 341 (1976).

19. Stukey v. United States Air Force, 809 F. Supp. 536 (S.D. Ohio 1992).

20. Anderson v. Bessemer, 470 V. S. 564 (1985).

21. Gobert v. Babbitt, 83 FEP Cases 1620 (E.D. La. 2000).

22. Greenbaum v. Svenska Handelsbanken , 67 F. Supp. 2d 228 (S.D.N.Y. 1999).

23. Edwards v. U.S. Postal Service, 909 F.2d 320 (8th Cir. 1990).

24. Rodriguez v. Board of Education of Eastchester Union Free School District, 620 F.2d 362 (2nd Cir. 1980).

25. Hearn v. General Electric Co., 927 F. Supp. 1486 (M.D. Ala. 1996).

26. EEOC v. Farmers Brothers Co., 31 F.3d 891 (9th Cir. 1994).

27. In one case, however, after a complainant was denied promotion on three occasions, her supervisors refused to talk to her and assigned her excessive work. When she left the company, the court ruled that she had been constructively discharged. Glass v. Petro-Tex Chemical Corp., 757 F.2d 1554 (5th Cir.1985).

28. West v. Marion Merrell Dow, Inc., 54 F.3d 493 (8th Cir. 1995).

29. Gartman v. Gencorp., Inc., 71 FEP Cases 937 (E.D. Ark. 1996), reversed 120 F.3d 127 (8th Cir.1997).

30. Chertkova v. Connecticut General Life Insurance Co., 92 F.3d 8 1 (2nd Cir. 1996).

31. Hurd v. JCB International Credit Card Co., Ltd., 923 F. Supp. 492 (S.D.N.Y. 1996).

32. Tunis v. Corning Glass Works, 698 F. Supp. 452 (S.D.N.Y. 1988).

33. EEOC Sex-Based Charges,1997–2012. Available at eeoc.gov/eeoc/statistics/enforcement/sex.

34. Liz Kowalczyk, "Doctor Gets $7m in Gender Bias Lawsuit," *Boston Globe*, February 17, 2013.

12. CURRENT TRENDS IN THE LAW PROHIBITING DISCRIMINATION OF PREGNANT WOMEN

1. 42 U.S.C. § 2000e (k).

2. Urbano v. Continental Airlines, Inc., 138 F.3d 204 (5th Cir. 1998). Ms. Urbano's given name is Mirtha, not Martha.

3. Geier v. Medtronic, Inc., 99 F.3d 238 (7th Cir. 1996).

4. EEOC v. Hacienda Hotel, 881 F.2d 1504 (9th Cir. 1989).

5. EEOC v. Continuity Programs, Inc., 841 F. Supp. 218 (E.D. Mich.1993).

6. EEOC v. Yenkin-Majestic Paint Corp, 112 F.3d 831 (6th Cir. 1997).

7. EEOC v. Red Baron Steak House, 47 FEP Cases 49 (N.D. Cal. 1988).

8. Sheehan v. Donlen Corp., 173 F.3d 1039 (7th Cir. 1999).

9. Tamimi v. Howard Johnson Co., Inc., 807 F.2d 1550 (11th Cir. 1987).

10. Ahmad v. Loyal American Life Insurance Co., 767 F. Supp. 1114 (S.D. Ala. 1991).

11. Bainlardi v. SBC Warburg, Inc., 78 FEP Cases 122 (S.D.N.Y. 1998).

12. Pacourek v. Island Steel Co., Inc., 858 F. Supp. 1393 (N.D. Ill. 1994).

13. Fejes v. Gilpin Ventures, Inc., 960 F. Supp. 1487 (D. Colo. 1997).

14. Piantanida v. Wyman Center, Inc., 116 F.3d 340 (8th Cir. 1997).

15. Turic v. Holland Hospitality, Inc., 63 FEP Cases 1267 and 64 FEP Cases 786 (W.D. Mich. 1994), affirmed 85 F.3d 1211 (6th Cir. 1996).

16. Bergstrom-Ek v. Best Oil Co., 153 F.3d 851 (8th Cir. 1998).

17. Gloria Allred and Dolores Y. Leal, "Employment: A BFOQ Defense," *National Law Journal*, February 22, 1999, referring to Tylo v. Spelling, 55 Cal. App. 4th 1379 (1997).

13. CURRENT TRENDS IN THE LAW PROHIBITING DISCRIMINATION OF WOMEN WITH CHILDREN

1. Muller v. Oregon, 208 U.S. 412 (1908).

2. Jurinko v. Edwin L. Wiegand Co., 477 F.2d 1038 (3d Cir. 1973).

3. EEOC Title VII Regulations, 29 C.F.R. § 1604.4.

4. U.S. Census Bureau, *Statistical Abstract of the United States* (2011), table 599.

5. Trezza v. The Hartford, 78 FEP Cases 1826 (S.D.N.Y. 1998).

6. Bass v. Chemical Bank Corp., 1996 WL 374151 (S.D.N.Y. 1996).

7. McGrenaghan v. St. Denis School, 979 F. Supp. 323 (E.D. Pa. 1997).

8. Many legal writers have commented upon these circumstances. See, e.g., Kathryn Abrams, "Gender Discrimination and the Transformation of Workplace Norms," *Vanderbilt Law Review* 42, no. 4 (1989): 1183, 1223; and Mary Ann Mason, "Beyond Equal Opportunity: A New Vision for Women Workers," *Notre Dame Journal of Law, Ethics and Public Policy* 6 (1992): 393.

9. Fisher v. Vassar College, 852 F. Supp. 1193 (S.D.N.Y. 1994).

10. *Fisher*, 114 F.3d 1332 (2d Cir. 1997).

14. SEXUAL HARASSMENT AND THE SEX DISCRIMINATION PROHIBITIONS OF TITLE VII

1. Mona Harrington, *Women Lawyers: Rewriting the Rules* (New York: Plume, 1995) 97–98, 105,115–16.

2. Barbara A. Gutek, *Sex and the Workplace* (San Francisco: Jossey-Bass, 1985), 8–9.

3. Catherine A. MacKinnon, *Sexual Harassment of Working Women* (New Haven, CT: Yale University Press, 1979), 4.

4. Barnes v. Train, 13 FEP Cases 123 (D. D.C. 1974).

5. Corne v. Bausch and Lomb, Inc., 390 F. Supp. 161 (D.C. Ariz. 1975), reversed on other grounds 562 F.2d 55 (9th Cir. 1977).

6. Tomkins v. Public Service Electric & Gas Company, 568 F.2d 1044 (3rd Cir. 1977).

7. Barnes v. Costle, 561 F.2d 983 (D.C. Cir. 1977).

8. *Tomkins*.

9. Henson v. Dundee, 682 F.2d 897 (11th Cir. 1982).

10. Meritor Savings Bank v. Vinson, 477 U.S. 57 (1986).

11. 29 C.F.R. § 1604.11 (a) (1) and (2).

12. EEOC Policy Guidelines on Current Issues of Sexual Harassment. Available at http://www.eeoc.gov/doc. See also Lancaster v. Sheffler Enterprises, 19 F. Supp.2d 1000 (W.D. Mo. 1998).

13. Stephen Franklin, "More Women Speak about Harassment—and Sue," *Chicago Tribune,* January 8, 1999; Sexual Harassment Charges: EEOC and FEPAs Combined: FY 1992–FY 2000, available at www.eeoc.gov/stats/harass.

14. EEOC, Sexual Harassment Charges: EEOC and FEPAs Combined: FY 2010–FY 2012, available at http://www.eeoc.gov/eeoc/statistics/enforcement/sexual_harassment.cfm.

15. Anne C. Levy and Michele A. Paludi, *Workplace Sexual Harassment* (Upper Saddle River, NJ: Prentice Hall, 1997), 50.

16. Nijole V. Benokraitis and Joe R. Feagin, *Modern Sexism: Blatant, Subtle, and Covert Discrimination* (Englewood Cliffs, NJ: Prentice Hall, 1995), 31.

17. Marni Halasa, "Officer Wins $2.2 Million In Harassment Suit," *New York Law Journal,* October 2, 2000.

18. Weeks v. Baker & McKenzie, 76 FEP Cases 1219 (Cal. Ct. of Appeals, 1998).

19. "$21 Million Award in Sex-Harassment Case," *New York Times,* July 20, 1999.

20. Monte Williams, "$2.6 Million to End Sex Harassment Suit," *New York Times,* June 4, 1999.

21. EEOC Press Release, September 7, 1999.

22. Reed Abelson, "Can Respect Be Mandated? Maybe Not Here," *New York Times,* September 10, 2000.

23. EEOC Policy Guidance 915-050, Current Issues of Sexual Harassment, available at http://www.eeoc.gov/policy/docs/currentissues.html

24. Harris v. Forklift Systems, Inc., 510 U.S. 17 (1993).

25. Burns v. McGregor Electronic Industries, Inc., 989 F.2d 959 (8th Cir. 1993).

26. Ellison v. Brady, 924 F.2d 872 (9th Cir. 1991).

27. EEOC Guidelines on Discrimination Because of Sex, 29 C.F.R. § 1604; EEOC Policy Guidance 915-050, "Current Issues of Sexual Harassment."

28. *Meritor Savings Bank v. Vinson,* 477 U.S. 57 (1986).

29. *Meritor* at 66–67.

30. Bishop v. Interim Industrial Services, 77 FEP Cases 1598 (N.D. Tex. 1998).

31. McKenzie v. Illinois Department of Transportation, 92 F.3d 473 (7th Cir. 1996).

32. EEOC v. A. Sam & Sons Produce Co., Inc., 872 F. Supp. 29 (W.D.N.Y. 1994).

33. Mallinson-Montague v. Pocrnick, 224 F.3d 1224 (10th Cir. 2000).

34. Fall v. Indiana University Board of Trustees, 12 F. Supp. 2d 870 (N.D. Ind. 1998).

35. EEOC Policy Guidance, "Current Issues of Sexual Harassment."

36. Henson v. Dundee, 682 F.2d 897 (11th Cir. 1982).

37. Kotcher v. Rosa & Sullivan Appliance Center, Inc., 957 F.2d 59 (2d Cir. 1992).

38. Gan v. Kepro Circuit Systems, Inc., 28 FEP Cases 639 (E.D. Mo. 1982).

39. Kahn v. Objective Solutions, 82 FEP Cases 495 (S.D.N.Y. 2000).

40. Wolak v. Spucci, 217 F.3d 157 (2d Cir. 2000).

15. EMPLOYER LIABILITY FOR EMPLOYEE ACTS OF SEXUAL HARASSMENT

1. Meritor Savings Bank v. Vinson, 477 U.S. 57 (1986).

2. Burlington Industries, Inc. V. Ellerth, 524 U.S. 743 (1998).

3. Faragher v. City of Boca Raton, 524 U.S. 775 (1998). The Court held that an employer may not rely on the affirmative defense if it is unable to establish that its antiharassment policy was effectively communicated to its employees.

4. EEOC Enforcement Guidance, "Vicarious Employer Liability for Unlawful Harassment," available at http://www.eeoc.gov/docs/harassment.

5. EEOC Enforcement Guidance, "Vicarious Employer Liability for Unlawful Harassment."

6. Durham Life Insurance Co. v. Evans, 166 F.3d 139 (3d Cir. 1999).

7. Molnar v. Booth, 229 F.3d 593 (7th Cir. 2000).

8. EEOC Enforcement Guidance, "Vicarious Employer Liability for Unlawful Harassment."

9. EEOC Enforcement Guidance, "Vicarious Employer Liability for Unlawful Harassment."

10. Desmarteau v. City of Wichita, 64 F. Supp. 2d 1067 (D.C. Kan. 1999).

11. Van Steenburgh v. Rival Co., 171 F.3d 1155 (8th Cir. 1999).

12. Scrivner v. Socorro Independent School District, 169 F.3d 969 (5th Cir 1999).

13. McCrackin v. LabOne, Inc., 74 FEP Cases 1018 (D.C. Kan. 1995),' later dismissed on other grounds 903 F. Supp. 1430 (D. Kansas 1995).

14. Smith v. Bath Iron Works Corp., 943 F.2d 164 (1st. Cir. 1991).

15. EEOC Enforcement Guidance on Harassment by Supervisors, 8 FEP Manual (BNA), Guidance 405:7654 (1999), available at http://www.eeoc.gov/policy/docs/harassment.html.

16. Vance v. Ball State University, 133 S.Ct. 2434 (2013).

16. CURRENT TRENDS IN THE LAW PROHIBITING NATIONAL ORIGIN DISCRIMINATION ISSUES

1. The materials on national origin discrimination in this chapter closely follow the rules set forth in the EEOC Compliance Manual.

2. EEOC v. Premier Operator Services, Inc., 113 F. Supp.2d 1066 (2000).

3. Terry Pristin, "Jury Finds Baccarat Discriminated against Spanish-Speaking Worker," *New York Times*, February 10, 1998.

4. EEOC Press Release, May 5, 2013.

5. EEOC Press Release, August 30, 2011.

6. Lam v. University of Hawaii, 40 F.3d. 1551 (9th Cir. 1994).

17. CURRENT TRENDS IN THE LAW PROHIBITING RELIGIOUS DISCRIMINATION

1. Georgette F. Bennett and Myrna Marofsky, *Religion in the Workplace: A Guide to Navigating the Complex Landscape* (New York: Tanenbaum Center for Interreligious Understanding, 2003), 7.

2. Bennett and Marofsky, *Religion in the Workplace*.

3. Douglas A. Hicks, *Religion and the Workplace: Pluralism, Spirituality, Leadership* (New York: Cambridge University Press, 2003), 102.

4. EEOC Charge Statistics, FY 1197 through FY 2011, available at http://eeoc.gov/eeoc/statistics/enforcement/charges.cfm.

5. Bennett and Marofsky, *Religion in the Workplace*, 14–15.

6. Steven Greenhouse, "Muslims Report Rising Discrimination at Work," *New York Times*, September 23, 2010.

7. Hicks, *Religion and the Workplace*, 103.

8. Chalmers v. Tulon Co. of Richmond, 101 F.3d 1012 (4th Cir. 1996).

9. Banks v. Service America Corp., 73 FEP Cases 173 (D. Kans. 1996).

10. Johnson v. Hale Merchandising, 49 FEP Cases 527 (W.D. Mo. 1989).

11. *Banks*, 73 FEP Cases at 176.

12. EEOC v. Townley Engineering & Manufacturing Co., 859 F.2d 610 (9th Cir. 1988).

13. Title VII, § 702(a), 42 U.S.C. § 2000e-1(a).

14. Title VII, § 703(e)(2), 42 U.S.C. § 2000e-2(e)(2).

15. Rayburn v. General Conference of Seventh-Day Adventists, 772 F.2d 1164 (4th Cir. 1985).

16. Little v. Wuerl, 929 F.2d 944 (3d Cir. 1991).

17. Feldstein v. Christian Science Monitor, 555 F. Supp. 974 (D. Mass. 1983).

18. Title VII, § 703(e)(1), 42 U.S.C. § 2000e-2(e)(1).

19. Pime v. Loyola University of Chicago, 803 F.2d 351 (7th Cir. 1986).

18. THE MINISTERIAL EXCEPTION

1. McClure v. Salvation Army, 460 F.2d 553 (5th Cir. 1972), quoting Sherbert v. Verner, 374 U.S. 398 (1963).

2. Rayburn v. General Conference of Seventh-Day Adventists, 772 F.2d 1164 (4th Cir. 1985).

3. EEOC v. Catholic University of America, 83 F.3d 455 (D.C. Cir. 1996).

4. Alicia-Hernandez v. The Catholic Diocese of Chicago, 320 F. 3d 698 (7th Cir. 2002).

5. EEOC v. Southwestern Baptist Theological Seminary, 651 F.2d 277 (5th Cir. 1981).

6. Bollard v. California Province of the Society of Jesus, 196 F.3d 940 (9th Cir. 1999).

7. Diana B. Henriques, "Where Faith Abides, Employees Have Few Rights," *New York Times,* October 9, 2006.

8. The facts recited here are based on those set forth in various court documents filed in the United States District Court, Northern District of Ohio, Western Division, Docket No. 3:02CV7171, for Rosati v. Toledo, Ohio Catholic Diocese, 233 F. Supp. 2d 917 (N. D. Ohio 2002) including the Affidavit of Mary Rosati, the Affidavit of Dr. Candilee Butler, the Affidavit of Sister Sharon Elizabeth Gworek, and Plaintiff's Memorandum in Opposition to Defendants' Motion for Summary Judgment.

9. *Rosati,* Complaint.

10. *Rosati,* Defendants' Memorandum in Support of Motion for Summary Judgment.

11. *Rosati,* Plaintiff's Memorandum in Opposition to Motion for Summary Judgment.

12. *Rosati,* Defendants' Reply Memorandum in Support of Motion for Summary Judgment.

13. *Rosati.*

14. Stanley Fish, "Is Religion Above the Law?" *New York Times,* October 17, 2011.

15. Hosanna-Tabor Evangelical Lutheran Church and School v. EEOC, No. 10-553, 565 U.S. __ (2012).

16. Caroline Mala Corbin, "The Irony of Hosanna-Tabor Evangelical Lutheran Church and School v. EEOC," *Northwestern University Law Review* 106, no. 2 (2012): 951.

19. ACCOMMODATING EMPLOYEE RELIGIOUS BELIEFS AND PRACTICES

1. Trans World Airlines, Inc. (TWA) v. Hardison, 432 U.S. 63 (1977).

2. *Trans World Airlines* (Marshall, J., dissenting).

3. EEOC Guidelines on Discrimination Because of Religion, 29 C.F.R. 1605 (1980).

4. Proctor v. Consolidated Freightways Corp. of Delaware, 795 F.2d 1472 (9th Cir. 1986).

5. Anderson v. U.S.F. Logistics (IMC), Inc., 274 F.3d 470 (7th Cir. 2001).

6. Brener v. Diagnostic Center Hospital, 671 F.2d 141 (5th Cir. 1982).

7. Ansonia Board of Education v. Philbrook, 479 U.S. 60 (1986). This decision appears to undermine EEOC Guidelines that provide that when there is more than one means of accom-

modating an employee's religious beliefs and practices, the employer must offer the alternative with the fewest disadvantages to the employee being accommodated.

8. Josh Schopf, "Religious Activity and Proselytization in the Workplace: The Murky Line between Healthy Expression and Unlawful Harassment," *Columbia Journal of Law and Social Problems* 31 (1997): 39, 43.

9. David L. Gregory, "The Role of Religion in the Secular Workplace," *Notre Dame Journal of Law, Ethics and Public Policy* 4 (1990): 749.

10. Smith v. Pyro Mining Co., 827 F.2d 1081 (6th Cir. 1987).

11. Shelton v. University of Medicine and Dentistry of New Jersey, 223 F.3d 220 (3d Cir. 2000).

12. Eversly v. MBank Dallas, 848 F.2d 172 (5th Cir. 1988).

13. EEOC Guidelines on Discrimination Because of Religion, 29 C.F.R. § 1605.2(e)(1).

14. Protos v. Volkswagen of America, Inc., 797 F.2d 129 (3d Cir. 1986).

15. Wangsness v. Watertown School District, 541 F. Supp. 332 (D. S.D. 1982).

20. CURRENT TRENDS IN THE LAW PROHIBITING AGE DISCRIMINATION

1. Daniel P. O'Meara, *Protecting the Growing Number of Older Workers: The Age Discrimination in Employment Act* (Philadelphia: University of Pennsylvania, Wharton School, Industrial Research, 1989),1.

2. Walter K. Olson, *The Excuse Factory* (New York: Free Press,1997), 145.

3. Punahele v. United Airlines, Inc., 756 F. Supp. 487 (D.C. Colo. 1986).

4. Reed v. Signode Corp., 652 F. Supp. 129 (D.C. Conn. 1986).

5. Senner v. Northcentral Technical College, 113 F.3d 750 (7th Cir. 1997).

6. Hertz v. The Gap, 75 FEP Cases 1883 (S.D.N.Y. 1997).

7. Palmiero v. Western Controls, 809 F. Supp. 341(M.D. Pa.1992); affirmed 8 F.3d 812 (3d Cir. 1993).

8. Sischo-Nownejad v. Merced Community College, 934 F.2d 1104 (9th Cir. 1991).

9. EEOC v. Independent Stave Co., Inc., 754 F. Supp. 713 (E. D. Mo.1991).

10. Proffitt v. Anacomp, Inc., 747 F. Supp. 421 (S. D. Ohio 1990).

11. Betty Friedan, *The Fountain of Age* (New York: Simon and Schuster,1993), 197.

21. LATER DEVELOPMENTS IN PROVING DISCRIMINATION IN TITLE VII CASES

1. McDonnell Douglas Corp. v. Green, 411 U.S. 792 (1973).

2. St. Mary's Honor Center v. Hicks, 509 U.S. 502 (1993). The case is examined in greater depth later in this chapter and in chapter 22.

3. Sprint/United Management Co. v. Mendelsohn, 552 U.S. 379 (2007).

4. Price Waterhouse v. Hopkins, 490 U.S. 228 (1989).

5. Desert Palace Inc., dba Caesars Palace Hotel & Casino v. Costa, 539 U.S. 90 (2003).

6. Texas Department of Community Affairs v. Burdine, 450 U.S. 248 (1981).

7. Anderson v. Baxter Healthcare Corp., 13 F. 3d 1120 (7th Cir. 1994).

8. *St. Mary's Honor Center*.

9. Reeves v. Sanderson Plumbing Products, Inc., 530 U.S. 133 (2000).

10. Stanley Fish, "Because of Race: Ricci v. DeStefano," *New York Times*, July 13, 2009.

11. Griggs v. Duke Power Co., 401 U.S. 424 (1971).

12. Watson v. Fort Worth Bank & Trust, 487 U.S. 977 (1988).

13. Wards Cove Packing Co. v. Atonio, 490 U.S. 642 (1989).

14. Ricci v. DeStefano, No. 07-1428, 557 U.S. 557 (2009).

22. LATER DEVELOPMENTS IN PROVING DISCRIMINATION IN ADEA CASES

1. St. Mary's Honor Center v. Hicks, 509 U.S. 502 (1993).
2. Hazen Paper Co. v. Biggins, 507 U.S. 604 (1993).
3. Metz v. Transit Mix, Inc., 828 F.2d 1202 (7th Cir. 1987).
4. Graefenhain v. Pabst Brewing Co., 827 F.2d 13 (7th Cir. 1987).
5. Holt v. The Gamewell Corp., 797 F.2d 36 (1st Cir. 1986).
6. Bay v. Times Mirror Magazines, Inc., 936 F.2d 112 (2d Cir.1991).
7. *Hazen Paper Co.* The Court was careful to note that its decision did not mean that an employer could, under the circumstances, lawfully fire a worker solely in order to prevent his pension rights from vesting. An employer, so motivated, would violate ERISA.
8. EEOC v. Francis W. Parker School, 61 FEP Cases 967 (N.D. Ill. 1993).
9. Judith J. Johnson, "Reasonable Factors Other Than Age: The Emerging Specter of Ageist Stereotypes," *Seattle University Law Review* 33 (2009): 49, 50.
10. Smith v. City of Jackson, 544 U.S. 228 (2005), and Meacham v. Knolls Atomic Power Laboratory, No. 06-1505, 128 S. Ct. 2395 (2008).
11. Jeffrey S. Klein and Rose E. Morrison, "Courts Rethink ADEA Disparate-Impact Claims," *National Law Journal,* June 30, 1997, B-10.
12. *Smith.*
13. *Meacham.*
14. R. Henry Pfutzenreuter IV, "The Curious Case of Disparate Impact under the ADEA," *Minnesota Law Review* 92, no. 2 (2009): 467, 469.
15. Tyler v. Bethlehem Steel Corp., 958 F.2d 1176 (2d Cir. 1992).
16. Gross v. FBL Financial Services, Inc., No. 08-441, 129 S.Ct. 2343 (2009).
17. "Preventing Age Discrimination" (editorial), *New York Times*, October 13, 2009.
18. "Combating Age Discrimination" (editorial), *New York Times*, March 29, 2012.
19. Price Waterhouse v. Hopkins, 490 U.S. 228 (1989).
20. Aungst v. Westinghouse Electric Corp., 937 F.2d 1216 (7th Cir. 1991).
21. Berkowitz v. Allied Stores of Penn-Ohio, Inc., 541 F. Supp. 1209 (E.D. Pa. 1982).
22. Haskell v. Kaman Corp., 743 F.2d 113 (2d Cir. 1984).
23. Atkin v. Lincoln Property Co., 991 F.2d 268 (5th Cir. 1993).
24. Ryder v. Westinghouse Electric Corp., 74 FEP Cases 1867 (3d Cir.1997).

23. THE GENDER PAY GAP AND THE LILLY LEDBETTER CASE

1. 42 U. S. C. § 2000e-5(e)(1).
2. Ledbettter v. Goodyear Tire & Rubber Co. Inc., 550 U.S. 618 (2007).
3. Justice Ginsburg, dissenting opinion.
4. "Injustice 5, Justice 4" (editorial), *New York Times*, May 31, 2007.
5. Tristin K. Green, "Insular Individualism: Employment Discrimination Law after Ledbetter v. Goodyear," *Harvard Civil Rights-Civil Liberties Law Review* 43 (2008): 353.
6. Lilly Ledbetter Fair Pay Act of 2009, Pub. L. 111-2, 123 Stat. 5 (2009).

24. SAME-SEX SEXUAL HARASSMENT

1. Wright v. Methodist Youth Services, Inc., 511 F. Supp. 307 (N.D. Ill. 1981).
2. 42 U.S.C. § 2000e-2(a)(1).
3. Meritor Savings Bank v. Vinson, 477 U.S. 57 (1986).
4. Oncale v. Sundowner Offshore Services, 523 U.S. 75 (1998).
5. Davis v. Coastal International Security, Inc. 275 F.3d 1119 (D.C. 2002).
6. Nichols v. Azteca Restaurant Enterprises, Inc., 256 F.3d 864 (9th Cir. 2001). Sanchez and two other Azteca employees brought this action. This opinion considered only Sanchez's claim.
7. Rene v. MGM Grand Hotel, Inc., 305 F.3d 1061 (9th Cir. 2002).

25. RETALIATION

1. Other Unlawful Employment Practices, 42 U.S.C. § 2000e-3(a) (2010).
2. Prohibition of Age Discrimination, 29 U.S.C. § 623 (d) (2011).
3. Burlington Northern & Santa Fe Railway Co. v. White, 548 U.S. 53 (2006).
4. 42 U.S.C. § 2000e-3(a).
5. Crawford v. Metropolitan Government of Nashville and Davidson County, 129 S. Ct. 846 (2009).
6. 42 U.S.C. § 2000e-3(a).
7. *Burlington Northern & Santa Fe Railway Co.*
8. 42 U.S.C. § 2000e-5(f)(1).
9. Thompson v. North American Stainless, LP, 131 S. Ct. 863 (2011).
10. University of Texas Southwestern Medical Center v. Nassar, 133 S. Ct. 978 (2013).

26. ARBITRATION

1. Gilmer v. Interstate/Johnson Lane Corp., 500 U.S. 20 (1991).
2. Pat K. Chew, "Arbitral and Judicial Proceedings: Indistinguishable Justice or Justice Denied." *Wake Forest Law Review* 46 (2011): 185, 204.
3. DiRussa v. Dean Witter Reynolds, Inc., 121 F.3d 818 (2nd Cir. 1997).
4. The quoted material is from Federal Judge Nancy Gertner's opinion in Rosenberg v. Merrill Lynch, 965 F. Supp. 190 (D.C. Mass. 1997). Judge Gertner's decision, barring arbitration in that case, was later reversed by an appellate court, 170 F.3d 1 (1st Cir.1999).
5. Stuart H. Bompey and Michael P. Pappas, "Is There a Better Way? Compulsory Arbitration of Employment Discrimination Claims after Gilmer," *Employee Relations Law Journal* 19, no. 3 (Winter 1993–94): 197. See also Stuart H. Bompey and Andrea H. Stempe, "Four Years Later: A Look at Compulsory Arbitration of Employment Discrimination Claims after Gilmer v. Interstate/Johnson Lane Corp.," *Employee Relations Law Journal* 21, no. 2 (Autumn 1995): 21.
6. Kinnebrew v. Gulf Insurance Co., 1994 WL 803508 (N.D. Tex. 1994).
7. Nghiem v. NEC Electronics, Inc., 25 F.3d 1437 (9th Cir.1994).
8. EEOC, "EEOC Policy Statement on Mandatory Arbitration," EEOC Notice No. 915.002, July 10, 1997, reprinted in BNA's *Employment Discrimination Report,* July 16, 1997, p. 166.
9. Circuit City Stores, Inc. v. Adams, 532 U.S. 105 (2001).
10. *Statement of Senator Leahy,* Senate Judiciary Committee, October 7, 2009.
11. Rosenberg v. Merrill Lynch, Pierce, Fenner & Smith, 170 F.3d 1 (1st Cir. 1999).

12. Hooters of America, Inc. v. Phillips, 173 F.3d 933 (4th Cir. 1999).

13. Cole v. Burns International Securities Services, 105 F.3d 1465 (D.C. Cir. 1997).

14. Penn Plaza LLC v. Pyett, 556 U.S. 247 (2009).

15. Alexander v. Gardner-Denver Co., 415 U.S. 36 (1974).

16. Drew S. Days, III, "Employment Discrimination Decisions from the October 2008 Term," *Touro Law Review* 26, no. 2 (2010): 491, 501.

17. Arbitration Fairness Act of 2013, H.R. 1844, Senate Bill 878.

27. POLITICAL AND JUDICIAL OPPOSITION TO THE EMPLOYMENT DISCRIMINATION LAWS

1. Drew S. Days, III, "The Court's Response to the Reagan Civil Rights Agenda," *Vanderbilt Law Review* 42 (1989): 1003, 1008, 1016.

Drew S. Days, III, "The Court's Response to the Reagan Civil Rights Agenda," *Vanderbilt Law Review* 42 (1989): 1003, 1008, 1016.

2. David I. Rose, "Twenty-Five Years Later: Where Do We Stand on Equal Employment Opportunity Law Enforcement?" *Vanderbilt Law Review* 42 (1989): 1121, 1169.

3. Alfred W. Blumrosen, "The EEOC at the End of the First Clinton Administration," in Citizens' Commission on Civil Rights, *The Continuing Struggle: Civil Rights and the Clinton Administration* (New York: Ford Foundation, 1997), 72.

4. Ferriol v. Brink's Incorporated, 841 F. Supp. 411 (S.D. Fla.1994).

5. Kristoferson v. Otis Spunkmeyer, Inc., 965 F. Supp. 545 (S.D.N.Y. 1997).

6. Reported by Howard C. Eglit, "The Age Discrimination in Employment Act at Thirty: Where It's Been, Where It Is Today, Where It's Going," *University of Richmond Law Review* 31 (1997): 591n47.

7. Eglit, "The Age Discrimination in Employment Act at Thirty," 651.

8. William P. Murphy, "Meandering Musings about Discrimination Law," *The Labor Lawyer* 10, no. 4 (1994): 649, 654.

9. Charles B. Craver, "Radical Supreme Court Justices Endeavor to Rewrite the Civil Rights Statutes," *The Labor Lawyer* 10, no. 4 (1994): 727, 728.

10. University of Texas Southwestern Medical Center v. Nassar, 133 S. Ct. 978 (2013).

11. Adam Liptak, "Corporations Find a Friend in the Supreme Court," *New York Times*, May 4, 2013.

12. Lee Epstein, William M. Landes, and Richard A. Posner, "How Business Fares in the Supreme Court," *Minnesota Law Review* 97 (2013): 1431.

28. THE ROLES OF THE EEOC AND THE PRIVATE ATTORNEY

1. EEOC Race-Based and Sex-Based Charges, FY 1997–FY 2012, available at eeoc.gov// eeoc/statistics/enforcement.

2. EEOC Race-Based and Sex-Based Charges, FY 1997–FY 2012.

3. EEOC Race-Based and Sex-Based Charges, FY 1997–FY 2012.

4. The jury's verdict was later overturned by the court, thus making it necessary to try the case a second time. On the second trial, AHP did not even bother to offer the testimony of the EEOC investigator, and thus her testimony ultimately was not a factor in the second jury's decision in favor of AHP.

5. EEOC Press Release, January 28, 2013.

6. Michael Selmi, "The Value of the EEOC: Reexamining the Agency's Role in Employment Discrimination Law," *Ohio State Law Journal* 57, no. 1 (1996): 6n17.

7. Selmi, "The Value of the EEOC," 50.

8. National Employment Lawyers Association, http://www.nela.org.

29. WHAT LAYS AHEAD FOR THE EMPLOYMENT DISCRIMINATION LAWS

1. Kevin M. Clermont and Stewart J. Schwab, "Employment Discrimination Plaintiffs in Federal Court: From Bad to Worse?" *Harvard Law and Policy Review* 3 (2009): 103, 111.

2. Clermont and Schwab, "Employment Discrimination Plaintiffs in Federal Court."

3. Clermont and Schwab, "Employment Discrimination Plaintiffs in Federal Court," 112.

4. Clermont and Schwab, "Employment Discrimination Plaintiffs in Federal Court," 127.

5. Clermont and Schwab, "Employment Discrimination Plaintiffs in Federal Court," 115.

6. Michael Selmi, "Why Are Employment Discrimination Cases So Hard to Win? *Louisiana Law Review* 61 (2001): 555, 561–62; David Benjamin Oppenheimer, "Verdicts Matter: An Empirical Study of California Employment Discrimination and Wrongful Discharge Jury Verdicts Reveals Low Success Rates for Women and Minorities," *University of California, Davis Law Review* 37 (2002): 511, 559–560; Judge Nancy Gertner and Melissa Hart, "Implicit Bias in Employment Discrimination Litigation," University of Colorado Law School Legal Research Paper Series, Working Paper Number 12-07, June 7, 2012.

7. Gertner and Hart, "Implicit Bias in Employment Discrimination Litigation."

8. David A. Schkade and Cass R. Sunstein, "Judging by Where You Sit," *New York Times*, June 11, 2003.

9. Selmi, "Why Are Employment Discrimination Cases So Hard to Win?"

10. Adam Liptak, "Business Finds Receptive Ear in Roberts Court," *New York Times*, December 18, 2010.

11. McDonnell Douglas Corp. v. Green, 411 U.S. 792 (1973).

12. St. Mary's Honor Center v. Hicks, 509 U.S. 502 (1993).

13. Hazen Paper Co. v. Biggins, 507 U.S. 604 (1993).

14. Gross v. FBL Financial Services, Inc., 557 U.S. 167 (2009).

Index

About the Author

For more than thirty-five years, **Raymond F. Gregory** focused his law practice on the litigation of employment discrimination cases. He has subsequently written extensively about the federal laws that bar such discrimination; this is his fifth book on the subject. He lives with his wife, Mary, outside of Boston.

CPSIA information can be obtained at www.ICGtesting.com
Printed in the USA
BVOW04*1305010814

361114BV00001BB/1/P